LYDIA SIGOURNEY
SELECTED POETRY AND PROSE

broadview editions
series editor: L.W. Conolly

Portrait used by Lydia Sigourney in her publications for many years.

LYDIA SIGOURNEY
SELECTED POETRY AND PROSE

edited by Gary Kelly

broadview editions

Library and Archives Canada Cataloguing in Publication

Sigourney, L.H. (Lydia Howard), 1791-1865
Lydia Sigourney : selected poetry and prose / edited by Gary Kelly.

Includes bibliographical references.
ISBN 978-1-55111-620-4

I. Kelly, Gary. II. Title.

PS2833.A5K44 2008 811′.3 C2008-903131-8

Broadview Editions
The Broadview Editions series represents the ever-changing canon of literature in English by bringing together texts long regarded as classics with valuable lesser-known works.

Advisory editor for this volume: Jennie Rubio

Broadview Press is an independent, international publishing house, incorporated in 1985. Broadview believes in shared ownership, both with its employees and with the general public; since the year 2000 Broadview shares have traded publicly on the Toronto Venture Exchange under the symbol BDP.

We welcome comments and suggestions regarding any aspect of our publications—please feel free to contact us at the addresses below or at broadview@broadviewpress.com.

North America
Post Office Box 1243, Peterborough, Ontario, Canada K9J 7H5
2215 Kenmore Avenue, Buffalo, NY, USA 14207
Tel: (705) 743-8990; Fax: (705) 743-8353;
email: customerservice@broadviewpress.com

UK, Ireland, and continental Europe
NBN International, Estover Road, Plymouth, UK PL6 7PY
Tel: 44 (0) 1752 202300 Fax: 44 (0) 1752 202330
email: enquiries@nbninternational.com

Australia and New Zealand
UNIREPS, University of New South Wales
Sydney, NSW, Australia 2052
Tel: 61 2 9664 0999; Fax: 61 2 9664 5420
email: info.press@unsw.edu.au

www.broadviewpress.com

This book is printed on paper containing 100% post-consumer fibre.

Broadview Press gratefully acknowledges the support of the Government of Canada through the Book Publishing Industry Development Program (BPIDP) for our publishing activities.

Typesetting and assembly: True to Type Inc., Claremont, Canada.

PRINTED IN CANADA

Contents

Acknowledgements

I am grateful to the increasing number of scholars and critics who are recovering the lives and work of Lydia Huntley Sigourney and her contemporaries; without their pioneering efforts this edition would not have been possible. I am also grateful to staffs of the University of Alberta Library and Beinecke and Stirling Memorial Libraries, Yale University, and the Harriet Beecher Stowe Centre and Connecticut Historical Society, Hartford, Connecticut; their help was indispensable to this project. I gratefully acknowledge permission of the Connecticut Historical Society and the Harriet Beecher Stowe Center to publish from manuscripts in their collections. For funding I am grateful to the Canada Research Chairs program and the Standard Research Grants program of the Social Sciences and Humanities Research Council of Canada. "Thanks" can hardly express what I owe to Kirsten MacLeod for her interest and support. Thanks to Broadview Press for letting me do this, for being so patient, and just for being.

I dedicate this book to my colleague Patricia Demers in gratitude for her wise counsel and exemplary scholarship and professionalism.

NORWICH, CONN. BIRTHPLACE OF MRS. SIGOURNEY.

Lydia Huntley's birthplace, the house of Mrs Lathrop, Norwich, Connecticut.

COLONIAL MANSION, HARTFORD, CONN.
Once the home of Mrs. Lydia Huntley Sigourney, poetess, and later the residence of
Ex-Lieutenant-Governor Catlin.
Adopted as a model for the Connecticut State Building at the Louisiana Purchase
Exposition at St. Louis, Mo.

Sigourney house, Hartford, home from a year after marriage until 1838.

Introduction

Lydia Huntley Sigourney (1791–1865) was the most popular American woman poet on both sides of the Atlantic through the first half of the nineteenth century. The editor of an 1852 anthology containing her work declared, "When account shall be made of the various agencies, moral and intellectual, that have moulded the American mind and heart during the first half of the nineteenth century, few names will be honoured with a larger credit than that of Lydia H. Sigourney."[1] Though she made herself well known in Britain and the United States, Sigourney was a specifically American woman writer for these reasons: she was a writer of American birth, education, and culture, and she mobilized that identity in her writing; she persistently addressed concerns—social, cultural, political, and literary—of the American reading public; she helped create a vision of the United States as a new and exemplary kind of nation in world history; she contributed to an emergent American literary idiom in both prose and verse to affirm that vision; and she did so particularly from the perspective and on behalf of American women.

Sigourney and her work have long lain in obscurity and have been overshadowed by a century and a half of relentless disparagement, however. Recovery is still in progress. Sigourney published a great deal, and the work of her and her contemporaries is in many ways still remote from present-day literary and academic culture. Accordingly, I provide here both a selection of her primary texts and appropriate contextual material to enable better understanding of her work. There is a selection of her poetry and prose texts, in approximately chronological order, representing both the span of her literary career and the diversity of themes and forms she attempted, with appropriate notes. There is a small selection of her letters and other documents illustrating her life and work; and there is a selection from reviews and other comments on her. In order to assist understanding of her writing, this introduction offers different contexts from which to approach her poetry and prose. I provide an outline of her career, based on recent research; this outline is keyed to my selection of texts. I provide an outline of the vision that informed all her work, of the United States as a republican nation with a

1 *The Female Prose Writers of America*, ed. John S. Hart (Philadelphia: E.H. Butler & Co., 1852), 76.

unique historical destiny; this, too, is keyed to the selection of texts. Finally, I provide accounts of her literary poetics and practice and of her critical reception, also keyed to the selections.

Formation and Career of an American Woman Author

At a time when few women had access to authorship, and even fewer could make a living from it, Lydia Sigourney sustained a remarkable professional literary career. By her own accounting, in the course of half a century she published over two thousand poems as well as prose pieces in almost three hundred newspapers, magazines, and annuals, from the local and ephemeral to the established and national, from the Western frontier to fashionable London, from the flimsy to the substantial, the shoddy to the refined.[1] She selected various combinations from this output for almost sixty books of several kinds and diverse formats, from small and cheap, through neat and elegant, to large and sumptuous. From the 1820s through the 1850s she contributed her work to a series of anthologies designed to create and at the same time profit from an emergent United States national literature. She purposefully exploited every niche in the magazine and book market. She achieved this career by self-discipline and hard work, assistance of socially prominent patrons, astute management of social networks, deft handling of the cultural and social discourses of femininity and domesticity, persistent practice of and experiment with her literary craft, close observation of literary trends and the tastes of the reading public, steady attention to the physical features of books and the operations of the book trade, aggressive marketing and distribution of her books, and careful maintenance of her public identity as a model and voice of an American republican culture that she helped to invent.

Early Years: Norwich, Connecticut

Lydia Howard Huntley was born on 1 September 1791, the only child of working-class parents in Norwich, Connecticut.[2] She grew

1 Lydia Sigourney, *Letters of Life* (1866), 366; 299 here.

2 Information from Sigourney's autobiography, *Letters of Life* (New York: D. Appleton and Co., 1866); Gordon S. Haight, *Mrs. Sigourney: The Sweet Singer of Hartford* (New Haven: Yale UP, 1930); and Melissa Ladd Teed, "Work, Domesticity and Localism: Women's Public Identity in Nineteenth-Century Hartford, Connecticut," unpub. PhD diss., University of Connecticut, 1999.

up in a time of critical transition in the state's society, economy, and culture, and this fact shaped her outlook. Connecticut's historic agricultural base was declining because of exhausted soil and large families. Many people migrated west, while others diversified into manufacturing, trade, and seafaring. Norwich was a small inland seaport mainly trading to the West Indies and serving the plantation slave economy there. Near Norwich were iron, cutlery, and pottery manufacturing, oil and chocolate milling, hemp spinning, and stocking weaving, and much home industry for commercial sale. The Huntleys had little to do directly with this side of Norwich, however, and later in life Lydia would repeatedly celebrate the passing agrarian way of life and disdain commerce and industrialization.

Her family, though humble, was associated with the Norwich gentry—a small elite of well-educated, socially prominent professionals, landholders, and business people. Her father, Ezekiel (born 12 April 1752),[1] had been an odd-jobs man for Dr. Daniel Lathrop, who was an important figure in the American Revolution, landholder, and the town's and region's apothecary. After Lathrop's death in 1782, Ezekiel Huntley remained as gardener for the widow at her extensive property on the edge of Norwich. Ezekiel Huntley himself volunteered for military service in the American Revolution and on returning to Norwich married Lydia Howard (born 1759) on 17 December 1786. She died of consumption the following year, and on 28 November 1790 he married Zerviah (or Sophia) Wentworth, who bore their only child. The Huntleys lived in part of the Lathrops' large house. For a time Lydia attended a school for girls and boys.[2] At home she learned domestic skills and did household tasks. She liked to write and at age eight began a novel, set in Italy. Already, her life and writing were inspired by religion.

The Huntleys belonged to the Congregationalist church, at that time the constitutionally established Connecticut state church. Congregationalists were Calvinists, believing that individual salvation or damnation depended on God's grace and was pre-ordained by His foreknowledge of all things. Congregationalists as a community were inward looking and exclusionary. During Lydia's childhood and youth, however, the Congregationalist church, like

---

1 Dates of family births, deaths, and marriages are taken from a transcript of entries in the Huntley family Bible, LHS Papers (US/CTH/SIGOL/1865—I.1A), CHS.

2 Francis M. Caulkins, *History of Norwich, Connecticut* (1866), 544.

other Protestant denominations, was transformed by the "Second Great Awakening." This was one of a series of religious revivals that swept through America, Britain, and parts of Europe from the seventeenth to the early nineteenth centuries, and that enabled the assumption of a public voice, supposedly under divine inspiration, by those otherwise socially subordinate and marginalized.[1]

Like the First Great Awakening of the 1730s and '40s, the Second was spearheaded by the mainly lower- and middle-class Methodists, but it affected all Protestant denominations. Sects dominated by the middle class and well-to-do, such as the Congregationalists, met this challenge in various ways. In the booming new town of Rochester, New York, the middle class transformed the Second Great Awakening into a "shopkeeper's millennium." They used the Awakening to develop class identity, discipline, and solidarity among themselves, and to control an otherwise unruly working class by basing employment on evidence of a "serious" or religious character, including good work habits, social deference, and abstention from work-disrupting activities such as drinking and "immoral" behaviour.[2] In Connecticut, the Second Great Awakening loosened Congregationalists' sectarian, social, and economic domination, leading to their disestablishment as the state church in 1818, but it also modified their beliefs and behaviour. It softened their insistence on predestination; it led them to promote "good works," or charitable and philanthropic causes, as a way of maintaining their social, cultural, and economic domination; and it brought them into social coalition with other predominantly middle-class sects

In this transformation, middle-class women acquired new opportunities for social and public participation through the extension of their conventionally accepted domestic roles as educators, nurturers, healers, and conciliators. As a young woman and member of the Congregationalist church, Lydia Huntley adapted the religious discourse of the Second Great Awakening to exploit the social and professional opportunities before her. After her marriage took her into the Protestant Episcopalian church, she continued to exploit this religious discourse in both her active community social life and her prolific professional literary work, to become a major voice of the dominant, religiously-inspired, middle-class culture of the early American republic.

1 Nancy Ruttenburg, *Democratic Personality: Popular Voice and the Trial of American Authorship* (Stanford: Stanford UP, 1998).

2 See Paul E. Johnson, *A Shopkeeper's Millennium: Society and Revivals in Rochester, New York 1815–1837* (New York: Hill and Wang, 1978).

Meanwhile, she was positioning herself for upward social mobility through self-education and self-culture. She was encouraged to read and write by her mother, an avid reader of Sentimental and Romantic literature. Apart from the books in Mrs Lathrop's house, Norwich could offer young Lydia a commercial circulating library with over four hundred volumes, mostly entertaining literature; a subscription library with about 250 volumes of more serious literature; and a bookseller.[1] Mrs Lathrop encouraged her gardener's clever daughter—patronizing lower-class merit was expected of the genteel and well-to-do—and Lydia often read aloud to the widow from devotional works such as the English poet Edward Young's *Night Thoughts* (1742). At one school she showed an aptitude for arithmetic and her teacher enthusiastically led her through the levels of mathematics. Later, at a school established by Daniel Lathrop, she began Latin and then undertook Hebrew in order to read the Old Testament Bible in its original language. From an early age she kept detailed journals of events, reflections, and spiritual and moral self-examination—a practice she later recommended to all girls as a way to develop self-discipline, self-knowledge, and self-control, and thus subjective autonomy.

Sigourney's published works show that during these years and thereafter she acquired a solid, religiously oriented, moralistic literary and historical knowledge. The Bible is a ubiquitous presence in her work. She had a good knowledge of eighteenth-century British moralists from Alexander Pope to Samuel Johnson. She knew classic English writers such as John Milton and William Shakespeare, and one of her favourite writers was the moral philosopher and essayist Francis Bacon. She read much history and biography—her favourite historian was the French republican Charles Rollin—and regarded history as religion teaching by examples. Later she sifted this reading into several books for young readers and promoted biography as a major educational and moral discourse. Another important influence on her themes and verse form was William Cowper's *The Task* (1785), a blank verse Christian moral epic of everyday life. She knew a broad range of devotional literature, including anthologies of moral anecdotes and maxims. She knew the work of British women writers, particularly those of religious and moral purpose, such as Joanna Baillie, Maria Edgeworth, and especially Hannah More. Later she would read the British Romantics William Wordsworth,

---

1 Caulkins, *History of Norwich*, 514.

Robert Southey, Walter Scott, and Felicia Hemans. She also knew the work of the American poets and novelists, including her female contemporaries. She rarely referred to Romantic writers who represented conflicted subjectivity, religious scepticism, social evils, or the erotic. Though she kept up with "books of the day" throughout her life, later quoting Charles Dickens, Alfred Tennyson, and Charlotte Brontë, among others, her primary literary sources remained the Bible, religious and moral writers in prose and verse, religious biography, and republican history from ancient times to the present.

Schoolteaching, Social Work, and First Publications

Lydia Huntley was soon able to make the most of this early education, wide reading, and exposure to genteel manners, culture, and society. Planning to help her parents by opening a school in Norwich with a friend, she studied "ornamental" subjects such as painting, embroidery, and filigree work to attract a genteel clientele. She and Nancy Maria Hyde opened their Norwich school in 1811,[1] though two years later they decided to operate independently.[2] At this time Lydia made a vow, kept through her life, to devote at least ten percent of her earnings to charity. Earlier, while visiting Hartford in 1806, she had met another widow, Mrs Wadsworth, and her nephew, Daniel.[3] Like other cultivated and wealthy Americans, Daniel Wadsworth exercised his social position by promoting projects of social and cultural improvement. One of these was a school organized in 1814 for fifteen girls from leading Hartford families. Believing there was increasing need for educated and professionalized wives and mothers to sustain a distinctive American middle-class culture and economy, Wadsworth prescribed a curriculum similar to that provided for boys. Recognizing in Lydia Huntley an exemplar of cultivated American femininity, he asked her to conduct the school.

Her pupils came from New England, the Southern States, and the West Indies.[4] She taught reading, spelling, penmanship, arithmetic, grammar, geography, natural and moral philosophy, and

---

1 1812 according to Caulkins, *History of Norwich*, 547.

2 Biographical sketch of Lydia H. Sigourney, *Female Prose Writers of America*, ed. John S. Hart (Philadelphia: E.H. Butler & Co., 1852), 79.

3 Sketch of Sigourney, *Female Prose Writers*, 80.

4 Catalogue of her pupils, LHS Papers (US/CTH/SIGOL/1865—II.2), CHS.

history.[1] She was thorough, preparing, for example, a list of 102 "Questions in Grammar" and extensive notes on trade, shares, and currencies.[2] She also organized her students for the kind of local charitable work stimulated by the Second Great Awakening. In 1815, their first year, they altered 160 items of their own clothing for distribution to the poor, knitted 35 pairs of stockings for the same purpose while listening to the regular afternoon history recitation, contributed $10 to the Asylum for the Deaf and Dumb and $5 toward a school for Cherokee Indians, and distributed $10 worth of books "among the children of poverty and ignorance."[3] Her pupils promoted similar activities wherever they settled across the United States. Such female social activism was becoming a major way for women to participate in the public sphere and civil society, despite not having the vote.[4] In 1815 Lydia Huntley extended her educational role by publishing a selection of her writings, titled *Moral Pieces, in Prose and Verse*; this collection was overseen by Daniel Wadsworth, with numerous subscribers from across Connecticut.

At this time, Hartford was already a major New England centre, but unlike Boston and New York in many ways. Like Norwich, Hartford was an inland port, shipping out agricultural goods from the hinterland, importing and distributing manufactures, and providing banking, insurance, and other financial services.[5] There was gradual growth in manufacturing in and near Hartford, including silver and Britannia ware, bells, cordage, pottery, and watches, and tanning, barrel-making, ship-building, and engraving. This commercial activity provided the foundation of Hartford's development as a major financial centre, a position it still holds. Sea-trade was risky and the business of marine underwriting was the basis of Hartford's pre-eminence in the insurance industry. Capital accumulation by insurance companies and banks financed new enterprises in Hartford and across the nation.

---

1 See "Rules of the School," 305.

2 LHS Papers (US/CTH/SIGOL/1865—I.24), CHS.

3 Lydia Sigourney, "Address to the former scholars of Miss Huntley's school on their meeting to form a Charitable and Literary Society" (1822), LHS Collection, HBSC.

4 See Catherine E. Kelly, *In the New England Fashion: Reshaping Women's Lives in the Nineteenth Century* (Ithaca and London: Cornell UP, 1999).

5 Ellsworth Strong Grant and Marion Hepburn Grant, *The City of Hartford 1784–1984* (Hartford: Connecticut Historical Society, 1986), 25.

Changes in transport and technology accelerated Hartford's manufacturing, industrial, and financial expansion. Steam-powered ships increased river traffic from the 1810s. A railway connected Hartford to New Haven in 1839 and Connecticut's network expanded rapidly to become one of the densest in the nation.[1] Steam-power enabled expansion in cotton and woolen processing, iron casting, publishing cheap books, making machinery, and manufacturing tools and guns.[2] Economic expansion stimulated increase in population, which nearly doubled from 1820 to 1840 and more than doubled from 1840 to 1860. In 1865, the year of Sigourney's death, Hartford's population approached 40,000, half of whom worked in the city's several hundred factories. Sigourney rarely refers to these remarkable developments in her writing, but in both her writing and her local social activism she repeatedly addressed their social and political consequences.

Inevitably, social tensions increased as workers defended their interests against employers by forming mutual benefit societies and trade unions.[3] Hartford also became more disparate socially. Immigration increased from the 1820s, led by Irish Catholics, straining established social and religious hierarchies, customs, and culture, and influencing local politics. This impact in turn aroused opposition and led to the election in 1854 of a state governor from the anti-immigrant Know-Nothing party.[4] These economic and social changes also had an impact on women, especially those from the working class, providing new opportunities for wage labour in factories and enabling them to become more independent in traditionally subservient occupations such as domestic service.

The transformation of Hartford during Sigourney's lifetime conditioned her professional and private life, taught her a businesslike approach to literary production, informed the major themes of her writing, and thereby enabled her success as an American poet. The transformation of Hartford and Connecticut was representative of the transformation of New England and the United States—indeed, the Western world. Though Americans boasted of their society's freedom from European social distinc-

---

1 Grant and Grant, *City of Hartford*, 27–31.

2 P. Henry Woodward, "Manufactures in Hartford," *Hartford in History: A Series of Papers by Resident Authors*, ed. Willis I. Twitchell, 1899), 171–73.

3 Grant and Grant, *City of Hartford*, 50.

4 Grant and Grant, 14, 16, 47, 57.

tions and hierarchies, in practice Americans, like Europeans, distinguished those in "trade," or manufacturing and business, from those in professions, government, and finance. The latter often used their education, cultivation, and cultural and social philanthropy to display their social distinction and exercise their social influence. While servicing and financing "trade," they also distinguished themselves from it by promoting an idealized image of a United States that was agrarian, Christian, and republican yet also cultivated, in a distinctively American way.

Hartford was an expanding industrial and commercial centre, and alternating state capital with New Haven. Consequently it was home to many property owners, financiers, and entrepreneurs as well as professional men such as lawyers, judges, educators, and clergy. Through the Wadsworths and her well-to-do pupils, Lydia Huntley could associate with the families of this inter-locking network of upper middle-class elite, or what she referred to as Hartford's "aristocracy."[1] Here were many professional and personal opportunities for a talented, cultivated, and attractive young woman like Lydia Huntley. She led an active social life and attended many parties. She was not averse to love and marriage, received tempting offers, and considered becoming a missionary's wife, but resolved to remain unmarried for her parents' sake. In January 1819, however, she received a letter of proposal from the well-to-do widower Charles Sigourney (1778–1854) and, after securing the approval of the Wadsworths and her parents, she closed her school; she and Sigourney married on 16 June.

Marriage versus Writing: Founding a Literary Career

Charles Sigourney (the accent is on the first syllable) exemplified the town gentry of Hartford and of the early American republic. He had distinguished early-American forbears in seventeenth-century Huguenot (French Protestant) immigrants, he was born and raised in Boston, and he was partly educated in England. In the new, progressive "romantic" fashion, he married for love, not money. His first wife, Jane Carter Sigourney (born 1787), died in 1818 leaving him with three children—Charles Henry (born 11 January 1811), Elizabeth Carter (born 6 August 1813), and Jane Carter (born 9 April 1815). Lydia Huntley already knew the

---

1 Sigourney, *Letters of Life*, 266.

family, and had written a poem on Mrs Sigourney after her death.[1]

Charles Sigourney's business and social involvements were typical of Hartford's social elite. With his brother in Boston, he owned an importing and distribution business based on the hardware used to build Hartford's and Connecticut's manufacturing infrastructure,[2] and he invested in other businesses, such as a dry goods store. He was a prominent layman in the Protestant Episcopal Church, which was dominated by Hartford's social elite.[3] When local resentment at the way Congregationalists favoured each other in business led to the founding of the Phoenix Bank in 1814, Charles Sigourney promoted it and became its president in 1820. Like many middle-class people motivated by the Second Great Awakening, he also promoted charitable projects. He was a vice-president of the Connecticut Asylum for the Instruction of Deaf and Dumb Persons, a cause his wife would also support with her energies and her pen.[4] In 1823 his large donation helped found Washington (later Trinity) College of theology in Hartford. He enjoyed literature and had authored at least one poem, "The Belles of Hartford."[5]

In social and economic terms this was an extremely good marriage for someone of Lydia Huntley's background, as people noted. Mary Porter, a Hartford working-class woman, commented in a letter to a friend:

> our Dear Mrs [Jane] Sigourney has long Slept in Death he [Charles Sigourney] is agone to Mary Miss Huntly you have heard of the Poet Miss Huntly kept School in Hartford – has now close. Mr Sigourney has carried her to Norwich to her Parents They are poor folks. he has not lookt for riches in neither of his Wifes. she is a Professor of religion.[6]

---

1 "On finding the grave of Mrs Sigourney, marked by a Rose," LHS Papers (US/CTH/SIGOL/1865—I.27), CHS.

2 *Connecticut Mirror* (Hartford) 4 (28 December 1812): 4.

3 Nelson Rollin Burr, *The Story of the Diocese of Connecticut* (Hartford: Church Missions Publishing Company, 1962), 331–33; 474.

4 Disability History Museum: <http://www.disabilitymuseum.org/lib/docs/1734.htm?page=1>.

5 "The Belles of Hartford in 1802. A Vision," in the Charles Sigourney papers, LHS Papers (US/CTH/SIGOL/1865—II.13), CHS.

6 Mary Porter to unnamed correspondent; East Hartford, 30 May [1819]; Kingsbury Collection, HBSC.

Perhaps aware of such attitudes, soon after her marriage the new Mrs Sigourney published anonymously a little magazine containing satires on mercenary marriages (p. 68 here). The Sigourneys apparently attracted a certain amount of envious or malicious gossip over the years.

Marriage into a prominent and established family placed heavy demands on the new wife. Her responsibilities included managing a household that consisted of her husband, his three children, the late Mrs Sigourney's unmarried sister, two of her husband's clerks, and two men and three women servants. She performed numerous household tasks. She supervised the children's home education. She made new clothes and recycled old ones. A year after the marriage, the family moved into an elegant mansion with extensive grounds. The couple planned for children of their own, and Lydia had a stillborn daughter on 10 May 1820. Hard pressed by these new burdens, one Sunday in 1821 she drew up a list of twenty questions to ask herself each week by way of "Self-Examination" on her spiritual, charitable, domestic, intellectual, and literary life (p. 306 here). A son born prematurely on 8 December 1821 soon died, as did another born prematurely on 3 January 1823.[1] Lydia Sigourney turned to writing and charitable social work.

Thanks partly to her husband's social position and partly to her own growing fame as a writer, she became a leading figure in charitable activities directed by wives of prominent Hartford men and carried out by their daughters and sisters, schoolmates and friends.[2] Female philanthropy in Hartford was socially hierarchical and denominationally exclusionary. The Episcopalian and Congregationalist "ladies" of Hartford directed their efforts at those regarded as potential social "problems," such as poor Protestant women and children; poor African Americans; the disabled, such as the deaf and dumb; the insane; and jail prisoners. Sigourney and the Hartford ladies also participated in national and international philanthropy as a form of American moral, ideological, and cultural imperialism, directing their efforts at other cultures, races, and religions, including immigrants and settlers in the American west, American aborigines, women in South America and Greece, and peoples in Asia and Africa. Sigourney used her writings to promote public awareness of and raise funds

---

1 Dates here from transcript of entries in the Huntley family Bible, LHS Papers (US/CTH/SIGOL/1865—I.1A), CHS.

2 See Melissa Ladd Teed, "Work, Domesticity and Localism," ch. 1.

for these efforts, while her charitable networks reinforced her literary and public reputation and helped sell her books.

Sigourney's marriage gave her social prominence and scope for social activism, but it also restricted her literary ambitions. Charles Sigourney considered female authorship to be unfeminine, inappropriate for a married woman and mother, likely to distract her from the domestic supervision that helped sustain his own career, and liable to public controversy. He agreed to allow his wife to publish anonymously, and helped her for a time, providing learned notes to her ambitious poem, *Traits of the Aborigines of America: A Poem* (1822; here p. 70). The poem did not sell well; but, with an eye for literary trends, she quickly turned to the vogue for regional local-colour writing with *Sketch of Connecticut, Forty Years Since* (1824; p. 81). She energetically promoted herself and her work, sending out a stream of contributions to newspapers and magazines, corresponding with editors and writers, and forming personal literary relationships in Hartford. Her husband's business commitments gave her freedom for writing, but, anticipating his disapproval, she tried to hide her increasing literary activity from him. He clearly loved her, and when away on business sent affectionate letters. But his discovery of her secrecy caused estrangement. In 1827 she published *Poems* "By the Author of 'Moral Pieces in Prose and Verse'" without consulting him. This precipitated a marital crisis.

Feeling torn between her marriage and her writing, burdened by household responsibilities, and abandoning prospect of motherhood, Sigourney asked her husband for a formal separation. He refused, stating his own grievances in an "Appeal" dated October 1827 (p. 310). Here he complained of her absorption in literary work and society; consequent neglect of domestic duties; unseemly pursuit of praise and publicity; preference for the company of literary men over the company of her own husband; secret correspondence with male editors, publishers, and writers; and what neighbours saw as her airs as a poet and Romantic "genius," with resulting public criticism and ridicule. He accused her of intellectual and imaginative adultery, and hinted that worse could follow. He warned her to avoid appearing to be a Romantic poetess, a feminist such as Mary Wollstonecraft, or a utopian socialist such as Frances Wright. He did not forbid her to publish, but urged her to reduce her literary activity, to be open with him about it, to avoid indecorous relations with literary men, to resume her domestic roles, and to bear children of her own. "Something must be created, which may be in common between us," he implored, in place of what he saw as the intensely self-absorbing and destabilizing feelings aroused in her by poetry, admiration and flattery, and desire for public distinction.

Lydia Sigourney granted her husband's "Appeal." Nine months after he wrote it she bore a daughter, Mary Huntley (3 August 1828), and later a son, Andrew Maximilian (11 July 1830). She continued publishing, and with increasing frequency, but did so anonymously for the next few years. She continued publishing poetry and literary prose in magazines and in books, but she also published books on acceptably feminine subjects such as education, moral reform, and female conduct. She posed as a part-time author, telling editors, publishers, and other correspondents that her literary activity was carried out in spare moments from domestic duties. Picking up the theme of her husband's appeal, she made the domestic role of women and its conventionally accepted extensions into the public sphere a central theme of her writing. Finally, she represented herself in her writing as the embodiment of this role.

Moving into more acceptably "feminine" kinds of writing was also good business. Since the late eighteenth century, increasing numbers of women writers, exploiting acceptance of women's expertise as mothers and home educators, turned to the expanding market in books for children and youth. American States and Territories developed public education systems, creating a major market for women writers—especially those like Sigourney with a background in teaching and with children of their own. In the decade from 1829 Sigourney quickly published a dozen books for this market (see Bibliography). She also took up another line that women writers had made their own: the "advice" or "conduct" book prescribing the education, social and cultural formation, and domestic responsibilities of young middle-class women. This, too, turned out to be an excellent business decision. Though modest looking, Sigourney's *Letters to Young Ladies* (1833; p. 110), "By a Lady," helped her become a national public figure. Her husband tolerated her contributions to periodicals, published with her initials only, and through the early 1830s she obeyed his wish to keep her name off the title pages of her books. *Letters to Young Ladies* became a bestseller, however, and her literary adviser, Theodore Dwight, Jr., urged her to put her name on the title page of her next poetry collection. Meanwhile, her husband's business interests were struggling, and she told Dwight, "I have felt it my duty to aid him, by pursuing more as a trade, what had previously been only a recreation or solace."[1] Her *Poems* (1834) announced on its title page, "By Mrs L.H. Sigourney."

"Mrs Sigourney" would henceforth become the major national female poetic voice for the middle-class American public. By the late 1820s her poetry was already appearing in anthologies promoting a new, specifically American national literature, and she was being called "our American Hemans," after the Englishwoman who was the most widely read and respected woman poet on both sides of the Atlantic.[2] Though the nickname was meant as a compliment, a few, such as Edgar Allan Poe (p. 331), considered it derogatory, indicating a derivativeness that many in Britain and the United States saw as a trait of emergent American literature. The association with Hemans also indicates the tendency of critics in her time and since to characterize her and Hemans' work narrowly but inaccurately as merely pious, feminine, domestic, and patriotic. Sigourney extended her "feminine" themes in many directions and continually tried new forms of verse and prose, for good reasons. As a literary businesswoman she had to catch new trends and try new "lines" on editors, publishers, and the reading public. To be respected as a literary artist she had continually to demonstrate versatility if not virtuosity. As an American writer she had to Americanize forms originated or pioneered in the "mother country" and Europe. As a woman writer she had to give a feminine or feminist turn to the forms and themes she used. As a religious writer, she had to infuse literature—otherwise a secular cultural institution—with religious-patriotic purpose.

These imperatives are evident in three major literary collections and another advice book. *Sketches* (1834; p. 124) collected diverse prose tales, from the psychological Gothic to the historical and comic, representing American life, culture, and identity, past and present. *Poems* (1834), retitled *Select Poems* in 1838, contained some of her most reprinted and anthologized pieces (p. 141), went through successive editions and augmentations in the following decades, and helped secure her prominence in American literary culture. *Zinzendorff, and Other Poems* (1835) collected previously published magazine pieces with new ones. "Zinzendorff" was another attempt at a specifically Christian American

---

1 Letter of 27 October 1834, quoted in Haight, *Mrs. Sigourney*, 36.

2 E.g., by Samuel Kettel, editor of *Specimens of American Poetry* (1829), vol. 2, 207; cf. Haight, *Mrs. Sigourney* (185 n. 185), who finds the first such reference in *Blackwood's Magazine*, 1834.

epyllion, or "smaller" epic, portraying a historical mission to convert the Indians rather than adventures of warriors and conquerors. The "Other Poems" included some of Sigourney's best known pieces (p. 152) and illustrate such central themes of "Zinzendorff" as the transformative, inspiring, and instructive power of the American landscape; pacifism as a Christian imperative distinguishing the New World from the Old; the centrality of evangelization and social charity to the national enterprise; and the agrarian way of life as the foundation of American values and identity. The volume exemplified Sigourney's self-appointed literary mission to Americanize Romantic culture, and Sigourney soon called on American women to join this mission with *Letters to Mothers* (1838; p. 173), an advice book addressing the issue of woman's power in society and the state and drawing on a late eighteenth-century discourse of republican motherhood.

Sigourney's success as the poet and instructor of American republican domesticity increased in proportion to her real domestic difficulties, however. In 1836 Charles Sigourney lost his bank position, the financial crisis of 1837 depressed business, and in 1838 the Sigourneys moved to a smaller house and retrenched domestic expenses. Fortunately, by now Sigourney could barely keep up with demand for her work from editors of periodicals, anthologies, and literary annuals. She was paid just to have her name on the title page of two women's magazines, Louis Godey's *Magazine and Lady's Book* and W.W. Snowden's *Ladies' Companion*, though the editors ignored her attempts to replace the magazines' sensational and fashionable material with that reflecting her national vision. She did edit the annual *Religious Souvenir* for 1838 and 1839, until finding that the pay did not compensate the work required. As she recycled clothes and household articles, so she recycled her writings for different venues, receiving payment for each, first publishing in periodicals and then selecting for her books. Even poems written for personal occasions were hurried into print: writing a note of condolence, with an appropriate poem, to a man whose wife had just died, she added in a postscript, "As little poems are very apt to find their way to the publick papers,—permit me to ask that this may not be printed, at present, as I should like to make use of it first for an Annual for children, which will appear in the course of next autumn or winter."[1]

---

1 Sigourney to unnamed correspondent, 22 March 1837; LHS Papers (US/CTH/SIGOL/1865—I.5), CHS.

Sigourney's standing as the "American Hemans" was affirmed in 1840 when she contributed an essay and a verse "Monody" to an American edition of Hemans. Revealingly, Sigourney's "Essay on the Genius of Mrs Hemans" (p. 178) celebrates the English writer as Sigourney represented herself—not the poetess of Romantic subjectivity and European literary and political investments that Hemans actually was, but a poetess of piety, domesticity, sympathy, and conciliation. Sigourney's Hemans is not only a Hemans for Americans, but a version of Sigourney as she constructed herself for her reading public. In this, Sigourney's model was not Hemans but the English Evangelical writer Hannah More (1745–1833)—appropriately, Sigourney had contributed a biographical sketch of More to an 1832 American edition of her works. Like More, Sigourney worked in various genres regardless of their literary and cultural status, and infused these works with religious evangelicalism. Like More, she was transformed personally and professionally by the religious "awakening" of the late eighteenth and early nineteenth centuries, and she developed a model of public identity based on religiously inspired "democratic personality" rather than on the European liberal ideology of the sovereign subject. Like More, she envisioned women's contribution to the national cause as domestic, educational, philanthropic, and cultural; she promoted a feminism—or femininism—rooted in the domestic ideology of her time; and she rejected forms of feminism, such as that of Mary Wollstonecraft or American suffragists, claiming political and electoral rights for women.

Sigourney's literary success was based on her promotion of an ideal of middle-class, American, republican domestic womanhood, but her home reality was again conflicting with that ideal. Her husband felt marginalized and neglected by her social activity and literary acclaim, and the couple seemed to lead separate lives in the same house. Worse, gossip circulated in Hartford about family hostility and even violence towards her. In July 1840 Charles Sigourney wrote out a legalistic document containing a "list of calumnies" circulating in Hartford, with a declaration signed by his wife agreeing to refute them.[1] These "calumnies" included reports that he had starved her, denied her writing

1 "'List of Calumnies &c,' submitted for Contradiction. July 22, 1840"; LHS Papers (US/CTH/SIGOL/1865—I.26), CHS; two versions of a document purporting to be by Lydia Sigourney but in her husband's handwriting.

paper, sold the big house to spite her, tried to eject her parents (whom he had agreed to support), taken money from her, threatened her with a sword, and tried to push her down stairs, and that one or other of his daughters had danced around the room in mockery when Lydia Sigourney's mother died, put shot pellets on the stairs to cause her to fall when she was pregnant, and bought arsenic to poison her and her infant daughter Mary. A month after this strange document was written and signed, Lydia Sigourney left on a long-planned extended trip to Europe.

A National and International Literary Figure

Her motives were not just escape or diversion. Being a national literary figure, she could anticipate becoming, like Felicia Hemans, an international one. By traveling to Europe, she could gather material for new books, make new connections, and secure new markets. A London firm had published a selection of her poems, mostly religious, as *Lays from the West* (1834), and she was anthologized in *The Columbian Bard: A Selection of American Poetry* (London, 1835), but there was no international copyright agreement and she likely received nothing from these. With the Rev. John Williams and his mother she toured picturesque places in England and Scotland and met authors such as William Wordsworth. She went on to Paris for two months and was introduced at the court of King Louis Philippe. She returned to London for three months, staying with the family of Evangelical philanthropist W.B. Gurney. She sent out work to publishers, witnessed Queen Victoria's opening of Parliament, and visited literary lions such as the Carlyles, Joanna Baillie, Samuel Rogers, Maria Edgeworth, Mrs S.C. Hall, the Countess of Blessington, and the prison reformer Elizabeth Fry, who showed her around Newgate prison. She made arrangements with London firms to publish her work, and returned to the United States in April 1841, embarking on the technologically advanced steamship, the *Great Western*—a good decision, as the ship had to navigate through an ice field of a kind that would have crushed a sailing ship (in fact, seventy-one years later the same kind of ice would sink the *Titanic*).

Before Sigourney left England she wrote the preface for a London edition of her *Pocahontas, and Other Poems*. A New York edition with this title appeared almost simultaneously, but with a different selection of "other poems." The title poem, "Pocahontas," is another annotated poem, representing seventeenth-century conflict between aborigines and settlers, centred on the familiar though fictionalized figure of Pocahontas. As usual, Sigourney's work addressed a major national issue. Sigourney opposed the forced removals of aborigines from their lands in the 1820s and 1830s, such as the infamous "Trail of Tears" in 1838–39. "Pocahontas" continued Sigourney's protest in *Traits of the Aborigines* against settler exploitation, public incomprehension, and government neglect and abuse of aboriginal peoples. "Pocahontas" was also a literary substitution, by which the poem's protagonist becomes Sigourney herself—mediator and exemplar of an idealized, proto-paradisal American nationhood yet to be realized.

Having taken herself and America to Britain literally and literarily, Sigourney then took Britain to America in her travelogue, *Pleasant Memories of Pleasant Lands* (1842), published simultaneously in Boston and London (pp. 189, 197). The book made her claim to mediate a transatlantic cultural traffic that remained a major force in American life and development.[1] It was well received, but created controversy for including parts of private letters from prominent people—regarded in Britain as a breach of etiquette. Worse, in 1843 she almost became involved in a threatened lawsuit against the editor of the *Ladies' Companion*. This passed, and Sigourney soon produced another book aimed at a transatlantic readership, *Scenes in My Native Land* (1845; p. 203), again published at Boston and London and, like *Pleasant Memories of Pleasant Lands*, comprising a series of linked pieces of poetry and prose describing a site or an event, almost all from New England.

Sigourney also continued to be sought by leading magazines, editors, and publishers. She dealt with this traffic in a characteristically business-like way, constantly circulating her work among editors, demanding a good price, and expecting prompt payment. Her manuscript record of contributions for 1847 shows her contributing over seventy pieces to some forty newspapers, magazines, and annuals in Hartford, Boston, New York, Philadelphia, London, Buffalo, Richmond (Virginia), and elsewhere,[2] and a record of receipts for 1847 (p. 307) shows her meticulously track-

---

1 See Christopher Mulvey, *Anglo-American Landscapes: A Study of Nineteenth-Century Anglo-American Travel Literature* (Cambridge: Cambridge UP, 1983).

2 Lydia Huntley Sigourney Papers (US/CTH/SIGOL/1865—I.31), at the Connecticut Historical Society.

ing payments. She attended carefully to hints about the reading public's interests and tastes. She responded diligently to numerous requests for poems for public or private anniversaries, inaugurations, commemorations, interments, and so on. She sent copies of her new books to anyone she thought might help promote them through personal networks or mention in periodicals. During the business and publishing slump of the late 1830s and early 1840s, she suggested to publishers ways of cutting costs so as to maintain sales. She demanded careful printing, offered to supervise production, and complained about shoddy work. Understanding the book as an article of fashionable cultural consumption, she urged publishers to provide elegant bindings, gilding, paper, and illustrations. She closely followed the production and distribution of her books, suggested new avenues for sales, and when publishers seemed unresponsive, she would distribute her books herself, using her literary, philanthropic, and personal networks, and taking her commission.[1]

Though now a transatlantic literary figure, Sigourney continued to explore any corners of the book market, however small, so long as useful and profitable. *Water-Drops* (1843) collected her pieces advocating temperance—now a national mass movement. *The Child's Book* (1844) addressed the market for school readers. The first run of *Poetry for Seamen* (1845) was purchased by reformers for distribution to the famously hard-living and hard-drinking sailing profession during a boom in New England whaling. *Myrtis; with Other Etchings and Sketchings* (1846) again promoted temperance, opposition to war, and national unity. *The Voice of Flowers* (1846), *The Weeping Willow* (1847), and *Whisper to a Bride* (1850) were collections suitable as gift-books or for copying individual poems on appropriate occasions. Reputation uncompromised, Sigourney had a town in Iowa named after her in 1844; in return, she paid for trees to be planted around the town square. Her national importance was again demonstrated in 1847 when the newly elected president of the United States, James Polk, turned aside while on a parade through Hartford particularly to greet her. The ultimate tribute to Sigourney's popularity and marketability came with the lavishly produced *Illustrated Poems* (1849), in a series that included Henry Wadsworth

1 Melissa Ladd Teed, "A Passion for Distinction: Lydia Huntley Sigourney and the Creation of a Literary Reputation," *New England Quarterly* 77:1 (March 2004): 51–69.

Longfellow, William Cullen Bryant, and Nathaniel Willis—at that time the most popular American male poets.[1]

Sigourney's national and international eminence was, however, based on her place in Hartford and its values, as illustrated by her and Hartford's response to two related issues—race and women's suffrage.

Sigourney sympathized with the condition of slaves and condemned racism in such poems as "Africa" (p. 100), "Difference of Color" (p. 140), and "Slavery" (p. 147). These were reprinted with other of her poems in the anti-slavery paper *The Liberator* and in African-American papers such as the *Colored American*, the *National Era*, and *Frederick Douglass' Paper*. In 1853 the *National Era*, which had first published Harriet Beecher Stowe's *Uncle Tom's Cabin* serially in 1851, reported approvingly that Sigourney contributed $25 to an appeal to purchase the freedom of a family of thirty slaves in Virginia, while Stowe herself contributed nothing.[2] Like most residents of Hartford, Sigourney was relatively conservative on the abolition of slavery, however. Boston-based abolitionists encountered difficulty campaigning and recruiting in Hartford, and most prominent Hartford people advocated assisted emigration of freed slaves to Africa rather than outright abolition. Sigourney supported the Hartford Female African Society, which promoted this option. Only when prominent Hartford men, antagonized by the Fugitive Slave Act and conflict over slavery in the western territories, took up active opposition to slavery in the 1850s, did the Hartford "ladies" join in.

Many women were active abolitionists, and some linked emancipation of slaves to emancipation of women. After the Americans Lucretia Mott and Elizabeth Cady Stanton were prevented from speaking at an 1842 anti-slavery congress in England because they were women, they organized a women's suffrage movement, leading to a convention at Seneca Falls, New York, in 1848.[3] Sigourney opposed such political activism in later editions of her *Letters to Young Ladies*, in the poem "Woman's Patriotism" (p. 225), and in her autobiographical novel, *Lucy*

---

1 In 1861 the book was priced at $3 bound in "half morocco" (a hand-processed cover made of goat-skin), $3.50 in full cloth "elegantly gilt," and $5 in Turkey morocco (advertisement, *Christian Recorder*, Philadelphia, 19 January 1861)—about half a week's wages for a skilled male worker, twice to four times that for a female worker.

2 *National Era* 7 (5 May 1853): 70.

3 Blanche Glassman Hersh, *The Slavery of Sex: Feminist-Abolitionists in America* (Urbana: U of Illinois P, 1978).

Howard's Journal (p. 260). She did so because she had much to lose, privately and publicly, locally and nationally, from supporting women's suffrage. Women of her class had a social prominence and political influence that would be compromised or lost were all adult women to have the vote.[1] At the time, women suffragists were a minority, were widely ridiculed, and seemed unlikely to achieve their objective in the foreseeable future—in fact, women did not get the vote across the United States until 1920. Like most other women writers, Sigourney had long promoted women's education, responsibilities, dignity, and even sanctity, within the domestic ideology of that time, as the more promising option for advancing the condition of women.

Last Years: Useful Books and Literary Experiments

During the last fifteen years of Sigourney's life, national politics were dominated by disagreement between North and South over the related issues of slavery, economic divergence, and Western settlement; these disputes were followed by a bloody Civil War. As always, Sigourney addressed these and other national issues in literary forms both familiar and innovative. At the same time, there were major shifts in the literary field and market for literature, with the emergence of a "high" artistic national literature dominated by men on one hand, and on the other hand a popular mass literature in which women writers were prominent. The 1850s have been called "the feminine fifties" because of the prominence and popularity of women authors;[2] but this decade also saw the publication of works such as Ralph Waldo Emerson's *Representative Men* (1850), Herman Melville's *Moby Dick* (1851), Nathaniel Hawthorne's *The Scarlet Letter* (1850), Henry David Thoreau's *Walden* (1854), and Walt Whitman's *Leaves of Grass* (1855). Little noticed at the time, these would eventually be canonized as America's national literature and oblivionize Sigourney and her women contemporaries. During the 1850s, too, some men achieved sales of poetry that far exceeded Sigourney's, such as Henry Wadsworth Longfellow with *Hiawatha* (1855) and James Gilbert Holland with *Bitter-Sweet* (1858). At the same time, the popular novel increased its dominance of the book

---

1 Susan E. Marshall, *Splintered Sisterhood: Gender and Class in the Campaign against Woman Suffrage* (Madison: U of Wisconsin P, 1997).

2 Fred Lewis Pattee, *The Feminine Fifties* (New York: D. Appleton-Century, 1940).

market, led by women writers such as Fanny Fern, Susan Warner, Mrs E.D.E.N. Southworth, Elizabeth Oakes Smith, Maria Susanna Cummins, and Sigourney's friend Ann Sophia Stephens, all exceeded by Harriet Beecher Stowe with her international bestseller, *Uncle Tom's Cabin* (1851–52).

Sigourney remained a popular and honoured writer, however. In 1853 Franklin Female College awarded her and Sarah Josepha Hale, editor of *Godey's Magazine*, honorary degrees of "Mistress of Arts." *The Ladies' Repository* noted, "So far as we recollect, this is the first instance in which honorary degrees of this kind have been conferred," and added, "Few ladies of the present age are more fairly entitled to literary distinction than Mrs Hale and Mrs Sigourney."[1] Students at the recently founded Butler University in Indiana started a Sigourneyan Society. Sigourney's name usually appeared whenever an essayist, American or foreign, asserted the existence of an American national literature, its democratic accessibility to both women and men writers, and its moral and religious potential to change the world. An 1855 essay on "The Literary Women of America" (p. 343) eulogized "the healthy moral energy which is diffused throughout" her work, "imparting greater strength and a holier tone to the better sentiments and sympathies of the heart." Across the Atlantic three months later, an essay (p. 344) placed Sigourney in the "first class" of the American poets whose influence would effect "the transfiguration of humanity ... from the degrading stigma of its present vices...."

With such validation, it is not surprising that Sigourney continued publishing the kind of magazine pieces and books already familiar to the reading public. There were broadly educational books of various kinds, including *Letters to My Pupils* (1851), *Examples of Life and Death* (1852), and *Examples from the Eighteenth and Nineteenth Centuries* (1857). There were moral and didactic poems and tales, collected in *Olive Leaves* (1852) and *Mary Rice and Other Tales* (1855). There was a commonplace book, *Selections from Various Sources* (1863). There were more books of edification and consolation, including *The Faded Hope* (1853), a memoir and anthology of writings of her son Andrew, who died in 1850; *Past Meridian* (1854; p. 248), an advice book on old age; *Sayings of the Little Ones, and Poems for Their Mothers* (1855; p. 250); and *The Daily Counsellor* (1859; p. 280), comprising a Bible passage and poem for each day in the year.

---

1 *Ladies' Repository* 13 (September 1853): 425.

There were three more collections of her magazine pieces, with further attempts at the long poem. The title poem of *The Western Home, and Other Poems* (1854) splices together a narrative of heroic western settlement and a fact-based Gothic story of moral and political corruption. The "Other Poems" reprise Sigourney's familiar themes: lessons in the book of nature ("Wild Flowers" and "Fallen Forests," pp. 241 and 243 here); female domestic heroism; the heroism of common folk; the importance of maintaining national unity; opposition to war; the United States' republican heritage; art as moral and republican education ("Powers's Statue of the Greek Slave," p. 244); moral topics such as good use of time, the dangers of "luxury," and consolation at the death of loved ones; and poetry itself ("The Muse," p. 245). *Gleanings* (1860) was a collection of shorter poems on such subjects as the virtues of an agrarian republic, but the title piece in *The Man of Uz, and Other Poems* (1862) was her most coherent long poem, retelling the Biblical book of Job, perhaps as counsel to the nation in the midst of the Civil War.

Sigourney also took some new directions. There was a new line of writing for wealthy friends, possibly on commission, including the introduction to Mrs C.M. Badger's *Wild Flowers Drawn and Colored from Nature* (1859), and *The Transplanted Daisy: Memoir of Frances Racillia Hackley* (1865). Sigourney also turned to a form new for her but that her women contemporaries were making their own—the novel of private life. Though she had published many short prose fictions, *Lucy Howard's Journal* (1858; p. 260) is a full-length, partly autobiographical fiction, returning to the theme of American western settlement as a test and renewal of the national character. By now Sigourney was also preparing her last book. Throughout her career she had made extensive use of exemplary lives in her literary program for educating her reading public. After her death on 10 June 1865, her posthumously published *Letters of Life* (1866; p. 295) subsumed her own autobiography into that program.

The Mission of Literature: Sigourney's National Vision

Sigourney's literary production was extensive and diverse, but informing it was a vision of America that changed little over her career. She envisioned a republican, agrarian, Christian United States as a new kind of nation, inspired by a specifically American landscape and nature—as close as God would permit fallen and sinful humanity to come to creating a heaven on earth, an exemplary paradise regained. Sigourney developed a form of feminism within this vision, proposing a central role for women in building this new kind of nation. In this task, she was concerned with the politics or structures of power in local, everyday life, operating through social practices, cultural values, and economic relations. This was also the sphere of political action most accessible to upper middle-class women like Sigourney herself. Accordingly, in her national vision, republicanism was less a set of political processes guaranteed by a written constitution than an ethos and ideal. Citizenship was less a matter of possessing the constitutional right to vote than a religiously inspired moral, intellectual, and cultural qualification to participate in the public sphere for the good of the republic. Agrarianism was less an economic structure and mode of production than a culture and set of values. Christianity was less a particular theology or church than a faith and morality unifying and validating the nation.

The vision of America that Sigourney performed in her personal and local life and embodied in her writings had several related aims—to create a national consensus across social and regional differences, to contribute to a specifically American national literary culture embodying that consensus, to raise the educational and cultural level of American society, to serve charitable causes, to make money for herself, and to establish herself as a public figure and force. Sigourney's national vision was also designed to serve the class that had employed her father and encouraged her as a girl and young woman, and that, Cinderella-like, she had joined through marriage.

This was a class historically based on wealth in land, but increasingly using that wealth to engage in commerce and finance, and displaying wealth in properly republican style, through education, taste, and cultural distinction. Historically, American values had discouraged the exercise of social distinction through luxury and conspicuous consumption. Such values persisted through Sigourney's lifetime, though increasingly challenged by new generations of those enriched by American economic expansion, led and financed by Sigourney's own Hartford, Connecticut. In reaction, Sigourney contributed largely to the reinvention of earlier republican agrarian values as the national "tradition." This invented tradition was implicitly Protestant, for most Americans could not see Catholic Christians, with their supposed obedience to a foreign Pope, or Jews, with their supposedly closed community, as part of their agrarian republic. This "tradition" was also a Northern one, for many Northerners could not see the South's plantation slave economy as part of republican agrarianism. Recognizing this, one Southern commentator attacked Sigourney for representing not the United States but the North, while another called for a "Mrs Sigourney" to represent the South as positively as Sigourney had done the North (see pp. 341, 335). Sigourney's vision of America also served the women of her adoptive class, because her vision rested on values that, historically and conventionally, were seen as "feminine," and that were in practice the province of educated and genteel women such as herself. Sigourney's challenge as a writer was to construct a vision of America that would make the interests of her adoptive class seem like the interests of most Americans and of America itself.

Sigourney's National Vision and Republican Identity

Her success in this task owed much to her formulation of a republican identity that could create a common American national consciousness. Such a republican identity would subsume social, economic, cultural, religious, political, and regional differences—as the motto on the Great Seal of the United States put it, *e pluribus unum*: one from many. For Sigourney, such an identity was not created in the fractious public political sphere, and was inadequately defined by Enlightenment, Revolutionary, or liberal political theory promoting political identity based on property qualification, individual rights, or a secularized sovereign subjectivity. Her vision of America promoted an inclusive republican identity derived from an American tradition of "democratic personality," or moral, intellectual, and religious qualification. Democratic personality was created in the religious revivals of the seventeenth to nineteenth centuries, invoking divine validation as the individual's conviction that he or she was speaking and acting with divine sanction. Democratic personality particularly empowered the subordinate and marginalized, including women and the lower classes, to speak and act in the public sphere, from which they were otherwise conventionally excluded by gender, class, or other social difference.[1] By Sigourney's day, however, democratic personality was invoked and practised by many middle-class people in their own interests. Sigourney and other women writers and activists of her time invoked such validation to claim not only a public voice for them-

1 Ruttenburg, *Democratic Personality*, 3–6.

selves, but also a right to speak for others, especially the marginalized and "unfortunate," in a way denied them by both constitution and social convention. This work is seen clearly in her approach to the related issues of class and gender.

Republican Identity, Class, and Gender

Class conflict was a national preoccupation during Sigourney's lifetime, and discussion of it took two different forms: one constitutional and electoral, and the other socio-economic. The constitutional discourse addressed the problem of prescribing the electorate for federal, state, and local governments. The socio-economic discourse understood class in terms of social and economic differences including occupation, income, and status. The two discourses interacted because the task of the constitution and electoral system was seen as balancing the "naturally" divergent social and economic interests of the propertied and propertyless, employers and employed—thereby avoiding social conflict and descent into "extremes" of tyranny or radical democracy. These issues were exacerbated by immigration from non-British and non-Protestant countries, the rise of trade unionism, exploitation of class conflict by political factions such as the Jacksonians (whom Sigourney detested), conflict over slavery in states newly admitted to the Union, and the tendency of alienated social groups to move westward and establish utopian, classless model communities of various kinds, possibly disintegrating national identity and unity.

One prominent response was the argument that, unlike other countries where class conflict was the norm, the American republic fostered a "harmony of interests" between classes.[1] This argument was advanced mainly by men of letters including several Sigourney knew, such as the Rev. Francis Wayland, who was on her voyage back from Europe in 1842; T.P. Kettell, editor of the *Democratic Review*, which published many of her poems; and Henry C. Carey, publisher of several of Sigourney's books. According to them, both employers and labourers depended on each other and so had a harmony if not commonality of interests; therefore, these commentators concluded, employers and capitalists should be free to pursue their interests and workers need not organize to defend theirs. "Harmony of interests" side-

1 Martin J. Burke, *The Conundrum of Class: Public Discourse on the Social Order in America* (Chicago and London: U of Chicago P, 1995), 108–32.

stepped arguments that the vote should be related to social class through property qualification, and avoided liberal arguments for representative constitutionalism based on possession of sovereign subjectivity. Sigourney often promoted the theory of "harmony of interests" in her work, as in her poem "The Thriving Family" (p. 234) and her novel *Lucy Howard's Journal* (p. 260). More important, the idea that the United States fostered harmony of class interests offered a role for the conventionally accepted promoters of social harmony—women, especially upper- and upper middle-class women. Sigourney exercised this role in her educational and charitable activities, recommended it in her writings, and fashioned her public image around it.

Sigourney also felt that women, especially of her class, had more to gain from a republican identity based on an ideology of democratic personality than from theories of political rights, liberal constitutionalism, or qualification to vote, which stirred up class conflict. As the electoral privileges and power of the social elite to which she belonged were weakened by expansion of the franchise, the role of that elite's social status and cultural prestige became more critical in maintaining their power and influence. This was the sphere in which Sigourney worked, both as local social activist and as national moral and cultural influence. She believed that women's direct involvement in electoral politics, with their divisiveness, demagoguery, controversy, conflict, and scandals, would sully the image and vitiate the role of women in her national vision, as seen in "Privileges of the Mother" (p. 173), "Woman's Patriotism" (p. 225), and Lucy Howard's declaration after visiting Washington:

> Politics seem to me but another name for strife.... One of the privileges of our sex is that they may keep clear of such matters.... Thrice blessed is our own quiet sphere of duty, where, in making others happy, we find our own truest joy. (p. 269)

Sigourney showed how to form women for this role in "On the Policy of Elevating the Standard of Female Education" (p. 133), *Letters to Young Ladies*, and *Letters to Mothers*. Examples of the role are presented in numerous exemplary lives, American and foreign, recent and ancient, famous and obscure, such as an American missionary's wife (p. 164); George Washington's mother (p. 97); and Cornelia, mother of the ancient Roman republican heroes the Gracchi (pp. 135, 175). Sigourney gave her fictional female characters a similar republican identity—religiously motivated, divinely validated, acquired through self-discipline and education, and performed through domestic management and care, often extended into the local community. In these lives, female republican identity is usually confirmed by personal and domestic affliction, as in *Lucy Howard's Journal*, numerous biographical subjects, numerous elegies, and poems and stories of bereaved mothers and widows, including herself. Together, these portraits constitute a female republic persisting through history, from past to future.

Margins of Republican Identity: Race, Ethnicity, Disability, and Criminality

Sigourney applied her version of republican identity to further issues of social difference, including race, ethnicity, and the socially marginalized. To each group she gave a different place in her national vision—to be marginalized and contained, converted to a limited form of American republican identity, managed and controlled through charity, or excluded.

Apart from people like herself, those most acceptable in Sigourney's national vision were aboriginal peoples. Like most, Sigourney believed that marginalization and perhaps extinction of aborigines was inevitable in face of the United States' historical destiny. Like some, she protested the treatment of aborigines, especially forced removals to make way for white settlement. Like many, she urged Christianization of aborigines as a prelude to their assimilation by republican America. Against popular antipathy to Indians, however, she also constructed them as a "positive stereotype":[1] she romanticized them, appropriated what she saw as their virtues, attributed to them a form of republican identity, and represented their way of life as an anticipation of her national vision. Thus she participated in the tendency of settler culture to appropriate aboriginal peoples as America's "folk." In European Romantic nationalism the folk were a supposedly original common people with shared culture, values, and religious beliefs, distinct from all other peoples and nations, thereby justifying their formation into an autonomous state with a distinct "national" identity, history, culture, and destiny. Americans both white and black all originated elsewhere, however, leaving abo-

1 Scott B. Vickers, *Native American Identities: From Stereotype to Archetype in Art and Literature* (Albuquerque: U of New Mexico P, 1998), 4.

rigines to be fashioned into the national folk.[1] But in order for aborigines to serve this function, they had to be portrayed as inevitably disappearing, receding ever westward or dying out. With but a spectral existence, they could better serve as a fantasy of qualities supposedly absorbed into American republican identity, illustrated in Sigourney's *Traits of the Aborigines of America*, "Indian Names" (p. 149), and "Oriska" (p. 227).

Sigourney could not imagine a similar role for African Americans. For her, they remained alien and, if free or freed, should be helped to return to Africa. Her poem "Africa" (p. 100) recalls the learning and heroism of ancient Africans but sees those of her own day as subjects for Christianization, and calls those enslaved in her own country an "exiled race," to be returned to their original home. Sigourney's protests against slavery, such as "Difference of Color" (p. 140), were relatively muted, and in the 1840s and 1850s she expressed more concern that the issue would break up the Union, in poems such as "The Thriving Family" (p. 234). On the threshold of the Civil War and during it, she did try to imagine African Americans as part of the American national identity. The narrator of *Lucy Howard's Journal* takes into her new home in the West, as servants, both an abandoned Indian woman, Orra, and an African American servant, Amy, thereby modeling her national vision's hierarchy of class and race.

Sigourney was less ambivalent about accommodating ethnic and religious difference in her national vision. Like many native-born Americans, she disdained the Irish Catholic immigrants who began appearing in numbers in Hartford and elsewhere in the 1830s.[2] By the 1850s a backlash produced the chauvinistic anti-immigrant Know-Nothing Party and the wars of the immigrant and anti-immigrant "gangs of New York" depicted in Herbert Asbury's 1927 book and Martin Scorsese's 2002 film of that title. In *Sketch of Connecticut* Sigourney depicts a rebellious Irish immigrant refusing to pay a road toll to the English immigrant toll keeper (p. 96). In "Miss Tabitha's Farming" (p. 254), she devises satirical names for the Irish labourers. *The Wide-Awake Gift*, a Know-Nothing gift book annual, republished

---

1 Robert F. Berkhofer, Jr., *The White Man's Indian: Images of the American Indian from Columbus to the Present* (New York: Alfred A. Knopf, 1978), 86–96.

2 Leonard Dinnerstein, Roger L. Nichols, and David M. Reimers, *Natives and Strangers: A Multicultural History of Americans*, 4th ed. (New York and Oxford: Oxford UP, 2003), ch. 3–4.

Sigourney's patriotic poem, "Grave of the Mother of Washington" (p. 97). In *Lucy Howard's Journal*, the Scottish immigrant gardener is depicted positively, the aboriginal domestic servant sentimentally, and Lucy says of her African American servant, "Methinks the African race have warmer affections and more lasting attachments than our hirelings of other nations" (p. 272). Degrees of republican identity are ordered by class, race, and ethnicity. Because of the demands of America's expanding economy, people from "other nations"—readers would understand them to be Catholics from Ireland and elsewhere—cannot be excluded, but they are merely "hirelings," apparently incapable of full republican identity.

Sigourney also tried to place another set of groups in relation to republican identity and her national vision—the socially marginalized, including abandoned or widowed mothers and orphaned children, the disabled, and prison convicts. All were cause of public concern in the formation of the American republic,[1] and all were addressed by Sigourney in her charitable work and her writing. Abandoned mothers and children—if Protestant and "respectable"—were targeted by several of Sigourney's charities, and her writings gave them several functions in her national vision. They were exemplary figures of female domestic heroism, victims of the accidents of mortality and of human (usually male) excesses, from drunkenness to warfare. Like aborigines and slaves, they also provided opportunities for exercise of the social charity and sympathy central to a feminized republican identity. Examples range from the long-suffering wife in Sigourney's widely distributed temperance tale, "The Intemperate," to the aboriginal heroine of her poem "Oriska" (p. 227). Sigourney also devoted much charitable energy and a number of poems to the disabled, in particular the deaf and dumb, and her writings on the subject appear on disability history websites today. For Sigourney, these groups, too, existed to exercise charity and sympathy, as in the poem, "The Deaf, Dumb and Blind Girl" (p. 156).

Sigourney represented the girl as a prisoner in her body awaiting liberation by death, and often used the prisoner or exile to represent the human condition in the light of eternity and in relation to the American republican freedom which, according to Sigourney, approximates the freedom of the eternal life hereafter. Sigourney's writings featured famous historical prisoners and exiles,

---

1 David J. Rothman, *The Discovery of the Asylum: Social Order and Disorder in the New Republic*, rev. ed. (New York: Aldine de Gruyter, 2002).

including victims of Old World tyrants, of religious persecution, of earlier European imperialism in the New World, and of masculine monarchic politics, such as Queen Caroline Matilda of Denmark (p. 101). These figures represented kinds of imprisonment supposedly abolished by the United States as a new kind of republican nation in history. Some unrepublican forms of imprisonment remained, especially slavery, though Sigourney did not envision freed slaves as capable of full republican identity. Imprisoned white Americans were another matter. "The Liberated Convict" (p. 148) engaged with an intense national debate as to whether the object of the prison was to reform outward behaviour or the inner person.[1] The poem depicted the convict as temporarily and regrettably, though nevertheless justly, removed from republican society, but still having roles in it—to exercise social sympathy and charity, to symbolize the fallen and sinning condition of humanity, and, most important, to illustrate the consequences of failure to sustain the moral, intellectual, social, and economic discipline of American republican identity, showing that imprisonment of the right kind could be an instrument for restoring that identity.

Teaching Republican Identity: Insects, Animals, Plants, and Children

Even the animal and vegetable creation had a place and function in Sigourney's national vision, as a school and test of republican identity. Humble or noxious creatures such as "The Coral Insect" (p. 99), "The Wasp" (p. 103), "The Rat" (p. 138), or "The Crushed Mouse" (p. 236) could teach the omnipresence and wisdom of divinity as well as patience, kindness, and sympathy. Useful plants such as those detailed in *Traits of the Aborigines of America* show divine wisdom in providing materials for human healing and comfort, while flowers such as "The Rose" (p. 65), "The Rose-Geranium" (p. 197), and "Wild Flowers" (p. 241) provide pleasure, consolation, and instruction. Children in their helplessness and innocence can nevertheless instruct and even redeem, as in "The Deaf, Dumb and Blind Girl," "The Father" (p. 124), *Sayings of the Little Ones* (p. 250), and Sigourney's numerous poems on dead children.[2]

---

1 Thomas L. Dumm, *Democracy and Punishment: Disciplinary Origins of the United States* (Madison: U of Wisconsin P, 1987), ch. 5.

2 See Elizabeth A. Petrino, "'Feet So Precious Charged': Dickinson, Sigourney, and the Child Elegy," *Tulsa Studies in Women's Literature* 13:2 (Fall 1994): 317–38.

These themes had been made the special province of women writers in Britain from the late eighteenth century, indicated in Anna Laetitia Barbauld's poem "The Mouse's Petition" and Sarah Trimmer's children's story *The History of the Robins*. Kindness to animals and insects was also a major topic in middle-class moral and social reform movements, with their many stories in which the cruel child grows up to become the adult murderer, slave-driver, or war-monger. Sigourney gave these themes a particular republican turn, however, as in "Be Kind to Animals" (p. 108) from her children's book *How To Be Happy*, where Benedict Arnold, the archetypal traitor in American republican history and mythology, began his career of infamy by tormenting birds, small animals, and cattle. Kindness and gratitude to the "inferior" creation, Sigourney often insisted, was a duty to the God "the Father of us all" and thereby an exercise of divinely sanctioned republican identity.

Republican Religion

A powerful religious evangelicalism sustained Sigourney's all-inclusive national vision, then, in four major ways. Christianity, or rather Protestantism, was central to Sigourney's vision of the United States as a republican nation of millennial possibilities, unprecedented in history, potentially a new promised land. This vision was based on a limited tolerationist approach to religious differences that had divided both Old World and New for three centuries and that led to the seventeenth-century settlement of New England and Sigourney's own Connecticut. She was raised a Congregationalist and became an Episcopalian through marriage. Congregationalists and Episcopalians were on opposite sides of a great theological, ecclesiastical, and political divide; Sigourney crossed that divide in her own life, and in her writings she avoided religious doctrine and promoted religious toleration—at least among Protestants, as in chapter 8 of *Sketch of Connecticut* (p. 81) and "The Yankee," a comic rendering of the seventeenth-century Salem witch trials (p. 212). As she wrote to a friend in 1827, "I have been in the habit of reading but little controversial theology, from the impression that it sometimes leads us either to foster or repel peculiar opinions, to the detriment of christian charity ..." (p. 309 here).

Second, as noted earlier, religion was central to Sigourney's national vision less as a particular theology or denomination than as the necessary condition of republican identity. This was the "democratic personality" validated by (Protestant) religious faith, qualifying the individual for membership and a voice in the republic, regardless of social difference, status, or electoral entitlement—in fact, supplanting these, to constitute her reading public as a supposedly inclusive and egalitarian, divinely sanctioned republic, with a divine mission in history to help redeem humanity.

Third, religious evangelicalism provided Sigourney and most of her contemporaries with a program for social action converging the sacred and the secular. Evangelicals emphasized religious observances and services, and Sigourney wrote many poems for these. Evangelicals promoted the use of hymns, and Sigourney wrote many of these. They promoted a wide range of social philanthropy of kinds which Sigourney founded, promoted, and led locally and contributed to nationally. They opposed particular social "vices," such as drinking, gambling, duelling, violence, and warfare, and Sigourney often discussed these topics in her writings. They promoted education, with religious foundation, for all; Sigourney was not only a teacher with a religious-social program but a tireless advocate of religion-based education for aborigines, Western settlers, the poor, the disabled, women, and foreign peoples, devoting much of her writing to these causes. Evangelicals had deep confidence in the power of print to transform individuals and hence society; Sigourney participated enthusiastically in this print culture, across the span of her writing and in particular contributions to religious tract societies, witnessed by her poem "Religious Tracts" (p. 165).

Finally, Evangelicalism was a transatlantic movement and culture, and gave Sigourney access to an American and also a British reading public, for whom she remained a mainly religious poet—for example, the "Other Poems" in the London edition of her *Pocahontas, and Other Poems* were more predominantly religious than in the New York edition. After her death, Sigourney was seen as a mainly religious poet, and her work was paired with that of the English devotional poet Frances Ridley Havergal in an 1885 collection. In the late nineteenth and twentieth centuries, this image would result in Sigourney's marginalization by the rise to dominance of a secular and liberal literary culture.

Republican Economy: Agrarian America

In Sigourney's national vision, the idea of democratic personality validated by republican religion is necessarily entwined with a model of the harmonization of individuals and classes in the domestic, familial productive unit of an agrarian economy. Sigourney, like many of her contemporaries, envisioned the United States as foundationally and essentially an agrarian republic, one that was in reality receding ever more into the past and to the West. Her celebrations of the agrarian way of life, artisanship, and home manufacture spanned her career, from *Sketch of Connecticut* (p. 81) to *Lucy Howard's Journal* (p. 260). She symbolized the agrarian republic through humble domestic objects, as in "To an Ancient Rocking Chair" (p. 105), or "To a Shred of Linen" (p. 168), contrasted to products of luxury, as in "To a Fragment of Silk" (p. 107). For Sigourney, the agrarian economy was not only an inexhaustible source of solid rather than ephemeral, commercial wealth, but also a nursery of republican virtues. In her often reprinted poem, "Agriculture" (p. 155), the agrarian economy not only provides plenty but nurtures simple living, contentment, and peace, in contrast to the destruction caused by warfare, born of ambition. Another much reprinted poem, "The Thriving Family" (p. 234), envisioned the various States as a harmonious rural family, the agrarian unit of production.

By contrast, she dealt seldom and indirectly with the reality of America's expanding commercial and trading economy. For example, "Connecticut River," one of her most reprinted poems (p. 141), ignored the fact that the river had already become a major New England channel of commerce, and instead emphasized the republican agrarian way of life along its shores. Her representation of urban life was persistently negative. The city is the scene and the source of luxury, vanity, temptation, and vice, as in "The Intemperate"; or a scene of brutalizing competition, as in "The Father" (p. 241); or an oppressively overcrowded scene of anomie, as in "Westminster Abbey" (p. 196) and Lucy Howard's impression of New York (p. 269). Sigourney was critical of the increased immigration that industrial expansion stimulated. She was sardonic about technological advances such as steam power, the telegraph, and machinofacture. She viewed ambivalently even an invention such as the sewing machine (p. 289), which lightened an onerous form of women's domestic labour but also reduced that labour's artisanship and opened the way for its industrialization in sweatshops.

Many others idealized agrarian America as the "real" America in the face of a spreading urban and industrial reality.[1] Along

---

1 David E. Shi, *The Simple Life: Plain Living and High Thinking in American Culture* (New York and Oxford: Oxford UP, 1985), ch. 5.

with these other observers, Sigourney was not ignorant of that reality. Her husband, his banking and business associates, and his social class were busy creating it all around her in Hartford, where her social philanthropy addressed its negative social consequences. In her early career she sympathized with the Jeffersonian vision of agrarian democracy, but she was not clinging to this vision against economic and social change and Hamiltonian assertions of the need for industrial development and commercial expansion. Nor would her reading public take her representation of this vision literally. She and they knew that this was less a representation of an actual or desired reality than it was a myth of an imagined moral and cultural condition—a vision to live *by* rather than *in*.

Republican Nature: Sublime, Beautiful, and Picturesque America

Reinforcing Sigourney's representation of the United States as ideally and ideologically an agrarian republic was her representation of American nature. For Sigourney, a Protestant agrarian republic with a divinely appointed mission in history would not destroy American nature but transform part of it into the republic's agrarian "home," through Western settlement, while leaving other parts to instruct and inspire American republican identity. Her writings on this topic were numerous and diverse, and contributed to a broad movement in the arts to represent America as a distinctive physical and social space.[1] This movement adapted the work of European Romantic historians, novelists, poets, and artists in representing the nation-state's topography as the shaper of the "national" character, history, culture, and destiny.

Sigourney's representations of American nature ranged across the established aesthetic categories of the sublime, beautiful, and picturesque. Her construction of a specifically American and republican natural sublime is seen most clearly in her texts on Niagara (pp. 152, 203, 210), part of an extensive American literature and iconography on the famous falls.[2] Picturesque nature blends into agrarian landscape in the poem "Connecticut River"

---

1 Charles L. Sanford, *The Quest for Paradise; Europe and the American Moral Imagination* (Urbana: U of Illinois P, 1981), ch. 8; David Bjelajac, *American Art: A Cultural History* (New York: Harry N. Abrams, 2001), ch. 5.

2 Elizabeth McKinsey, *Niagara Falls: Icon of the American Sublime* (Cambridge: Cambridge UP, 1985).

(p. 141), and "civilized" and civilizing nature carved from wilderness is represented in the later sections of *Lucy Howard's Journal*. New World nature represented in these texts is contrasted with, on the one hand, urban scenes in both New and Old Worlds and, on the other hand, Old World nature and landscape drenched in history that is dominated by men and their conflicts, as in "Carlisle" (p. 189). In Americanizing European Romantic discourses of national nature, Sigourney also Americanized genres well established in European culture, including the georgic, the loco-descriptive poem, the travelogue, and the sentimental narrative poem, while developing forms associated more with America itself, such as "local colour" prose, the Indian captivity narrative ("Oriana" from *Sketches*),[1] and the Western adventure story (*Lucy Howard's Journal*).

Republican Education, Culture, Literature, and the Arts

Such naturalization of cultural themes and literary forms was part of Sigourney's self-appointed task of forming a national literature against American imitation of European literature, massive republication by American publishers of foreign works, and widespread admiration of foreign literature by the American reading public.[2] For Sigourney, the formation of an American literature was a political and patriotic act promoting American professional authorship in a program to educate the American public, in the sense of fashioning, improving, and disciplining a specifically American republican national culture. In this respect, Sigourney merged her identities as teacher and writer,[3] seen in her early poem, "The Desertion of the Muse" (p. 63). In her writing she repeatedly referred to her experience, knowledge, and function as a teacher. She wrote numerous books for schools, dealing mainly with American themes; and she was often anthologized in school readers. She often raised issues in education, especially of women, for the national interest, as in her address

---

1 Richard VanDerBeets, *The Indian Captivity Narrative: An American Genre* (Lanham: UP of America, 1984).

2 Meredith L. McGill, *American Literature and the Culture of Reprinting, 1834–1853* (Philadelphia: U of Pennsylvania P, 2003); Ronald J. Zboray, *A Fictive People: Antebellum Economic Development and the American Reading Public* (New York and Oxford: Oxford UP, 1993).

3 Mary Loeffelholz, *From School to Salon: Reading Nineteenth-Century American Women's Poetry* (Princeton and Oxford: Princeton UP, 2004), ch. 2.

"On the Policy of Elevating the Standard of Female Education" (p. 133). She promoted teaching as a patriotic profession for women. She supported institutions of higher education for women, such as Mount Holyoke College. She depicted mothers forming the republican nation through domestic education, as in *Letters to Mothers* (p. 173), and represented teaching as an extension of "naturally" feminine and domestic expertises and knowledges. She depicted women instructing adults in republican values, as in *Sketch of Connecticut*. Sigourney represented republican woman as a fusion of wife, mother, and teacher, and frequently cited the ancient Roman Cornelia, mother and educator of the Gracchi brothers, heroes of republican history.

In Europe and Britain, the cultivated woman was often figured as a custodian of aesthetic taste, and "poetesses" such as Germaine de Staël's fictional Corinne, in the novel of that title (1807), and the Englishwoman Felicia Hemans promoted the "national" arts, past and present, and the role of the arts in social improvement. Sigourney differed from them, however, in her treatment of "high" culture and the arts. De Staël and her Corinne were formidable intellectuals discoursing widely on the arts; Hemans represented herself as charged with aesthetic sensibility, referred to a wide range of British and European literature, celebrated and contributed to the repertory of "national" song, and wrote frequently about her response to music, painting, sculpture, and other arts. In contrast, Sigourney employed a narrow range of literary reference and allusion, and wrote seldom about the other arts—one exception being her poem on the American Hiram Powers' sculpture, "The Greek Slave" (p. 244). Though some of Sigourney's poems, such as "Charter Oak," were set to music, her contributions to "national" song were few.

Unlike her European Romantic contemporaries, and in accordance with her promotion of an idealized agrarian culture, Sigourney associated the "high" arts with a decadent, corrupting, modern commercialized culture of consumption, luxury, and fashion—unsuitable and dangerous for a republic. Though Sigourney's work often appeared in magazines that displayed and discussed the latest fashions, she frequently criticized the fashion system that commercialized and popularized the arts through manufacturing, as in her poems "To a Fragment of Silk" (p. 107) and "The Milliners and Fishes" (p. 185). Instead, Sigourney celebrated articles of domestic artisanal production from the agrarian economy, as in "To an Ancient Rocking Chair" (p. 105) and the description of the Larkins' home in *Sketch of Connecticut* (p. 91).

Sigourney represented her own cultural production as a similar form of specifically feminine and domestic artisanship. In her autobiography, *Letters of Life*, she declared, "If there is any kitchen in Parnassus, my Muse has surely officiated there as a woman of all work, and an aproned waiter" (p. 301). The statement simultaneously domesticates Parnassus, mythical home of the muses, and ennobles the kitchen, centre and symbol of women's role as domestic producers. The statement also accords with Sigourney's refusal to pose as a Romantic "genius" or European-style poetess,[1] and with her pragmatic, utilitarian, and professional approach to literature as a form of domestic production for home and public use, in the national interest. Sigourney depicted the republican woman writer and poet, in her own person, not as a national poetess and female bard like Felicia Hemans or Germaine de Staël's fictional Corinne, but as a woman working domestically in her "kitchen in Parnassus." Whereas European writers such as de Staël and Hemans depicted the relationship between domesticity and literature, femininity and fame, as an anguished conflict destructive to the poetess, Sigourney depicted the relationship as a problem of domestic time management that the woman writer must resolve out of republican duty, as seen in her poem, "The Muse" (p. 245).

Sigourney was a prolific, diverse, and often experimental writer who kept her eye on new literary trends, so generalizations about her work will have limits. Nevertheless, it is clear that she fashioned her American literary poetics and language from particular lines of English and American writers, and that she understood literary poetics and language as her contemporaries did, in political terms, as matters of the national interest.[2] She drew her central themes, forms, and poetics from devotional poets, from John Milton through Edward Young to William Cowper, and from Evangelical prose writers, particularly Hannah More. Her models were English and American moral writers in the "plain style" tradition, and eighteenth-century poets in the tradition of

---

1 See Victoria Olwell, "'It Spoke Itself': Women's Genius and Eccentric Politics," *American Literature* 77:1 (March 2005): 33–63.

2 See David Simpson, *The Politics of American English, 1776–1850* (New York: Oxford UP, 1986); Michael P. Kramer, *Imagining Language in America From the Revolution to the Civil War* (Princeton: Princeton UP, 1992).

Alexander Pope. These writers favoured simple, unadorned language and limited literary diction, as seen in Sigourney's *Letters to Young Ladies* (p. 110) or "Connecticut River" (p. 141). They employed a "middle" style between the elevated and the colloquial, the courtly and the plebeian, as seen in Sigourney's "Carlisle" (p. 189). They deployed devices of "articulate energy" appealing to both feeling and intellect,[1] such as active verbs that personify abstractions, and syntax and verse-line structures that dramatize the sense of the passage, seen for example in the opening lines of Sigourney's *Traits of the Aborigines of America* (p. 70). To a degree, this kind of poetics was associated with moral, social, and political reform, designed to enable a more democratic and civil society, and was promoted by English reformists such as Joseph Priestley (who immigrated to the United States in the 1790s), and by early American republicans such as Thomas Jefferson. In her later work such as her revised *Letters to Young Ladies* and *Past Meridian* (p. 248), Sigourney did develop a more belletristic style, partly to keep up with literary fashion, but her literary practice remained within what she would consider an American republican poetics.

For the same reason, Sigourney devoted most of her literary production to several related kinds of writing. First, she represented America, past and present, in a wide variety of works. These include longer historical verse narratives such as "Zinzendorff," "Pocahontas," and "The Western Home"; the verse survey, *Traits of the Aborigines* (p. 70); regional and local-colour writing such as *Sketch of Connecticut* (p. 81) and "The Yankee" (p. 212); travelogue such as *Pleasant Memories of Pleasant Lands* (p. 189), which applies an American perspective to Europe, and *Lucy Howard's Journal* (p. 260); and loco-descriptive and nature writing in both verse and prose such as "Connecticut River" (p. 141) and *Scenes in My Native Land* (p. 203). Second, she commented on many issues of the day in shorter poems, prose fiction, and essays, from "Africa" (p. 100) through "The War-Spirit" (p. 145) to "Woman's Patriotism" (p. 225). She also provided moral and social instruction in many forms, including prose manuals and advice books of different kinds, from the satirical "Advice of Tabitha Thistle" (p. 68) through the horta-

1 Donald Davie, *Articulate Energy: An Enquiry into the Syntax of English Poetry* (New York: Harcourt, Brace and Company, 1958); also Davie, *The Purity of Diction in English Verse* (London: Chatto and Windus, 1952).

tory *Letters to Young Ladies* (p. 110) to the belletristic *Past Meridian* (p. 248); prose essays such as those on the education of women (p. 133) and the social status of the aged (p. 238); many didactic poems; prose and verse adaptations of parts of the Bible, from "The Creation" (p. 66) through *The Daily Counsellor* (p. 284) to "The Man of Uz"; books for children; prose biography; numerous verse elegies; and her own commonplace book, *Selections from Various Sources* (p. 292). She celebrated the trivial, humble, and everyday in numerous shorter poems from "To an Ancient Rocking Chair" and "To a Shred of Linen" to "The Sewing Machine" and "Breakfast" (p. 289). In a parallel vein, she produced at request a great many occasional poems, or poems for particular occasions from deaths and funerals to public celebrations, ceremonies, and observances.

Sigourney would know that efficient kitchens and households, even in Parnassus, recycle. She wrote for recycling, by herself and by others. She would re-use the same work several times, in different ways. She would usually publish first in a newspaper, magazine, literary annual, event program, or other ephemeral venue. She would then republish the work, often slightly revised, in a book collection or anthology, itself reprinted and revised. Local periodicals commonly reprinted pieces from other periodicals, though without payment, circulating Sigourney's work even farther. Her revisions were usually designed less to refine and improve than to refurbish and readdress, as seen in "Connecticut River" and "The Milliners and Fishes" (pp. 141, 185).

Appropriately for a "kitchen in Parnassus," many of her occasional pieces, especially those on important life events, were designed as recyclable literature in another sense. One reviewer noted that the tendency of many of Sigourney's poems was to represent types, even when particular individuals were being depicted: "With remarkable distinctness of conception and decision of expression, we have presented to us the type, but it is given in its simple unity, abstracted from all individuality." The reviewer saw this trait as "probably a chief source of [Sigourney's] influence over the hearts of her readers" (p. 341 here). Such poems, especially her elegies and odes, were written as pattern pieces, assimilating the individual person, event, or loss to a formula of edification, as seen in "On the Death of an Infant" (p. 151) or "Thoughts in a Church-yard" (p. 253). As Sigourney knew, readers could in their turn assimilate events in their own lives to such poems, which would be copied and circulated among those whom Sigourney would never meet, providing forms of "sentimental collaboration"[1]—a currency of popular literary artifacts for use in everyday life, thereby creating a national community through recycled verse. Sigourney collected her work of this kind into a literary counterpart to needlework pattern books, including pieces for copying out as valentines (*The Voice of Flowers*, 1846), consolatory mourning poems (*The Weeping Willow*, 1847), edifying wedding verses (*Whisper to a Bride*, 1850), and devotional religious poetry (*Poems*, 1842).

Many of her readers, like the teenage daughter of a Confederate army colonel in rural Georgia or the friend of a grieving mother in Pennsylvania,[2] would copy these and similar poems from Sigourney's books or clip them from newspapers and magazines, to insert in their commonplace books and scrapbooks, or to forward to friends. Sigourney intended such verse, along with her shorter poems on national and public themes, for use and re-use in everyday life. She did persist in attempting major, formally innovative poems on important national topics, from *Traits of the Aborigines* to "The Man of Uz"; but unlike contemporaries such as Longfellow (whose narrative verse form she imitated in part of her long poem "The Rural Life in New-England"), she achieved little critical or popular success in this line. These poems show considerable literary skill, if uncertain construction, but Sigourney remained, for critics and reading public alike, a poet of shorter pieces most likely encountered in newspapers and magazines—what Edgar Allan Poe, speaking of Sigourney, called "the newspaper iteration."[3]

Nevertheless, Sigourney, along with many of her critics, editors, publishers, and readers, considered this sustained ephemerality a major national literary achievement. As an early commentator on her career remarked, "There is indeed, no other shape, in which the widest popularity may so well be combined with the most permanent endurance" (p. 326 here). This may seem a paradox, but Sigourney's literary poetics and practice were designed to instill in her readers, by repetition, her version of republican identity for her vision of America. Her poetics were designed to form an American public literary style able to reach and educate a wide readership. Her practice of classical European literary forms, ranging from the

1 See Mary Louise Kete, *Sentimental Collaborations: Mourning and Middle-Class Identity in Nineteenth-Century America* (Durham and London: Duke UP, 2000).

2 Documents in the possession of the editor.

3 Reported in Nathaniel Parker Willis, *Dashes at Life with a Free Pencil* (New York: J.S. Redfield, 1845), part 4, "Ephemera," 201.

brief epic and long narrative through the ode, georgic, and elegy, was designed to democratize, vernacularize, and domesticate—to Americanize—these forms. Even her commonplace book, *Selections from Various Sources* (p. 292), assimilated past and contemporary European authors, many with values and visions different from Sigourney's, into her American literary republic simply by excerpting congenial passages from them. She also preferred informal genres developed or favoured by American writers and particularly suited to her national literary purpose, such as the loco-descriptive and local-colour piece, the travelogue, the sketch and the tale, the song for public occasions, the familiar essay. Her extensive and diverse practice of occasional poetry, especially for private occasions, was designed to poeticize everyday and public life in republican America for her readers, dignifying them through literary treatment, elevating them above the mundane, removing them, like the poem clipped out of a newspaper and pasted in a scrapbook, from the relentless flow of time and transience, in order to address repeatedly the passing events, emotions, issues and events of every day. In doing so in the ways she did, Sigourney aimed to transcendentalize this America for her reading public, ostensibly bringing America closer to and in communication with the divine, and thereby legitimating it as the divinely chosen nation in history, while insisting that this America must be lived out every day, in common life.

"The Sweet Singer of Hartford": Sigourney's Critical Reception

Sigourney's national vision, based on her version of a specifically American republican identity and embodied in the culturally prestigious forms of poetry and imaginative prose, made her the most widely read and respected American woman poet in the English-speaking world during her lifetime. Most of her contemporary critics approved this success as evidence of her and her reading public's moral and religious elevation (p. 344 here), while some saw it as evidence of low American taste responding to merely sentimental themes and mediocre literary skill (p. 337). The American Civil War, which ended just before her death, seemed to have dislocated the social and cultural patterns that formed Sigourney and her national vision, and her writing was marginalized by the growth of a mass popular culture on the one hand and an elite literary culture on the other. Her name continued to sell her books for barely a decade after her death. Some aspects of her work, such as her religious poetry, celebrations of domesticity, representations of aborigines as the American folk, and depictions of American nature, continued to hold a place for her in American and British popular literature through the nineteenth century and into the twentieth.

But the rise to hegemony of a secular liberal ideology of the sovereign subject, served by literature as high art, made Sigourney's work and its model of republican identity based on democratic personality seem crude and vulgar. A few of her poems continued to circulate in cheap poetry anthologies and in collections on subjects such as motherhood, and scraps of her verses continued to appear on articles such as souvenirs of Niagara in the form of paperweights and teapot stands.[1] In 1910, a short film titled *Pocahontas* was produced, with script by the prolific Lloyd Lonergan, apparently based on her poem of the same title. In the early twentieth century, literary Modernism rejected the themes and poetics of writers such as Sigourney. In 1930 Gordon S. Haight, a promoter of literary Modernism and of another Hartford poet, Wallace Stevens, published an academic biography of Sigourney suggesting that her success was achieved by crass self-promotion, commercial opportunism, and a rhetorically insincere sentimentalism appealing to the unschooled and gullible reading public of her day. This view of Sigourney prevailed until the 1970s.[2] In the middle and late twentieth century the formation of an early American literary canon based on Sigourney's formerly neglected male contemporaries of the 1850s, such as Emerson, Hawthorne, Melville, and Whitman, left her and her female contemporaries in obscurity. Those educated to the thematics and poetics of Modernism and trained in academic literary criticism found Sigourney and other popular Antebellum writers to be religiose, sentimental, chauvinistic, superficial, and inartistic. To such readers, Sigourney seemed to be only what Wallace Stevens called "A High-Toned Old Christian Woman." In these respects, Sigourney's critical reception resembled that of most women writers of her day.[3]

1 Objects in the possession of the editor.

2 Haight, *Mrs. Sigourney*; Ann Douglas Wood, "Mrs Sigourney and the Sensibility of the Inner Space," *New England Quarterly* 45:2 (June 1972): 163–81.

3 See the valuable overview by Dana D. Nelson, "Women in Public," in *The Cambridge Companion to Nineteenth-Century American Women's Writing*, ed. Dale M. Bauer and Philip Gould (Cambridge and New York: Cambridge UP, 2001), 38–68.

In the 1970s, however, feminist critics and historians turned to nineteenth-century movements, in which Sigourney participated, that promoted women's roles in the domestic sphere and in ameliorating a conflicted and war-torn public sphere dominated by men.[1] As early as 1947 the poet Louise Bogan, writing of critical condescension to women poets who write of the feelings, remarked drily that "The great importance of keeping the emotional channels of a literature open has frequently been overlooked,"[2] and in the 1980s and 1990s, literary historians and critics pointed out that Modernist disparagement of sentimentalism was self-serving and ignored its role as a force for cultural and social reform in which women played a major role.[3] More recently, some scholars have placed Sigourney in a "transatlantic poetess" tradition that challenged the male-dominated literary and critical institutions of the time.[4] A female poetic tradition different from that of the poetess has also been identified, one that originated in Britain and engaged the public sphere critically,[5] and that Sigourney and her American contemporaries took up.[6] Others have examined the important ideological and cultural work of Sigourney and her female contemporaries in the struggle during the first decades of American independence to create a distinct American cultural identity, construct an open yet

---

1 Ann Douglas, *The Feminization of American Culture* (1977; New York: Doubleday, 1988); Glenna Matthews, *"Just a Housewife": The Rise and Fall of Domesticity in America* (New York: Oxford UP, 1987), 25–26.

2 Louise Bogan, "The Heart and the Lyre," in *Selected Criticism* (New York: Noonday Press, 1955), 341.

3 Cheryl Walker, *The Nightingale's Burden: Women and American Culture before 1900* (Bloomington: Indiana UP, 1982); Suzanne Clark, *Sentimental Modernism: Women Writers and the Revolution of the Word* (Bloomington and Indianapolis: Indiana UP, 1991).

4 "The Transatlantic Poetess," ed. Laura Mandell, *Romanticism on the Net* 29–30 (February–May 2003); Amy S. Kolker, "The Circumscribed Path: Nineteenth-Century American Poetesses," unpub. PhD diss., University of Kansas, 1999; Annie Finch, "The Poetess in America" <http://www.ablemuse.com/critique/a-finch_poetess.htm>, *Able Muse*; *The Poetess Archive*, ed. Paula Feldman, Katherine Harris, Laura Mandell; also Patrick H. Vincent, *The Romantic Poetess: European Culture, Politics, and Gender 1820–1840* (Durham NH: U of New Hampshire P, 2004).

5 Anne K. Mellor, "The Female Poet and the Poetess: Two Traditions of British Women's Poetry, 1780–1830," *Studies in Romanticism* 36.2 (1997): 261–76.

6 Paula Bennett, *Poets in the Public Sphere: The Emancipatory Project of American Women's Poetry, 1800–1900* (Princeton: Princeton UP, 2003).

stable social order, sustain territorial expansion, and maintain national unity.[1] Whereas advocates of literary values serving educated cultural and professional elites commonly disparaged or ignored the work of Sigourney and her female contemporaries, this work is now acknowledged to be not only amenable to "close reading" but to require different reading strategies that engage both aesthetic and social considerations.[2]

These developments have enabled new understandings of Sigourney's writing, and since the early 1990s, her work has begun appearing in academic and educational literature anthologies and on academic websites, especially on women writers.[3] At the same time, a different readership is rediscovering Sigourney, apparently independently of academic scholarship and criticism, and her work can be found in a variety of popular collections and populist, religious, and philanthropic websites.[4] Sigourney is

1 Sandra A. Zagarell, "Expanding 'America': Lydia Sigourney's *Sketch of Connecticut*, Catharine Sedgwick's *Hope Leslie*," *Tulsa Studies in Women's Literature* 6:2 (Autumn 1987): 225–45; Nina Baym, "Reinventing Lydia Sigourney," *American Literature* 62:3 (September 1990): 385–404.

2 Mary Loeffelholz, *From School to Salon*, 3.

3 *American Women Poets of the Nineteenth Century: An Anthology*, ed. Cheryl Walker (New Brunswick, NJ: Rutgers UP, 1992); *American Poetry: The Nineteenth Century*, ed. John Hollander (New York: Library of America, 1993); *Rediscoveries: American Short Stories by Women*, ed. Barbara H. Solomon (New York: Mentor, 1994); *She Wields a Pen: American Women Poets of the Nineteenth Century*, ed. Janet Gray (Iowa City: U of Iowa P, 1997); *Nineteenth-Century American Women Poets: An Anthology*, ed. Paula Bennett (Malden, MA: Blackwell, 1997); *Water Drops from Women Writers: A Temperance Reader*, ed. Carol Mattingly (Carbondale: Southern Illinois UP, 2001); *Poetry for Young People: American Poetry*, ed. John Hollander (New York: Scholastic, 2004).

4 E.g., *Golden Thoughts of Mother, Home & Heaven*, ed. Gene Fedele (Gainesville: Bridge-Logos, 2003); *A Connecticut Christmas: Stories, Poems and Sermons, 1774–1918*, ed. Edward Ifkovic (New York: IUniverse, 2004); *The Aunt Lute Anthology of U. S. Women Writers*, vol. 1, ed. Lisa Maria Hopeland and Mary Klages (San Francisco: Aunt Lute Books, 2004); Lydia Sigourney, "The Noble Sailor," <http://seacoastnh.com/The_Arts/For_Better_or_Verse/The_Noble_Sailor/>; *GIGA Quotes*, <http://www.giga-usa.com/gigaweb1/quotes2/quautsigourneylydiahx001.htm>; *Poet's Corner*, <http://www.theotherpages.org/poems/sigour01.html>; *Sonnet Central*, <http://www.sonnets.org/sigourney.htm>; *The Words of a Woman*, <http://www.photoaspects.com/lilip/sigourney.shtml>; *SoJust.net*, <http://www.sojust.net/poems/sigourney_indians_welcome.html>; *Disability History Museum*, <http://www.disabilitymuseum.org/lib/subjects/Lydia_H_Sigourney/>.

again being read and valued, not only by academic and student readers, but by the kind of readers who used and use poetry—as most people use popular literature, music, and other arts—for their own purposes and real material interests, in everyday life.

Sigourney in old age: a "carte de visite" probably given away to those who asked for a souvenir of her.

Lydia Huntley Sigourney: A Brief Chronology

1791 born 1 September, only child of Ezekiel and Zerviah (or Sophia) Wentworth Huntley, Norwich, Connecticut

1806 visits Mrs Wadsworth at Hartford, Connecticut

1809 founds Hartford Female Benevolent Society

1811 opens school at Norwich with Nancy Maria Hyde

1814 asked to head school opened by Daniel Wadsworth for girls of elite Hartford families

1815 publishes *Moral Pieces, in Prose and Verse*, by subscription

1819 closes school; marries Charles Sigourney, widower, 16 June

1820 bears stillborn daughter 10 May; Charles Sigourney becomes president of Phoenix Bank; 1 August: first of 41 annual reunions with former pupils

1821 bears premature son, 8 December, who soon dies

1822 1 August: former pupils constitute Hartford Charitable Society, with Sigourney as president

1823 bears premature son, 3 January, who soon dies

1824 publishes *Traits of the Aborigines of America*

1825 helps form charitable Widows' Society; the Sigourneys visit Virginia, meeting Jefferson, Hamilton, and Adams

1827 publishes *Poems*; asks husband for separation; he refuses (October)

1828 bears a daughter, Mary, 3 August; leads Hartford campaign to aid Greeks in their War of Independence

1829 helps form charitable Hartford Female African Society, and Hartford County Temperance Society

1830 bears a son, Andrew, 11 July

1832 organizes fundraising to send a woman teacher to Greece

1833 publishes *Letters to Young Ladies*

1834 husband's business losses; publishes *Poems*, later retitled *Select Poems* (1838); publishes *Sketches*

1835 publishes *Zinzendorff, and Other Poems*

1836 Charles Sigourney ousted from Phoenix Bank

1837 failure of Sigourney's Philadelphia publisher, Key and Biddle, during economic recession

1838 edits the *Religious Souvenir*, giftbook annual; husband's business losses require sale of their country home, and moving to a smaller house in Hartford

1839 leads incorporation of Ladies Beneficent Society for the Relief of Colored Children; husband's two daughters marry

1840 rumours circulate in Hartford of conflict in the Sigourney family; leaves on extended trip to England and France, 1 August

1841 returns to the United States (April); publishes *Pocahontas, and Other Poems* almost simultaneously at London and New York

1842 publishes travelogue *Pleasant Memories of Pleasant Lands* at London and Boston; controversy over her publication of private letters of famous correspondents

1843 almost involved in libel claim against another editor of the *Ladies Companion*

1844 settlement of Sigourney, Iowa, named after her; one of 2100 women petitioning Connecticut General Assembly to regulate sale of alcohol

1845 publishes *Scenes in My Native Land* at Boston and London

1849 publication of her *Illustrated Poems*

1850 death of son, Andrew (June)

1853 awarded honorary degree of Mistress of the Arts by Franklin Female College; publishes *The Faded Hope*, memoir and writings of son, Andrew

1854 publishes *Past Meridian*; husband dies 31 December

1855 death of stepson, Charles; marriage of daughter, Mary

1857 visits Washington; house burgled

1865 dies at Hartford, 10 June

1866 autobiography, *Letters of Life*, published

A Note on the Texts

Sigourney published most of her work first in newspapers, magazines, or annuals, and then assembled selections in various collections in book form. These in turn she altered and republished over the years. She and her contemporaries regarded periodical publication as relatively ephemeral; book publication they saw as being more prestigious and presenting a claim for more permanent value for the work. Accordingly, I have reproduced the first versions published in book form, where this was the case. Sigourney revised her work for successive publication and republication, mainly to refurbish for a different venue rather than to refine toward some ideal form. Including revisions for all texts selected here would take too much space, but to illustrate Sigourney's revision practice I have included variants for several of her texts, including "Connecticut River" and "The Milliners and Fishes."

This is not a facsimile edition, but in setting up the texts I have tried to give an impression of the structure and look of Sigourney's printed texts and pages. The design of these remained remarkably consistent across her publishing career, and she gave great attention to the printing of her works when she could. Accordingly, I have retained as much as possible of her books' layout, headings, use of capitals, paragraphing, and so on.

I have selected from Sigourney's work so as to represent the span of her prolific output over her career and the diversity of the subjects she treated and the forms she used.

LYDIA SIGOURNEY
SELECTED POETRY AND PROSE

[Editor's elisions and emendations are enclosed in square brackets. For publication details of Sigourney's books, see Bibliography, p. 349.]

1. From *Moral Pieces in Prose and Verse* (1815).[1]

THE employment of transcribing, and the various concerns of a school, having rendered it almost impossible to invent or arrange any thing new, gave rise to the following effusion.[2]

THE DESERTION OF THE MUSE.

'TWAS night! but by an airy form,
  My eye was waking kept,
Which gliding near me, seem'd to seek
  The pillow where I slept.

She strove to frown, but still her brow
  Was innocent and mild;
And though her words were somewhat stern,
  Their tones were sweet and wild.

"Cast not," she said, "a stranger's glance;
  Not thus we us'd to greet,
We know each other well, although,
  Of late we seldom meet.

I saw you, when a child you sat,
  And ponder'd o'er the fire;
And deign'd to stoop that you might see,
  And try to reach my lyre.[3]

You prest its strings with so much joy,
  And such a smile serene,
I fondly hop'd you soon would learn,
  What gratitude might mean.

---

1 Sigourney's first collection of prose and verse, published by subscription, organized and overseen by her patron, Daniel Wadsworth.

2 Sigourney's headnote.

3 lyre] In classical legend, poets accompanied their chanting on this harp-like instrument, which hence became a commonplace symbol for poetry.

Amid your light domestic toils,
  I rov'd with footstep free,
And oft you laid your needle down,
  To take the pen from me.

When lonely, pausing o'er your book,
  You walk'd at close of day,
Well pleas'd to trace my dawning smile,
  You threw that page away.

I met you in my mountain dress,[1]
  And sandals wet with dew,
All unadorn'd, and yet I thought
  That I was fair to you.

My lyre was often out of tune,
  Its tones were rude[2] and small,
Yet were they e'er so weak or rough,
  You gladly heard them all.

But now how chang'd! for when I smile,
  And bring my sweetest rhyme,
You coldly bid me 'go my way,
  And come another time.'

For you must stay to 'copy off'
  And polish what you wrote,
And try to soften if you can
  My unharmonious note.

Even when I come, in all my charms,
  To catch your fickle view,
You, starting, turn your back, and cry,
  'The clock is striking two.'

Now, what has two, or nine o'clock
  To do with you and me?
And what delights you in your school,
  I'm sure I cannot see.

---

1 In ancient legend, mountains, particularly Mount Helicon, were supposed to be the haunt of the muses, inspiring poets.

2 rude] unpolished

Yet, when your strange excuses o'er,
  You sit and muse alone,
And seem to look as if you wish'd
  Again to hear my tone.

I come; and then with curious glance,
  My scanty robe you eye,
And count my curls, and measure where,
  Each flowing tress should lie:

And wonder why such tasteless wreaths[1]
  Of faded flow'rs I wear,
And chide because I could not stay,
  To dress myself with care.

And when you ask to hear my song,
  And I begin to play,
You utter, 'that is out of tune,'
  And snatch the lyre away.

Now since you have so soon forgot,
  My service, and my truth,
My kindness to your childhood shewn,
  My friendship for your youth;

Go, seek some other muse, who loves
  Your heavy task to bear;
For since your ways so much are chang'd,
  I cast you from my care."

She spake, and hid her glowing face,
  Within the veil of night,
And gazing as the vision fled,
  I trembled with affright;
Then rose in sadness from my bed,
  And lo! I could not write.

THE ROSE.[2]

I SAW a rose perfect in beauty; it rested gracefully upon its stalk, and its perfume filled the air. Many stopped to gaze upon it, many bowed to taste its fragrance, and the owner hung over it

1 wreath] symbol of poetic achievement, from classical myth

2 The rose was a long established literary symbol for the female beloved.

with delight. I past by again, and behold, it was gone—its stem was leafless—its root had withered; the enclosure which surrounded it was broken down. The spoiler[1] had been there; he saw that many admired it—he knew it was dear to him who planted it, and beside it he had no other plant to love. Yet he snatched it secretly from the hand that cherished it; he wore it on his bosom till it hung its head and faded, and when he saw that its glory was departed, he cast it rudely away. But it left a thorn in his bosom, and vainly did he seek to extract it, for now it pierces the spoiler, even in his hour of mirth. And when I saw that no man, who had loved the beauty of the rose, gathered again its scattered leaves, or bound up the stalk which the hand of violence had broken, I looked earnestly at the spot where it grew, and my soul received instruction. And I said, let her who is full of beauty and admiration, sitting like the queen of flowers in majesty among the daughters of women, let her watch lest vanity enter her heart, beguiling her to rest proudly upon her own strength; let her remember she standeth upon slippery places,[2] "and be not high minded, but fear."[3]

THE CREATION.[4]

BEING the first number selected as a specimen of a series of pieces on scripture subjects, intended for the use of young people.[5]

WHEN night and Chaos reign'd with awful sway,
And o'er the unform'd earth thick darkness lay,
The Almighty voice awoke the kindling strife,
And call'd the dormant elements to life.

"*Let there be light;*" a sudden ray there came,
Like ether, pure, and piercing as the flame;
"*Let day arise;*" a blush of purple flow'd;
The young dawn trembled, and the morning glow'd;
"*Let night divide the empire of the day,*"
And frowning darkness claim'd his ancient sway.

1 the spoiler] Biblical term for oppressor, ravager, or death

2 she ... places] echoing the Bible, Psalms 73.18: Surely thou didst set them in slippery places: thou castedst them down into destruction.

3 The Bible, Paul's letter to the Romans, 11.20

4 Verse paraphrase of the Bible (Genesis 1–2), a form often practised by women writers.

5 Sigourney's headnote.

Then like an arch the azure skies were rear'd,
The seas were gather'd, and the earth appear'd;
Clad with fresh flowers, and plants of gentle root,
Herb yielding seed, and tree presenting fruit.

Then, where the curving skies the Ocean prest,
The Sun, all glowing, darted from his rest;
Pale cast the moon her first, and timid glance,
And the stars sparkled o'er the blue expanse.

Mild Ocean's waves with scaly silver glow'd,
Birds soar'd in air, and hover'd o'er the flood;
Above, around, the tones of rapture sigh'd,
"*Live, and rejoice,*" the forming God reply'd,
"*Sport on the cloud, and thro' the waters glide.*"

Next, rising slow, a mix'd and varied birth,
Unnumber'd beasts came roving o'er the earth,
They crept, they sported wild, they stalk'd with pride,
Or cropt the grass, or drank the limpid tide;
Some, with aw'd gaze, the wondrous scene survey'd,
And some slept fearless, in the cooling shade.

Serene, the great Creator clos'd his plan,
And stamp'd his image on the form of man;
Gave life and motion to a mass of clay,
Eye speaking thought, and brow denoting sway,
Reason to judge, and majesty to awe,
Sole monarch, holding sway o'er all he saw.

Last, came a female form, more soft and fair,
And Eden smil'd to see the stranger there.

Then tones of joy, from harps seraphic rung,
The stars of Morning in their courses sung,
Earth echo'd back the shout of grateful love,
From hill and valley, cavern, stream and grove;
Man fill'd with praise in silent rapture stood,
God bow'd to view his work, and God pronounc'd it good.

2. From *The Square Table*, number 2 (1819).[1]

THE ADVICE OF TABITHA THISTLE, TO YOUNG WOMEN, WHO ARE DESIROUS OF GETTING MARRIED.

1.

It is necessary first of all, that a woman should have money;—this, as the ancient orator said of action, is the first—the second—the third requisite. This will supply all other deficiencies.

2.

If you possess no personal charms, be not discouraged; those days of romance are past, when the eye was suffered to affect the heart. Women, now, like a bale of merchandize, are weighed in the scale of cool calculation.

3.

Should you unhappily be destitute of a large fortune—though this is the greatest obstacle to your attempt that could possibly occur—still by strict observance of the following rules, especially if you will fly from the city to a country residence, some ray of hope may remain.

4.

If by any chance you have read any thing besides the last new novel, be careful to conceal it closely, and it would be well to confess a dislike to reading, and an unconquerable aversion to writing.

5.

If you hear any literary conversation, or if a question bearing upon such a subject, should accidentally be addressed to you, answer it by a vacant stare—an interesting simper, or a declaration of profound ignorance, observing to fix a silly gaze upon your fan or work, if you should happen to have any.

6.

Should your family boast, though in its most remote connection, of some member once ennobled by wealth, title, or fashion-

1 A satirical little magazine of two issues (September and November 1819) written by Sigourney, responding to another Hartford magazine, the *Round Table*.

able distinction, talk incessantly of that personage:—a principle of pride mingles with the avarice of the age, which you may possibly turn to some advantage.

7.

Affect an extravagant fondness for children; run after, and kiss all the dirty babes you may chance to meet in the street:—it signifies more than you imagine.

8.

Endeavour to gain the reputation of being a notable housewife. Be seen at an open street-door, with a broom, or at a chamber window brandishing a brush. No matter whether you know how to sweep clean or not, if you can only render it probable, that you would save the expense of an extra servant.

9.

Let your conversation be with great gravity of household matters. Tell how many shirts you are in the habit of plaiting[1] before breakfast, and how often you have lain sleepless, studying the science of *saving*, and the best method of lowering servants' wages.

10.

Commit to memory some choice recipes from the cookery book, and repeat them with a loud voice in company. Ten to one, you may thus entrap some old bachelor, who has been long a boarder, and always dissatisfied with his table—or inveigle some perfect epicure: for luxury is strangely compounding itself with avarice, in the hearts of the modern lords of creation.

11.

Don't affect frights at trifles—spasms at a spider—sudden faintness, &c. &c. The day for these devices is past. You had better pretend to be vigorous and brave. Who wants the burden of a sick wife?

12.

Take particular notice, that the *very first* time you are asked, whether you will exchange your situation,[2] that you answer, "*Yes*

---

1 plaiting] folding, an Americanism by this time

2 exchange your situation] accept a proposal of marriage

Sir," with a courtesy. If from any foolish scruple whatever, you should think of waiting for a second offer, I have no further remedy to propose, and dare not flatter you with even a shadow of hope.

3. From *Traits of the Aborigines of America: A Poem* (1822).[1]

From CANTO FIRST.

O'ER the vast regions of that Western world,
Whose lofty mountains hiding in the clouds
Conceal'd their grandeur and their wealth so long
From European eyes, the Indian rov'd,
Free and unconquered. From those frigid plains
Struck with the torpor of the Arctic pole,
To where Magellan lifts his torch to light
The meeting of the waters;[2]—from the shore
Whose smooth green line the broad Atlantic laves,[3]
To the rude borders of that rocky strait[4]
Where haughty Asia seems to stand and gaze
On the New Continent, the Indian reign'd

---

1 Sigourney's first major work, this is an ambitious blank-verse survey-poem, a genre practised by eighteenth-century male philosophical poets. It also resembles the epyllion, or short epic (women were thought to be incapable of achieving a full-scale epic), and its language often echoes Milton's Christian epic, *Paradise Lost*—*Traits* surveys the history, culture, religions, and condition of native peoples in America, as a lost paradise, despoiled by white settlers. The poem opposes American hostility to aborigines and celebrates their social, religious, and domestic virtues as important elements of republican identity in Sigourney's national vision, as in later works by Sigourney such as "Pocahontas" and "Oriska." Sigourney's husband supplied many historical and botanical notes (summarized here in footnotes), but the annotated poem was developed by the English writer Felicia Hemans, with whom Sigourney was soon compared, and *Traits* picks up a central theme of Hemans' *Tales, and Historic Scenes* (1819)—the disappearance of tribes, nations, and civilizations in the violent process of male-dominated history. An "Advertisement" followed the title page: "The avails of this work are devoted exclusively to religious charities."

2 Magellan ... waters] Magellan Strait, where Atlantic and Pacific Oceans meet at the southernmost tip of South America; lifts his torch: Tierra del Fuego (Land of Fire), the island south of the Strait

3 laves] washes, a common poeticism

4 rocky strait] Bering Strait, between present day Alaska and Russia

Majestic and alone. Fearless he rose,
Firm as his mountains, like his rivers, wild,
Bold as those lakes, whose wondrous chain controuls
His northern coast.[1] The forest and the wave
Gave him his food; the slight-constructed hut
Furnish'd his shelter, and its doors spread wide
To every wandering stranger. There his cup,
His simple meal, his lowly couch of skins
Were hospitably shared. Rude[2] were his toils,
And rash his daring, when he headlong rush'd
Down the steep precipice to seize his prey;
Strong was his arm to bend the stubborn bow,
And keen his arrow. This the Bison knew,
The spotted Panther, the rough, shaggy Bear,
The Wolf dark-prowling, the eye-piercing Lynx,
The wild Deer bounding through the shadowy glade,
And the swift Eagle, soaring high to make
His nest among the stars. Cloth'd in their spoils
He dar'd the elements; with eye sedate
Breasted the wintry winds; o'er the white heads
Of angry torrents steered his rapid bark[3]
Light as their foam, mounted with tireless speed
Those slippery cliffs, where everlasting snows
Weave their dense robes, or laid him down to sleep
Where the dread thunder of the cataract lull'd
His drowsy sense. The dangerous toils of war
He sought and lov'd. Traditions, and proud tales
Of other days, exploits of chieftains bold,
Dauntless and terrible, the warrior's song,
The victor's triumph,—all conspired to raise
The martial spirit, kindling in his breast
With life's first throb. Oft the rude,[4] wandering tribes
Rush'd on to battle. Their aspiring chiefs
Lofty and iron-fram'd, with native hue
Strangely disguised in wild and glaring tints,
Frown'd like some Pictish king.[5] The conflict rag'd

1 lakes ... northern coast] the Great Lakes

2 rude] here: rough, harsh

3 bark] vessel; also particularly the canoe of birch bark

4 rude] here: unlearned, violent, turbulent, rugged, robust, vigorous

5 Pictish king] The Picts or Gaels were ancient natives of Scotland and Ireland; here the allusion, reinforced by the subject and language of the passage, would recall the poems of "Ossian"—partly fake prose "transla-

Fearless and fierce, 'mid shouts and disarray,
As the swift lightning urges its dire shafts
Through clouds and darkness, when the warring blasts
Awaken midnight. O'er the captive foe
Unsated vengeance storm'd. Flame and slow wounds
Rack'd the strong bonds of life; but the firm soul
Smil'd in its fortitude to mock the rage
Of its tormentors; when the crisping nerves
Were broken, still exulting o'er its pain[1]
To rise unmurmuring to its father's shades,
Where in delightful bowers the brave and just
Rest and rejoice.
Thus stood stern Regulus,[2]
When furious Carthage urg'd her torturing darts,
Transfix'd with dark, demoniac rage to find
Her quiver all exhausted, and that soul
Proudly unhurt.
Yet those untutor'd tribes,
Bound with their stern resolves and savage deeds
Some gentle virtues; as beneath the gloom
Of overshadowing forests, sweetly springs
The unexpected flower. Oft to their homes
The captive youth they led, into his wounds
Pouring the oil of kindness, and with love
Alluring him to fill the vacant place
Of brother, or of son, untimely slain
In the dread battle.[3] Their uncultur'd hearts
Gave a strong soil for Friendship, that bold growth
Of generous affection, changeless, pure,
Self-sacrificing, counting losses light,
And yielding life with gladness. By its side
Like sister-plant, sprang ardent Gratitude,

---

tions" of ancient Gaelic heroic poems (published 1760–63) by James Macpherson, enormously popular, especially in the United States.

1 still exulting o'er its pain] reference to ritual torture of captives practised by some aboriginal peoples—a topic of fascination to Europeans

2 Regulus] During the Punic War (third century BCE), the Roman captive Regulus was sent back to Rome by the Carthaginians to argue for peace, on condition he return to captivity if he failed; he urged the Romans to continue the war, returned to Carthage, and was tortured to death.

3 A long endnote compares adoption practices of American aborigines and various peoples of Europe, Africa, and Asia.

Vivid, perennial, braving winter's frost
And summer's heat; while nurs'd by the same dews
Unbounded Reverence for the form of Age,
Struck its deep root spontaneous, and display'd
Its fair, decumbent[1] petals. The dim eye,
The furrow'd brow, the temples thinly clad,
The wasted page of man's infirm decline
Awake that deep respect, not always trac'd
'Mid those whom Science[2] nurtures, whom the arts
Of smooth refinement polish, and a voice
Sublime instructs, "Honour the head that bears
The hoary crown of Age."[3]
With pious awe
Their eye uplifted sought the hidden path
Of the Great Spirit.[4] The loud midnight storm,
The rush of mighty waters, the deep roll
Of thunder, gave his voice; the golden sun,
The soft effulgence of the purple morn,
The gentle rain distilling, was his smile
Dispensing good to all. The Spirit of Ill,
Base foe to man, they dreaded; and the cry
Of his vile legions shrieking on the blast,
Shuddering they heard. In various forms arose
Their superstitious homage. Some[5] with blood
Of human sacrifices sought to appease
That anger, which in pestilence, or dearth,
Or famine stalk'd; and their astonish'd vales
Like Carthaginian altars,[6] frequent drank
The horrible libation. Some,[7] with fruits,
Sweet flowers, and incense of their choicest herbs,

---

1 decumbent] trailing on the ground, with the tip raised

2 Science] learning of all kinds

3 Paraphrase of the Bible, part of Leviticus 19.32.

4 Great Spirit] commonly used as supposed translation of aboriginal terms for the supreme deity; ll. 92–100: description of aboriginal religious beliefs in terms similar to those found in the Old Testament of the Bible

5 An endnote compares the Aztecs' beliefs and practice of human sacrifice with those of ancient Europeans such as the Scythians.

6 Carthage] powerful ancient city-state, crushed by its rival Rome in 146 BCE after a series of costly wars

7 An endnote describes Peruvians' peacefulness and mildness, based on their religion.

Sought to propitiate HIM,[1] whose powerful hand
Unseen, sustain'd them. Some[2] with mystic rites,
The ark, the orison, the paschal feast,[3]
Through glimmering tradition seem'd to bear,
As in some broken vase, the smother'd coals,
Scatter'd from Jewish altars.

[The poem considers the theory that North American aborigines were a lost tribe of Biblical Israel, then resumes representing the aboriginal way of life.]

Though his stern heart
Seem'd cold and fixed as adamant, its cell
Conceal'd the warm fount of parental love,
And felt its thrilling tide. The lofty chiefs,
Inur'd by frowning hardship to despise
The lineaments of joy, found o'er their souls
Strange softness stealing, as they mutely gaz'd
Upon the smile of infancy, or saw,
Waking from its sweet dream, the joyous babe
Reach forth its little hands. The warrior bold,
Who vanquish'd toil and famine, bore unmov'd
The battle-shock, or with calm, changeless brow
Endur'd the keenest tortures, writh'd in pangs
Over his children lost; while bitter drops
Wrung forth by anguish stain'd his furrow'd cheeks.
In that dire struggle when relentless Grief
Confronts strong Nature, the heart cherish'd nerve
Broken and bleeding, rent the stubborn breast,
As uptorn roots dislodge the iron oak
Which tempests could not bend. A prey to grief
Seem'd the sad mothers. The first-rising storm
Of sorrow, passionate and wild, burst forth,
And in that deadly calm which Reason dreads
Shuddering, their weak, exhausted hands they prest

1 HIM] the Judeo-Christian God, which Sigourney suggests may be the same God worshipped by American aborigines

2 An endnote summarizes arguments that American aborigines are "the mingled offspring of different nations" of ancient Europe, Africa, and Asia.

3 paschal feast] celebration of Easter

On their wan[1] lips, and in the lowly dust
Laid them despairing.
——O'er the dreaded grave
Mist and thick darkness brooded; trembling Hope
Vision'd futurity;[2] but Fancy wrought
Incessant, peopling it with airy shapes
Fantastic as her own.[3]
Now the fair clime
Was bright with verdure, lofty forests wav'd
In the pure breeze, gay deer with branching horns
Allur'd the hunter, through clear, sparkling streams
Glided the scaly tribes, and thronging seals
Innumerous, sporting 'mid the emerald isles
Fled not the barbed lance. The Arctic sky
Kindling at evening with resplendent hues
Crimson and gold, in changeful wreaths combin'd,
To the poor Greenlander reveal'd the dance
Of happy spirits,[4] who in fields of bliss
Weave their light measures. But anon, pale Fear
With trembling pencil trac'd a gulph of woe
Throng'd with unearthly shapes, whose dizzy bridge
Tottering, and guarded by a monster fierce,
How few could pass! The first sad days of grief,
Were dark and dreadful. The tear-blinded eye
Pursues the wanderer, as he seems to urge
His toilsome journey. His adventurous foot,
Uncertain, slides upon that slippery bridge
Which like a tremulous and shrivell'd thread
Shoots the abyss of flame. Falling he rolls
Upon the fiery flood, struggling to gain
The far, dim coast, where angry dragons wait
With jaws distain'd[5] and scaly strength to attack
The weary traveller, ere he reach the abode
Of happy spirits. Hence the mourners place
By their lamented friend, his trusty bow,
Arrows and food, and closely wrapt in skins

1 An endnote compares American aborigines' and ancient Jews' gestures of bereavement.

2 futurity] life after death

3 Various aboriginal notions of heaven and hell are now described.

4 An endnote describes Greenland natives' concepts of heaven and hell.

5 distain'd] discoloured, but also defiled

They leave him standing in his narrow cell
Prepar'd for combat. [...]
Thus the natives dwelt,
Fearless, nor asking aught save what their realm
Amply supplied. They had not learnt to change
Heaven's gifts to poisons, nor the aliment
That cheers the body, to th' imprisoning bond
Of th' ethereal mind. No baleful arts
Of chymistry transform'd the staff of life
To Riot's weapon, and the tottering props
Of Death's dark throne. They knew not then to mark
With sparkling eye the transmigration foul
Of Earth's blest harvest melted in the bowl
Inebriate.[1] Nor had the fatal charm
Of Luxury seduced them to subject
Spirit to sense, binding the lofty soul
A vassal at the revel and the feast,
Like purple Dives.[2] Temperance was theirs;
Theirs the elastic, the unruffled flow
Of spirits and of blood, the nerve firm-brac'd,
The vigorous mind, th' undreaded day of toil,
And the pure dream. Say, can the eye that mark'd
Their simple majesty, and their bold hearts
Free and unfettered, as the wind that swept
Their cloud-capt mountains, bear to turn and trace
The dark reverse? [...]

From CANTO THIRD.

[...] While with insatiate zeal
The Red Man roam'd the forest, or from floods
Allur'd the finny spoil, the toil-worn hand
Of his more weak companion, wrought to win
In scanty harvest from the tardy earth,
The swelling legume, and that tub'rous root
Which in their clay-built cells, the hardy sons
Of emerald Erin bless.[3] Like modest worth

1 blest harvest ... inebriate] alcoholic drinks made from grain or corn

2 purple Dives] the Bible, gospel of Luke 16.19–31: Dives "was clothed in purple and fine linen, and fared sumptuously every day," ignoring the starving leper Lazarus

3 sons of emerald Erin bless] the peasants of Ireland (Erin) depended on the potato, originally from America

Oft shrouded in a plain and homely garb,
'Neath its rough leaf, and lurid flow'r, it hides
Pale Penury's blessing. This the New World gave
When in the cradle of her innocence
To haughty Europe, who with curious eye,
As peers the miser at some new-found hoard,
Survey'd the infant stranger, and her gift
Grasp'd as the bane of Famine.[1] By its side
The fruitful maize,[2] in verdant vistas rear'd
Its spire majestic, to the playful breeze
Spreading its loosely-waving panicles,[3] while low
The purple anthers bending o'er to kiss
The silken, tassel'd styles, delight the eye
Of watchful Ceres.[4] Autumn's earliest call
Demands its treasures, and the caskets pour
Forth from their silver cones, in streams profuse,
The vegetable gold. Its lingering wealth
Spreads in rich tribute at the icy throne
Of that swart form, the licens'd King of storms,[5]
For whose support, soft Spring in tears awakes
The infant germ, bright Summer toiling wastes
Her fervid beauty, and grave Autumn roams
As a tax-gatherer, o'er the vast domain,
Heaping his revenue.

While warlike zeal
Nerv'd the bold sons of Nature, as they rush'd
In that red path, where Earth's proud heroes roll
The car[6] o'er trampled life, with silent step
The softer sex, still unregarded, cull'd
From wild, or fountain side, such plants as aid
The healer's art. And might they hope to shun
The cup of scorn, because they meekly went
On Mercy's mission? Does a sapient world,[7]

---

1 An endnote cites differing accounts of how the potato was introduced into the British Isles from America.

2 An endnote scientifically validates the nutritious properties of maize, which "has so sensibly diminished the ravages of famine" in Europe.

3 panicles] branching clusters of flowers

4 Ceres] goddess of crops in Roman mythology

5 King of storms] Aeolus, in ancient myth ruler of the four winds

6 car] common poeticism for chariot

7 sapient world] learned men, scientists in the modern sense

Ev'n at her noon-tide beam, accord her meed[1]
To the mild race, whose heav'n-taught Science heals
The rankling wound, extracts from stern disease
Its sting, and props frail Man to cope with Death?
No! to the licens'd[2] murd'rer, to the wrath
Of Cesar's wild ambition, to the scourge
Of bleeding Cambria, ruthless Tamerlane,
The Swedish mad-man, and the tyrant son
Of Corsica. When the stern warrior fell,
Writhing in agony, the patient hand
Of those despis'd restorers, knew to check
The purple tide, and bind the throbbing chasm
With happy skill.

[The poem describes aboriginal use of other plants for medicinal purposes, then turns to the present condition of the aborigines.]

When rising cities shone
In wealth and splendour, the poor natives rov'd
Around their bounds, amaz'd. Fall'n Pride, represt
The words of admiration; but strange awe,
Slavish degeneracy, and the dark frown
Of banish'd men, sat heavier on their brow.
Once, to the mart which favouring Commerce rear'd
On fair Manhattan, their sad Chiefs repair'd
To seek an audience. From a tow'ring height
They mark'd the goodly prospect. Lofty spires,
Vast domes, delightful villas, clust'ring roofs,
Streets, where the countless throng incessant pour'd,
As pleasure, pomp, or business mov'd their tides
In murmuring fluctuation; distant dales,
Slumbering in verdure; the majestic flood,[3]
Crown'd with tall masts, and white with snowy sails,

---

1 meed] reward, recompense; a poeticism

2 licens'd] given permission, but also privileged, free to; the next lines catalogue military conquerors: Julius Caesar (100–44 BCE), Roman conqueror of Gaul; Edward I of England (CE 1239–1307), conqueror of Wales (Cambria); Tamerlane (CE 1336–1405), conqueror of Asia; Charles XII of Sweden (CE 1682–1718), whose military career left no legacy; Napoleon Bonaparte, originally a Corsican, whose European empire collapsed with his defeat at Waterloo in 1815

3 flood] river, a poeticism here

Thoughtful they view'd. Unmov'd, the men of wealth,
Who mark'd their own possessions, lightly ask'd,
"Why are ye sad?" as once Chaldea's bands
Inquir'd of wasted Judah, where their mirth
And songs had vanish'd, when their unstrung harps
Hung on the willows, and their exil'd feet
Roam'd in captivity.[1]
——To them replied
The elder Chief:[2] "We bear upon our minds
Past times, and other days. This beauteous land
Was once our fathers'. Here, in peace they dwelt;
For the Great Spirit gave it as a gift
To them, and to their sons. But to this shore
Once came a vast canoe, which white men steer'd
Feebly, against the blast.
Driv'n by rude storms,
They sought permission on our coast to land,[3]
And how could we refuse? Their sick, they brought,
And in our soft shades, fann'd by gentle gales,
Laid them, and they reviv'd. But wintry winds
Soon swept the waste, and humbly they besought
Leave to erect a wigwam,[4] while the frost
And snows were raging. Could our hearts refuse
The stranger shelter? to our Chiefs they said
With solemn words, that when the soft'ning spring
Dissolv'd the wrath of winter, they would seek
Their distant homes, and leave us to ourselves;
And we were satisfied. With pitying eye
Their wasted frames we saw, by Famine smit;
We gave them corn, and fed them. When fair spring
Shone sweetly on the budding earth, we claim'd
Their promise to depart. But they had rear'd
Strange iron ramparts,[5] which at their command
Breath'd flame and death. Pointing to these, they said
'We will not!' and indignantly they glanc'd

1 The Bible, Psalms 137.1–3, the lamentation of the Jews (Judah) after their defeat and enslavement by the Babylonians, or Chaldeans.

2 In the following lines the Chief recounts the well-known history of English arrival and settlement, but from the aboriginal point of view.

3 on our coast to land] The Pilgrims who landed in Massachusetts in 1620 had originally set out for Virginia.

4 wigwam] lodge, from an Algonquian word

5 iron ramparts] fortifications with cannon

Defiance on us. Other bands arriv'd
Strength'ning their purpose. Mad, enticing draughts[1]
Deceitfully they gave us, till the cup
Reft us of reason. Then they forc'd us back
From field to field, from forest, and from flood,
Where our subsistence lay. And you, their sons,
Still drive us onward. You enjoy the land
Of luxury; while we, wasted and scorn'd,
Herd in the wilderness. But ye will cease
Ere long to press us, for our fading race
Will cease to be. Think ye, that we can view
These beauteous shores, and yon proud swelling flood,
And not remember that they once were ours?
And thus rememb'ring, need ye wond'ring ask
Why sorrow clothes our brow?"
Full many a strain
Of native eloquence, simple and wild,
Has ris'n in our dark forests,[2] which the winds
Unheeded, swept away. Yet, had it broke
From bold Demosthenes,[3] when Athens fear'd
The distant step of Philip, had it burst
From the impetuous Hannibal, when Rome
Muster'd at Zama[4]—it had been enroll'd
In History's choicest annal, the pure eye
Of Taste had trickled o'er it, and the lip
Of the young student, had been proud to pour
Its treasur'd pathos. But thy slighted words,
Untutor'd Red Man!—Ah! how few will trace
Their chronicle obscure, and fewer still
Accord the meed of just applause, unmix'd
With scorn upon thy nation. [...]
Driven back
From wild to wild, the natives yield, and sink
In cold oblivion. We, who ought to weep
O'er their deep woes, and send a cordial balm

1 enticing draughts] alcoholic drinks

2 An endnote cites accounts of aboriginal oratory indicating it equalled that of famous British statesmen.

3 Demosthenes] Greek orator (384–322 BCE) who exhorted Athenians to resist Philip of Macedon, father of Alexander the Great

4 Before the battle of Zama (202 BCE), the Roman general Scipio Africanus and the Carthaginian general Hannibal addressed each other, as imagined by the Roman historian Livy (*Histories*, book 30, section 30).

To heal the wounds, made by our fathers' swords,
Lift up the hand against them, stain our page
Not with their wrongs, but with their dark reproach
Industriously sought. We teach our babes
Not to lisp prayers for them, but join their names
With baseness, treachery, and the shuddering
Of dread disgust. We take away their food,
Their hunting forests, and their broad lakes throng'd
With scaly tribes. Their meagre forms we see
Withering with famine, and to their parch'd lips
Hold that enchanted cup, whose fearful dregs
Like those of Circe,[1] change the form erect,
To grov'lling beastliness. [...]
Still we boldly say,
The Indian cruelty, untam'd and fierce,
Can find no parallel, in any age,
Or any nation. This strong charge is brought,
And they deny it not. What page have they,
Or what historic pen to palliate,
To justify or blazon?[2] To the lists[3]
We dare the unarm'd, and conquer them at once.
We cite them to their trial, where they stand
Silent and we condemn.

[The poem calls for "some friend, some advocate" of the aborigines to tell them of the long history of war, devastation, and cruelty by European and Asian peoples; the description of these atrocities closes by asking, "And thou,/My Country! what has thy example been?" (ll. 835–36)]

4. From *Sketch of Connecticut, Forty Years Since* (1824).[4]

CHAPTER VIII.

A man I am, of quaint, uncourtly speech,
And uncouth manners, nurtur'd from my youth
To bide the buffet of the wintry blast,

---

1 Circe] in Greek mythology and Homer's *Odyssey*, a sorceress who turned men into animals

2 blazon] boast of

3 lists] barriers for ritual combat of medieval knights

4 The American "sketch" achieved transatlantic popularity with Washington Irving's *Sketch Book of Geoffrey Crayon* (1819–20), but women

And toil unshrinking when the sultry skies
Scorch'd the green verdure of the earth I till'd;
Yet not by health, or peace, or sweet content
Unvisited, nor yet by patient trust
In Him, the harvest's universal Lord,
Uncheer'd. ———[1]

THE agricultural part of Madam L——'s possessions, or as it is styled in New-England "landed estate," was situated in one of the smaller towns in the vicinity of that where she resided. It was under the care of a farmer of undoubted integrity, and industry, who rendered her, with great punctuality, her stipulated share of its products. His father had been, for many years, tenant of the same estate. After him a younger son succeeded to this trust, but died at an early age. The present occupant, being the only remaining branch of the family, and feeling an affection for the abode of his infancy, returned from "upcountry,"[2] where, to use his own expression, he had "moved to make room for brother Zedekiah;"[3] and resumed with delight the culture of those fields, where he had "driv-team when a leetle boy."

---

writers also specialized in such "local colour" writing. It was characterized by brevity, informality, anecdotal tone, and representation of incidents, settings, and characters in common life, and depicted bygone or disappearing cultures and customs. *Sketch of Connecticut* was published as the northern United States were rapidly urbanizing, industrializing, and beginning to receive new waves of immigrants, giving rise to new social tensions. In such change, the book assigns an educative, conciliating role for women. Chapter 8 deals with religious and social tensions caused by the Second Great Awakening, an early nineteenth-century religious revival. Chapter 10 depicts agrarian life "forty years since" as Madam L—— (based on the Huntleys' patroness, Mrs Lathrop) stealthily observes the Larkins' modest home and family dinner, symbolizing the virtues of agrarian republican economy and culture against increasing "luxury" and decadence from urbanization and industrialization. Here quotation marks have been adjusted for clarity, and a printing error corrected. Title-page epigraph: "Land of my sires!—What mortal hand/Can e'er untie the filial band/That knits me to thy rugged strand!"/[Walter] SCOTT. [*The Lay of the Last Minstrel* (1805), 6.21–23.]

1 The lines may be Sigourney's own.

2 upcountry] land remote from any town; an Americanism

3 New England Puritans and Evangelicals named children from the Bible to indicate character or aspiration; in the Bible, a Zedekiah is the last king of Judah, another is a priest, two are nobles, and two are false prophets.

Madam L—— had often taken pleasure in his conversation, which was marked with that plain common-sense, which seems the birthright of the New-England farmer, while the simplicity of his opinions on some subjects, and the oddity of his dialect, administered to her entertainment.

Calling one morning on his patroness, for whom he cherished a respect, almost bordering upon adoration, he was requested to walk into her parlour. This he had ever refused to do, under pretence that his "shoes were clumsy, and he was afraid of meeting some of the gentlefolks, whose ways he was not used to." But she being somewhat indisposed, and declining to go into her kitchen, he appeared at the door, with a well meant bow, which the dandies of the present day, who deal principally in nods and shrugs, might consider a semi-prostration. The revolution, which in giving us liberty, obliterated almost every vestige of the politeness of the "old school," had not then done its work completely. Individuals were found, forty years since, in every grade of society, who, having been educated when a bow was not an offence to fashion, nor respect for age a relic of monarchy, continued the exercise of both, without being hooted at as aristocrats, or "quizzed"[1] as antidiluvians.[2]

Farmer Larkin was dressed in a suit of stout cloth, whose deep brown colour was produced by an infusion of the bark of the butternut. It had grown the preceding summer upon his own sheep, and after sustaining many processes of mutation in the domestic laboratory, now appeared upon his own person. The mail[3] of Diomede was not more invulnerable to the shafts of the Trojans,[4] than this to the attacks of winter; and if a crevice ever appeared in it, the arts of housewifery were in instant requisition, like "armourer accomplishing the knight, with busy hammers closing rivets up."[5]

A neat broad brimmed hat, which his father had worn on great occasions for half a score of years, a drab coloured great-coat, with deep cuffs, and huge buttons, both taken from the Sunday wardrobe, out of reverence to "the Lady," and vast shoes of the skin of that animal whom the Brahmins worship,[6] completed his

---

1 quizzed] mocked

2 antidiluvians] antediluvians: those before the Biblical flood, i.e., the aged

3 mail] armour

4 Diomede ... Trojans] In Homer's *Iliad* Diomed is a Greek warrior; Diomede is the mistress of Achilles.

5 Shakespeare, *Henry V*, act 4, Prologue, lines 12–13, spoken by the Chorus.

6 animal ... worship] circumlocution for "cow," considered a sacred animal by Hindus; Brahmins: the highest or priestly caste in Hindu society

array. His countenance, where the blasts of winter, and heats of summer had long set their seal, exhibited that decision, and contempt of bodily hardship, which in ancient Sparta[1] was dignified as a virtue. It also displayed that mixture of sobriety with contentment, resting on the basis of moderated desires, and humble piety, which often gives the agriculturist of our country a dignity, which Sparta in her pride never knew.

Mr. Larkin, at entering the apartment, seemed desirous to make his way on that narrow stripe[2] of the floor, which in those days was always permitted to surround the carpet. At length a large table, which he doubted whether it were decorous for him to move, obstructed his course, and he exclaimed with some perplexity,—

"I *must* tread on the kiverlid." The Lady suppressing a smile, said,—

"I beg, good Mr. Larkin, that you would step on the coverlet. It would save Beulah[3] some labour, who prides herself on the whiteness of the floor, which she daily scours."

Thus assured, he made one or two strides towards a chair which she placed for him, walking on tiptoe, and murmuring with some regret, as he rested his heels upon the hearth,—

"Your ha-ath too, is as clean as a cheeny tea-cup, Ma'am. I hate to put my coarse huffs on it. But I ha'nt been used to seein' kiverlids spread on the floor to walk on. We are glad to get 'em to kiver us up with a nights. This looks like a boughten one," he added, examining the figure, and feeling its texture. "'Tis exceedin' curous. They must have had a pretty many treadles in the loom, that wove this."

The Lady remarked that the use of carpets, like other luxuries, was gaining ground too rapidly among those who were often deficient in real comfort. "Silks and satins put out the kitchen-fire, as a wise man has said."[4]

"Ay, Ma'am, he answered, just so I tell my young gals, when they get a teasin' their mammy, for somethin' fine and gay. See to

---

1 Sparta] ancient city-state, famous for simple life and martial prowess; defeated Athens, known for wealth and luxury, in the Peloponnesian War (431–404 BCE) and was briefly the dominant power in Greece

2 stripe] strip

3 Beulah] Hebrew name meaning married; in the Bible, Isaiah 62.4, a name to be given to Jerusalem after the end of the Jews' exile, accordingly often given to African-American female slaves or former slaves

4 Benjamin Franklin, *The Way to Wealth* (1758), citing "Poor Richard"; also a German proverb, signifying that artificial wants exceed natural ones

your under-riggin',[1] I tell 'em, and keep yourselves whole and neat. It's as much as I can do, to get along, says I, in any comfortable kind of a way with such a snarl on[2] ye. And if there was'nt so many, says I, and I was a monied man, ye should not go a flauntin' around with your top-knots,[3] for there's no use in 'em, but to make young folks vain, and silly ones stare. If ye larn to be extravagant, ye'll be likely to be old gals all your days, for men are afeard to marry women who spend money, and never make it."

The Lady expressed her approbation of his correct judgment, and inquired after the welfare of his family.

"All stout and hearty, thank'e Ma'am. My wife sent compliments to you, and Molly tell'd me to say, that she was a thousand times beholden to you, for your good present. She, and all on 'em, wishes you a happy New-Year."

"I thank them for their kind recollections. Molly, I think, is the plump girl with such rosy cheeks."

"Why, as for that matter, they're all in the same situation, as plump as patridges, and swarmin' round like bees. Molly's the oldest on 'em, and as fat as butter. She'll be fourteen years old, come the tenth day o' February—and that will be Sabba-day[4] arter next. She weighs about twice as much as you do, Ma'am, I guess. She's rather more stocky than her mother, and I hope will be as smart for bizness. She'll spin her run o' tow-yarn,[5] or woollen, afore dinner; and she has wove six yards a day, of yard-wide sheetin'. She takes in weavin', when any body will hire it done, and so buys herself her bettermost cloes, which is a help to me. Jehoiakim,[6] the oldest boy—he's named arter his grandaddy—and is a stout, stirrin' youngster. He'll hoe near-about as much corn in an hour, as I can; and cold winter days, he'll chop and sled wood through the snow, without frettin' a bit. But I s'pose 'tant right and fittin' to brag about my children, Ma'am. It seems as if I thought my geese were all swans."

"It gives me pleasure, my good friend, to hear of the welfare of your family, and the habits of industry in which you are training them. I hope that you are also careful, that their minds are stored with useful knowledge."

---

1 under-riggin'] underclothes (rigging: clothes)

2 snarl on] traffic jam of (the many Larkin children)

3 top-knots] ribbon bows in a lace cap, or knobs of hair on top of the head

4 Sabba-day] Sabbath-day, an Americanism

5 tow] fibre of flax, hemp, or jute prepared for making cloth

6 Jehoiakim] in the Bible, a king of Judah (second book of Kings)

"O yes Ma'am. They all go to the deestrict-school,[1] more than ha-af o' the winter; though it's nigh upon two mild from the house. In the summer time, it's kept a leetle spell by a woman—and then the younger ones go, to keep 'em out o' the way o' them who are glad to work at home. I s'pose they larn somethin' about sewin' and readin'. But Tim, the third child, he's the boy for larnin'. He took a prodigious likin' to books, when he was a baby; and if you only show'd him one, he'd put it rite into his mouth, and stop squallin'. He 'ant but eleven year old now; and when he gets a newspaper, there's no *whoa*[2] to him, no more than to our black ox when he sees the haystack, till he's read it clear through, advertisements and all. The Master says that he's the smartest of all the boys about spellin', and now he takes to cypherin'[3] marvellously. So that I don't know but sometime or other, he may be hired to keep our deestrict-school. But I hope my heart a'nt lifted up with pride, at sich great prospects, for I know that 'God resisteth the proud, and giveth grace unto the humble.'"[4]

"I trust you will always remember that humility is necessary to our religion. But it is equally your duty to receive the gifts of God with gratitude, and to enjoy them with a cheerful spirit. I know not that I recollect the names of all your children."

"It's no wonder that ye don't Ma'am, there's such a neest on 'em. They're as thick as hops round the fire[5] this winter. There's Roxey and Reuey, they're next to Tim,[6] and look like twins. They pick the wool, and card tow, and wind quills,[7] and knit stockins and mittins for the fokes in the house; and I've brought some down with me to day, to see if they'll buy 'em to the marchants' shops, and let 'em have a couple o' leetle small shawls. Then there's Keziah,[8] she 'ant but a trifle over six year old, and I recken she has a kind of a hard time on't; for she takes most o' the care o' the three youngest ones. Jehu[9] is about as big as she is, and pretty obstropolous,[10] so that I have to take him in hand, once in

1 A Connecticut law of 1766 enabled towns to form school districts under local control and financing.

2 whoa] stop (to a horse or draught animal); at this time an Americanism

3 cypherin'] ciphering: arithmetic

4 The Bible, Paul's first letter to Peter, 5.5.

5 hops ... fire] Hops are dried to make beer and medicines.

6 In the Bible, Timothy is a faithful associate of the apostle Paul.

7 wind quills] coil yarn around a reed or hollow stem

8 Keziah] in the Bible, the second of Job's three daughters

9 Jehu] in the Bible, a king of Israel who expelled the worshippers of Baal

10 obstropolous] obstreperous

a while. Then there's young Tryphena, and the baby Tryphosa,[1] who's rather tendsome,[2] and Keziah's tied to 'em a'most every minute when she 'ant abed. So her Mammy is able to see to the cheese-tubs, for you know, sich a dairy as we have keeps a woman pretty tight to't. There's nine o' the young ones, Ma'am, and as I said afore, the oldest is but e'en a just fourteen. Yet I should be sorry to have one less, though I should work off my fingers' eends clear[3] to the bone to maintain 'em. I'm willin' to slave for 'em, but I mean they shall do their part, and not grow up in idleness to laff, and make game[4] of their old hard-workin' parents, and be moths[5] in the world, arter they get to be men and women."

The paternal narrative was interrupted by Cuffe bearing refreshments; for the Lady seldom permitted any one to leave her mansion, without partaking its hospitality. A well warmed mince-pye, and a mug of sparkling cider, she had supposed would be useful in guarding the farmer from the extreme cold of his ride; and he soon convinced her, by his formidable attacks upon both, that she had not misjudged in the question of what was palatable. After despatching his refection, and some business respecting the farm, he hesitated slightly and said—

"I wonder now, if you'd take it hard, Ma'am, if I should trouble you with some o' my own family consarns, and ax your advice about 'em, seein' you've had more years, and experunce than I?" The Lady assured him of her willingness both to listen, and to serve him, according to her ability.

"Well then, it's all about my nephew, Amariah Stutson.[6] He's liv'd with me now goin' on ten year. About the time o' my movin' into York State, his daddy died, and the children was all necessiated to be put out.[7] My old woman, she set on me to take this boy, cause he was her sister Jemima's[8] son, and she always set great store by 'Mima. I tell'd her he was a spindlin', white-liver'd[9]

---

1 Tryphena ... Tryphosa] In the Bible, Romans 16.12, Paul greets Tryphena and Tryphosa, "who labour in the Lord."

2 tendsome] needing a lot of attention; an Americanism

3 clear] completely; an Americanism by this period

4 game] jest

5 moths] here, parasites

6 Amariah] in the Bible, a Levite, sect known for its religious zeal

7 put out] sent to work as live-in servants or labourers

8 Jemima's] In the Bible, Jemima is Job's eldest daughter.

9 white-livered] deficient in the bile choler, so supposedly lacking spirit

thing, and never'd stand the fever and agy[1] in the new countries. But she kept at me, till she had her way, as women are pretty apt to do; and he did better than I expected, and grow'd up to a chunked,[2] healthy youngster. He'll be 19 year old, come next April-fool-day; and I meant to a done well by Amariah, when he got to be of age, and give him a decent settin' out, and then hired him by the month, if so be that he was agreeable to't, and pay him the money.

"But he's growin' despate unstiddy of late, ever since the judgment o' God upon our church, and congregation, in lettin' the Methodist[3] loose among us. You ha'nt heard of our chastisement for our backslidins, and lukewarmness, have ye, Ma'am? Poor Deacon Bump takes it to heart so sadly, that he's grown as thin as a June-shad.[4] Why these people have hired a room rite over acrost the way from our meetin-house, and when our worthy minister begins the sarvice a Sabba-day mornin', they begin what they call their *exercises*,[5] and what with their screechin' and scramin', and singin' and tumlin' down, they make sich a racket, that it's utterly unpossible, for us to hear any thing to be edified with. They hold out longer than we too, and have love-feasts,[6] and night-meetins, and a deal that I cant make neither head nor tail on, and I grieve to say that Amariah is gittin' bewitched arter 'em. I'm sure I don't know what religion there can be in sich actions, and as for their lungs, if they wa'nt made o' soal-luther,[7] I'm sure they'd be wore into holes like a honey-comb."

"The Methodists, my good friend, though their manner of worship differs from ours, must not be thought destitute of true piety. They sometimes exhibit an excess of that zeal, which we are reproached for being deficient in. We should guard against condemning those, who differ from us in opinions, or forms. They

---

1 agy] ague (a term describing a fever marked by bouts of shivering, fever, and sweating at regular intervals)

2 chunked] stoutly built; early nineteenth-century Americanism

3 Methodism] mid eighteenth-century, mainly working-class movement in England, taken to America by George Whitefield (1714–80), reinforcing the "First Great Awakening" (1730s–1740s); the "Second Great Awakening" followed from the 1790s to the 1820s, also led by Methodists (see above, p. 14)

4 shad] a kind of herring plentiful in American rivers in May and June

5 exercises] religious observances

6 love-feasts] communal meals, imitating early Christians, from *agape*: social love

7 soal-luther] shoe-sole leather, necessarily resistant to wear

may have as much sincerity as ourselves, and though 'man judgeth according to the outward appearance, you know who looketh upon the heart.'"[1]

"Land o' Goshen![2] why Lady! You don't think that all the crutters, who call themselves Christians, are as right as we, do ye? There's the Episcopalians,[3] I went to their church, once at the landin' a' Christmas I think they call'd it. I took it at first, for a merry-makin', there was so many green branches plastered up here and there; but they kept such a perpechual jumpin' up, and sittin' down, that afore they'd done it made my bones ache as bad as a hard day's work. What religion there is in readin' prayers out of a book,[4] I never could see. Then there's the Baptists, who think a man is to be saved, by sousing over head and ears in cold water.[5] But these Methodist folks seem to me the most strangest of all. Why they don't hold to the doctrine o' lection,[6] and them that won't believe the Bible, when it's as plain to 'em as the nose on their face, have denied the faith, and are worse than an infidel. They make a long talkin' too, about arrivin' at parfection,[7] and Amariah he holds forth consarnin' it. But I'm sure he's a great deal more unparfect than he was, when he was just a larnin' by heart in his catechise, that 'no meer man since the fall is able to keep the commandaments.'"[8] Now, he must go racin' to all the night meetin's, and that makes my boys unstiddy, and teaze to go long with him. They shan't stir a step while I live. Was'nt their honoured grandaddy deacon in the Presbyterian meetin' fifteen years and better? They sha'nt scandalize[9] him, while I have the rule over 'em.

---

1 The Bible, 1 Samuel, 16.7: "for man looketh on the outward appearance, but the Lord looketh on the heart."

2 Goshen] in the Bible, book of Genesis, a fertile region in Egypt from which Moses led his people out of bondage to the promised land; "land of Goshen": supposedly a common American oath

3 Episcopalians] American branch of the Anglican church, believing in salvation by individual free-will choosing good and effected by divine grace, in contrast to Larkin's Calvinist Presbyterian church, asserting individual predestination to salvation or damnation

4 prayers out of a book] Episcopalians' "Book of Common Prayer"

5 cold water] Baptists practised adult baptism by full immersion

6 election] the Calvinist doctrine that God has chosen ("elected") or preordained the individual to salvation or damnation

7 parfection] Methodists emphasized striving for "perfection" in the sense of living a holy life

8 A principle found in the Presbyterian catechism, or instruction manual.

9 scandalize] disgrace

"But as I was a sayin' of Amariah, he tells his experunces[1] at their meetin's, and sometimes at twelve o'clock at night, he'll wake up in his bed, and scrame some o' the Methodist hymns so loud, that he sets the baby a roarin', bein' scared, and no crutter in the house can get one wink o' sleep till he's a mind to give over. Then if I, or his A-ant, open our heads to say one word to him about it, then he makes a towse,[2] and is parsecuted, and I s'pose tells an experunce out on't to Mr. Snortgrass, his minister, who is a terrible tonguey[3] man."

"Your situation, good Mr. Larkin, requires considerable delicacy. Yet I can assure you, that Mr. Whitfield, the leader of a great part of the sect of Methodists, was a man of real excellence and piety. My husband, who was educated in the same faith which we profess, and was sincerely attached to its precepts, possessed that liberality of soul which I strive to imitate, and gave to differing sects the praise of whatever virtue they displayed. Mr. Whitfield was always an honoured guest at our house, when he made his excursions through this part of the country. I will relate a little anecdote of him, which may prove to you, how much his thoughts were fixed upon a future state. Soon after the death of our three little sons, he breakfasted with us. Some Chocolate was brought in, and the recollection of their fondness for that beverage, and of their recent burial, brought tears to my eyes. My husband explained the emotion by saying, 'she thinks of the olive-plants that once flourished around our table,[4] and in one week were smitten.' The Divine for a moment raised his eyes upwards, then laying his hand upon the head of my husband said, with a vivacity and earnestness which characterized him, 'My dear Doctor! what a lift is this towards heaven.'"

"Well Ma'am, I s'pose that was clever enough since you think so. But most folks would say it sounded despate like want o' feelin', not to seem to be sorry for you, nor nothin' sich-like. Now, what would ye have me to do about Amariah's business, for it's high time for me to be a gittin' under way, Ma'am."

"Mr. Larkin, your own good sense will guard you against any violent opposition to a young man who, if he is deceived, deserves

---

1 experunces] In "experience-meetings" Methodists recounted incidents of their religious life.

2 towse] fuss

3 tonguey] talkative

4 The Bible, Psalms 128.3: "Thy wife shall be as a fruitful vine by the sides of thine house: thy children like olive plants round about thy table."

pity, if sincere, candour.[1] This strong excitement will be likely to pass away, if you do not nourish it by waking angry passions. Extremes are not apt to be lasting, and, in any case, moderation will be most effectual. Remember, my friend, that contention about doctrines, is neither that love which is the evidence of the Spirit, nor that holiness, without which no man shall see God. And I doubt not that you will feel, after a little more reflection, that, as long as we are so compassed about with infirmity, we should dread to judge, lest we also be judged, or to condemn, lest we be condemned."[2]

From CHAPTER X.

[With winter over, Madam L—— visits the Larkin farmhouse.]

As Madam L—— entered she heard, in the clattering of knives and forks, the reason, why she was not as usual welcomed at the door. Unwilling to interrupt the refection of the family, she took a seat unobserved. She found herself in the best room of the mansion, but to this the inhabitants of the neighbouring villages would assign, neither the name of "parlour, hall, or drawing-room,"[3] avoiding the example of their city acquaintance, as the ancient reformers did the abominations of the Church of Rome.[4] Adhering to their habits of precision as tenaciously as to their ideas of simplicity, they gave to this most honourable room an appellation derived from its bearing upon the cardinal points. The one under present consideration, being visited by the latest beams of the setting sun, and the first breathings of the summer breeze, was denominated the "south-west room." As the furniture of this best apartment of Farmer Larkin may serve as a sample of the interiour of most of the Sanctum Sanctorums[5] of the better

---

1 candour] impartiality

2 Echoing the Bible, Luke, 6.37.

3 Names for the main room in houses of families pretending to gentility; drawing-room: originally "withdrawing-room," the room to which the ladies withdrew after dinner while the gentlemen drank and smoked.

4 abominations ... Rome] During the early sixteenth-century Protestant Reformation some wished to replace Roman Catholic ritual with the supposed primitive simplicity of early Christianity.

5 Holy of Holies] in the Biblical Temple of Jerusalem, the innermost and hence most sacred room, to be entered only by the purified; hence any room closed to all but a few or not for everyday use

sort of agriculturists at that early period, it may be well to add a brief description.

The bed, an indispensable appendage, was without either curtains, or high posts, and decorated with a new woollen coverlet, where the colour of red gorgeously predominated over the white and green, with which it was intermingled. So small a space did it occupy, that if, like Og, king of Bashan, whose gigantic height was predicated from his bedstead of nine cubits,[1] the size of our farmers should have been estimated by the dimensions of their places of repose, posterity would do them immense injustice.[2]

A buffet, or corner-cupboard was a conspicuous article, in which were arranged a set of bright, pewter plates, some red and white cups and saucers, not much larger than what now belong to a doll's equipage, and a pyramidal block-tin tea-pot.[3] The lower compartment of this repository, which was protected by a door, furnished a receptacle for the Sabbath-day hats and bonnets of the children, each occupying its own place upon the shelves. In the vicinity was what was denominated "a chist o' draws,"[4] namely, a capacious vault of stained pine, which, opening like a chest, contained the better part of the wardrobe of the master and mistress of the family; while, beneath, space was left for two or three drawers, devoted to the accommodation of the elder children. But the masterpiece of finery was a tea-table, which, elevating its round disk perpendicularly,[5] evinced that it was more for show than use.

Its surface displayed a commendable lustre, protected by a penal statute from the fingers of the children. But an unruly kitten used to take delight in viewing, on the lower extremity of that polished orb, a reflection of her own round face, and formidable whiskers. Unhappily mistaking the appearance of these for an adversary, she imprinted thereon the marks of her claws, too deeply for all the efforts of the good housewife to efface, and soon

---

1 Og ... cubits] In the Bible, Og is the last of a race of giants defeated by the Israelites; his bed is described in Deuteronomy 3.11. Cubit: ancient measure equal to the length of the forearm and hand.

2 size ... injustice] In earlier times beds were often shorter, as most people slept semi-upright out of the belief that those lying prone were more likely to die while asleep.

3 block-tin] Britannia metal, or white metal, a cheap substitute for silver, with an important manufacturing centre at Meriden, Connecticut

4 chist o' draws] chest of drawers, originally used to keep money, valuables, and so on but later, enlarged, used to keep clothing

5 The table-top folded up when not in use.

after expiated her crime upon the scaffold. A looking-glass, much smaller than the broad expansion of the Farmer's face, hung against the roughly plastered, yet unsullied wall.[1] A few high, strait-back'd chairs, and a pair of small andirons nicely black'd, whose heads bore a rude resemblance to the "human form divine,"[2] completed the inventory of goods and chattels. Over the low, wide fire-place, hung in a black frame, without the superfluity of a glass, the family record, legibly penned, with a space very considerately left for future additions. The apartment had an air of neatness, beyond what was then generally observed in the houses of those who made the dairy, and spinning-wheel, their prime objects of attention. The white floor was carefully sanded,[3] and at each door a broad mat, made of the husks of the Indian corn, claimed tribute from the feet of those who entered. Where Madam L—— was seated, she had a full view of the family, surrounding their peaceful board, and so cordially engaged in doing justice to its viands, that not a glance wandered to the spot which she occupied.

The table, covered with a coarse white cloth, bore at the head a large supply of boiled beef, and pork, served up in a huge dish of glazed ware, of a form between platter and bowl, though it probably would rank with the latter genus. A mass of very fine cabbage appeared in the same reservoir, like a broad, emerald islet, flanked with parsnips and turnips, the favourite "long and short saace"[4] of the day. At the bottom of the board was an enormous pudding of Indian meal, supported by its legitimate concomitants, a plate of butter, and jug of molasses. Four brown mugs of cider, divided into equal compartments the quadrangle of the board, and the wooden trenchers, which each one manfully maintained, were perfectly clean and comfortable.

Farmer Larkin, and his wife, not deeming it a point of etiquette to separate as far as the limits of the table would permit,[5] shared together the post of honour by the dish of meat. At the left hand of the father, sat his youngest son, and at the right hand of

1 Large mirrors were very expensive until a chemical process for coating glass was devised in 1835.

2 A phrase used by Robert Southey, William Wordsworth, and William Blake.

3 sanded] sprinkled with sand

4 long ... saace] "Long sauce" included beets, carrots, and parsnips; "short sauce" included potatoes, turnips, and onions.

5 Disregardful or ignorant of fashionable manners, Mr and Mrs Larkin do not sit at opposite ends of the dining table, but side by side.

the mother, her youngest daughter. Thus the male line, beginning at Jehu, and touching every one according to his age, passed over the heads of Timothy and Jehoiakim, ending in Amariah, the nephew, and would-be Methodist. On the other hand, the female line, from the mother, who held in her lap the chubbed Tryphosa, passed with geometrical precision through the spaces allotted to Tryphena, Keziah, Roxey and Reuey, terminating with buxom Molly. She was indeed a damsel of formidable size, but of just proportions, and employed her brawny arm, in cutting slices from a large loaf of brown bread, which she distributed with great exactness by each trencher, as soon as her father had stocked it with meat, and her mother garnished it with vegetables. There was something pleasing in the sight of so many healthy and cheerful faces, and in the domestic order which evidently prevailed. The first course past in silence, except that Farmer Larkin said to his wife,—

"Do pray, Mammy, put down Tryphosa on the floor, and give her a crust o' bread to gnaw. I can't bear to see ye always a carryin' some burden or other, so that ye get no rest even at meal times."

The wife obediently placed the plump infant in a humbler station, who lifted up its broad blue eyes, as if it thought itself aggrieved, until the father reaching it a piece of bread, said,—"there, baby, larn to take care o' yourself."

It soon became so much absorbed with its fragment of the staff of life, as to make no overtures to return to the arms of its mother. In a short time, each trencher, neatly scraped, was presented to Molly for a slice of the pudding in her vicinity, to which Amariah carefully added the usual condiments. When Tim's plate, in due rotation, was replenished, the farmer said,—

"Amariah, that boy did not do his ta-a-sk this mornin'. Don't ye put any lasses[1] on his puddin'. Lazy folks sha-ant fare so well as others in my house. That's right an't it Tim, to larn ye to be industrious?"

"Yes Father," said the boy, eating his dry pudding without complaint, and with the air of one who intended to profit by the justice which he acknowledged. The meal was accompanied by a few questions from the parents, to which the younger members returned brief answers; but refrained from holding light conversation among themselves, with far greater sense of propriety, than is always witnessed at the tables of the professedly polite. At the

1 lasses] molasses

close of the repast, the Father, bowing his head, uttered brief but hearty thanks to the Giver of all Mercies, during which even the youngest children stood as if in an act of devotion. They had been taught that the food of each day, however homely, was a favour; that it was both a duty and pleasure to thank Him[1] who bestowed it; and that it was sinful to do this with a light, irreverent deportment. Madam L——, touched at this scene of domestic order, harmony and devotion, thought that the careless, the proud, or the epicure, who would scorn these humble inmates, might still receive from them a salutary lesson. Perchance, in her mind was a train of thought, similar to what inspired the ploughman-poet, when he exclaimed—

> "From scenes like these, old Scotia's grandeur springs,
> Which makes her lov'd at home, rever'd abroad—
> Princes and lords are but the breath of kings,
> *An honest man's the noblest work of God.*"[2]

[Madam L—— enters, concludes her business with Mr Larkin, and distributes gifts to the children. The narrator reflects on the changing tastes and material culture of American farmers.]

Since that period, those luxuries and refinements, which spread so rapidly in our cities, have pervaded, in some degree, the abodes of the tillers of the earth. They are becoming a more enlightened race than their fathers, and from their habitations have issued some of our most distinguished merchants, statesmen, and divines. Their sons have been distinguished in our seminaries of science, for the zeal with which they have pursued knowledge, and the indefatigable application with which they have supplied the defects of early culture. When the sons of rich men, languid from indulgence, have shrunk from mental effort as insupportable hardship, and fallen prey to those vices which indolence creates, the offspring of those who hold the plough have wrested from their feeble hands the prize of honour, and pressed on in the path of their country's praise and pride. There is, in the pursuits of agriculture, a salutary discipline both for the body and mind, as they are gradually developed. That hardihood of frame, which despises privation, or change of elements, is more congenial to elevation of character, than the enervating nurture

1 Him] God

2 Robert Burns (1759–96), "The Cotter's Saturday Night," 163–66.

of patrician families, where animal tastes are pampered, at the expense of vigour of intellect, and ease of body promoted, even to the bondage of the free spirit. Possibly also, in the simplicity of man's primeval occupation, there may be, like the angels hovering over Eden, natural and invisible guards around the avenues of innocence, cheerfulness, and that religion which springs from a view of the Creator in his works.

Agriculture has been, in the New-England States, a source of wealth, less splendid indeed than some others, but far less fluctuating. It has been a fountain, not always as profuse in its streams as avarice or ambition might desire, but perennial when sought by industry and prudence. How frequently does it happen, in our republican government, that a fortune, acquired by the economical agriculturist, furnishes the means of vanity and pride to his son; who, removing to the city, and educating his children in indolence, prepares them to squander the inheritance of their ancestors. The next generation, born in poverty, seek an antidote in labour, and find that "tide in the affairs of men, which taken at the flood leads on to fortune."[1]

Many such instances had fallen under the observation of Madam L——, and her silent reflections upon them were not interrupted, until her approach to the Turnpike, and few miles from her residence.

[The chapter ends with an anecdote of an Irish immigrant refusing to pay a toll for use of a road, enraging the English immigrant toll-keeper. The chapter closes when Madam L—— comes along: "The Lady suddenly changed the fierce expression of his countenance, by putting into his hand, with her own toll, the sum for which his recreant brother of Erin was indebted; and kindly wishing him a good afternoon, departed with a smile of that conciliating spirit, which prompted the patriarch's exhortation to his kinsmen, 'let there be no strife, I pray thee, between me and thee, and my herdsman and thy herdsmen, for we be brethren.'"[2]]

---

1 Shakespeare, *Julius Caesar*, 4.3.215–16.

2 The Bible, Genesis 13.8.

5. From *Poems* (1827).[1]

GRAVE OF THE MOTHER OF WASHINGTON.[2]

MOTHER of him whose godlike fame
  The good throughout the world revere,
Ah! why, without a stone, or name.
  Thus sleep'st thou unregarded here?

Fair pensile branches o'er thee wave
  And Nature decks the chosen dell;
Yet surely o'er thy hallow'd grave
  A nation's mournful sighs should swell!

Rome, with a burst of filial pride,
  The mother of her Gracchi[3] view'd;
And why should we restrain the tide
  Of reverential gratitude?

She to sublime Volumnia[4] paid
  Her tribute of enraptured tears,
When the dread chief that voice obey'd
  Which sternly curb'd his infant years.

Thou in the days of Sparta's[5] might,
  Had'st high on her illustrious roll
Been rank'd, amidst those matrons bright,
  Who nobly nursed the great of soul.

---

1 Sigourney's second major collection.

2 The first poem in the collection, reprinted in *The Wide-Awake Gift: A Know-Nothing Token for 1855*, pp. 44–45, possibly without Sigourney's permission; the Know-Nothing movement saw Catholic immigrants as a threat to emergent American "national" culture, and made an icon of George Washington (1732–99), military leader of the American Revolution and first president of the United States; his mother, Mary Ball (1708–89), was idealized as a model of republican motherhood.

3 mother ... Gracchi] The Gracchi brothers, second century BCE, were supposed to have learned republican virtues from their mother, Cornelia.

4 Volumnia] in Shakespeare's *Coriolanus*, mother of the stoical Roman general whom she dissuades from destroying Rome in revenge for the plebeians' rejection of him

5 Sparta] ancient Greek city-state renowned in legend for simple life and martial prowess, inspired by patriotic mothers

For disciplined in Wisdom's school,
  The lofty pupil own'd thy sway;
And well might he be skill'd to rule,
  So early nurtured to obey.

No enervating arts refined
  To slumber lull'd his heaven-born might;
No weak indulgence warp'd thy mind,
  To cloud a hero's path of light.[1]

Say,—when upon thy shielding breast
  The saviour of his country hung,
When his soft lip to thine was prest,
  Wooing the accents from thy tongue,

Saw'st thou, prescient, o'er his brow,
  The shadowy wreath of laurel[2] start?
Or, did thy nightly dream bestow
  High visions of his glorious part?

And when his little hands were taught
  By thee, in simple prayer to rise,[3]
Say,—were thy own devotions fraught
  With heighten'd incense for the skies?

Well may that realm confiding rest,
  Heroes, and mighty chiefs to see,
Which finds its infant offspring blest
  With monitors and guides like thee.

A future age, than ours more just,
  With his, shall blend thy honor'd name,
And rear, exulting, o'er thy dust,
  The monument of deathless fame.[4]

---

1 indulgence ... light] Republicans since ancient times maintained that luxury weakened a nation's moral fibre, public spirit, and martial values.

2 laurel] In ancient Rome laurel wreaths were awarded to victors.

3 simple prayer to rise] George Washington was barely religious, but was later—and is still—represented by many as a devout Christian.

4 monument ... fame] The obscurity of Mary Washington's grave was deplored by the marquis de Lafayette, hero of the American and French Revolutions, in his *Memoirs* (translated 1825); a monument was begun in 1833 but abandoned; another was completed in the 1890s.

And thither bid young mothers wend,
To bless thy spirit as they rove,
And learn, while o'er thy tomb they bend,
For heaven to train the babes they love.

THE CORAL INSECT.[1]

Toil on! toil on! ye ephemeral train,
Who build in the tossing and treacherous main;
Toil on,—for the wisdom of man ye mock,
With your sand-based structures and domes of rock;
Your columns the fathomless fountains lave,[2]
And your arches spring up to the crested wave;—
Ye're a puny race, thus to boldly rear
A fabric so vast, in a realm so drear.

Ye bind the deep with your secret zone,
The ocean is seal'd, and the surge a stone;
Fresh wreaths from the coral pavement spring,
Like the terraced pride of Assyria's king;[3]
The turf looks green where the breakers roll'd,
O'er the whirlpool ripens the rind of gold;—
The sea-snatch'd isle is the home of men,
And mountains exult where the wave hath been.

But why do ye plant 'neath the billows dark
The wrecking reef for the gallant bark?—[4]
There are snares enough on the tented field,
Mid the blossom'd sweets that the valleys yield;
There are serpents to coil, ere the flowers are up;
There's a poison-drop in man's purest cup,
There are foes that watch for his cradle breath,
And why need ye sow the floods with death?

---

1 Reprinted in *Specimens of American Poetry, with Critical and Biographical Notices*, ed. Samuel Kettel, 3 vols. (Boston: S.G. Goodrich, 1829), an early "national" anthology; "coral insect" was a name for coral polyp.

2 lave] wash, a common poeticism

3 terraced pride ... king] the "hanging gardens" of Babylon created by Nebuchadnezzar II; one of the "seven wonders" of the ancient world

4 bark] ship, a poeticism

With mouldering bones the deeps are white,
From the ice-clad pole to the tropicks bright;—
The mermaid hath twisted her fingers cold
With the mesh of the sea-boy's curls of gold,
And the gods of ocean have frown'd to see
The mariner's bed in their halls of glee;—
Hath earth no graves, that ye thus must spread
The boundless sea for the thronging dead?

Ye build,—ye build,—but ye enter not in,
Like the tribes whom the desert devour'd in their sin;[1]
From the land of promise ye fade and die,
Ere its verdure gleams forth on your weary eye;—
As the kings of the cloud-crown'd pyramid,
Their noteless bones in oblivion hid;[2]
Ye slumber unmark'd 'mid the desolate main,
While the wonder and pride of your works remain.

AFRICA.

Land of the wise!—where science broke[3]
  Like morning from chaotic deeps,
Where Moses, holy prophet, woke,[4]
  Where Parsons, youthful martyr, sleeps;—

Land of the brave!—where Carthage rear'd
  'Gainst haughty Rome a warrior's crest,[5]
Where Cato,[6] like a god revered,
  Indignant pierced his patriot breast;—

---

1 tribes ... sin] In the Bible, book of Exodus, Moses led the Jews from bondage in Egypt to the promised land of Israel, but those God considered sinful (including Moses himself) were excluded

2 pyramid ... hid] Huge pyramids were built as tombs by ancient Egyptian rulers, but their names remained unknown in Sigourney's day.

3 science broke] Many credited ancient Egypt as the birthplace of civilization and "science" in the broad sense of knowledge.

4 Moses ... woke] In the Bible, Exodus 20.1–17, Moses took God's law to the Jews in ten commandments central to the Judaeo-Christian tradition.

5 Carthage ... crest] Carthage, on the north coast of Africa, controlled a Mediterranean empire until finally defeated by its rival Rome in 146 BCE.

6 Cato] Marcus Porcius Cato (95–46 BCE), or Cato the Younger, hero of republican history; opposed Julius Caesar's pursuit of despotic power, fled to Africa, and killed himself rather than live in a world ruled by Caesar

Land of the scorn'd, the exiled race,
Who fainting 'neath oppressive toil,
With never-ceasing sighs retrace
Their palm-tree's shade, their fathers' soil;

Shall blest Benevolence extend
Her angel reign from sea to sea,
Nor yet one glance of pity bend
Deserted Africa! on thee?—

Did Nature bid the torrid skies
Glare fiercely o'er thy desert glade?—
In heathen gloom benight thine eyes
And cloud thy brow with ebon[1] shade?—

And must thy brother's hatred find
A doom that Nature never gave?—
A curse Creation ne'er design'd,—
The fetter, and the name of slave?—

Haste! lift from Afric's wrongs the veil,
Ere the Eternal Judge arise,
To list the helpless prisoner's wail,
And count the tears from misery's eyes.

Oh! ere the flaming heavens reveal
That frown which none can meet and live,
Teach her before the Throne to kneel
And like her Saviour pray,—"*Forgive.*"

CAROLINE MATILDA, TO CHRISTIAN THE SEVENTH OF DENMARK.[2]

From gloomy Zell, where shades usurp the day,
Where hopeless grief in secret pines away,

1 ebon] ebony

2 Caroline (1751–75), grand-daughter of George II of Britain, was married to Christian of Denmark in 1766 but, alienated by his debauchery and court politics, she became the lover of J.F. Struensee (1737–72), reforming prime minister. After a popular uprising, Struensee was executed, Caroline was divorced and exiled to Celle (here, Zell) in Germany, and died there. In Sigourney's day she was a figure for woman as pawn and victim in the male-dominated political sphere, for example in Mary Wollstonecraft's *Letters* from Scandinavia (1796), letter 18.

To Denmark's distant clime these lays I send,
To *seek the husband, not to find the friend.*—
—How hard my fate! although to power allied,
A monarch's daughter, and a monarch's bride,
Torn from those joys that strew'd my path with bloom,
And sternly coffin'd in a living tomb.—
——Oh! by the memory of that love which bore
My early youth from Albion's sacred shore,[1]
By that first ardour guiltless and divine,
Which moved to leave a parent's arms for thine,
By all the hopes that lured my trusting mind,
By all thy vows, if vows thy soul can bind,
Bend to my woes!—but ah, how vain the plea
That summons pity or remorse from thee.—
—Cold as the icy girdle of thy shores,
Deaf as the storm that o'er thy mountains pours,
I see thee wield the sceptre, scourge and chain,
And rule despotic o'er a trembling train.—
—Unfading traces of thy cruel sway
Glare in my soul and fright mild sleep away,—
Thy victim's throng,—I mark the ghastly train,
Their straining eye-balls start with bloodshot pain,
The brave Struensee!—say,—what crime had he
To kindle hatred or revenge in thee?—
He mounts the scaffold,—dark with curdled gore;
He falls,—he bleeds,—his bosom heaves no more;[2]
And I,—alas!—but stay thou fleeting line,
Why is Struensee's image link'd with mine?—
Think not that guilt this artless bond has wove
Nor blot my friendship with the name of love.—[3]
——But me, sad victim of thy jealous strife,
Rent in my youth from all the joys of life,
My last retreat a mightier foe invades,
And darkly dooms me to impervious shades.
From my blanch'd cheek the color fades away,
Mysterious bands my buoyant footsteps stay;
While Spring's young flowers that erst my path did strew,
Unnoticed wither in their fragrant dew,
Uncheer'd I view their graceful beauties wave
And start to gather what may deck my grave.—

1 Albion] poetic name for England

2 no more] Struensee was executed by being dismembered in public.

3 Nor blot ... love] Caroline and Struensee were in fact lovers.

—Unfeeling consort!—shroud my life with gloom,
Scorn, hate, condemn, and curse me in the tomb,
Wreak all thy malice on my wretched name,
But spare my infant,[1]—spare thy daughter's fame,
Spare the fond babe who foster'd in my breast,
Smiles at my tears, or sinks in balmy rest,
Marks not the anguish on my brow that preys,
Nor shares the grief that blasts her mother's days.

TO A WASP.[2]

Bless me, kind friend!—who canst thou wish to see?
Thus climbing onward with untiring labor,
A deal of friendship thou must have for me,
To take such wondrous pains, obliging neighbour,
What may thy business be, a formal call?
Then take a chair and sit, as if thou 'dst none at all.

Be amiable, I pray thee now, sweet guest!
I would not harm thee, that were sport unkind,
Thou cam'st, Sir Wasp, like knight with lance in rest,
Hoping perchance, some tournament to find,
But yet I mean not thou my veins shalt probe,
So find some other tilt-yard, prithee, than my robe.

Thou giv'st a warrior's warning, bold and fair,
Like Ajax valiant, or Achilles proud,[3]
Thou lay'st no ambush, no deceitful snare,[4]
But sound'st thy tiny trumpet long and loud,
Through which, a moral lesson thou art teaching
Backbiters and false friends.—Would that they heeded preaching!

Who knows but what among thy kindred brood
Some *leech*[5] thou art, of credit and renown,
And so thou com'st, forsooth, to let me blood!—

---

1 infant] princess Louisa Augusta, born 1771, possibly Struensee's child

2 One of several poems by Sigourney humanizing insects and small animals.

3 Ajax ... Achilles proud] heroes of the Trojans and the Greeks respectively in the Homeric epic, the *Iliad*, about the siege of Troy

4 ambush ... snare] The Greeks captured Troy by pretending to abandon the siege, leaving a large wooden horse concealing warriors, which the Trojans took into the city as a trophy.

5 leech] physician, incorrectly based on physicians' use of leeches to treat patients by drawing their blood

Haste—leave my arm, or I must help thee down!
I've fear'd the doctors marvellously, ever
Since they gave brandy in the spotted fever.—[1]

Mayhap I do misconstrue thee.—Well! well—
The best are fallible,—and I will strive
If but thy hidden virtues thou wilt tell,
To be as just as any one alive;—
I would not, even fly or flea should say,
I took their reputations wilfully away.—

Dost thou make honey? Sure! I had not thought it,
Such beverage must be exceeding rare,
I trow[2] the critic gentry may have bought it,
To neutralize their very acid fare.—[3]
Some cordial[4] they must need, who toil so hard
To pickle and to hack[5] each poor adventurous bard.—

I've read in school-boy days,—thy cousin bees,
(Mauger[6] the din of warming-pans and matrons[7])
Would swarm around the lips of Sophocles[8]
Mistaking the sweet muses for their patrons;
But thou, more wise, dost better things secure,
Trucking[9] thy surplus wares with some well-paid Reviewer.

Good bye!—but why that angry hiss? I pray,
Go vent in thy own nest, thy heighten'd spleen,[10]
Upon thy wife and babies, *that's the way*,
It breaks the dulness of too tame a scene,
But if they chance to sting, as well as thee,
Thou'lt need the stock of venom thou hast spared from me.

---

1 spotted fever] term once used for cerebro-spinal meningitis and typhus

2 trow] believe, here a humorous archaism

3 acid fare] Critics were commonly portrayed as embittered because envious of authors, and hence bitter or acid in their criticism.

4 cordial] an invigorating medicinal drink

5 pickle] apply salt and vinegar (i.e., acid remarks); hack: mangle or mutilate, but also apply a hackle, or wire brush, to process flax or hemp

6 Mauger] in spite of; a deliberate archaism

7 din ... matrons] In popular lore, wasps were chased away by loud noise.

8 Sophocles] famous fifth-century BCE Greek playwright; in ancient legend, honey-bees touched the lips of infants destined to be poets

9 Trucking] dealing or bartering

10 spleen] ill temper, supposedly caused by excess of bile from the spleen

TO AN ANCIENT ROCKING CHAIR.[1]

Whom have thy curving arms embraced
  Thou ancient, stately chair?
Since first thy form the parlor graced
  And claim'd the housewife's care.

For full a century,[2] I ween,
  Its mighty round has made,
Since first thy columns black and sheen
  Their maker's skill display'd.

The slippery Sofa's glossy dress
  Allures the weary wight,[3]
But soon his sliding limbs confess
  Their most uneasy plight,—

Though still it decks the modern hall
  The eye of taste to please:
While thou, a favourite art of all
  Who love the balm of ease.

On thee, the invalid reclined,
  His form by sickness chain'd,
Though haply still, his soaring mind
  Its prison house disdain'd,—

And wandering wide o'er fairy land
  Collected rainbow rays,
Or waked with memory's magic wand
  Fair forms of other days.

Here has some ancient maiden bright
  Repell'd encroaching Time,
Ensconced in stiff-laced stays[4] upright
  With high-heel'd shoe sublime.

---

1 One of Sigourney's poems celebrating common household objects.

2 full a century] Rocking chairs only began to appear in the late eighteenth century and were especially popular in the United States.

3 wight] person; a deliberate archaism

4 stays] corset stiffened with whalebone or metals rods

And here the meeker matron view'd
  Her children trooping round,
Who guide with shouts of laughter rude
  The ball's elastic bound,—

Anon to aid their sports would spread
  Her gay-flower'd ample gown,
Or at their quarrels shake her head
  And awe them with a frown.

Here, in thy arms,—the nodding nurse
  Has slumber'd out the night,
Regardless of the mutter'd curse
  Of the poor, gouty wight;

Or frighten'd from her stolen dream
  Has heard in deep dismay
The falling infant's piteous scream
  Who on her bosom lay.

Here beauty, like some blighted flower
  Smit by unfriendly sky,
Consumed the wakeful,—restless hour
  With bright, unearthly eye,

While on her cheek, the hectic glow
  Dire symbol of decay,
Reveal'd how fast the treacherous foe
  Was mining on his way.[1]

Ah!—wouldst thou speak,—thou ancient Chair,
  What secrets couldst thou tell?
Of hidden Love's mysterious care
  Breathed in thy hermit cell.

What mad resolves,—what deep-laid schemes
  What fancies bold and free,—
What dazzling hopes, and airy dreams
  Were born and died with thee.

1 mining on his way] reference to pulmonary consumption (i.e., tuberculosis) or phthisis

Then wouldst thou chide her idle rhyme,
  Who lolling thus at ease,
Mispends the untold wealth of time
  In lays so light as these.

6. From *The Token* (1833).[1]

TO A FRAGMENT OF SILK.[2]

WELL, radiant shred of silk, is it your choice,
  Here on my carpet, thus at ease to lay?
I've heard the veriest trifles have a voice
  Unto the musing mind; what can you say?
You seem to wake a dream of southern bowers,
Where sprang your rudiments, among Italian flowers.

Who were your ancestors? Methinks you pause!
  Excuse me, Yankees always ask the question;
What! those unsightly worms, with tireless maws,
  And such a very marvellous digestion?
Their spinning wheels, no doubt, their health supply;
But lo! in cone-like urns they fold themselves to die.

Perchance, to reel their slight cocoons did foil
  The patient skill of many a purblind dame,
While firmer nerves essayed the shuttle's toil,
  From whence your rainbow tinted tissue came;
Bound on a voyage o'er the boisterous ocean,
Quite snugly packed in bales, secure from all commotion.

What was your destiny in this New World?
  In dazzling robe to make young beauty vain?
Or for some waning lady pranked and curled
  To hide time's ravage from the giddy train?
Or bid pale Envy's pang the bosom swell,
That erring deems true bliss with outward show doth swell.

---

1 *The Token and Atlantic Souvenir: A Christmas and New Year's Present*, ed. S.G. Goodrich (Boston: Gray and Bowen, 1833), 335–36.

2 One of several rag poems by Sigourney; see "To a Shred of Linen" (p. 168) and "To a Fragment of Cotton" (p. 183).

Your history's not complete. Your second birth
  Is in bank-paper, to allure the eyes,
Making the rich o'erprize the gifts of earth,
  And the poor covet what his God denies:
Man's vanity from a vile worm may grow,
And paper puff his pride; go, gaudy fragment, go!

7. From *How to Be Happy* (1833).[1]

SECOND PART.

---

1. Be kind to Animals.

There are few things more disgraceful in children than to be cruel to those harmless creatures, which are unable to defend themselves. If I see a child pull off the wings of an insect, or throw stones at a toad, or take pains to set his foot upon a worm,—I am sure there is something wrong about him, or that he has not been well instructed. There was once a boy who loved to give pain to every thing that came in his way, over which he could get any power. He would take the eggs from the mourning Robin,—and torture the unfledged Sparrow.—Cats and Dogs, the peaceable Cow, and the faithful Horse, he delighted to worry and distress. I do not like to tell you of the many cruel things that he did. He was told that such deeds were wrong. An excellent lady with whom he lived used to warn and reprove him for his evil conduct. But he did not reform. When he grew up he became a soldier. He was never sorry to see men wounded, and blood running upon the earth. He became so wicked as to lay a plan to betray his country, and sell it into the hands of the enemy. This is to be a traitor. But he was discovered and fled. He never dared to return to his native land, but lived despised, and died miserably in a foreign clime. Such was the end of the cruel boy, who loved to give pain to animals. His name was Benedict Arnold.[2]—He was

---

1 One of Sigourney's several books for children.

2 Arnold (1741–1801) served with Connecticut forces during the Seven Years War between Britain and France and was an officer in the American army during the Revolution. Believing the war lost, he defected to the British and his name became a byword for traitor in American mythology.

born at Norwich, in Connecticut, and the beautiful city of his birth is ashamed of his memory.

We are bound by gratitude to be kind to the domestic animals, because they add so much to our comfort. Were it not for the sheep, how should we bear the winter's cold? How would journies, and the business of our vast country, and even the affairs of its government go on, without the aid of the Horse? How much does the comfort of families depend upon the patient and orderly Cow? When the first settlers in New England came to Plymouth, in the winter of 1620, *four years* elapsed before any Cows were brought to them from England. During all that time, while their bread was made of pounded corn, they had not a drop of milk for the weaned infant, or the feeble child, or to make any little delicacy for the sick, and aged. Every time you see a pudding or a custard, remember our good pilgrim Fathers, who patiently endured so many hardships, that we might dwell in plenty in this goodly land. And when you take your nice supper of milk, dear children, remember to be kind to the animal from whom you obtain it. Domestic animals are sensible of kindness and improved by it. They are made happier and more gentle, by being caressed and spoken to, with a kind voice. Food, shelter, needful rest, and good treatment are all they ask for their labors, for our benefits.

Many of the inferior creation display virtues which are worthy of respect. You have doubtless read many stories of the sagacity of the Elephant. The grateful disposition and strong attachment of the Dog, are well known. In a church yard, in London, a Dog was seen continually stretched upon a grave. He could not be persuaded to leave it. It was his master's grave. The people in the neighborhood pitied him, and daily gave him food. The sexton made him a little kennel, to which he might go for shelter, from cold and from the storm,—but he would not forsake the lowly bed of his master. It seemed as if he expected him to return,—and feared to be long absent, lest he should miss of him. He was not very unhappy, though he sometimes moaned. And there for years, night and day he watched for his beloved master. When a footstep was heard suddenly among the tombs, he started up, but it was not the step he longed for. Then he would lay his head patiently down upon the long grass, and watch again, and so watching, he died. The birds, who sing among the branches, give us examples of tender affection. There is no warfare in their nests. The little brothers and sisters live in harmony, till they are able to stretch out the newly-plumed wing, and quit the care of the parent. The Dove, by its affectionate and innocent character, is cited as an example in the Book of God, "Be ye harmless as doves,"—said our benevolent Savior to his disciples.[1] The Stork spreads out its broad pinions, and bears its aged parents on their journey through the air.[2] It feeds and cherishes them with the same tenderness which it received in its own helpless infancy. My dear children, do not despise to take a lesson of filial love, from these birds. Never distress any of the tenants of the air, by taking their eggs or their young,—and never see it done by others without remonstrating against such cruelty. It is wrong to disturb or injure the insect-race. The Bee and the Ant are entitled to respect. So doubtless, would others be found, if you knew more of their habits and character. They are delicately and wonderfully formed. A fine writer has called insects, the "winged jewelry of Heaven." A microscope would display to you bodies of such exquisite workmanship, that you would regret to deface or destroy them. The embroidery of a Beetle's wing has never been equalled by any robe that princes wear. Since the Almighty has seen fit to create and adorn them,—it is for some wise purpose. You must not carelessly destroy what He has made. Never kill any harmless creature, nor delight to give pain to the vilest and most deformed. "I would not have for my friend," says the excellent Cowper, "one who carelessly sets foot upon a worm."[3] Live in kindness and peace with the inferior creation. The Father of us all, hath given them for our use,—but not for the exercise of savage power, or malevolent dispositions.

8. From *Letters to Young Ladies* (1833).[4]

From LETTER I.

ON THE IMPROVEMENT OF TIME.

NOTHING truly valuable, my dear young friends, is to be attained without industry; nor can there well be persevering industry, without a sense of the value of time. [...]

---

1 The Bible, gospel of Matthew 10.16.

2 The stork ... air] a legend found in the Roman writer Pliny the Elder (CE 23–79), *Natural History*, book 3

3 Paraphrase of William Cowper, *The Task* (1785) 6.560–63.

4 Often reprinted, *Letters* is a female "advice" or "conduct" book on the education and socialization of young women. Following Mary Wollstonecraft's feminist *Vindication of the Rights of Woman* (1792) and

Lost wealth may be regained by a course of industry; wasted health repaired by temperance; forgotten knowledge recalled by study; alienated friendship soothed into forgiveness, even forfeited reputation restored by penitence and virtue: but who ever looked again upon his wasted hours? called back his slighted years, and stamped them with wisdom? or effaced from heaven's record, the fearful blot of a lost life? [...]

Though the path of distinction in science and literature, is not the object of our ambition, yet in the humbler sphere allotted to our sex, order and method are of essential importance. The assigning daily duty to particular hours, as far as may be practicable, helps to ensure its performance. The system must often yield to circumstances, and be subject to interruptions, yet by keeping its general features steadily in view, more will be accomplished, and to better purpose than by desultory effort.

Consider every day, my dear young friends, as a sacred gift from the author of your being. Divide it between the duties you owe to *Him*, to *yourselves*, and your *fellow creatures*. Remember that you are held responsible at a higher tribunal than that of earth, for the manner in which they are discharged. Keep these three great divisions before the eye of the mind. Proportion the day between them, as the promised land was divided by lot among the chosen tribes. Consult those whom it is your duty to obey or to please, respecting the appropriation of particular hours to particular employments. Use discretion and kindness in not interfering with the convenience of those around, and then evince decision in not yielding to slight obstacles. When your system is once correctly established, let it be understood that it is not lightly to be set aside. When it must unavoidably yield, let it be done with patience and sweetness.

Hannah More's conservative *Strictures on the Modern System of Female Education* (1799), it promotes the professionalization of women as domestic managers, educators, philanthropists, cultural censors, and promoters of civil society—roles requiring training in independent critical thinking similar to that needed by middle-class men in business, professions, and public office. In subsequent editions, Sigourney added new letters, expanded existing ones with literary and historical references and discussion of current social issues, and aimed more at the well-to-do middle class, emphasizing the dangers of "luxury," indifference to religion, neglect of the unfortunate, and materialism resulting from industrial and commercial expansion. The direct, laconic style of the first edition was gradually replaced by a more "literary" style, reflecting changing taste in her reading public and Sigourney's status as an author of national importance. The text here is from the first edition.

When the light of the morning first meets your eye, say to your waking heart, "behold another day, to be divided between the giver, your own improvement, and the good of those with whom you are associated." Secure by early rising those hours, when the frame is refreshed by repose, and the mind clear and vigorous with the consciousness of renovated existence. Commence your day with devotion, the reading of the Scriptures, and meditation. As far as possible, let these sacred duties be in solitude and secrecy between yourself and your Maker. [...]

The second division of the duties of the day, regards *yourself.* Much is required of the young to fit themselves for respectability and usefulness in life. Much is required of our sex, in the present state of society, and by the spirit of an age rapidly advancing in improvement. Be true to every just expectation. Regard it as a privilege that much is expected of you. The care of your health, the advance of your mind in knowledge by study and contemplation, dexterity and diligence in the varied circle of domestic employment, attention to such accomplishments as your station may require, the whole field of physical, mental and moral culture, which opens before her who is determined that her husbandry shall not be faithless, nor her harvest light, is too wide and diversified to admit of rules being given you by another, except the injunction that as far as is in your power, each department should have its allotted period.

The third department of daily duty regards our *fellow beings.* To be engrossed wholly by our own pursuits, though their object be improvement, may create selfishness. It is possible for the intellect to be cultivated at the expense of the heart. [...]

Duties to brothers, sisters and companions, culture of social feelings, punctuality in promises, kindness and courtesy to all, open an important and interesting sphere of exertion. I should delight to think that each of you were capable of firm and confiding friendship for one of your own sex. [...] Services to the poor, the uneducated, the afflicted, you will also, as you have opportunity, comprehend within your daily department of duty, to your fellow beings.

Close the day by the same sacred services with which it commenced. Add also the exercise of self-examination. Compare the performances in each division of duty with the requisitions enforced in the morning. Inquire of the first allotted period, what hast thou done to render the *soul* more acceptable to pure eyes?—of the second, what armor hast thou given the *mind* for life's warfare?—of the third, how hast thou aided the *heart* to advance the happiness of others? [...]

One useful adjunct in this work of self-inspection is a Journal. It seems like the sensible presence of a friend, whose frown makes folly ashamed, and whose smile gives confidence to virtue. It preserves what else might be forgotten, and plants waymarks and scatters mementos, at every footstep of our pilgrimage. It gives an artificial length to life, by clothing the buried past in fresh and living imagery, and aiding us to retrace

> "As in a map, the voyager his course,
> The windings of our way for many years."[1]

Though in the seclusion of the domestic sphere, the course of passing events will usually be too monotonous to justify narration, yet the current of feeling and sentiment, the authors with whom we are conversant, and the reflections of a mind in the search of knowledge and truth, will always furnish something worthy of memorial [...].

From LETTER II.

ON FEMALE EMPLOYMENTS.

[...] Since the domestic sphere is entrusted to our sex, and the proper arrangement and government of an household is so closely connected with our enjoyments and virtues, nothing that involves the rational comfort of home, is unworthy of attention. The science of housekeeping affords exercise for the judgment and energy, ready recollection, and patient self-possession, that are the characteristics of a superior mind. Its elements should be acquired in early life; at least, its correspondent tastes and habits, should never be overlooked in female education. [...]

It has been sometimes urged as an objection against the modern system of female education, that the wide range of science which it comprises, turns the attention of the young from household duty, and renders them impatient of its details and labors. This argument seems to address itself to mothers. It might be in their power to refute it, and to associate in the minds of their daughters, with a love of study, a knowledge of the unpretending pursuits of their own future province. Their affection for them would naturally prompt them to the wish to save them from the mistakes and perplexities to which ignorance might in future

1 William Cowper, *The Task* (1785), 6.17–18.

expose them. Though perhaps little native affinity exists between intellectual pursuits and household cares, they may doubtless be united so as to relieve each other; and she will give strong proof of the best education and the best regulated mind, who neglects the fewest duties, and despises none. [...]

In our state of society, where equality so visibly prevails, and where the desire of living without labor, is but too common, servants faithful, and thoroughly trained in their several departments, are not always to be found. To instruct those who are ignorant; to know when they have done well, and when they have done enough; when they have reason to be weary, or a right to complain, it is necessary to have had some personal experience of what is required of them. Complaints of the errors of domestics are very common, and with none more so than with those who are least qualified to direct them. Perhaps too much is expected of them; perhaps we neglect to make due allowance for their causes of irritation, or to sympathize in the hardships of their lot. Possibly we may sometimes forget that the distinctions in society are no certain test of intrinsic merit, and that we "all have one Master, even Christ."[1]

Yet admitting that the grades of rank and station are not very clearly defined, and that the lower classes sometimes press upon the higher. This is in accordance with the spirit of a republic, and all should be willing to pay some tax for the privileges of a government, which admits such an high degree, and wide expansion, of happiness. If our domestics draw back from the performance of what the spirit of feudal times, or aristocratic sway might exact, a remedy still remains; to moderate our wants, and study simplicity in our style of living. Much time will be rescued for valuable pursuits, when the love of show and vanity, with their countless expenses and competitions, are stricken from our household lists. She who is contented to live more plainly than her neighbors, and dress more simply than her associates, when reason, or the wishes of her friends require it, has gained no slight ascent in true philosophy. [...]

I have ever thought it desirable that young ladies should make themselves the mistresses of some attainment, either in art or science, by which they might secure a subsistence, should they be reduced to poverty. Sudden and deep reverses are not uncommon in the history of affluence. To sustain them without the means of lessening the evils of dependence, when health and

1 · The Bible, Matthew 23.10.

intellect are at our command, is adding helplessness to our own affliction, and increasing the burden of others. [...] Such is now the variety of departments open to females, as instructors in the schools and seminaries of their own sex, that they may follow the impulse of their genius in the selection of a study or accomplishment, and while they pursue it as a pleasure, be prepared to practise it as a profession.

[...] The sphere of Woman is eminently practical. There is much which she will be expected to do, and ought therefore to learn, and to learn early, if she would acquit herself creditably. Though to combine the excellences of a housekeeper, especially in New England, with much eminence in literature or science, cannot rationally be attempted, still there is no need that domestic duties should preclude mental improvement, or extinguish intellectual enjoyment. They may be united by diligence and energy, and the foundation of these qualities should be laid *now, in youth.* [...]

From LETTER III.

ON DRESS, MANNERS, AND ACCOMPLISHMENTS.

ON the subject of Dress, I am aware that much has been said and written to little purpose. The laws of fashion are often so preposterous, and her dominion so arbitrary, that Reason and Philosophy can have little hope of gaining ground in her empire. Neither is it wise to expect of the young, a superiority to reigning modes. Singularity is never desirable. Still it is possible not to be eccentric, and yet to avoid such a style of dress, as opposes taste, produces deformity, or leads to unnecessary expense. There are a few rules which ought never to be violated by females.

1st. *Not to permit fashion to impair health.* [...]
2nd. *Dress should never infringe on delicacy.* [...]
3rd. *Dress ought not to involve unnecessary expense.* [...]
4th. *Dress should not engross too much time.* [...]

With regard to accomplishments,[1] as they are popularly termed, so much depends upon circumstances, the wishes of those who direct your education, and the impulse of taste, that it

---

1 accomplishments] ornamental skills designed to display a young woman's cultivation and taste for the marriage market

would be impossible to give any definite rule, except that they do not interfere with the attainment of solid learning. The true order of acquisition seems to be, *first*, what is necessary; *second*, what is useful; *third*, what is ornamental. To reverse this arrangement, is like beginning to build at the top of the edifice. [...]

A taste for Drawing, heightens the admiration of Nature by enforcing a closer examination of her exquisite workmanship, from the hues of the wild flower, to the grandeur of the forest, and the glowing beauties of the extended landscape. [...]

Music, at present the most popular of all accomplishments, is a source of surpassing delight to many minds. From its power in soothing the feelings and modifying the passions, it seems desirable to understand it, if this can be accomplished without too great an expense of time. [...]

Dancing, which from ancient times ranked high among accomplishments, has occasionally fallen into disrepute, from the late hours, and display in dress, with which it has been associated. [...] Dancing, in itself considered, is a graceful and elegant accomplishment, and as a species of exercise in the domestic circle, healthful, and favorable to a cheerful flow of spirits.

Reading aloud, with propriety and grace, is an accomplishment, worthy the acquisition of females. [...]

The acquisition of Languages has of late been considered an essential part of an accomplished female education. [...] Still, I press the monition, *avoid being superficial.* It is the danger of females of the present age. [...]

From LETTER IV.

ON BOOKS.

A taste for reading is important to all intellectual beings. To our sex, it may be pronounced peculiarly necessary. It is important to all, because it is the way in which aliment is conveyed to the mind; and to our sex peculiarly necessary, because, dwelling much in the contemplation of little things, they are in danger of losing the intellectual appetite. Their sphere of household employment, engrossing much attention to its cardinal points, "what shall we eat, and wherewithal be clothed,"[1] sometimes disposes the mind to be puffed up with the vanity of superficial knowledge, or willingly to pine away in the atrophy of ignorance.

1 The Bible, Matthew 6.31.

A taste for reading is therefore to them, an armor of defence. It is also a resource, when the world reveals its emptiness, or the things of the world confess their inability to satisfy the heart. Men go abroad into the busy current of life, and throw aside their chagrins and disappointments, and lose the narrowness of personal speculation, in its ever-fluctuating tide. Home, the woman's province, admits of less variety. She should therefore diversify it by an acquaintance with the world of intellect, and shed over it the freshness derived from the exhaustless fountains of knowledge. She should render herself an entertaining and instructive fire-side companion, by daily replenishing her treasury, with that gold which the hand of the robber may not waste, nor the rust of time corrode. The love of books is also a refuge in those seasons of indisposition, when active duties are laid aside, when even conversation is a burden, and that gaiety of heart which was as sunshine to life's landscape, has taken its flight. [...]

[...] I hope to persuade you to establish a systematic course of reading. Set apart a stated period of each day for this employment. Have it understood, that it is not to be dispensed with, except from imperative necessity. Do not dismiss your habits of study, when you cease to attend school. [...]

But while the value of knowledge renders a *taste for reading* so important, *the choice of books* is equally so. They produce the same effect on the mind, that diet does on the body. [...]

Works of imagination usually predominate in the libraries of young ladies. To condemn them in a mass, as has been sometimes done, is hardly just. Some of them are the productions of the finest minds, and abound with the purest sentiments. Yet discrimination, with regard to them, is exceedingly important, and such discrimination as a novice cannot exercise. The young should therefore ask guidance of an experienced and cultivated mind, and devote to this class of reading, only a moderate portion of time, as to a recreation. Frequent and long indulgence in it, creates disgust at the patient acquisition of solid learning, as compound and poignant dishes destroy a relish for plain and healthful food. It forms habits of desultory thought, and uproots mental discipline. [...]

History is replete with moral lessons. The instability of human power, the tyranny of man over his brother, and the painful truth that the great are not always the good, mark almost every feature of its annals.

Read History, with candor and independence of mind. The opinions of the historian should be examined, and the gilding stripped from false glory. The admiration so profusely bestowed on warriors and conquerors, should be analyzed. And if conquerors are discovered to have wrought more evil than good, to have polluted the fountains of peace and liberty, and to have wantonly shed blood and caused misery for their own aggrandizement, let the sentence upon their deeds be given in equity, though the heathen world counted them as gods, and Christendom blindly sanctioned the homage.

Next in intellectual interest to History, and superior to it in its influence upon the heart, is the study of Biography. The wise and good are thus brought into familiar intercourse with us. We forget the difference of rank, or the distance upon earth's surface that divided us. We almost listen to their voices, and number them among our household friends. [...]

Mental Philosophy,[1] claims a high rank among the studies of youth. It promotes self-knowledge, one of the direct avenues to wisdom. [...]

I am persuaded that you would find Logick, a subject of sufficient interest, to enter into your course of reading. The *art of thinking*, so important to all who have the power of thought, is possibly too little studied by our sex. Our inverted mode of reasoning, and the slight structure of our arguments, often expose us to the criticism even of school-boys. A science, which according to the concise definition of Watts, "teaches to use reason well, in inquiries after truth,"[2] is an important aid in the acquisition of all other sciences.

[...] Let the Scriptures form a part of the study of every day. Read a stated portion in the morning, with the aid of some commentary, and let its spirit go with you as a guide and a counsellor. Those who have excelled in the knowledge of the Inspired Volume, have usually perused it in course, year after year. It may be completed in thirteen months, by reading three chapters daily. Never read the Book of Heaven in haste, or as a task, with a wandering intellect, or without subsequent meditation. [...]

To facilitate the management of Memory, it is well to keep in view, that her office is three fold. Her first effort is to *receive* knowledge; her second, to *retain* it; her last, to *bring it forth*, when it is needed. The first act is solitary, the silence of fixed attention. The next is also sacred to herself and her ruling power, and con-

---

1 Mental Philosophy] older name for psychology

2 Isaac Watts, *Logick; or, The Right Use of Reason in the Enquiry after Truth* (1725), opening sentence.

sists in frequent, thorough examination of the state and order of the things committed to her. The third act is social, rendering her treasures available to the good of others. [...]

Weekly societies, organized on the plan of recapitulation, render very important assistance to those who are earnestly engaged in a course of History. They should comprise but few members, and those of somewhat congenial taste and feeling, that no cause of restraint or reserve may impede the free action of the mind. Three or four young ladies, with one or two older ones, will be found an agreeable and profitable number. Let the system to be pursued, and the authors to be studied, be a subject of mutual arrangement, and at the stated meeting, let each compress the substance of what she has read during the week, relate the principal events with their chronology, and as far as possible mention what was taking place at the same period of time, in the annals of other nations. Opinions dissenting from those of the historian should be freely given, with the reasons for such variation, and the discussions which arise, will both serve to fix knowledge firmly in the memory, and to aid in forming a correct judgment of the character and deeds of those, whom History has embalmed. [...]

From LETTER V.

ON CONVERSATION.

[...] Conversation, to be interesting, should be sustained with animation. Warmth of heart must put in motion the wheels of intellect. [...]

Those, who would please others, should never talk for display. [...]

Avoid exaggeration in discourse. [...]

Spare to use the language of flattery. [...]

You are doubtless aware that our sex have been accused of a tendency to remark with severity upon the foibles of character. It has been gravely asserted that we were prone to evil-speaking. *Is it so?* Let us candidly canvass the point. We may have temptations to this vice, peculiar to ourselves. We have more leisure for conversation than men. Our range of subjects is more limited. The multifarious pursuits of business and politics, or the labors of scientific and professional studies, engross their thoughts, and necessarily lead them to more elevated and expansive channels. Women, acting in a narrower sphere, examine with extreme ardor, whatever falls under their observation, or enters into competition with them. When employments weary, or amusements fail, *character* is a favorite field in which to expatiate. By nature they are gifted with a facility for reading its idioms. But if they indulge themselves in searching out only its weaknesses,—if they form a taste for hunting down its deformities, and feeding, like the Hyena, upon its fleshless, lifeless carcase, are they not in danger of perverting the tides of benevolent feeling, and tinging the fountains of the heart with bitterness.

My dear young friends, for *you* there is a remedy. Education has provided you with a shield against this danger. [...]

[...] Before we dismiss the subject, let us turn our attention to that modification of it, which regards the intercourse of young ladies, with those of their own age, among the other sex. [...]

I would not seek to disguise the degree of influence, which in the radiant morning of your days, you possess over young men. [...]

You have it in your power to give vigor to their pursuit of respectability, to fix their attention on useful knowledge, to fortify their wavering opinions, and to quicken or retard their progress in the path of benevolence and piety. [...]

[...] Every night, in the silence of your apartment, let the heart question the lips of their part in the day's doings. Recall the instances in which they have been trifling, profitless, or recreant to the law of kindness, and thus gather deeper contrition for the prayer with which you resign yourself to sleep. Lest this work be done lightly or carelessly, endeavor to make it a faint emblem of that tribunal before which we must all stand at last; and engrave indelibly on your memory the solemn assurance that for "*every idle word, we must give account in the day of judgment.*"[1]

From LETTER VI.

ON DOING GOOD.

[...] Resolve, therefore, *this day*, that you will not live exclusively for your own gratification, but that the good of others, shall be an incentive to your studies, your exertions, your prayers. If you will be persuaded thus to enroll yourselves among the students of Heaven, consider attentively your own powers, situation, and opportunities of doing good.

---

1 The Bible, Matthew 12:36.

Take a view of the ground which you occupy. Look around on every member of your own family. Contemplate all among whom you reside, and with whom you particularly associate. Are any ignorant, whom you might instruct; unhappy, whom you might console; in error, whom you might reclaim? Make acquaintance with the poor. See with your own eyes, the deficiency of their accommodations, and the nature of their sorrows. [...]

From among the many charitable societies of the day, select one, whose design is most congenial to your feelings, or most approved by your older friends. Enroll yourself among its members, and study its management, and become familiar with the detail of its operations. Thus you will preserve your own interest from languishing, and gather instruction from the associated wisdom of others. Whatever income you may possess, or whatever stipend is allowed you, set apart *one tenth* for charitable purposes. [...]

As a part of the science which we contemplate, let us now bestow some attention on the *manner* of doing good. In imparting relief to the poor, always regard their feelings. Let the law of kindness dwell on your lips whenever you address them. Are we better than they, because a larger proportion of this world's fleeting possessions have fallen to our share? He who "maketh us to differ,"[1] will surely be displeased, if there is pride in our heart, or unkindness on our lips, towards our poor brother. [...]

From LETTER VII.

ON SELF-GOVERNMENT.

THAT self regulating power, by which the affections and passions are rendered subservient to the dictates of reason, and the precepts of inspiration, should be earnestly sought after by woman. Appointed to be all her life "under tutors and governors,"[2] it is for her comfort and well being, that the principle of discipline have root in her own heart. As government is best administered by those who have themselves learned subordination, so she should govern herself, that she may be better able to obey. The foundation of the unity and strength of nations, is laid in the discipline of well ordered families; and the consistence and beauty of a well balanced character may be resolved into the element of self control. Other checks are of unequal operation.

---

1 The Bible, Paul's first letter to the Corinthians, 4.7.

2 The Bible, Paul's letter to the Galatians, 4.2.

The eye of authority cannot always be vigilant. The heart that we love to make happy, cannot always be near. The desire that the community may speak well of us, may produce an artificial goodness, and stir up hypocrisy to adorn a "whited sepulchre."[1] But that power which subjugates the warring factions of the soul, commands silence when reason speaks, and obedience when virtue lifts her sceptre, is the highest power of our nature, and must derive strength from above. [...]

It has been urged as a reproach to our sex, that we were prone to be discomposed by trifles. Our business is among trifles. Household occupations, to men engrossed by the sublime sciences, seem a tissue of trifles. Yet, as "trifles make the sum of human things,"[2] so the comfort of a family is affected by the touching, or not touching, many minute springs, which like a "wheel within a wheel,"[3] are of secret operation, but essential importance. Susceptible as we are, by our original construction, and often rendered more so, by delicate health, or nervous temperament, trivial obstacles are sometimes encountered with less calmness, than heavy adversities. Our danger from slight causes of irritation, is obvious. So also is the remedy. Suffer not the heart to be fixed on trifles. If our sphere of action comprises them, there is no reason that they should destroy our capacity for enjoyment. Supply the thoughts with nobler subjects of contemplation. When the little angry billows beat against the bark, *look aloft*. The Pilot is always the same. [...]

The first effectual step towards self government, is *self knowledge*. [...]

I cannot feel, my dear friends, that self government is perfect without religion, for since there are agents within us, whose force we may fail to estimate, and which, springing suddenly into action, may destroy the fabric on which philosophy has labored for years,—and since we have not the gift of prescience, and cannot always measure the future by the past, is it not safest to rely for aid on the Former of our bodies, the Father of our spirits, who hath said, "if any lack wisdom, and ask of Him, he giveth liberally and upbraideth not."[4]

---

1 The Bible, Matthew 23.27, referring to the use of whitewash to brighten the appearance of a tomb; i.e., something beautiful outside but concealing corruption within.

2 Hannah More, "Sensibility: An Epistle to the Honourable Mrs. Boscawen" (1782), l. 293.

3 Echoing the Bible, Ezekiel 1.16.

4 The Bible, Paul's letter to James, 1.5.

From LETTER VIII.

ON MOTIVES TO EXERTION.

THE age in which we live, is replete with motives to intellectual and moral effort. The continually advancing state of society, requires that the mind should never slumber at its post. What was considered a good education, twenty, or even ten years since, would now be visibly deficient. [...]

From the *nature of our government*, an argument is derived for persevering energies. To a republic, whose welfare depends on the intelligence, and virtue of the people, the character and habits of every member of its family are of value. Possibly some of you may reply, "I am not a politician, therefore I have nothing to do. My station is subordinate: what share can I have in the destinies of my country?" The same share that the rill has in the rivulet, and the rivulet in the sea. Should every little shaded streamlet tarry at its fountain head, where would be the river, that dispenses fertility,—the ocean, bearing commerce and wealth upon its never resting tide? Woman possesses an agency which the ancient republics never discovered. The young fountains of the mind are given in charge to her. She can tinge them with sweetness or bitterness, ere they have chosen the channels where to flow, or learned to murmur their story to the time-worn pebbles. [...] But our country has conceded every thing; the blessings of education, the equality of companionship, the luxury of benevolence, the confidence of a culturer's office, to those young buds of being, in whom is her wealth and her hope. What does she require of our sex, in return for these courtesies? Has she not a right to expect that we give our hands to every cause of peace and truth,—that we nurse the plants of temperance and purity,—that we frown on every inroad of disorder and vice,—that we labor in all places where our lot may be cast, as gentle teachers of wisdom and charity, and that we hold ourselves, in domestic privacy, the guardians of those principles which the sage defends in the halls of legislation, and the priest of Jehovah upon the walls of Zion?[1]

Gratitude for the religion of Jesus Christ, inspires another motive for exertion. Not only are we indebted for that hope of salvation which we share in common with all who listen to the gospel, but our obligations as a sex are peculiar and deep. It has broken down the vas-

1 Zion] a mount with a fortress, near Biblical Jerusalem, holy city of the Jews, later standing for Jerusalem itself

salage, which was enforced even in the most polished heathen climes. Its humility hath taught man to give honor to the weaker vessel. That policy, which, for ages, regarded women as toys of fancy for a moment, and then slaves forever, "hewers of wood, and drawers of water,"[1] so vile as to be shut from the consecrated temple on earth, and so devoid of soul as to be incapable of an entrance into Heaven, is "abolished by Him, who hath made both one, and broken down the middle wall of partition between us."[2] [...]

And now, my daughters, farewell! In pursuing with you, objects of tender and high concern, my heart has been drawn towards you, with something of a mother's love. The hand that traces these lines, will soon moulder in dust, and the eye that peruses them, however radiant with hope, or brilliant in beauty, must wear the seal of clay. Though we never meet in the flesh, yet at that day when the "dead, small and great, shall stand before God,"[3] may it be found that we have so communed in spirit, as to aid in the blessed pilgrimage to "glory,—honor, immortality,—eternal life."[4]

9. From *Sketches* (1834).[5]

THE FATHER.

"Yes,—I am he,—who look'd and saw decay
Steal o'er the lov'd of earth,—the ador'd too much.—
It is a fearful thing, to love what Death may touch."

MRS. HEMANS.[6]

I WAS in the full tide of a laborious and absorbing profession,—of one which imposes on intellect an unsparing discipline, but ultimately opens the avenues to wealth and fame. I pursued

1 hewers ... water] used numerous times in the Bible, e.g., Joshua 9.21

2 The Bible, Paul's letter to the Ephesians, 2.14.

3 The Bible, book of Revelation, 20.12.

4 The Bible, Paul's letter to the Romans, 2.7.

5 A collection of prose tales of various kinds including, in order, a study of obsession ("The Father"), a historical tale of New England settlement ("Legend of Oxford"), a courtship tale ("The Family Portraits"), an Indian captivity narrative ("Oriana"), a pro-temperance story ("The Intemperate"), and a story of North Carolina settlement ("The Patriarch").

6 Felicia Hemans, *The Forest Sanctuary* (1825), part 2, stanza 50, describing the narrator-protagonist's grief as he watches his wife dying.

it, as one determined on distinction,—as one convinced that *mind* may assume a degree of omnipotence over matter and circumstance, and popular opinion. Ambition's promptings were strong within me, nor was its career unprosperous.—I had no reason to complain that its promises were deceptive, or its harvest tardy.

Yet as my path was among the competitions and asperities of men, a character combining strong elements might have been in danger of becoming indurated, had it not been softened and refined by the domestic charities.[1] Conjugal love, early fixing on an object most amiable and beautiful, was as a fountain of living water,[2] springing up to allay thirst, and to renovate weariness. I was anxious that my home should be the centre of intellectual and polished society, where the buddings of thought should expand unchilled, and those social feelings which are the life-blood of existence, flow forth, unfettered by heartless ceremony.—And it was so.

But my present purpose is to delineate a single, and simple principle of our nature,—the most deep-rooted and holy,—*the love of a father for a daughter.* My province has led me to analyze mankind; and in doing this, I have sometimes thrown their affections into the crucible. And the one of which I speak, has come forth most pure, most free from drossy admixture. Even the earth that combines with it, is not like other earth. It is what the foot of a seraph might rest upon, and contract no pollution. With the love of our sons, ambition mixes its spirit, till it becomes a fiery essence. We anticipate great things for them,—we covet honors,—we goad them on in the race of glory;—if they are victors, we too proudly exult,—if vanquished, we are prostrate and in bitterness. Perhaps we detect in them the same latent perverseness, with which we have waged warfare in our own breasts, or some imbecility of purpose with which we have no affinity; and then, from the very nature of our love, an impatience is generated, which they have no power to soothe, or we to control. A father loves his son, as he loves himself,—and in all selfishness, there is a bias to disorder and pain. But his love for his daughter is different and more disinterested; possibly he believes that it is called forth by a being of a higher and better order. It is based on the integral and immutable principles of his nature. It recognizes the sex[3] in hearts, and from the very gentleness and mystery of

1 charities] affections

2 fountain of living water] Biblical phrase; see Jeremiah 2:13

3 sex] sexual difference

womanhood, takes that coloring and zest which romance gathers from remote antiquity. It draws nutriment from circumstances which he may not fully comprehend, from the power which she possesses to awaken his sympathies, to soften his irritability, to sublimate his aspirations;—while the support and protection which she claims in return, elevate him with a consciousness of assimilation to the ministry of those benevolent and powerful spirits, who ever "bear us up in their hands, lest we dash our foot against a stone."[1]

I should delight longer to dwell on this development of affection, for who can have known it more perfectly in its length and breadth, in its depth and height? I had a daughter, beautiful in infancy, to whom every year added some new charm to awaken admiration, or to rivet love. To me, it was of no slight import, that she resembled her mother, and that in grace and accomplishment, she early surpassed her contemporaries. I was desirous that her mind should be worthy of the splendid temple allotted for its habitation. I decided to render it familiar with the whole circle of the arts and sciences. I was not satisfied with the commendation of her teachers. I determined to take my seat in the sacred pavilion of intellect, and superintend what entered there. But how should one buried beneath the ponderous tomes and Sysiphean toils[2] of jurisprudence, gain freedom, or undivided thought, for such minute supervision? A father's love can conquer, if it cannot create. I deprived myself of sleep: I sat till the day dawned, gathering materials for the lectures that I gave her. I explored the annals of architecture and sculpture, the recesses of literature and poetry, the labyrinthine and colossal treasure-houses of history,—I entered the ancient catacombs of the illustrious dead, traversed the regions of the dim and shadowy past, with no coward step,—ransacked earth and heaven, to add one gem to her casket. At stated periods, I required her to condense, to illustrate, to combine, what I had brought her. I listened, with wonder, to her intuitive eloquence: I gazed with intense delight upon the intellect that I thus embellished,—upon the Corinthian

---

1 Echoing Bible passages: Psalms 91.11–12, promising that angels shall "keep thee in all thy ways," bearing "thee up in their hands, lest thou dash thy foot against a stone," and gospels of Matthew (4:6) and Luke (4:11) where Satan tempts Christ to test this promise by throwing himself from the top of the temple.

2 Sysiphean toils] In Greek myth, Sisyphus' punishment in the afterlife is repeatedly to roll a stone up a hill only to have it roll down again.

capital[1] that I had erected and adorned. Not a single acanthus-leaf started forth, but I cherished and fostered it with the dews of a father's blessing.

Yet while the outpoured riches of a masculine understanding were thus incorporating themselves with her softer structure, I should not have been content, unless she had also borne the palm of female grace and loveliness. Was it therefore nothing to me, that she evinced in her bloom of youth, a dignity surpassing her sex, that in symmetry she restored the image of the Medicean Venus,[2] that amid the circles of rank and fashion, she was the model—the cynosure? Still was she saved from that vanity which would have been the destroyer of all these charms, by the hallowed prevalence of her filial piety. It was *for my sake*, that she strove to render herself the most graceful among women,—*for my sake*, that she rejoiced in the effect of her attainments. Her gentle and just nature felt that the "husbandman who had labored, should be the first partaker of the fruits."[3] Returning from these scenes of splendor, where she was the object of every eye, the theme of every tongue, when the youthful bosom might be forgiven for inflation from the clouds of incense that had breathed upon it, to the inquiry of her mother, if she had been happy, the tender and sweet reply was, "Yes,—because I saw that my dear father was so."

Sometimes, I was conscious of gathering roughness from the continual conflict with passion and prejudice, and that the fine edge of the feelings could not ever be utterly proof against the corrosions of such an atmosphere. Then I sought my home, and called my bird of song, and listened to the warbling of her high, heaven-toned voice. The melody of that music fell upon my soul, like oil upon the troubled billows,[4]—and all was tranquil. I wondered where my perturbations had fled, but still more, that I had even indulged them. Sometimes, the turmoil and fluctuation of the world, threw a shade of dejection over me: then it was her pride to smooth my brow, and to restore its smile. Once, a sorrow of no common order had fallen upon me; it rankled in my breast,

---

1 Corinthian] most ornate of three ancient Greek orders of architectural decoration, with stylized acanthus leaves on capitals of columns

2 Medicean Venus] the Venus de' Medici, Roman-era copy of a Greek statue of the goddess Venus, later owned by the Medici family of Florence

3 Paraphrasing the Bible, Paul's second epistle to Timothy, 2.6.

4 oil ... billows] Oil was used to calm turbulent waters.

like a dagger's point; I came to my house, but I shunned all its inmates. I threw myself down, in solitude, that I might wrestle alone with my fate, and subdue it; a light footstep approached, but I heeded it not. A form of beauty was on the sofa, by my side, but I regarded it not. Then my hand was softly clasped, breathed upon,—pressed to ruby lips. It was enough. I took my daughter in my arms, and my sorrow vanished. Had she essayed the hackneyed expressions of sympathy, or even the usual epithets of endearment, I might have desired her to leave my presence. Had she uttered only a single word, it would have been too much, so wounded was my spirit within me. But the deed, the very poetry of tenderness, breathing, not speaking, melted "the winter of my discontent."[1] Ever was she endued with that most exquisite of woman's perfections, a knowledge both *when* to be silent, and *where* to speak,—and *so* to speak, that the frosts might dissolve from around the heart she loved, and its discords be tuned to harmony.

Thus was she my comforter, and in every hour of our intercourse, was my devotion to her happiness richly repaid. Was it strange that I should gaze on the work of my own hands with ineffable delight? At twilight I quickened my homeward step, with the thought of that countenance, which was both my evening and morning star; as the bird nerves her wearied wing, when she hears from the still-distant forest, the chirpings of her own nest.

I sat in the house of God, in the silence of sabbath meditation, and tears of thrilling exultation moistened my eyes. I gazed upon my glorious creature, in the stainless blossom of unfolding youth, and my whole soul overflowed with a father's pride. I said, *What more can man desire?* I challenged the whole earth to add another drop to my cup of felicity. Did I forget to give glory to the Almighty, that his decree even then went forth, to smite down my idol?[2]

I came from engrossing toil, and found her restless, with strange fire upon her cheek. Fever had lain rankling in her veins, and they had concealed it from me.[3] I raved. I filled my house with physicians. I charged them wildly to restore her to health and to me. It was in vain. I saw that God claimed her. His will

1 Well worn phrase from Gloucester's speech opening Shakespeare's *Richard III*, expressing his resentment at exclusion from favour and power.

2 Did I forget ... my idol] Many Christians believed it sacrilegious to love an earthly thing or person above God.

3 Yellow fever and scarlet fever were common in children and greatly feared, though not as deadly as tuberculosis, also accompanied by fever.

was written upon her brow. The paleness and damps of the tomb settled upon her.

I knelt by the bed of death, and gave her back to her Creator. Amid the tears and groans of mourners, I lifted up a firm voice. A fearful courage entered into me. I seemed to rush even upon the buckler[1] of the Eternal. I likened myself unto him who, on Mount Moria, "stretched forth his hand, and took the knife to slay his son."[2] The whole energy of my nature armed itself for the awful conflict. I gloried in my strength to suffer. With terrible sublimity, I stood forth, as the High Priest of my smitten and astonished household. I gave the lamb in sacrifice, with an unshrinking hand, though it was my own heart's blood, that steeped, and streamed over the altar.

It was over. She had gone. She stayed not for my embraces. She was permitted to give me no parting-token. The mind that I had adored, shrouded itself and fled. I knew that the seal upon those eyes must not be broken, till the trump of the Archangel.[3]

Three days and nights, I sat by the dead. Beauty lingered there, in deep, and solemn, and sacred repose. I laid my head upon her pillow. I pressed my lips to hers, and their ice entered into my soul. I spoke to her of the angels, her companions. I talked long to the beautiful spirit, and methought, it answered me. Then I listened breathlessly, but "there was no voice, nor any that regarded."[4] And still, I wept not.

The fatal day came, in which even that clay was to be no longer mine. The funeral knell, with its heavy, yet suppressed summons, came over me like the dividing of soul and body. There was a flood of weeping, when that form, once so replete with every youthful charm, so instinct with[5] the joyous movement of the mysterious principle of life, was borne in marble stillness from its paternal halls. The eye of the mother that bore her, of the friend that had but casually beheld her, even of the poor menial

1 buckler] warrior's shield

2 The Bible, Genesis 22.10, describing Abraham about to sacrifice his son at God's command, a test of his faith that is reversed at the last moment.

3 trump of the Archangel] reference to the end of time and the angel's trumpet summoning the dead to divine judgment, described in the Bible

4 Echoing the Bible, 1 Kings 18.29, describing what happened when, at the prophet Elijah's challenge, the priests of Baal called on their god to send fire to consume their sacrificial offering; when Elijah in turn called on his god, a fire descended to consume his offering.

5 instinct with] imbued with, impelled by

that waited upon her, knew the luxury of tears. All were wet with that balm of sorrow, to overflowing—*all save mine.*

The open grave had a revolting aspect. I could not bear that the form which I had worshipped, should be left to its cold and hideous guardianship. At the hollow sound of the first falling clod,[1] I would fain have leaped into the pit, and demanded her. But I ruled myself. I committed her to the frozen earth, without a tear. There was a tremendous majesty in such grief. I was a wonder to myself.

I returned to my desolated abode. The silence that reigned there was appalling. My spirit sank beneath it, as a stone goes down into the depths of ocean, bearing the everlasting burden of its fathomless tide.[2] I sought the room where I had last seen her, arrayed in the vestments of the tomb. There lay the books which we had read together. Their pages bore the marks of her pencil. I covered my eyes from them, and turned away. I bowed down to inhale the fragrance of her flowers, and felt that they had no right to bloom so fair, when she, their culturer and queen, was blighted. I pressed my fingers upon the keys of her piano, and started back at the mournful sound they made. I wandered to her own apartment. I threw myself on the couch where from infancy she had slumbered. I trusted to have wept there. But my grief was too mighty, to be thus unchained. It disdained the relief of tears. I seemed to rush as upon a drawn sword, and still it refused to pierce me.

Yet all this was when no eye saw me. In the presence of others, I was like Mount Atlas, bearing unmoved the stormy heavens upon his shoulders.[3]

I went forth, amid the jarring competitions and perpetual strifes of men. I adjusted their opposing interests, while I despised them and their concerns. I unravelled their perplexities. I penetrated their subterfuges. I exposed their duplicity. I cut the Gordian knots[4] of their self-conceit. I made the "crooked

---

1 first falling clod] Once the coffin was placed in the grave, mourners threw clods of earth on it to symbolize the finality of interment.

2 Stone ... fathomless tide] echo of Felicia Hemans, *Forest Sanctuary*, describing the burial of the narrator's wife at sea (part 2, stanzas 58–60)

3 Mount Atlas ... shoulders] conflation of Mount Atlas in Lebanon and the Titan named Atlas; in ancient legend, each held up the heavens

4 Gordian knots] in ancient legend, an intricate knot kept in the temple of Zeus at Gordium; whoever could undo it was destined to rule the world; finally, Alexander the Great "undid" it by cutting it with his sword

straight, and the rough places plain,"[1]—with an energy that amazed them and myself. It was like that of a spirit, which has nothing to do with the flesh. I suffered the tumult of my soul to breathe itself out in bursts of stormy declamation. I exerted the strength of a giant, when it was not required. I scorned to balance power with necessity. The calculations of prudence, and the devices of cunning, seemed equally pitiful, and despicable. I put forth the same effort to crush an emmet,[2] as to uproot the oak of a thousand centuries. It was sufficient for me always to triumph. While men marvelled at the zeal with which I served them, I was loathing them in my heart. I was sick of their chicanery, and their sabbathless rush after empty honors and perishable dross. The whole world seemed to me, "less than nothing, and vanity."[3] Still, I was sensible of neither toil, nor fatigue, nor physical exhaustion. I was like one, who in his troubled dream of midnight, treads on air, and finds it strangely sustaining him.

But every night, I went to my daughter's grave. I laid me down there, in unutterable bitterness. While the stars looked coldly on me, I spoke to her fondly and earnestly, as one who could not be denied. I said,—"Angel! who art mine no longer, listen to me. Thou, who art raised above all tears, cause *one tear* to moisten my burning brow. Give it to me, as a token that thou hearest me, that thou hast not forgotten me." And the blasts of Winter, through the leafless boughs, mocking replied,—"*Give it to me,—Give it to me.*" But I wept not. Ten days and nights passed over me,—and still I wept not.

My brain was heated to agony. The visual nerves were scorched and withered. My heart was parched and arid, as the Libyan desert. Then I knew that the throne of Grief was in *the heart*: that though her sceptre may reach the remotest nerve, and touch the minutest cell where the brain slumbers, and perplex every ethereal ambassador from spirit to sense,—yet the pavilion where her darkest dregs are wrung out, the laboratory where her consuming fires are compounded, is *the heart,—the heart.*

I have implied that my intellect faltered. Yet every morning I went to the scene of my labors. I put my shoulder to the wheel, caring not though it crushed me. I looked at men fixedly and

---

1 echoing the Bible, Isaiah 40.4; at the last judgment, "Every valley shall be exalted, and every mountain and hill shall be made low: and the crooked shall be made straight, and the rough places plain."

2 emmet] ant

3 Echoing the Bible, Isaiah 40.17.

haughtily with my red eye-balls. But I spoke no word to betray the flame feeding at my vitals. The heart-strings shrivelled and broke before it, yet the martyrdom was in silence.

Again, Night drew her sable curtain, and I sought my daughter's grave. Methought, its turf-covering was discomposed, and some half-rooted shrubs that shuddered and drooped when placed in that drear assemblage of the dead, had been trampled and broken. A horrible suspicion took possession of my mind.[1] I rushed to the house of the sexton.—"Has any one troubled my daughter's grave?" Alarmed at my vehemence, he remained speechless and irresolute.

"Tell me," I exclaimed, in a voice of terror, "who has disturbed my daughter's grave." He evaded my adjuration, and murmured something about an injunction to secrecy. With the grasp of a maniac, I bore him to an inner apartment, and bade him satisfy my question. Trembling at my violence, he confessed that the grave had been watched[2] for ten nights.

"Who has watched my daughter's grave?" Reluctantly he gave me the names of those friends,—names for ever graven upon my soul.

And so, for those ten long, wintry nights, so dreary and interminable, which I had cast away amid the tossings of profitless, delirious, despairing sorrow, they had been watching, that the repose of that unsullied clay might remain unbroken.

A new tide of emotion was awakened. I threw myself down, as powerless as the weaned infant. Torrents of tears flowed. The tenderness of man wrought what the severity of Heaven had failed to produce. It was not the earthquake, nor the thunder, nor the tempest, that subdued me. It was the still, small voice.[3] I wept until the fountains of tears failed. The relief of that hour of weeping, can never be shadowed forth in language. The prison-house of passionate agony was unlocked. I said to God that he was merciful, and I loved him because my angel lived in his presence. Since then, it would seem, that my heart has been made better. Its aspirations are upward, whither she has ascended, and as I tread the devious path of my pilgrimage, both the sunbeam

---

1 A horrible ... mind] At this period, increased demand for cadavers by commercial anatomy schools led to an increase in grave-robbing.

2 watch] observe, but also guard, or keep vigil over

3 The Bible, 1 Kings 19.11–12; after a tempest, an earthquake, and a fire, God speaks to the prophet Elijah in "a still small voice," instructing him how to return the children of Israel to their covenant with God.

and the thorn point me as a suppliant to the Redeemer of Man, that I may be at last fitted to dwell with her for ever.

Hartford, October 28, 1833.

10. From *American Annals of Education* (1834).

On the Policy of Elevating the Standard of Female Education. Addressed to the American Lyceum, May, 1834.[1]

THE importance of Education seems now to be universally admitted. It has become the favorite subject, of some of the wisest and most gifted minds. It has incorporated itself with the spirit of our vigorous and advancing nation. It is happily defined by one of the most elegant of our living writers,—as the "*mind of the present age, acting upon the mind of the next.*" It will be readily perceived how far this machine surpasses the boasted lever of Archimedes,[2]—since it undertakes not simply the movement of a mass of matter, the lifting of a dead planet from its place, that it might fall, perchance, into the sun and be annihilated,—but the elevation of that part of man whose power is boundless,—and whose progress is eternal,—the raising of a race "made but a little lower than the angels,"[3] to a more entire assimilation with superior natures.

In the benefits of an improved system of Education, the female sex are now permitted liberally to participate. The doors of the temple of knowledge, so long barred against them, have been thrown open. They are invited to advance beyond its threshold. The Moslem interdict that guarded its hidden recesses is removed.[4] The darkness of a long reign of barbarism, and the illusions of an age of chivalry, alike vanish,—and the circle of the sciences, like the shades of Eden, gladly welcome a new guest.[5]

---

1 *American Annals of Education and Instruction* 4 (August 1834): 361–65; reprinted in the *Southern Literary Messenger* 1 (December 1834): 169–70.

2 Archimedes] third-century BCE Greek scientist who declared he could move the Earth if he could place a lever for the purpose

3 Three similar phrases in the Bible: Psalms 8.5; Hebrews 2.7, Hebrews 2.9.

4 The common Christian belief that Islam denied education to women.

5 In the benefits ... a new guest] a common view of history as "progress" from barbarism (the "Dark Ages" after the Roman empire), when women were brutalized; through "chivalry" or courtly Medieval culture, when women were accorded delusory and corrupting homage; to

While gratitude to the liberality of this great and free nation is eminently due from the feebler sex, they have still a boon to request. They ask it as those already deeply indebted, yet conscious of ability to make a more ample gift profitable to the *giver* as well as to the *receiver*. It seems desirable that their education should combine more of thoroughness and solidity, that it should be expanded over a wider space of time, and that the depth of its foundation should bear better proportion to the height and elegance of its superstructure. Their training ought not to be for display and admiration,—to sparkle amid the froth and foam of life, and to become enervated by that indolence and luxury, which are subversive of the health and even the existence of a republic. They should be qualified to act as teachers of knowledge, and of goodness. However high their station, this office is no derogation from its dignity,—and its duties should commence whenever they find themselves in contact with those who need instruction. The adoption of the motto, that *to teach is their province*, will inspire diligence in the acquisition of a knowledge, and perseverance in the beautiful mechanism of pure example.

It is requisite that they who have, in reality, the *moulding of the whole mass of mind, in its first formation*, should be profoundly acquainted with the structure and capacities of that mind; that they who nurture the young citizens of a prosperous republic, should be able to demonstrate to them, from the broad annals of History, the blessings which they inherit, and the wisdom of preserving them, the value of just laws, and the duty of obeying them. It is indispensable that they on whose bosom the infant heart is laid, like a germ in the quickening breast of spring, should be vigilant to watch its first unfoldings, and to direct its earliest tendrils where to twine. It is unspeakably important, that they who are commissioned to light the lamp of the soul, should know how to feed it with pure oil; that they to whose hand is entrusted the welfare of a being never to die, should be able to perform the work, and earn the wages of heaven.

Assuming the position that *females are by nature designated as teachers*, and that the mind in its most plastic state is their pupil, it becomes a serious inquiry, *what they will be likely to teach.* They will, of course, impart what they best understand, and what they most value. They will impress their own peculiar lineaments upon

---

modern "Enlightenment," when educated women acquired a major role in sustaining civil society and republican government, here compared to Eve's situation in the Biblical Paradise

the next generation. If vanity and folly are their predominant features, posterity must bear the likeness. If utility and wisdom are the objects of their choice, society will reap the benefit. This influence is most palpably operative in a government like our own. Here the intelligence and virtue of every individual possesses a heightened relative value. The secret springs of its harmony may be touched by those whose birth-place was in obscurity. Its safety is interwoven with the welfare of all its subjects.

If the character of those, to whom the charge of schools is committed, has been deemed not unworthy the attention of lawgivers, is not *her* education of consequence, who begins her labor before any other instructor, who pre-occupies the unwritten page of being, who produces impressions which nothing on earth can efface, and stamps on the cradle what will exist beyond the grave, and be legible in eternity?

The ancient republics overlooked the worth of that half of the human race, which bore the mark of physical infirmity. Greece, so exquisitely susceptible to the principle of beauty, so skilled in wielding all the elements of grace, failed to appreciate the latent excellence of woman. If, in the brief season of youth and bloom, she was fain to admire her as the acanthus-leaf of her own Corinthian capital,[1] she did not discover, that like that very column, she might have added stability to the temple of freedom. She would not believe, that her virtues might have aided in consolidating the fabric which philosophy embellished and luxury overthrew.

Rome, notwithstanding her primeval rudeness,[2] and the ferocity of her wolf-nurs'd greatness,[3] seems more correctly, than polished Greece, to have estimated the "weaker vessel."[4] Here and there, upon the storm driven billows of her history, the form of woman is distinctly visible, and the mother of the Gracchi[5] still stands forth in strong relief, amid that imagery, over which time has no power. Yet where the brute force of the warrior was counted godlike, the feebler sex were prized, only in their approximation to the energy of a sterner nature, as clay was held in com-

---

1 Corinthian] the most elaborate order of ancient Greek architectural decoration, featuring acanthus leaves on column capitals

2 rudeness] lack of culture and refinement

3 wold-nurs'd greatness] Romulus and Remus in legend, abandoned as infants but suckled by a she-wolf, and later founded Rome

4 The Bible, 1 Peter, 3.7, describing the wife; a proverbial expression.

5 mother of the Gracchi] Cornelia (died 100 BCE), mother of brothers renowned for their republican values

bination with iron, in the feet of that mysterious image which troubled the visions of the Assyrian king.[1]

To some of the republics of South America, the first dawn of liberty gave a light which Greece and Rome, so long her favored votaries, never beheld. Even in the birth of their political existence, they discovered that the sex whose *strength is in the heart*, might exert an agency in modifying national character. New Granada[2] set an example which the world had not before seen. Ere the convulsive struggles of revolution had subsided, she unbound the cloistered foot of woman, and urged her to ascend the heights of knowledge. She established a college for females, and gave its superintendence to a lady of talent and erudition. We look with solicitude toward the result of this experiment.[3] We hope that our sisters of the "cloud-crowned Andes,"[4] may be enabled to secure and to diffuse the blessings of education, and that from their abodes of domestic privacy, a hallowed influence may go forth, which shall aid in reducing a chaos of conflicting elements to order, and symmetry, and permanent repose.

In our own country, man, invested by his Maker with the "right to reign,"[5] has nobly conceded to her, who was for ages a vassal, equality of intercourse, participation in knowledge, guardianship over his dearest possessions, and his fondest hopes. He is content to "bear the burden and heat of the day,"[6] that she may dwell in plenty, and at ease. Yet from the very felicity of her lot, dangers arise. She is tempted to rest in superficial attainments, to yield to that indolence

---

1 Reference to the Bible, book of Daniel (2:33), where the prophet Daniel construes king Nebuchadnezzar's dream of a huge figure with feet of iron and clay as a kingdom fatally weakened because two peoples will not mix.

2 New Granada] province of Spain's South American empire, now Colombia

3 this experiment] also celebrated in Sigourney's "Establishment of a Female College in New-Granada" (*Zinzendorff, and Other Poems*, 1837); reported in *American Annals of Education* 4 (February 1834): 97

4 John Neal (American, 1793–1876), *The Conquest of Peru* (1819), 1.79: "The cloudy Andes"; Sigourney, *Traits of the Aborigines* (1822), 2.1335: "cloud-encircled Andes."

5 Phrase used variously to justify the divine right of kings to reign, the divine right of Jesus to reign, or Jesus' natural right to reign through descent from ancient kings of Israel.

6 The Bible, Matthew, ch. 20, Jesus' parable of labourers in a vineyard, paid the same wage whether they began work early or late in the day, signifying Jesus' right to extend salvation regardless of degree of merit.

which spreads like rust over the intellect, and to merge the sense of her own responsibilities in the slumber of a luxurious life. These tendencies should be neutralized by an education of utility, rather than of ornament. Sloth and luxury, the subverters of republics, should be banished from her vocabulary. It is expedient that she be surrounded in youth with every motive to persevering industry, and severe application; and that in maturity she be induced to consider herself an ally in the cares of life, especially in the holy labor of rearing the immortal mind. While her partner stands on the high places of the earth,[1] toiling for his stormy portion of that power or glory from which it is her privilege to be sheltered, let her feel that to her, in the recesses of the domestic sphere, is entrusted the culture of that knowledge and virtue, which are the strength of a nation. Happily secluded from lofty legislation and bold enterprise, with which her native construction has no affinity, she is still accountable to the government by which she is protected, for the character of those who shall hereafter obtain its honors, and control its functions.

Her place is in the quiet shade, to watch the little fountain, ere it has breathed a murmur. But the fountain will break forth into a stream, and the swelling rivulet rush toward the sea; and she, who was first at the fountain head and lingered longest near the infant streamlet, might best guide it to right channels; or, if its waters flow complaining and turbid, could truest tell what had troubled their source.

Let the age which has so freely imparted to woman the treasures of knowledge, add yet to its bounty, by inciting her to gather them with an unremitting and tireless hand, and by expecting of her the highest excellence of which her nature is capable. Demand it as a debt.—Summon her to abandon inglorious ease.—Arouse her to practise and to enforce those virtues, which sustain the simplicity, and promote the permanence of a great republic. Make her answerable for the character of the next generation. Give her this solemn charge in the presence of "men and of angels,"[2] —gird her for its fulfilment with the whole armor of education and piety, and see if she be not faithful to her offspring, to her country, and to her God!

L.H.S.

---

1 high places of the earth] the Bible (Deuteronomy 32.13; Isaiah 58.14; Amos 4.13; Micah 1.3), signifying possession of power

2 Conflation of the Bible, 1 Corinthians 13.1 and the gospel of Luke 12.8.

11. From *Poetry for Children* (1834).

THE RAT.[1]

When others for their faults are blam'd,
'Tis a good rule to show
Some causes for defence or praise,
If any such we know.

Now *Rats* are usually condemn'd
As quite devoid of grace,
And yet I can a story tell
In honor of their race.

A gallant ship to Lisbon went,
And as it cross'd the sea,
It found increasing 'mid its freight
The rat fraternity.

And most uncomfortable friends
Those busy people were,
For nothing could be so conceal'd
But what they'd have a share.

Candles, and eggs, and cheese, and bread,
Off to their cells they bore,
And rifled every apple-cask,
And every sweet-meat store.

And though to punish thefts like these
The sailors oft would toil,
Yet still these cunning culprits hid
And fattened on the spoil.

But when the vessel reach'd the port,
Dark vengeance they secured,
And fill'd their hold with sulphur smoke
Too strong to be endured.

The rats not fancying such perfume,
Fled from their holes amain,

---

1 One of several poems humanizing small animals; dropped from the republished version of the book, titled *Poems for Children* (1836).

And hurrying headlong o'er the wharf,
  Were without mercy slain.

But one was seen with care to tread
  The path all red with gore,
And on his back, a rat quite grey
  And blind with age he bore.

Then some who mark'd this filial deed
  Did that good rat compare
To Eneas, who from flames of Troy,
  His sire, Anchises, bare.[1]

The astonish'd executioners,
  No longer bitter foes,
Did let the faithful creature pass
  In safety, where he chose.

This simple tale is true, my dears,
  And so here ends the strain;
For even if rats our candor[2] crave,
  They should not ask in vain.

WAR.[3]

War, is a wicked thing,
  It strikes the strong man dead,[4]
And leaves the trampled battle-field
  With blood and carnage red,
While thousand mangled forms
  In hopeless suffering bleed,
And vultures and hyenas throng
  Upon their flesh to feed.

See with what bitter grief
  Those widowed ones deplore;
And children for their father mourn,

---

1 To Eneas ... bare] as described in Vergil's Latin epic the *Aeneid*, when Aeneas fled Troy after it fell to the Greeks

2 candor] impartiality

3 Republished with a few alterations in Sigourney's *Olive Buds* (1836) and *The Child's Book* (1844).

4 It ... dead] *Olive Buds*: It strews the earth with dead

Who must return no more.
And aged parents sink
In penury and despair,
And sorrow dwells in many a home,—
War makes the weeping there.

It comes with sins and woes,
A dark and endless train,
It fills the breast with murderous hate
Where Christian love should reign,
It desolates the land
With famine, death, and flame,
And those are in a sad mistake
Who seek the warrior's fame.

Oh, may I guard my heart
From every evil thing,
From thoughts of anger and revenge
Whence wars and fightings spring.
And may the plants of peace
Grow up serene and fair,
And mark me for a child of heaven
That I may enter there.

DIFFERENCE OF COLOR.[1]

God gave to Afric's sons
A brow of sable dye,
And spread the country of their birth
Beneath a burning sky,
And with a cheek of olive, made
The little Hindoo child,
And darkly stain'd the forest-tribes
That roam our western wild.

To me he gave a form
Of fairer, whiter clay;
But am I, therefore, in his sight
Respected more than they?

---

1 Published the same year, with some differences in wording, in *Parley's Magazine, For Children and Youth* 6 (5 July 1834): 24.

No,—'tis the hue of deeds and thoughts
He traces in his Book,
'Tis the complexion of the heart[1]
On which he deigns to look.

Not by the tinted cheek
That fades away so fast,
But by the *color of the soul*,
We shall be judg'd at last.
And God, the Judge, will look at me
With anger[2] in his eyes,
If I, my brother's darker brow
Should ever dare despise.

12. From *Poems* (1834).[3]

CONNECTICUT RIVER.[4]

FAIR RIVER! not unknown to classic song;—[5]
Which still in varying beauty roll'st along,
Where first thy infant fount is faintly seen,
A line of silver 'mid a fringe of green;

---

1 A phrase used by many writers, including Francis Bacon, playing on "complexion" as "moral temperament" and as "skin-colour"; a similar play on "color" (l. 19) as "attribute" or "character" and "hue or tint."

2 anger] *Parley's Magazine*: sorrow

3 The major anthology of Sigourney's poems; retitled *Select Poems* in 1838 and often republished, with additions and deletions.

4 Published in *The Token: A Christmas and New Year's Present* (Boston: S.G. Goodrich, 1828), 110–13; *The Garland for 1830: Designed as a Christmas and New-Year's Present* (New York: Josiah Drake [1829]), 265–69; and *Specimens of American Poetry*, ed. Samuel Kettel (1829); republished as the first poem in *Poems* (1834), with variations—wording, lighter punctuation, changing some words ending in -or to -our (a reversal of emergent American spelling practice), and changing past participle endings (crown'd to crowned); to illustrate Sigourney's revision practice, verbal variations in *Specimens of American Poetry* given in footnotes here.

5 classic song] That is, American "classic" poetry (e.g., J.G. Brainerd, "On Connecticut River"; William Cullen Bryant, "Ode to the Connecticut River"), but also the European Georgic tradition, celebrating simple rustic life; Sigourney ignores the fact that the Connecticut River was by this time a major commercial waterway.

Or where near towering rocks thy bolder tide
To win the giant-guarded pass doth glide;
Or where in azure mantle pure and free
Thou giv'st thy cool hand to the fervent[1] sea.

Though broader streams our sister realms may boast,
Herculean[2] cities, and a prouder coast,
Yet from the bound where hoarse St. Lawrence roars[3]
To where La Plata rocks resounding shores,
From where the arms[4] of slimy Nilus shine,
To the blue waters of the rushing Rhine,
Or where Ilissus glows like diamond spark,
Or sacred Ganges whelms her[5] votaries dark,
No brighter skies the eye of day may see,
Nor soil more verdant, nor a race more free.

See! where amid their cultured vales they stand,
The generous offspring of a simple land;
Too rough for flattery, and all fear above,
King, priest, and prophet 'mid[6] the homes they love,—
On equal laws their anchored hopes are staid,
By *all interpreted*, and all obeyed.
Alike the despot and the slave they hate,
And rise firm columns of a happy state.
To them content is bliss,—and labour health,
And knowledge power; and meek[7] religion, wealth.

The farmer, here, with honest pleasure sees
The orchards blushing to the fervid breeze,
His bleating flocks, the shearer's care which[8] need,
His waving woods, the wintry hearth[9] that feed,

---

1 fervent] *Specimens*: waiting

2 From Hercules, strongman of ancient legend.

3 Rivers of four continents, famed in past and present: the St Lawrence, part of the border between Canada and the United States; the La Plata, border between Argentina and Uruguay; the Nile in Egypt; the Rhine in Germany; the Ilissus in Greece; and the Ganges in India.

4 arms] *Specimens*: urns

5 her] *Specimens*: its

6 'mid] *Specimens*: in

7 meek] *Specimens*: true

8 which] *Specimens*: who

9 wintry hearth] *Specimens*: winter fire

His hardy steers that break the yielding soil,
His patient sons, who aid their father's toil,
The ripening fields, for joyous harvest drest,
And the white spire that points a world of rest.

His thrifty mate, solicitous to bear
An equal burden in the yoke of care,
With vigorous arm the flying shuttle heaves,
Or from the press the golden cheese receives;
Her pastime when the daily task is o'er,
With apron clean, to seek her neighbour's door,
Partake the friendly feast, with social glow,
Exchange the news, and make the stocking grow;
Then hale and cheerful to her home repair,
When Sol's slant ray renews her evening care,
Press the full udder for her children's meal,
Rock the tired babe—or wake the tuneful wheel.

See, toward yon dome where village science[1] dwells,
When the church-clock its warning[2] summons swells,
What tiny feet the well-known path explore,
And gaily gather from each rustic[3] door.
The new-weaned child with murmuring tone proceeds,
Whom her scarce taller baby-brother leads,
Transferred as burdens, that the housewife's care
May tend the dairy, or the fleece prepare.
Light-hearted group!—who carol[4] wild and high,
The daisy cull,[5] or chase the butterfly,
Or[6] by some traveller's wheel[7] aroused from play,
The stiff salute, with deep demureness[8] pay,

Bare the curled brow,—or stretch the sunburnt[9] hand,
The home-taught[10] homage of an artless land.

---

1 science] knowledge
2 When ... warning] *Specimens*: What time the warning clock its
3 rustic] *Specimens*: sylvan
4 carol] *Specimens*: gambol
5 cull] *Specimens*: pluck
6 Or] *Specimens*: Till
7 wheel] *Specimens*: wheels
8 deep demureness] *Specimens*: face demure, they
9 sunburnt] *Specimens*: ready
10 home-taught] *Specimens*: untutor'd

The stranger marks amid their joyous line,
The *little baskets* whence they hope to dine,
And *larger books*, as if their dexterous art,
Dealt most nutrition to the noblest part:—
Long may it be, ere luxury teach the shame
To starve the mind, and bloat the unwieldy frame.

Scorn not this lowly race, ye sons of pride,
Their joys disparage, nor their hopes deride;
From germs like these have mighty statesmen sprung,
Of prudent counsel, and persuasive tongue;
Unblenching[1] souls, who ruled the willing throng,
Their well-braced[2] nerves, by early labour strong;
Inventive minds, a nation's wealth that wrought,
And white haired sages, sold to[3] studious thought,
Chiefs whose bold step the field of battle trod,[4]
And holy men, who fed the flock of God.

Here, 'mid the graves by time so sacred made,
The poor, lost Indian slumbers in the shade;—
He, whose canoe with arrowy swiftness clave
In ancient days yon pure, cerulean[5] wave;
Son of that Spirit,[6] whom in storms he traced,
Through darkness followed—and in death embraced,
He sleeps an outlaw 'mid his forfeit land,
And grasps the arrow in his mouldered hand.

Here, too, our patriot[7] sires with honour rest,
In Freedom's cause who bared[8] the valiant breast;—
Sprung[9] from their half-drawn furrow, as the cry
Of threatened Liberty went[10] thrilling by,
Looked to their God—and reared in bulwark round,
Breasts free from guile, and hands with toil embrowned,

1 Unblenching] *Specimens*: Bold patriot
2 well-braced] *Specimens*: powerful
3 sold to] *Specimens*: skill'd in
4 Chiefs ... trod,] *Specimens*: Chiefs, who the field of battle nobly trod
5 cerulean] sky-blue, a common poeticism
6 Spirit] *Specimens*: spirit
7 our patriot] *Specimens*: those warrior
8 In ... bared] *Specimens*: Who bared in freedom's cause
9 Sprung] *Specimens*: Sprang
10 Liberty went] *Specimens*: liberty came

And bade a monarch's thousand banners yield,
Firm at the plough and glorious in the field,
Lo! here *they* rest, who every danger braved,
Unmarked, untrophied, 'mid the soil they saved.

Round scenes like these doth warm remembrance glide,
Where emigration rolls its ceaseless tide,
On western wilds,[1] which thronging hordes explore,
Or ruder Erie's serpent-haunted shore,
Or far Huron, by unshorn forests crowned,
Or red Missouri's unfrequented bound,
The exiled man, when midnight shades invade,
Couched in his hut, or camping on the glade,
Starts from his dream, to catch, in echoes clear,
The boatman's song that charmed[2] his boyish ear;
While the sad mother, 'mid her children's mirth
Paints with fond tears a parent's distant hearth,
Or cheats[3] her rustic babes with tender tales
Of thee, blest River! and thy velvet vales;
Her native cot,[4] where luscious[5] berries swell,
The village school, and sabbath's tuneful[6] bell,
And smiles to see the infant soul expand
With proud devotion for that *fatherland*.

THE WAR-SPIRIT.[7]

WAR-SPIRIT! War-Spirit! how gorgeous[8] thy path,
Pale Earth shrinks with fear from thy chariot of wrath,
The king at thy beckoning comes down from his throne,
To the conflict of fate the armed nations rush on,
With the trampling of steeds, and the trumpet's wild cry,
While the folds of their banners gleam bright o'er the sky.

---

1 western wilds] lands that are now western New York and Ohio
2 charmed] *Specimens*: pleased
3 cheats] *Specimens*: charms
4 cot] cottage, a common poeticism
5 luscious] *Specimens*: ripening
6 tuneful] *Specimens*: holy
7 In spirit, metre, and allusions the poem echoes Byron's well known poem "The Destruction of Sennacherib."
8 gorgeous] splendid, magnificent, but also showy, gaudy

Thy glories are sought, till the life-throb is o'er,
Thy laurels[1] pursued, though they blossom in gore,
Mid the ruins of columns and temples sublime,
The arch of the hero doth grapple with time;
The Muse o'er thy form throws her tissue divine,[2]
And History her annal emblazons[3] with thine.

War-Spirit! War-Spirit! thy secrets are known,
I have looked on the field when the battle was done,
The mangled and slain in their misery lay,
And the vulture was shrieking and watching his prey;
But the heart's gush of sorrow, how hopeless and sore,
In the homes that those loved ones revisit no more.

I have traced out thy march, by its features of pain,
While Famine and Pestilence[4] stalked in thy train,
And the trophies[5] of sin did thy victory swell,
And thy breath on the soul, was the plague-spot of hell;
Death lauded thy deeds, and in letters of flame
The realm of perdition recorded thy name.

War-Spirit! War-Spirit! go down to thy place,
With the demons that thrive on the woe of our race;
Call back thy strong legions of madness and pride,
Bid the rivers of blood thou hast opened be dried—
Let thy league with the grave and Aceldama[6] cease,
And yield the torn world to the Angel of Peace.

---

1 laurels] in ancient times, a laurel wreath awarded to a victor

2 tissue] rich cloth, decorating yet concealing; but also paper used for printing; "divine" because the Muses were supposed to inspire the poet

3 emblazons] inscribes or adorns, but also celebrates, extols

4 Famine and Pestilence] with War and the False Prophet, the four "horsemen of the Apocalypse" (the Bible, Revelation 8.1–8)

5 trophies] spoils such as captured arms and treasure displayed at a victor's parade in ancient times

6 Aceldama] in the Bible, a field near Jerusalem purchased as a cemetery for foreigners with the pieces of silver given to Judas to betray Christ

SLAVERY.[1]

"Slavery is a dark shade on the Map of the United States."
La Fayette.[2]

WRITTEN FOR THE CELEBRATION OF THE FOURTH OF JULY.

WE have a goodly clime,
  Broad vales and streams we boast,
Our mountain frontiers frown sublime,
  Old Ocean guards our coast;
Suns bless our harvest fair,
  With fervid smile serene,
But a dark shade is gathering there—
  What can its blackness mean?

We have a birth-right proud,
  For our young sons to claim,
An eagle soaring o'er the cloud,
  In freedom and in fame;
We have a scutcheon bright,[3]
  By our dead fathers bought,
A fearful blot distains its white—
  Who hath such evil wrought?

Our banner o'er the sea
  Looks forth with starry eye,
Emblazoned glorious, bold and free,
  A letter on the sky,
What hand with shameful stain
  Hath marred its heavenly blue?
The yoke, the fasces,[4] and the chain,
  Say, are these emblems true?

---

1 Written for the celebration of the fourth of July. [Sigourney's note.]

2 The Marquis de La Fayette (1757–1834) served with American forces during the American Revolution. The phrase here was widely circulated.

3 scutcheon bright] coat of arms, symbolizing family identity, unstained by dishonour

4 fasces] bundle of rods with an axe in the middle; in ancient Rome, symbol of the magistrates' power to punish

This day doth music rare
Swell through our nation's bound,
But Afric's wailing mingles there,
And Heaven doth hear the sound:
O God of power!—we turn
In penitence to thee,
Bid our loved land the lesson learn—
To bid the slave be free.[1]

THE LIBERATED CONVICT.[2]

DARK prison-dome, farewell.
How slow the hours
Have told their leaden march within thy walls,
Toil claimed the day, and stern remorse the night,
And every season with a frowning face
Approached, and went unreconciled away.
Ah! who with virtue's pure, unblenching soul
Can tell how tardily old Time doth move,
When guilt and punishment have clogged his wings!
The winter of the soul, the frozen brow
Of unpolluted friends, the harrowing pangs
Of the lost prayer, learned at the mother's knee,
The uptorn hope, the violated vow,
The poignant memory of unuttered things,
Do dwell, dark dome, with him, who dwells with thee.
And yet, thou place of woe, I would not speak
Too harshly of thee, since in thy sad cell
Repentance found me, and did steep with tears
My lonely pillow, till the heart grew soft,
And spread itself in brokenness before
The Eye of Mercy. Now my penal doom
Completed, justice with an angel's face
Unbars her dreary gate. But when I view

1 Later printed in *The African Slave Trade* by the Rev. Rufus W. Clarke (Boston: American Tract Society, 1860), 68.

2 This is one of several poems by Sigourney addressing the condition of jail prisoners, a cause she also supported in her charitable work with Newgate prison near Hartford. The poem engages with an intense public debate over the best penal system for a republic, the "Auburn" system designed to "correct behaviour," or the "Pennsylvania" system designed to achieve moral repentance, and hence alter behaviour. At the time there were disclosures of widespread mistreatment of jailed prisoners.

Once more my home, when mild, forgiving eyes
Shall beam upon me, and the long-lost might
Of freedom nerve my arm, may the strong lines
Of that hard lesson sin hath taught my soul,
Gleam like a flaming beacon.
God of Heaven!
Who not for our infirmities or crimes
Dost turn thy face away, gird thou my soul
And fortify its purpose, so to run
Its future pilgrim-race, as not to lose
The sinner's ransom at the bar of doom.

INDIAN NAMES.[1]

"How can the red men be forgotten, while so many of our states and territories, bays, lakes and rivers, are indelibly stamped by names of their giving?"

YE say they all have passed away,
That noble race and brave,
That their light canoes have vanished
From off the crested wave;
That 'mid the forests where they roamed
There rings no hunter shout,
But their name is on your waters,
Ye may not wash it out.

'Tis where Ontario's billow[2]
Like Ocean's surge is curled,
Where strong Niagara's[3] thunders wake
The echo of the world.
Where red Missouri[4] bringeth
Rich tribute from the west,

---

1 One of Sigourney's most popular poems, later republished in *Selections from the American Poets* (1840) with slight variations, but omitting the last two stanzas; name translations from George R. Stewart, *American Place-Names* (New York: Oxford UP, 1970).

2 Ontario] beautiful lake (Iroquoian language)

3 Niagara] at the neck (of land) (Iroquoian); later stated to mean thundering waters

4 Missouri] canoe (Siouan); name of aboriginal people living near the river's mouth

And Rappahannock[1] sweetly sleeps
  On green Virginia's breast.

Ye say their cone-like cabins,
  That clustered o'er the vale,
Have fled away like withered leaves
  Before the autumn gale,
But their memory liveth on your hills,
  Their baptism on your shore,
Your everlasting rivers speak
  Their dialect of yore.

Old Massachusetts[2] wears it,
  Within her lordly crown,
And broad Ohio[3] bears it,
  Amid his young renown;
Connecticut[4] hath wreathed it
  Where her quiet foliage waves,
And bold Kentucky[5] breathed it hoarse
  Through all her ancient caves.

Wachuset[6] hides its lingering voice
  Within his rocky heart,
And Alleghany[7] graves its tone
  Throughout his lofty chart;
Monadnock[8] on his forehead hoar
  Doth seal the sacred trust,
Your mountains build their monument,
  Though ye destroy their dust.[9]

Ye call these red-browed brethren
  The insects of an hour,

---

1 Rappahannock] back-and-forth-stream, i.e., tidal river (Algonquian)
2 Massachusetts] place of big hills (Algonquian); name of the aboriginal people living there
3 Ohio] fine, beautiful river (Iroquoian)
4 Connecticut] place of the long river (Algonquian)
5 Kentucky] meadowland (Iroquoian)
6 Wachuset] mountain place (Algonquian)
7 Alleghany] beautiful stream (Algonquian)
8 Monadnock] island-like mountain (Algonquian)
9 dust] common poetic term for the mortal body

Crushed like the noteless worm amid
  The regions of their power;
Ye drive them from their father's lands,
  Ye break of faith the seal,
But can ye from the court of Heaven
  Exclude their last appeal?

Ye see their unresisting tribes,
  With toilsome step and slow,
On through the trackless desert pass,
  A caravan of woe;
Think ye the Eternal's ear is deaf?
  His sleepless vision dim?
Think ye the *soul's blood* may not cry
  From that far land to him?

13. From *Tales and Essays for Children* (1835).

HYMN
ON THE DEATH OF AN INFANT.[1]

Go to thy rest, my child,
  Go to thy lowly bed,
Gentle and undefil'd,
  With blessings on thy head,
Fresh roses in thy hand,—
  Buds on thy pillow laid,—
Haste from this fearful land,
  Where flowers so quickly fade.

Before thy heart had learn'd
  In sinful paths to stray,
Before thy feet had turn'd
  The dark and downward way,—
Ere care had mark'd thy breast,
  Or sorrow woke the tear,
Rise to thy home of rest
  In yon celestial sphere.

1 Representing a large body of elegies by Sigourney, most about ordinary people.

14. From *Zinzendorff, and Other Poems* (1835).[1]

NIAGARA.[2]

FLOW on forever, in thy glorious robe
Of terror and of beauty.—Yea, flow on
Unfathom'd and resistless.—God hath set
His rainbow on thy forehead:[3] and the cloud
Mantled around thy feet.—And he doth give
Thy voice of thunder,[4] power to speak of Him
Eternally, —bidding the lip of man
Keep silence,—and upon thy rocky altar pour
Incense of awe-struck praise.
                                        Ah! who can dare
To lift the insect-trump of earthly hope,
Or love, or sorrow,—'mid the peal sublime
Of thy tremendous hymn? Even Ocean shrinks
Back from thy brotherhood: and all his waves
Retire abash'd. For he doth sometimes seem
To sleep like a spent laborer,—and recall
His wearied billows from their vexing play
And lull them to a cradle calm:—but thou,
With everlasting, undecaying tide,
Dost rest not, night or day,—The morning stars,

---

1 The title poem, "Zinzendorff" is another of Sigourney's attempts at a specifically American epyllion, or "smaller" epic. It treats the mission of the historical German Count Zinzendorff (1700–60) to Christianize the Indians as "epic" in scope and heroizes ordinary life rather than historical or mythical figures—the traditional matter of epic. The "Other Poems" included some of Sigourney's best known shorter poems. Diverse in subject and form, these illustrate central themes of "Zinzendorff," including the transformative, religiously inspiring, and instructive power of the American landscape; pacifism as a Christian imperative distinguishing the New World from the Old; evangelization and social charity as central to the national enterprise; and the agrarian way of life as the foundation of American values and identity.

2 Also the theme of the opening piece of Sigourney's *Scenes in My Native Land* (1845)—see p. 203 here; one of Sigourney's most frequently reprinted and anthologized poems, with substantial alterations (e.g., *Select Poems*, 1841; *The American Female Poets*, 1848).

3 rainbow ... forehead] In the Bible, Genesis 9.12–13, after God has destroyed sinning humanity with a great flood he sets a rainbow in the sky as a covenant never to do the like again.

4 thunder] in the Bible, often represented as the voice of God

When first they sang o'er young Creation's birth,
Heard thy deep anthem, and those wrecking fires
That wait the archangel's signal to dissolve
This solid earth,[1] shall find Jehovah's name[2]
Graven, as with a thousand diamond spears
On thine unending volume.
Every leaf
That lifts itself within thy wide domain,
Doth gather greenness from thy living spray,
Yet tremble at the baptism.—Lo!—yon birds
Do boldly venture near, and bathe their wing
Amid thy mist and foam. 'Tis meet for them,
To touch thy garment's hem, and lightly stir
The snowy leaflets of thy vapour wreath,
For they may sport unharmed amid the cloud,
Or listen at the echoing gate of heaven,
Without reproof. But as for us, it seems
Scarce lawful, with our broken tones, to speak
Familiarly of thee.—Methinks, to tint
Thy glorious features with our pencil's point,
Or woo thee to the tablet of a song[3]
Were profanation.
Thou dost make the soul
A wondering witness of thy majesty,
But as it presses with delirious joy
To pierce thy vestibule, dost chain its step,
And tame its rapture, with the humbling view
Of its own nothingness, bidding it stand
In the dread presence of the Invisible,
As if to answer to its God, through thee.

DEATH AMONG THE TREES.[4]

DEATH walketh in the forest.
The tall pines
Do woo the lightning-flash, and through their veins

---

1 Creation's birth ... earth] The Creation and Apocalypse, or beginning and end of time in Genesis and Revelation, the Bible's first and last books.

2 Jehovah] Biblical name for God

3 tablet of a song] tablet: writing pad, or possibly stone; song: poem

4 One of several poems by Sigourney protesting ecological destruction caused by westward settlement; see "Fallen Forests" (p. 243).

The fire-cup, darting, leaves their blackened trunks
A tablet, for ambition's sons to read
Their destiny. The oak, that centuries spared,
Grows grey at last, and like some time-worn man
Stretching out palsied arms, doth feebly cope
With the destroyer, while its gnarled roots
Betray their trust. The towering elm turns pale,
And faintly strews the sere and yellow leaf,
While from its dead arms falls the wedded vine.
The sycamore uplifts a beacon brow,
Denuded of its honors, and the blast,
Swaying the withered willow, rudely asks
For its lost grace, and for its tissued leaf,
With silver lined.
I knew that blight might check
The sapling, ere kind Nature's hand could weave
Its first spring-coronal, and that the worm,
Coiling itself amid our garden-plants,
Did make their unborn buds its sepulchre.
And well I knew how wild and wrecking winds
Might take the forest-monarchs by the crown,
And lay them with the lowliest vassal-herb;
And that the axe, with its sharp ministry,
Might, in one hour, such revolution work,
As all Earth's boasted power could never hope
To re-instate. And I had seen the flame
Go crackling up, amid yon verdant boughs,
And with a tyrant's insolence dissolve
Their interlacing, till I felt that man,
For sordid gain would make the forest's pomp
Its heaven-raised arch and living tracery,
One funeral-pyre.
But, yet I did not deem
That pale Disease amid those shades would steal
As to a sickly maiden's cheek, and waste
The power and plenitude of those high ranks,
Which in their peerage and nobility,
Unrivalled and unchronicled, had reigned.
And so I said if in this world of knells
And open tombs, there lingereth one whose dream
Is of aught permanent below the skies,
Even let him come and muse among the trees,
For they shall be his teachers; they shall bow

To Wisdom's lessons his forgetful ear,
And, by the whisper of their faded leaves,
Soften to his sad heart the thought of death.

AGRICULTURE.[1]

THE hero hath his fame,
'Tis blazon'd[2] on his tomb,
But earth withholds her glad acclaim,
And frowns in silent gloom:
His footsteps on her breast
Were like the Simoom's[3] blast,
And Death's dark ravages attest
Where'er the Conqueror past.

By him her harvests sank,
Her famish'd flocks were slain,
And from the fount where thousands drank
Came gushing blood like rain;
For him no requiem-sigh
From vale or grove shall swell,
But flowers exulting lift their eye,
Where the proud spoiler fell.

Look at yon peaceful bands
Who guide the glittering share,[4]
The quiet labor of whose hands
Doth make Earth's bosom fair,
For them the rich perfume
From ripen'd fields doth flow,
They bid the desert rose to bloom,
The wild with plenty glow.

Ah! happier thus to prize
The humble, rural shade,

---

1 Reprinted with a few changes in Sigourney's *Olive Buds* (Hartford: William Watson, 1836), a collection of pacifist verse and prose, and in *Poems* (1842), a collection of her religious and elegiac poems.

2 blazon'd] represented according to rules of heraldry; inscribed appropriately; proclaimed boastfully

3 Simoom] hot dry African desert wind, in legend bringing plague

4 share] ploughshare, glittering because polished by abrasion of the soil

And like our Father in the skies
  Blest Nature's work to aid,
Than famine and despair
  Among mankind to spread,
And Earth our mother's curse to bear
  Down to the silent dead.

THE DEAF, DUMB AND BLIND GIRL OF THE AMERICAN ASYLUM AT HARTFORD, CON.[1]

SEE—while her mute companions share
  Those joys which ne'er await the blind,
A moral night of deep despair
  Descending, wraps her lonely mind.

Yet deem not, though so dark her path
  Heaven strew'd no comfort o'er her lot,
Or in her bitter cup of wrath
  The healing drop of balm forgot.

No! still with unambitious mind
  The needle's patient task to ply,
At the full board her place to find,
  Or close in sleep the placid eye,

With Order's unobtrusive charm
  Her simple wardrobe to dispose,
To press of guiding care the arm,
  And rove where autumn's bounty flows,

With touch so exquisitely true
  That vision stands astonish'd by,
To recognize with ardor due
  Some friend or benefactor nigh,—

Her hand 'mid childhood's curls to place,
  From fragrant buds the breath to steal,
Of stranger-guest the brow to trace,
  Are pleasures left for her to feel.

And often o'er her hour of thought
  Will burst a laugh of wildest glee,

---

1 Con.] Connecticut

As if the living gems she caught
  On wit's fantastic drapery,

As if at length, relenting skies
  In pity to her doom severe,
Had bade a mimic[1] morning rise,
  The chaos of the soul to cheer.

But who, with energy divine,
  May tread that undiscover'd maze,
Where Nature in her curtain'd shrine[2]
  The strange and new-born thought surveys?

Where quick perception shrinks to find
  On eye and ear the envious seal,
And wild ideas throng the mind,
  That palsied speech must ne'er reveal;

Where Instinct, like a robber bold,
  Steals sever'd links from Reason's chain,
And leaping o'er her barrier cold,
  Proclaims the proud precaution vain.

Say, who shall with magician's wand
  That elemental mass compose,
Where young affections slumber fond
  Like germs[3] unwak'd 'mid wintry snows?

Who, in that undecypher'd scroll,
  The mystic characters may see,
Save He who reads the secret soul,
  And holds of life and death the key?

Then, on thy midnight journey roam,
  Poor wandering child of rayless gloom,
And to thy last and narrow home,
  Drop gently from this living tomb.

---

1 mimic] here, imitation

2 curtain'd] concealed, but also referring to the curtaining of shrines and sacred places to conceal them from the unprepared or unpurified

3 germs] seeds

Yes,—uninterpreted and drear,
  Toil onward with benighted mind,
Still kneel at prayers thou canst not hear,
  And grope for truth thou may'st not find.

No scroll of friendship, or of love,
  Must breathe soft language o'er thy heart,
Nor that blest Book[1] which guides above,
  Its message to thy soul impart.

But Thou, who didst on Calvary die,[2]
  Flows not thy mercy wide and free?
Thou, who didst rend of *Death* the tie
  Is *Nature's* seal too strong for thee?

And Thou, Oh Spirit pure![3] whose rest
  Is with the lowly contrite train,
Illume the temple of her breast,
  And cleanse of latent ill[4] the stain,

That she, whose pilgrimage below,
  Was night that never hoped a morn,
That undeclining day may know
  Which of eternity is born.

The great transition who can tell!
  When from the ear its seal shall part,[5]
Where countless lyres seraphic swell,
  And holy transport thrills the heart:

---

1 blest Book] the Bible

2 on Calvary die] In the Bible, Jesus allowed himself to be crucified (on mount Calvary) to redeem the sins of all humanity.

3 Spirit pure] the Holy Spirit, part of the Trinity of Father (God), Son (Jesus), and Holy Spirit central to the theology of the Protestant Episcopalian (or Anglican) church to which Sigourney belonged

4 latent ill] original sin, the doctrine that all are sinners from birth because of the fall of Adam and Eve from paradise; in Sigourney's day, a doctrine held, though with diminishing tenacity, by Calvinists and Evangelicals

5 The last three stanzas allude to the religious belief that after the last judgment the imperfect bodily senses will be "unsealed" and the sanctified will perceive and communicate with divine and heavenly reality.

When the chain'd tongue, forbid to pour
The broken melodies of time,
Shall to the highest numbers soar
Of everlasting praise sublime:

When those veil'd orbs, which ne'er might trace
The features of their kindred clay,
Shall scan of Deity, the face,
And glow with rapture's deathless ray.

NAPOLEON'S EPITAPH.[1]

"The moon of St. Helena shone out, and there we saw the face of Napoleon's sepulchre, *characterless, uninscribed.*"

And who shall write thine epitaph? thou man
Of mystery and might.
Shall orphan hands
Inscribe it with their fathers' broken swords?
Or the warm trickling of the widows' tear,
Channel it slowly 'mid the rugged rock,
As the keen torture of the water-drop
Doth wear the sentenc'd brain?[2]
Shall countless ghosts
Arise from Hades,[3] and in lurid flame
With shadowy finger trace thine effigy,
Who sent them to their audit unanneal'd,[1]
And with but that brief space for shrift or prayer,
Given at the cannon's mouth?

---

1 Also published in the *New-England Magazine* 9 (Aug. 1835): 97–99; revised for *Select Poems* (1841), as "Napoleon at Helena." Napoleon Bonaparte (1769–1821) conquered Europe. After final defeat in 1815 he was exiled to St Helena in the south Atlantic, dying there in 1821; his tombstone was inscribed only "Ci-Git" ("Here Lies"). In 1840 his remains were taken to Paris and interred in an imposing monument. Compare Sigourney's depiction with Byron's in "Ode to Napoleon Bonaparte."

2 Water drops falling at regular intervals eventually drive the bound victim insane.

3 Hades] in classical mythology, the underworld inhabited by spirits of the dead, rather than Hell as a place of torment in Christian cosmology

4 to their audit unanneal'd] to judgment by God without benefit of the sacrament of extreme unction (unannealed: variant of unaneled)

Thou who did'st sit
Like eagle[1] on the apex of the globe,
And hear the murmur of its conquer'd tribes,
As chirp the weak-voic'd nations of the grass,[2]
Why art thou sepulchred in yon far Isle,
Yon little speck, which scarce the mariner
Descries mid ocean's foam? Thou who didst hew
A pathway for thy host above the cloud,
Guiding their footsteps o'er the frost-work crown
Of the thron'd Alps,[3]—why dost thou sleep unmark'd,
Even by such slight memento as the hind[4]
Carves on his own coarse tomb-stone!
Bid the throng
Who pour'd thee incense, as Olympian Jove,[5]
And breath'd thy thunders on the battle field,
Return, and rear thy monument. Those forms
O'er the wide vallies of red slaughter spread,
From pole to tropic, and from zone to zone,[6]
Heed not thy clarion call. But should they rise,
As in the vision that the prophet saw,
And each dry bone its sever'd fellow find,
Piling their pillar'd dust,[7] as erst they gave
Their souls for thee, the wondering stars might deem
A second time the puny pride of man
Did creep by stealth upon its Babel stairs,[8]
To dwell with them. But here unwept thou art,
Like a dead lion in his thicket-lair,

---

1 eagle] one of Napoleon's symbols, also used on his armies' standards, imitating ancient Roman emperors and armies

2 nations of the grass] grasshoppers, but also ephemeral generations

3 Alps] referring to Napoleon's Italian campaigns of the late 1790s, involving heroic passage over the Alps

4 hind] peasant

5 Jove] supreme deity in the ancient Roman pantheon of gods, dwelling atop mount Olympus in Greece; incense: used in pagan rituals of worship

6 zone to zone] Napoleon campaigned north and south with armies of conscripts from many lands ("zones") in a coalition of the unwilling.

7 pillar'd dust] probably referring to the Bible, Ezekiel 37.14, where God sends the prophet a vision of restoration of the Jews to their own land

8 Babel stairs] In the Bible, the Babylonians try to build a stepped tower to the heavens, but God causes each group to speak a different language and the project fails because of inability to communicate.

With neither living man, nor spirit condemn'd,
To write thine epitaph.
Invoke the climes,[1]
Who serv'd as playthings in thy desperate game
Of mad ambition, or their treasures strew'd[2]
Till meagre famine on their vitals prey'd,
To pay thy reckoning.
France! who gave so free
Thy life-stream to his cup of wine, and saw
That purple vintage shed o'er half the earth,
Write the first line, if thou hast blood to spare.
Thou[3] too, whose pride did deck dead Cæsar's tomb,
And chant high requiem o'er the tyrant band
Who had their birth with thee, lend us thine arts
Of sculpture and of classic eloquence
To grace his obsequies, at whose dark frown
Thine ancient spirit quail'd; and to the list
Of mutilated kings, who glean'd their meat
'Neath Agag's table,[4] *add the name of Rome.*
—Turn Austria! iron-brow'd and stern of heart,
And on his monument, to whom thou gav'st
In anger, battle, and in craft a bride,
Grave[5] *Austerlitz*, and fiercely turn away.[6]
—As the rein'd war-horse snuffs the trumpet-blast,
Rouse Prussia from her trance with Jena's name,[7]

1 climes] Napoleon's military campaigns ranged from tropical Egypt (1798) to wintry Russia (1812).

2 treasures strew'd] Napoleonic imperialism and the French economy were financed by appropriations, levies, and taxation of conquered countries.

3 Thou] Pope Pius VII, ruler of Rome (l. 54) and head of the Catholic church, suppressed by Napoleon, but Pius VII later signed a treaty with him allying church and state (the Concordat of 1801), and presided at his coronation as Emperor in 1804.

4 Agag's table] the Bible, Judges 1.7, where the king is Adonibezek, alluding to Napoleon's defeat or capture of many princes and kings

5 Grave] engrave

6 turn away] Napoleon defeated the Austrian empire several times, notably at Austerlitz (1805), but in a strategic alliance ("in craft"), Austrian archduchess Marie Louise became Napoleon's consort in 1810 after his first wife, Josephine, failed to bear him an heir.

7 Prussia ... Jena's name] referring to Napoleon's victories over Prussia, notably at the battle of Jena (1806), though at great cost

And bid her witness to that fame which soars
O'er him of Macedon,[1] and shames the vaunt
Of Scandinavia's madman.[2]
From the shades
Of letter'd ease, Oh Germany! come forth
With pen of fire, and from thy troubled scroll
Such as thou spread'st at Leipsic, gather tints
Of deeper character than bold romance
Hath ever imag'd in her wildest dream,
Or history trusted to her sybil-leaves.[3]
—Hail, lotus crown'd! in thy green childhood fed,
By stiff-neck'd Pharaoh, and the shepherd kings,[4]
Hast thou no tale of him who drench'd thy sands
At Jaffa and Aboukir?[5] when the flight
Of rushing souls went up so strange and strong
To the accusing Spirit?
Glorious Isle![6]
Whose thrice enwreathed chain, Promethean like[7]
Did bind him to the fatal rock, we ask
Thy deep memento for this marble tomb.
—Ho! fur-clad Russia![8] with thy spear of frost,

1 him of Macedon] Alexander the Great (356–323 BCE), from Macedonia, who conquered lands from Greece to the border of India, but who died young and his empire did not long survive him

2 Scandinavia's madman] Charles XII of Sweden (1682–1718), who resembled Alexander in his brief career and becoming a commonplace figure for the futility of military ambition

3 pen of fire ... sybil-leaves] German Romantic literature and historiography, highly regarded in the United States; Leipsic: or Leipzig, site of large annual publishers' fair, but also of German states' defeat of Napoleon at the "battle of the nations" (1813)

4 Hail ... kings] Egypt, ruled in ancient times by despotic Pharaohs and then a dynasty of kings descended from sheep-herding peoples

5 Jaffa and Aboukir] In his Egyptian campaign Napoleon was defeated by the British at Aboukir Bay (1798) and captured Jaffa (1799); blockaded by the British navy, he abandoned his forces and slipped back to France.

6 Glorious Isle] Britain

7 Promethean like] In ancient myth, Prometheus stole fire from heaven to benefit humanity and was punished by the gods, being chained to a rock where an eagle tore at his side each day. In Romantic literature he became a literary figure for ambition inevitably defeated by human, social, and institutional limitations. Napoleon was often called a "Prometheus."

8 Russia] scene of Napoleon's disastrous campaign of 1812

Or with thy winter-mocking Cossack's lance,
Stir the cold memories of thy vengeful brain,
And give the last line of our epitaph.
—But there was silence: for no sceptred hand
Receiv'd the challenge.
From the misty deep
Rise, Island-spirits! like those sisters three,[1]
Who spin and cut the trembling thread of life;
Rise on your coral pedestals, and write
That eulogy which haughtier climes deny.
Come, for ye lull'd him in your matron arms,
And cheer'd his exile with the name of king,[2]
And spread that curtain'd couch which none disturb;
Come, twine some trait of household tenderness
Some tender leaflet, nurs'd with Nature's tears
Around this urn. But Corsica,[3] who rock'd
His cradle at Ajacio, turn'd away,
And tiny Elba, in the Tuscan wave
Threw her slight annal with the haste of fear,
And rude[4] Helena sick at heart, and grey
'Neath the Pacific's smiting,[5] bade the moon
With silent finger, point the traveler's gaze
To an unhonor'd tomb.
Then Earth arose,
That blind, old Empress, on her crumbling throne,
And to the echoed question, "*who shall write*
Napoleon's epitaph?" as one who broods
O'er unforgiven injuries, answer'd, "*none.*"

---

1 sisters three] in ancient Greek mythology the Fates, daughters of Zeus and Themis, who controlled individual lives, Clotho weaving the web of life, Lachesis measuring it out, and Atropos cutting the thread at death

2 king] Napoleon's title during his first exile in 1814 as ruler of the small island of Elba off the coast of Italy, which was followed by his escape to France and final defeat at Waterloo in June 1815

3 Corsica] Italian-speaking French possession in the Mediterranean, place of Napoleon's birth and early life

4 rude] rough, savage

5 the Pacific's smiting] corrected in *Select Poems* to "rude Atlantic's scourging" (St Helena is in the Atlantic; Sigourney may at first have been lured by the play on Pacific and pacifism.)

DEATH OF MRS. HARRIET W.L. WINSLOW, MISSIONARY TO CEYLON.[1]

THY name hath power like magic. Back it brings
The earliest pictures hung in Memory's halls,
Tinting them freshly o'er:—the rugged cliff,
The towering trees, the wintry walk to school,
The page so often conn'd, the needle's task
Achiev'd with weariness, the hour of sport
Well earn'd and dearly priz'd, the sparkling brook
Making its slight cascade, the darker rush
Of the pent river thro' its rocky pass,
Our violet-gatherings 'mid the vernal banks,
When our young hearts did ope their chrystal gates
To every simple joy.
I little deem'd
'Mid all that gay and gentle fellowship
That Asia's sun would beam upon thy grave,
Tho' even then, from thy dark, serious eye
There was a glancing forth of glorious thought
That scorn'd earth's vanities. I saw thee stand
With but a few brief summers o'er thy head,
And in the consecrated courts of God
Confess thy Saviour's name. And they who mark'd
The deep devotion and the high resolve
Of that young half-blown bud, did wondering ask
What its full bloom must be. But now thy couch
Is with thine infant train, where the sad voice
Of the poor Ceylon mother tells her child
Of all thy prayers and labors. Yes, thy rest
Is in the bosom of that fragrant isle
Where heathen man with lavish nature strives,
To blot the lesson she would teach of God.
Thy pensive sisters pause upon thy tomb
To catch the spirit that did bear thee through
All tribulation, till thy robes were white,
To join the angelic train. And so farewell,
My childhood's playmate, and my sainted friend,
Whose bright example, not without rebuke
Admonisheth, that home and ease and wealth
And native land, are well exchang'd for Heaven.

1 One of a number of poems by Sigourney about American missionaries, especially in Asia; revised version published in *Poems* (1842).

RELIGIOUS TRACTS.

THEY descend to the humblest lot,
  They are found in the proudest dome,
And free to the hearth of the lowliest cot,[1]
  Like the beam of Heaven they come.

When the way-side beggar wails
  They are with him in his care,
To tell of a refuge that never fails,
  Of a wealth he may freely share.

In the sailor's chest they sleep,
  They check his ribald-song,
They kindle a flame in his musing breast,
  'Mid the night watch cold and long.

Like the light-wing'd bird they rove
  Untir'd from zone to zone,
With links of love they enchain the world
  To Mercy's changeless throne.

15. From *Olive Buds* (1836).[2]

WALKS IN CHILDHOOD.[3]

THE years of my childhood past away, in humble and peaceful simplicity. I loved the shadow of high rocks, and the free musick of the brooks in summer. My heart was full of gladness, though it scarcely knew why. I made to myself a companionship among the beautiful and tuneful things of Nature,—and was happy all the day. But when evening darkened the landscape, I sat down mournfully. There was no brother, into whose hand I might put my own, and say, "Lead me forth to look at the solemn stars,—and tell me of their names." Sometimes, too, I wept in my bed,—because I had no sister, to lay her gentle head upon the same pillow.

---

1 cot] cottage, a poeticism

2 A collection of Sigourney's pacifist writings.

3 Also published, with some differences, in *The Gift: A Christmas and New Year's Present for 1836*, ed. Eliza Leslie (Philadelphia: Carey and Hart [1835]), 50–56; punctuation regularized in two places.

Sometimes, at twilight, before the lamp was lighted,—there came up, out of my brotherless and sisterless bosom, what seemed to be a companion. I talked with it, and was comforted. I did not know that its name was *Thought*,—but I waited for it, and whatsoever it asked me,—I answered.

It questioned me of my knowledge. And I said,—"I know where the first fresh violets of spring grow,—and how the sweet lilly of the vale comes forth from its broad, green sheath—and where the vine climbs to hide its purple grapes,—and when the nut ripens in the forest, after autumn comes with its sparkling frost. I know how the Bee is nourished in Winter, by that essence of the flowers, which her industry embalms,—and I have learned to draw forth the kindness of the domestic animals,—and to know the names of the birds that build their houses in my father's trees."

Then Thought inquired, "What knowledge hast thou of those who reason,—and have dominion over the things that God has created?" And I confessed,—"of my own race, save those who have nurtured me,—I know nothing." I was troubled at my ignorance. So I went forth more widely,—and earnestly regarded what passed among men.

Once, I walked abroad, when the dews of the morning still lingered upon the grass, and the white lillies drooped their beautiful bells, as if shedding tears of joy. Nature breathed a perpetual song, into the hearts of her most silent children. But I looked towards those whose souls have the gift of reason, and are not born to die. I said if the spirit of joy is in the frail flower that flourishes but for a day,—and in the bird that bears to its nest a single crumb of bread,—and in the lamb that knows no friend but its mother,—how much purer must be their happiness, who are surrounded with good things as with a flowing river,—and whose knowledge need have no limit but life,—and who know that though they seem to die,—it is to live forever.

Then I looked upon a group of children. They were unfed and untaught,—and clamored loudly with wayward tongues. I asked them why they went not to school with their companions, and they mocked at me.

I heard two who were once friends, speak harsh and violent words to each other, and turned away affrighted, at the blows they dealt. I saw a man with a bloated and fiery countenance. He seemed strong as the Oak among trees,—yet his steps were more unsteady, than those of the tottering babe. He fell heavily,—and I wondered that no hand was stretched out to raise him up.

I saw an open grave. A poor widow stood near it, with her little ones. Yet methought their own sufferings had set a deeper seal upon them, than sorrow for the dead.

Then I marvelled what it was, thât made the father and mother not pity their children when they hungered, nor call them home, when they were in wickedness,—and the friends forget their early love,—and the strong man fall down senseless,—and the young die before his time. And a voice answered,—"*Intemperance* hath done these evils,—and there is mourning throughout the land because of this."

So I returned sorrowing. And if God had given me a brother or a sister,—I would have thrown my arms around their neck, and said,—"Touch not your lips, I pray you, to the poison-cup,—but let us drink the pure water which God has blessed,—all the days of our lives."

Again I went forth, and looked attentively on what was passing around. I met a beautiful boy weeping. I said, "Why dost thou mourn?" And he replied, "My father went to the wars,—and is dead. He will come back to me no more."

I saw a woman, pale and weak with sorrow. The sun shone upon her dwelling, and the woodbine climbed to its window, and blossomed sweetly. But she beheld not their brightness. For she was a widow. Her husband had been slain in battle,—and there was joy for her no more.

I saw a hoary man. He sat by the wayside. His head rested upon his bosom. His garments were old,—and his flesh wasted away. Yet he asked not for charity. I said, "Why is thy heart heavy?" And he answered, "I had a son,—an only one. I toiled from his cradle, that he might be fed, and clothed, and taught wisdom. He grew up to bless me, and all my labor, weariness, and care were forgotten. I knew no want for he cherished me. But he left me, to be a soldier. He fell on the field of battle. Therefore my eye runneth down with water,—because the comforter who should relieve my soul must return no more."

I said,—"show me a field of battle,—that I may know what war means."

And he said,—"Thou art not able to bear the sight. But I will tell thee what I have seen, when the battle was done. A broad plain, covered with dead bodies,—and those who struggled in the pains of death. The trampled earth red with blood. Mangled bosoms sending forth dreadful groans,—and broken limbs vainly reaching for some supporting hand. Wounded horses in their agony rolling upon their riders,—and tearing with their hoofs the faces of the dying. And for every man that lay there slaughtered,—how bitter must be the mourning of the parents who reared him,—and of the young children who sat upon his knee. Yet this is but a part of the misery that War maketh among mankind."

Then I said, "Tell me no more, I beseech thee, of battle or of war,—for my heart is sick."

But when I saw that the silver haired man raised his eyes and his hands upwards,—I kneeled down at his side. And he prayed, "Lord, keep this child from anger, and hatred, and ambition, which are the seeds of war,—and grant to all who take the name of Jesus Christ, peaceable and meek hearts, that shunning all deeds of strife, they may dwell at last in the country of unchanging peace,—even in heaven."

Hastening to my home, I said earnestly to my mother,—"Oh, shelter me, as I have been sheltered,—in solitude and in love. Bid me turn the wheel of industry,—or bring water from the fountain,—or tend the plants in the garden,—or feed a young bird and listen to its song,—but let me go forth no more,—to look upon the vices and miseries of man."

16. From *Select Poems*, 3rd edition (1838).[1]

TO A SHRED OF LINEN.[2]

WOULD they swept cleaner!—
Here's a littering shred
Of linen left behind—a vile reproach
To all good housewifery. Right glad am I,
That no neat lady, train'd in ancient times
Of pudding-making, and of sampler-work,[3]
And speckless sanctity of household care,
Hath happen'd here, to spy thee. She, no doubt,
Keen looking through her spectacles, would say,
"*This comes of reading books:*"—or some spruce beau,[4]

---

1 I.e., 3rd edition of *Poems* (1834); *Select Poems* became Sigourney's major reprinted collection.

2 One of several fabric poems by Sigourney; see "To a Fragment of Silk" (p. 107) and "To a Fragment of Cotton" (p. 183).

3 sampler] piece of embroidery with designs and mottoes as an example of a girl or woman's needlework skills

4 beau] elegant, even foppish man or suitor; spruce: dapper

Essenc'd[1] and lily-handed,[2] had he chanc'd
To scan thy slight superfices, 'twould be
"*This comes of writing poetry*."—Well—well—
Come forth—offender!—hast thou aught to say?
Canst thou by merry thought, or quaint conceit,
Repay this risk, that I have run for thee?
—Begin at alpha,[3] and resolve thyself
Into thine elements. I see the stalk
And bright blue flower of flax, which erst o'erspread
That fertile land, where mighty Moses[4] stretch'd
His rod miraculous.[5] I see thy bloom
Tinging, too scantly, these New England vales.
But, lo! the sturdy farmer lifts his flail,
To crush thy bones unpitying, and his wife
With 'kerchief'd head, and eyes brimful of dust,
Thy fibrous nerves with hatchel-tooth[6] divides.
——I hear a voice of music—and behold!
The ruddy damsel singeth at her wheel,[7]
While by her side the rustic lover sits.
Perchance, his shrewd eye secretly doth count
The mass of skeins,[8] which, hanging on the wall,
Increaseth day by day. Perchance his thought,
(For men have deeper minds than women—sure!)[9]
Is calculating what a thrifty wife
The maid will make; and how his dairy shelves
Shall groan beneath the weight of golden cheese,
Made by her dexterous hand, while many a keg
And pot of butter to the market borne,
May, transmigrated, on his back appear,
In new thanksgiving coats.
Fain would I ask,

---

1 Essenc'd] perfumed with an essence, or extract distilled from a plant or other substance

2 lily-handed] with white hands, i.e., unused to manual, outdoor work

3 alpha] first letter in the Greek alphabet

4 Moses] in the Bible, book of Exodus, a prophet who leads the Jews out of bondage in Egypt, famous in ancient times for linen textiles

5 rod miraculous] with which Moses struck a rock causing a spring of water so his people could drink (the Bible, Numbers 20.11)

6 hatchel] hackle, or heckle: tool for combing out fibres of flax or hemp

7 wheel] spinning wheel for combining flax fibres into thread

8 skeins] loops of thread

9 sure] surely

Mine own New England, for thy once loved wheel,
By sofa and piano quite displaced.[1]
Why dost thou banish from thy parlour-hearth
That old Hygeian harp,[2] whose magic rul'd
Dyspepsia,[3] as the minstrel-shepherd's skill
Exorcis'd Saul's ennui?[4] There was no need,
In those good times, of trim callisthenics,[5]
And there was less of gadding, and far more
Of home-born, heart-felt comfort, rooted strong
In industry, and bearing such rare fruit,
As wealth might never purchase.
                                                            But come back,
Thou shred of linen. I did let thee drop,
In my harangue, as wiser ones have lost
The thread of their discourse. What was thy lot
When the rough battery of the loom had stretch'd
And knit thy sinews, and the chemist sun
Thy brown complexion bleach'd?[6]
                                                            Methinks I scan
Some idiosyncrasy, that marks thee out
A defunct pillow-case.—Did the trim guest,
To the best chamber usher'd, e'er admire
The snowy whiteness of thy freshen'd youth
Feeding thy vanity? or some sweet babe
Pour its pure dream of innocence on thee?
Say, hast thou listen'd to the sick one's moan,
When there was none to comfort?—or shrunk back
From the dire tossings of the proud man's brow?
Or gather'd from young beauty's restless sigh
A tale of untold love?

---

1 displaced] displacement of home spinning by factory manufacture, in the transition from local to regional economy, domestic to industrial production, utilitarian to commercial and fashionable consumption

2 Hygeia] in ancient legend, the goddess of health, produced by the physical exercise of spinning, along with "music" from the wheel's hum

3 Dyspepsia] indigestion, usually involving depression

4 Saul's ennui] in the Bible (1 Samuel 16.23), Saul's weariness and dissatisfaction, soothed by David's harp playing

5 callisthenics] from Greek for "beautiful strength": physical exercises to develop the beauty of the human figure, introduced into girls' education in the second quarter of the nineteenth century

6 brown complexion bleach'd] Whereas the sun turns the human complexion brown, it turns the natural brown of linen to white.

Still, close and mute!—
Wilt tell no secrets, ha?—Well then, go down,
With all thy churl-kept hoard of curious lore,
In majesty and mystery, go down
Into the paper-mill, and from its jaws,
Stainless and smooth, emerge.[1]—Happy shall be
The renovation, if on thy fair page
Wisdom and truth, their hallow'd lineaments
Trace for posterity. So shall thine end
Be better than thy birth, and worthier bard
Thine apotheosis immortalize.

ON THE ADMISSION OF MICHIGAN INTO THE UNION.[2]

COME in, little sister, so healthful and fair,
Come take in our father's best parlor a share,
You've been kept long enough at the nurse's,[3] I trow,
Where the angry lakes roar and the northern winds blow;
Come in, we've a pretty large household, 'tis true,
But the twenty-five[4] children can make room for you.

A present, I see, for our sire you have brought,
His dessert to embellish, how kind was the thought;
A treat of ripe berries, both crimson and blue,
And wild flowers to stick in his button-hole too,
The rose from your prairie, the nuts from your tree;
What a good little sister—come hither to me.

You've a dowry besides very cunningly stor'd,
To fill a nice cupboard, or spread a broad board,
Detroit, Ypsilanti—Ann Arbour,[5] and more—
For the youngest, methinks, quite a plentiful store,
You're a prog,[6] I perceive—it is true to the letter,
And your sharp Yankee sisters will like you the better.

---

1 Stainless ... emerge] The best quality paper was made from linen rags.

2 Michigan was admitted in 1837 as a free state along with the slave state of Arkansas, by the compromise between pro- and anti-slavery sections of the United States; Sigourney ignores Arkansas' admission.

3 long enough at the nurse's] referring to the delay in Michigan's admission due to a dispute with Ohio over a strip of territory, almost leading to war

4 twenty-five] the number of States in the Union at that time

5 Detroit, Ypsilanti—Ann Arbour] prominent Michigan towns

6 prog] colloquial abbreviation of "progressive," here referring to education policy, in Michigan's comprehensive public education system

But where are your Indians—so feeble and few?[1]
So fall'n from the heights where their forefathers grew!
From the forests they fade, o'er the waters that bore
The names of their baptism, they venture no more—
O soothe their sad hearts ere they vanish afar,
Nor quench the faint beams of their westering star.

Those ladies who sit on the sofa so high,
Are the stateliest dames of our family,
Your thirteen old sisters,[2] don't treat them with scorn,
They were notable spinsters before you were born,
Many stories they know, most instructive to hear,
Go, make them a curtsy, 'twill please them, my dear.

They can teach you the names of those great ones to spell,
Who stood at the helm, when the war tempest fell,
They will show you the writing that gleam'd to the sky
In the year seventy-six, on the fourth of July,[3]
When the flash of the Bunker-Hill flame was red,[4]
And the blood gush'd forth from the breast of the dead.

There are some who may call them both proud and old,
And say they usurp what they cannot hold;
Perhaps, their bright locks have a sprinkle of gray,
But then, little Michy, don't hint it, I pray;
For they'll give you a frown, or a box on the ear,
Or send you to stand in the corner, I fear.

They, indeed, bore the burden and heat of the day,
But you've as good right to your penny[5] as they;
Though the price of our freedom, they better have known,
Since they paid for it, out of their purses alone,
Yet a portion belongs to the youngest, I ween,
So, hold up your head with the "Old Thirteen."

---

1 Indians ... feeble and few] chiefly the Chippewa, Ottawa, and Potawatomi, from whom concessions were extracted by a treaty of 1836

2 thirteen old sisters] the original thirteen colonies that formed the United States after independence

3 fourth of July] date in 1776 when delegates from thirteen British North American colonies ratified their Declaration of Independence

4 Bunker-Hill ... red] British forces took Bunker Hill on 17 June 1775, attempting to break the American siege of Boston, but at high cost.

5 penny] opinion

17. From *Letters to Mothers* (1838).[1]

LETTER I.

PRIVILEGES OF THE MOTHER.

My Friend, if in becoming a mother, you have reached the climax of your happiness, you have also taken a higher place in the scale of being. A most important part is allotted you, in the economy of the great human family. Look at the gradations of your way onward,—your doll, your playmates, your lessons,—perhaps to decorate a beautiful person,—to study the art of pleasing,—to exult in your own attractions,—to feed on adulation,—to wear the garland of love;—and then to introduce into existence a being never to die;—and to feel your highest, holiest energies enlisted to fit it for this world and the next.

No longer will you now live for self,—no longer be noteless[2] and unrecorded, passing away without name or memorial among the people. It can no more be reproachfully said of you, that you "lend all your graces to the grave, and keep no copy."[3] "My cousin Mary of Scotland, hath a fair son born unto her, and I am but a dead tree," said Queen Elizabeth,[4] while the scowl of discontent darkened her brow. In bequeathing your own likeness to the world, you will naturally be anxious to array it in that beauty of virtue, which fades not at the touch of time. What a scope for your exertions, to render your representative, an honour to its parentage, and a blessing to its country.

---

1 This advice book addresses the issue of woman's power in society and the state, drawing on a late eighteenth-century discourse of republican motherhood, which restricted women to the domestic sphere while sanctifying that sphere as the source of public virtue. The book applies republican motherhood to continuing issues in the early United States, given new edge in the 1830s—increased immigration of Irish and European Catholics, fractious and corrupt national politics, and increased participation by women in highly politicized public issues such as opposition to slavery. Though not as popular as *Letters to Young Ladies*, *Letters to Mothers* was reprinted several times.

2 noteless] unnoted

3 lend ... copy] echoing Shakespeare, *Twelfth Night*, 1.5.245–46, said by Viola to Olivia, and where "lend" is "lead."

4 Queen Elizabeth] Fleeing political enemies, Mary queen of Scots sought refuge with Elizabeth I of England, who had her imprisoned and eventually executed; Mary's son James, already king of Scotland, succeeded the unmarried and childless Elizabeth on the English throne in 1603.

You have gained an increase of power. The influence which is most truly valuable, is that of mind over mind. How entire and perfect is this dominion, over the unformed character of your infant. Write what you will, upon the printless tablet, with your wand of love. Hitherto, your influence over your dearest friend, your most submissive servant, has known bounds and obstructions. Now, you have over a newborn immortal, almost that degree of power which the mind exercises over the body, and which Aristotle[1] compares to the "sway of a prince over a bondman." The period of this influence must indeed pass away;—but while it lasts, make good use of it.

Wise men have said, and the world begins to believe, that it is the province of woman to teach. You then, as a mother, are advanced to the head of that profession. I congratulate you. You hold that license which authorizes you to teach always. You have attained that degree in the College of Instruction, by which your pupils are in your presence continually, receiving lessons whether you intend it or not, and if the voice of precept be silent, fashioning themselves on the model of your example. You cannot escape from their imitation. You cannot prevent them from carrying into another generation, the stamp of those habits which they inherit from you. If you are thoughtless, or supine, an unborn race will be summoned as witnesses of your neglect.

"Meantime, the mighty debt runs on,
  The dread account proceeds,
And your *not-doing* is set down
  Among your darkest deeds."[2]

In ancient times, the theory that the mother was designated by nature as an instructor, was sometimes admitted and illustrated. The philosopher Aristippus,[3] was the pupil of maternal precepts. Revered for his wisdom, he delighted in the appellation of Metrodidactos, the "taught of his mother."

"We are indebted," says Quintilian, "for the eloquence of the Gracchi, to their mother Cornelia," who though qualified to give publick lectures in philosophy at Rome, did not forget to be the faithful teacher in private, of those, whom she so justly styled 'her

1 Aristotle] Greek philosopher (384–322 BCE), author of works on politics, rhetoric, literature, ethics, logic, science, and other subjects

2 Echoing Edward Young (1683–1765), *Resignation* (1762) 1. 469–72.

3 Aristippus] the Elder (c. 435–365 BCE), Greek philosopher who taught that the purpose of life is pleasure

jewels.'"[1] St. Jerome also bears similar testimony. "The eloquence of the Gracchi, derived its perfection from the mother's elegance and purity of language."[2]

Should heathen mothers be permitted to be more faithful in their duties, than those who are under bonds to the life-giving Gospel? "A good mother, says the eloquent L'Aime Martin,[3] will seize upon her child's heart, as her special field of activity. To be capable of this, is the great end of female education. I have shewn that no universal agent of civilization exists, but through mothers. Nature has placed in their hands, our infancy and youth. I have been among the first to declare the necessity of making them, by improved education, capable of fulfilling their natural mission. The love of God and man, is the basis of this system. In proportion as it prevails, national enmities will disappear, prejudices become extinguished, civilization spread itself far and wide,—one great people cover the earth, and the reign of God be established. This is to be hastened, by the watchful care of mothers over their offspring, from the cradle upwards."

What an appeal to mothers! What an acknowledgement of the dignity of their office! The aid of the "weaker vessel,"[4] is now invoked by legislation and sages. It has been discovered that there are signs of disease in the body politick, which can be best allayed, by the subordination taught in families, and through her agency to whom is committed the "moulding of the whole mass of mind in its first formation."

Woman is surely more deeply indebted to the government that protects her, than man, who bears within his own person, the elements of self-defence. But how shall her gratitude be best made an operative principle? Secluded as she wisely is, from any share in the administration of government, how shall her patriotism find legitimate exercise? The admixture of the female mind in the ferment of political ambition, would be neither safe if it were permitted, nor to be desired if it were safe. Nations who have encouraged it, have usually found their cabinet-councils perplexed by intrigue, or turbulent with contention. History has recorded instances, where the gentler sex have usurped the scep-

---

1 Quintilian (CE 35–95), Roman rhetorical theorist, *Institutio oratoria*, book 1, ch. 1.

2 Jerome (c. CE 340–420), *Letters*, 107, section 4.

3 Martin] Louis-Aimé Martin (1781–1847), *De l'Éducation des mères de famille; ou, De la Civilisation du genre humain par les femmes* (1834)

4 The Bible, Paul's first letter to Peter 3.7, referring to the wife.

tre of the monarch, or invaded the province of the warrior. But we regard them either with amazement, as a planet rushing from its orbit, or with pity as the lost Pleiad,[1] vanishing from its happy and brilliant sisterhood.

Still, patriotism is a virtue in our sex, and there is an office where it may be called into action, a privilege which the proudest peer might envy. It depends not on rank or wealth, the canvassings of party, or the fluctuations of the will of the people. Its throne is the heart, its revenue in Eternity. This office is that of maternal teacher. It is hers by hereditary right. Let her make it an inalienable possession. Nature invested her with it, when giving her the key of the infant soul, she bade her enter it through the affections. Her right to its first love, her intuitive discernment of its desires and impulses, her tact in detecting the minutest shades of temperament, her skill in forming the heart to her purpose, are proofs both of her prerogative, and of the Divine Source, whence it emanates.

It seems now to be conceded, that the vital interests of our country, may be aided by the zeal of mothers. Exposed as it is, to the influx of untutored foreigners, often unfit for its institutions, or adverse to their spirit, it seems to have been made a repository for the waste and refuse of other nations. To neutralize this mass, to rule its fermentations, to prevent it from becoming a lava-stream in the garden of liberty, and to purify it for those channels where the life-blood of the nation circulates, is a work of power and peril. The force of public opinion, or the terror of law, must hold in check these elements of danger, until Education can restore them to order and beauty. Insubordination is becoming a prominent feature in some of our principal cities. Obedience in families, respect to magistrates, and love of country, should therefore be inculcated with increased energy, by those who have earliest access to the mind. A barrier to the torrent of corruption, and a guard over the strong holds of knowledge and of virtue, may be placed by the mother, as she watches over her cradled son. Let her come forth with vigour and vigilance, at the call of her country, not like Boadicea[2] in her chariot, but like the mother of Washington,[3] feeling that the first lesson to every incipient ruler should be, "*how*

---

1 lost Pleiad] In ancient mythology the seven stars of the constellation Pleiades represented seven sisters; the one faint star was called the lost Pleiad, favourite subject of Romantic poets including Felicia Hemans.

2 Boadicea] or Boudicca, British queen who led her people against first-century CE Roman invaders and later symbolized woman as patriot

3 mother of Washington] see "Grave of the Mother of Washington," p. 97

to obey." The degree of her diligence in preparing her children to be good subjects of a just government, will be the true measure of her patriotism. While she labours to pour a pure and heavenly spirit into the hearts that open around her, she knows not but she may be appointed to rear some future statesman, for her nation's helm, or priest for the temple of Jehovah.[1]

But a loftier ambition will inspire the christian mother, that of preparing "fellow citizens for the saints in glory." All other hopes should be held secondary, all other distinctions counted adventitious and fleeting. That she may be enabled to fulfil a mission so sacred, Heaven has given her priority and power, and that she may learn the nature of the soul which she is ordained to modify, has permitted her to be the *first* to look into it, as into the cup of some opening flower, fresh from the Forming Hand. The dignity of her office admits of no substitute. It is hers to labour day and night, with patience, and in joyful hope. It is hers to lead forth the affections in healthful beauty, and prompt their heavenward aspirings. It is hers to foster tenderness[2] of conscience, and so to regulate its balance that it swerve not amid the temptations of untried life. It is hers so to rivet principle, that it may retain its integrity, both "beneath the cloud, and under the sea."[3] And as she labours for God, so she labours for her country, since whatever tends to prepare for citizenship in heaven, cannot fail to make good and loyal subjects of any just government on earth.

This then, is the patriotism of woman, not to thunder in senates, or to usurp dominion, or to seek the clarion-blast of fame, but faithfully to teach by precept and example, that wisdom, integrity and peace, which are the glory of a nation. Thus, in the wisdom of Providence, has she been prepared by the charm of life's fairest season, for the happiness of love; incited to rise above the trifling amusements and selfish pleasures which once engrossed her, that she might be elevated to the maternal dignity; cheered under its sleepless cares by a new affection; girded for its labours by the example of past ages; and adjured to fidelity in its most sacred duties, by the voice of God.

Admitting that it is the profession of our sex to teach, we perceive the mother to be first in point of precedence, in degree of power, in the faculty of teaching, and in the department allotted. For in point of precedence, she is next to the Creator; in power

---

1 Jehovah] Biblical term for God

2 tenderness] sensitivity

3 Echoing the Bible, 1 Corinthians 10.1.

over her pupil, limitless and without competitor; in faculty of teaching, endowed with the prerogative of a transforming love; while the glorious department allotted, is a newly quickened soul, and its immortal destiny.

Let her then not be regardless of the high privileges conferred upon her, or seek to stipulate for a life of indolence and ease, or feebly say that her individual exertion can be of little value. Let her not omit daily to cast into the treasury of the unfolding mind, her "two mites."[1] The habits which she early impresses, though to her eye they seem but as the filmy line of the spider, scarcely clasping the spray, trembling at every breeze, may prove as links of tempered steel, binding a deathless being to eternal felicity or woe. A glorious aggregate will at last be formed by long perseverance in "line upon line, precept upon precept, here a little, and there a little."[2] As the termites patiently carry grains of sand, till their citadel astonishes the eye, as the coral insect toils beneath the waters, till reef joins reef, and islands spring up with golden fruitage and perennial verdure, so let the mother, "sitting down or walking by the way,"[3] in the nursery, the parlour, even from the death-bed, labour to impress on her offspring that goodness, purity, and piety, which shall render them acceptable to society, to their country, and to their God.

18. From *The Works of Mrs. Hemans* (1840).[4]

From ESSAY ON THE GENIUS OF MRS. HEMANS.

Seldom has the early possession of poetical genius been more clearly determined, than in the case of the gifted individual, whose collected works are here presented to the public. Its infantine

---

1 two mites] In the Bible (Mark 12.42 and Luke 21.2), the poor widow donates all she has—two mites, or small coins—to the Temple; Jesus tells his disciples that she donated more than the wealthy who donated much more, because she gave her all while they had more to give.

2 The Bible, Isaiah 28.13.

3 Echoing the Bible, Deuteronomy 6.7 and 11.19, referring to the ten commandments: And thou shalt teach them diligently unto thy children, and shalt talk of them when thou sittest in thine house, and when thou walkest by the way, and when thou liest down, and when thou risest up.

4 *The Works of Mrs. Hemans, with A memoir by Her Sister, and An Essay on Her Genius, by Mrs. Sigourney*, 7 vols. (Philadelphia: Lea and Blanchard, 1840); the Englishwoman Felicia Hemans (1793–1835) was the most respected and popular woman poet in the United States.

indications, both through the affections and the intellect, were too strong to be overlooked, and too peculiar to be mistaken. The temperament of that art, which has been styled by one of its masters, "the breath, and finer spirit of all knowledge,"[1] revealed itself, in tremulous sensibility—in deep love of the beautiful—in lonely and intense communings with nature—and in those restless aspirations, which earth can neither satisfy nor control. Passionate desires for knowledge,—rapid, almost intuitive appropriation of it,—and exceedingly strong retentive powers, were also precociously developed. The genius permitted thus vigorously to unfold, was also eminently fortunate, in the circumstances of its education, throughout the whole of life. It is pleasant to trace the influences, which both from "heaven above, and earth beneath,"[2] conspired to nurture, and mature it, for its high destiny.

First in order, we place maternal culture. The strength of this agency, none will question, who has beheld in the illustrious, from the Gracchi to him of Mount Vernon,[3] the hand of the mother, polishing the mental gem, or leading in paths of wisdom, the young footsteps of the Father of his Country. If such influence is so powerful, over the elements of masculine character, with how much more ease and certainty must it modify the plastic nature of woman! [...]

In happy combination with this hallowed influence of a mother, sustaining the enthusiasm in which herself participated, was the scenery by which the childhood of the poet was surrounded. The rushing streams and wild mountains of Wales, among which, at the age of seven years, she became a resident, hung up their strong, bold pictures, in her soul. The deep, shadowy dells, where she mused and wandered; the large, dimly-lighted hall, where she rehearsed her lessons; the echoed voice of the "melancholy main,"[4]—tinted her buoyant fancy with solemn hues of thought. [...]

---

1 William Wordsworth, Preface to *Lyrical Ballads* (1802).

2 The Bible, Joshua 2.11, describing where God is.

3 Gracchi] second-century BCE Roman brothers and heroes of American republican ideology, sons of Cornelia, Sigourney's favourite figure for republican motherhood; Mount Vernon: home of George Washington (1732–99), military leader of the American Revolution and first president of the United States, whose mother was another of Sigourney's figures of republican motherhood; see p. 97.

4 James Thomson (English, 1700–48), *The Castle of Indolence*, canto 1, stanza 30; also quoted by American Nathaniel Hawthorne (1804–64), "Foot-prints on the Sea-shore," *Twice-told Tales* (1837).

The nature of the education of Mrs. Hemans, was favourable to the development of her genius. A wide range of classical and poetical studies, with the acquisition of several languages, supplied both pleasant aliment and needful discipline. [...]

As youth advanced, her situation allowed her social feelings to receive discreet and healthful development. Thus the balance of character was preserved, and the eccentricity which has been sometimes supposed a concomitant of genius, had in her, no place. [...]

Her freedom, for many years, from those cares which usually absorb a wife and mother,—and her early participation of the unutterable sympathies which, flowing from those sources of affection, ripen and raise woman to her climax, exerted a decided influence on her poetical character. From the high and hallowed duties which in the bloom of youth she assumed, her lyre caught a deeper and more thrilling tone; while by her prolonged residence under the maternal wing, she was sheltered from the burden of those cares which sometimes press out the life of song.

"The Muses frowned on me, for keeping account-books," said a Spanish poet. Still more coldly may they be supposed to look, on the unending details of household occupation, which are wont to leave but little space for the laborious refinement which their art imposes. [...]

The last of the influences which we shall mention, as having conspired to educate her genius, is the infusion of sorrow. Its high harmonies could have been perfected by no other teacher. [...] Her lot of loneliness was an affliction,[1] which every passing year made more palpable and painful. She took the discipline to her heart, as a messenger from Heaven. [...]

The tendencies of a genius thus thoroughly educated, were pure and holy. With dark and stormy passions it had no affinity. To reveal the loveliness of nature, the endearments of home, the deathless strength of the affections, the noble aims of disinterested virtue, the power of that piety which plucks the sting from death, were its chosen themes. [...]

Another of its striking excellencies was freedom from bigotry. It was the echo of no sect nor party. [...] Peace, and good will, were its watch-words. With the true love of charity, it greeted all, who, through varying paths, advanced in Christian faith, towards the same heavenly home. [...] It saw in its own sweet art, a bond of union,—a green, quiet oasis, in which to hide from the strife of tongues. [...]

---

1 affliction] Hemans' husband abandoned her and their five sons.

The Possessor of this genius evinced both an innate consciousness of its powers, and a determination to devote them to their legitimate purposes. She held on her way, not in self-esteem, but in reverence for the loftiness of her vocation, and with a continually heightening gratitude for the entrusted treasure. She guarded her gift of melody, as the vestal-flame,[1] for whose debasement or extinction she was bound to give solemn account. So full and entire was she, in this consecration, as to resist the most tempting offers to write prose,—though moved to their acceptance by pecuniary need. She felt that she had a higher and holier calling, and with unwavering confidence pursued its upward promptings. [...]

Both critics and casual readers have united in pronouncing her poetry to be essentially feminine. The whole sweet circle of the domestic affections,—the hallowed ministries of woman, at the cradle, the hearth-stone, and the death-bed, were its chosen themes. [...]

It has been alleged that the warlike imagery, so predominant in her poetry, is a departure from its feminine elements. Yet was this the emanation of an indigenous, or an acquired taste? [...]

In which of the spirit-stirring, belligerent lays, does the trembling sweetness of the poet's own soul, irresistibly steal out, as in "The Voice of Spring," "The Graves of a Household," "The Homes of England," "The Treasures of the Deep," the thrilling sigh of the "Palm-Tree," or the full, sustained, sublime inspiration of the "Forest Sanctuary?" [...]

The genius of Mrs. Hemans was as pure and feminine in its impulses, as in its out-pourings. That ambition which impels the man of genius to "scorn delights, and live laborious days,"[2] that he may walk on the high places of the world's renown, and leave a name which shall be as a trumpet-tone to all time, woke no answering echo in her bosom. Sympathy, not fame, was the desire of her being. [...]

In Mrs. Hemans, we see the true poetic genius producing its highest effect, the sublimation of piety. Cheering, by its versatile powers, the darkness of her destiny, and gradually throwing off all stain of earthliness, it desired at length, to breathe only the songs of heaven. [...]

And now, we grieve to say farewell to thee, sweet ruler of the

1 vestal-flame] sacred fire kept burning by virgin-priestesses at the temple of the goddess Vesta in ancient Rome

2 scorn ... days] Milton, *Lycidas*, l. 72.

tuneful harp. The young, free-hearted West, is a weeper at thy grave. The hymns of the Pilgrim-Fathers have found an echo in thy lofty strain; and from the storm-beaten rock where they landed, to the Gulph where the Floridian orange-grove and the magnolia mingle their perfumes,—from the sounding shores of the Atlantic, to the lone wilds of the Oregon, where the red man wanders,—thine image is cherished, and thy memory dear.

The emigrant mother, toiling over steep, rugged mountains, reads thy poems in the rude vehicle which bears all her treasures to a stranger-land. The lisping child responds to her voice, amid those deep solitudes,—and the words are thine. Thou art with them, in their unfloored hut,—teaching them to love the home which God has given.

Why have we said farewell? We recall the word. Thou art still with us, gentle spirit. Race after race may fall like autumnal leaves, and our broad prairies become the site of thronged cities; but thou shalt still be there, undecaying, unchanged.

Yes,—sit by our hearth-stones, and sing there, when we shall be gathered to the fathers. When by our children's children our memory is forgotten, thou shalt not be forgotten:—thou shalt lift up thy voice of melody to unborn ages, and tell them of the Better Land.[1]

L.H.S.

Hartford, Conn., January, 1840

19. From *Pocahontas, and Other Poems* (1841).[2]

THE BUTTERFLY.

A BUTTERFLY bask'd on a baby's grave,
  Where a lily had chanced to grow:
"Why art thou here, with thy gaudy die,
When she of the blue and sparkling eye,
  Must sleep in the churchyard low?"

Then it lightly soar'd through the sunny air,
  And spoke from its shining track:
"I was a worm till I won my wings,
And she whom thou mourn'st like a seraph sings:
  Wouldst thou call the blest one back?"

1 Better Land] heaven

2 Editions published at London and New York in 1841, but with somewhat different contents; selections here are from the New York edition.

TO A FRAGMENT OF COTTON.[1]

METHINKS thou'rt indestructible. At first
But the slight remnant of a spruce cravat,
Thou cam'st unbidden to my premises,
And then the baby tore thee, and the dog
Did munch thee in a corner, where he play'd;
Next thou wert hanging at the housemaid's broom,
Yet here thou art, for all.
Hast e'er a tongue?
No doubt. The veriest triflers oft can boast
Great store of words. If thou hast aught to say,
I'll be a listener. Tell me of thy birth,
And all thy strange mutations, since the dow[2]
Of infancy was on thee, to thine hour
Of finish'd beauty 'neath the shuttle's skill.

So, thou wert known in history! and thy sire
The sounding name of Sir Gossypium[3] bore.
He was a younger brother of the fleece,
And of the flax of Egypt, and the silk
Which the poor spinning-worm doth die to make
A present of, to those who thank her not.
Thy race have multiplied exceedingly,
And sown themselves in every sunny zone
Of both the hemispheres. The planter's hand,[4]
Well pleased, doth play about their thickening beard
When its young promise tints the ripen'd cheek.
Thy name is mention'd where the merchants meet,
And Commerce loves thee well. Yea, thou dost make
Much clamour in the world, with thundering crash
Of water-wheel, and loom, and steaming smoke
From coal-fed chimneys, fusing to the skies
With blacken'd breath. Yet mid thy vassal throng
Of toiling artisans, 'tis sad to see

---

1 One of several fabric poems; see "To a Shred of Linen" (p. 168) and "To a Fragment of Silk" (p. 107).

2 dow] perhaps a variant of dough, or paste made of plants such as hemp

3 Gossypium] botanical name for cotton

4 planter] here probably plantation owner, especially in the southern United States where cotton was a cash crop grown on large estates by the labour of black slaves

Such troops of little ones,[1] with pallid cheek,
Yielding their joyous birthright at thy shrine,
And all sweet intercourse with fields and flowers,
That glads the peasant's child.
'Twere hard to count
Thy many transmigrations, or to keep
Tithe[2] of the dramas where thou dost enact
Most changeful parts. Thou in the vessel's hold
Dost slumber heavily, in ponderous bales,
Like precious ingots, or with winged sail
Impel its trackless journey o'er the deep,
Or, closely furl'd, embrace the groaning mast
That crouches to the tempest. Thou dost stoop,
With garment coarse, to wrap the labouring kind,[3]
And deck the country-dame in Sunday-gown
Of ample-flower'd and many-colour'd chints,[4]
Or, slow emerging from the Indian loom,[5]
Light as the texture of a dreamy thought,
Veil the fair bride, and drape the throned queen.
With man thou art when to the dust he goes,
And in thy snowy shroud[6] dost fold his brow
When friend and lover have forsaken him.

But yet thou hast a higher ministry
Of kindliness, and, when thou well hast served
His body's need, dost turn thy hand and touch
The ethereal mind.[7] Yea, when thou seem'st to die,
Thou only dropp'st thy grosser elements
To commune with the soul.
Mysterious Guest!
I seem to fear thee. Would that I had known
Thy lineage better, and been less remiss
In the good grace of hospitality.

---

1 little ones] the many children employed in cotton mills

2 Tithe] a tenth

3 kind] perhaps a misprint for "hind": peasant

4 chints] chintz: cotton cloth fast-printed with coloured designs of various kinds and usually glazed

5 Indian loom] India was famous for cottons with colourful printed designs.

6 snowy shroud] white sheet wrapping the dead for burial

7 ethereal mind] referring to the use of cotton rags in making paper, from which is made books that address the mind and spirit

I much bemoan myself that thou shouldst be
So treated in my house. With reverent hand
And genuflection, I do take thee up,
And straight bespeak for thee more fitting place
Mid thy compeers.
But who can say what form
Thou next may'st wear?
Perchance the pictured page
Through which the lisping and delighted child
Hath its first talk with knowledge, or the chart
That saves the mariner mid rocks and shoals
Upon the wrecking sea.
Or lov'st thou best
To be the tablet of the sage? or bear
The bard's rich music to another age?
Or with some message from the Book of Life,[1]
Wake the dead slumber of benighted lands?[2]

THE MILLINERS AND FISHES.[3]

COMMERCE and enterprise should be applauded,[4]
And so[5] the Paris milliners opine
It seems; for when their fashionable fabrics
Grow obsolete, 'tis said[6] they freight a vessel
Straight for the Baltic, and the Northern[7] belles
In the quaint fragments of the realm of taste,
Proudly array themselves. And yet 'twere sad,[8]

1 Book of Life] the Bible

2 benighted lands] referring to missionaries distributing Bibles and religious tracts

3 Women's magazines in which Sigourney published included illustrations of current fashions and patterns for lace, needlework, and so on. This poem was first published as "The Parisian Milliners and the Fishes" in *The Token and Atlantic Souvenir: A Christmas and New Year's Present*, ed. S.G. Goodrich (Boston: Gray and Bowen, 1833 [1832]), 180–83. Sigourney made many verbal changes and updated fashions for the version here; to illustrate her revision practice, verbal changes from the *Token* are noted.

4 line 1] *Token*: Commerce, they say, is quite a source of profit;

5 so] *Token*: thus

6 Grow obsolete, 'tis said] *Token*: Remain too long on hand,

7 Northern] *Token*: Swedish

8 ll. 6–7] *Token*: And Russian beauties haughtily do sport/Those antiquated matters. Yet 'twere sad,

Methinks, to see, at polar fête or ball,
Some shivering[1] Nova-Zemblan[2] lady[3] flaunt[4]
In robe of lace, short-sleeved, the purple bust
Reveal'd most liberally.[5]
Once a storm,
Hoarse from the Gulf of Finland, crossly wreck'd
The adventurous ship quite near her destined port,
And strew'd her riches o'er the admiring deep.
There[6] perish'd many a hope of many a fair
Young sempstress, by such cruel loss condemn'd[7]
To wear her cast-off dress[8] another year,[9]
Vamp'd up[10] as best she may.
'Tis an ill wind
That blows no good.[11] The watery realm rejoiced,[12]
For all its finny aristocracy
Of their oldfashioned suits had long complain'd.
Next day a Salmon at the Neva's mouth[13]
Was taken, very delicately clad
In a white lutestring[14] drapery,[15] with veil
Of costly blonde:[16] her wedding dress, no doubt.
The[17] bridemaid, Porpoise, wore a radiant zone[18]
Girt rather tight around[19] the slender waist,

---

1 shivering] *Token*: blue lipped
2 Nova-Zemblan] from Novaya Zemlya, a large island north of Russia
3 lady] *Token*: madam
4 *Token*: additional line: Shivering and shaking like an ague fit,
5 ll. 10-11] *Token*: In short sleeved barage dress, cut to reveal/The ankle liberally.
6 There] *Token*: Then
7 condemn'd] *Token*: constrained
8 dress] *Token*: frock
9 Before the advent of cheap cottons, most lower-class people dressed in cast-off clothes of the well-to-do.
10 vamp'd up] refurbished
11 Proverbial: it's a bad thing indeed that doesn't do good to somebody.
12 rejoiced] *Token*: was glad
13 Neva: river flowing through Petersburg, former capital of Russia
14 lutestring] from lustring, in turn from French *lustrine*: glossy silk fabric
15 drapery] *Token*: petticoat
16 blonde: a kind of lace
17 The] *Token*: Her
18 zone: belt or girdle.
19 tight around] *Token*: close about

While her embroider'd mouchoir[1] snugly hid
A bottle of Cologne[2] to cheer the bride
During the service. Ogling, near the shore
A Sturgeon[3] stole, her finery to display:
A very stiff brocade,[4] with bishop[5] sleeves,[6]
Making such huge circumference 'twere well
She had no neighbour near; while a smart hat
Envelop'd in its rich rotundity[7]
Her fairy brow.
                    The Seal was taking snuff,
And thrust his box in a bead reticule;[8]
The other rough paw held a parasol
Of parti-colour'd silk, and ivory-staff'd:
'Twas thought the Amphibia, one and all, would find
This fashion quite commodious, in their walks
To leave their cards[9] beneath the[10] summer sun.
—A Shark in a small boat's wake follow'd long;
The sailors[11] thought his purpose was to eat them,[12]
And spread all sail; *but 'twas to be unlaced,*
For he a pair of corsets had rigg'd on,
With busk and bones,[13] just fashionably tight,
But[14] could not bear the torture; so with haste
Panting and flouncing,[15] sought to be released.
Item:[16] Would it not be the surest way[17]

1 mouchoir] delicately fine handkerchief
2 Cologne-water, an alcohol based perfume used to soothe or revive.
3 Sturgeon] highly regarded food fish
4 brocade] rich fabric woven with raised pattern
5 A very stiff ... bishop] *Token*: A mighty robe of silk, with stiffened
6 bishop sleeves] wide sleeves, as on a bishop's attire
7 while a smart hat/Envelop'd in its rich rotundity] *Token*: and on her head/A jaunty bonnet's huge rotundity,/In this last item, her acknowledged taste/Was rendered dubious, as it somewhat hid
8 reticule] small woven bag for personal items, carried on the arm
9 leave their cards] calling on someone only to leave a calling-card
10 the] *Token*: a
11 sailors] *Token*: fisher
12 them] *Token*: him
13 busk] strip of whalebone in front of a corset to stiffen it; bones: strips of whalebone inserted around a corset to strengthen it
14 But] *Token*: Yet
15 flouncing] *Token*: floundering
16 Item] likewise; a term used to introduce a hint, suggestion, or query
17 l. 50] *Token*: Would it not be the surest mode to kill

To kill that[1] hardy and voracious fish,[2]
Which ofttimes foils the harpoon?
Mighty mounds
Of artificial flowers did make the deep
Glow like a greenhouse. Full frisets[3] and curls
Lay unregarded, till a prudish Pike,[4]
Suspected to be somewhat in her wane,
Assumed a wig, declaring[5] it more cool,
And vastly more delightful to the head[6]
Than was the natural hair.
Such varied stores[7]
Of gay gauze robes on seaweed hedges hung,
That the plebeians thought[8] to have a ball
In the old Coral Palace. Thither came
The Codlings,[9] deck'd with drooping Ostrich-plumes,
The purblind Lampreys,[10] each with opera-glass[11]
Uplifted pertly, and gay safety-chain
The gilded watch within their belts to guard;[12]
The Lobsters toiling their red arms to hide
'Neath long kid gloves, and their strange nether limbs
Ensconced in gaiter-boots;[13] while countless[14] shoals
Of Herrings flock'd, false brilliants in their heads[15]
In gorgeous knots; and Crabs with widespread fans,
Aping the elegant, but inly chafed
To find their retrograding step confound

1 To kill that] *Token*: That very
2 voracious fish] the whale
3 frisets] bands of (usually artificial) curls worn around the forehead
4 Pike] slender fish with pointed snout
5 declaring] *Token*: pronouncing
6 l. 58] *Token*: omitted
7 l. 59] *Token*: And pleasant than the natural hair. Such stores
8 That the plebeians thought] *Token*: The "middling interest" vowed
9 Codlings] young codfish
10 Lampreys] eel-shaped fish with sucker-like mouth
11 opera-glass] small telescope or binoculars, originally used for watching opera
12 ll. 64-6] *Token*: The purblind lampreys promenading round / With their pert eye glass and rich safety chain;
13 gaiter-boots] *Token*: satin slippers [gaiter-boots are cloth-covered ladies' boots with black-leather strap, fashionable in 1840]
14 countless] *Token*: such
15 l. 70] *Token*: Of herrings, flocked with ribands dizened out

Their partners, figuring in the favourite waltz.[1]
—A barge of Oysters reach'd St. Petersburgh:
Extremely loth they were to be dissected,
For those[2] sly people in their cloister'd cells,
Close-mouth'd as Achan with[3] his wedge of gold,[4]
Lock'd[5] hoards of jewelry, broaches and rings
Profuse as ancient Cannæ's battle spoil.[6]
—Even thus it is. What bodeth loss to one
Doth prove another's gain. The adversity
Of those French milliners did benefit
The commonwealth of fishes. A few tears,
Brief and soon dried, fill'd the broad sea with joy
And merry pastime. One small spot of earth
Was sad, but what a gorgeous[7] holyday
Held Ocean's myriads!
Sure the tuneful bard[8]
Of Twickenham hath not unjustly styled[9]
"All partial evil universal good."[10]

20. From *Pleasant Memories of Pleasant Lands* (1842).[11]

CARLISLE.[12]

HOW fair, amid the depth of summer green,
Spread forth thy walls, Carlisle! thy castled heights
Abrupt and lofty, thy cathedral dome

---

1 ll. 72-4] *Token*: That scarcely space in that vast hall was found / For one cotillion, or the favorite waltz.

2 those] *Token*: these

3 with] *Token*: o'er

4 In the Bible, Joshua ch. 7, Achan stole goods and was stoned to death.

5 Lock'd] *Token*: Hid

6 The Carthaginians crushed the Romans at the battle of Cannae (216 BCE), taking tens of thousands of gold rings from the dead.

7 gorgeous] *Token*: glorious

8 Sure the tuneful bard] *Token*: Hath not tuneful Pope

9 l. 89] *Token*: In his well measured maxim justly styled

10 English poet Alexander Pope (1688–1744) had a villa at Twickenham, near London; *Essay on Man*, Epistle I, l. 284.

11 Sigourney's account in verse and prose of her tour of Britain and France.

12 American tourists and travel writers were fascinated by European scenery because it seemed steeped in history and treated in literature to

Majestic and alone, thy beauteous bridge
Spanning the Eden, where the angler sits
Patient so long, and marks the browsing sheep
Like sprinkled snow amid the verdant vales.
—Old time hath hung upon thy misty walls
Legends of festal and of warlike deeds.
King Arthur's wassail-cup; the battle-axe
Of the wild Danish sea-kings; the fierce beak
Of Rome's victorious eagle; Pictish spear,
And Scottish claymore, in confusion mixed
With England's cloth-yard arrow. Every helm
And dinted cuirass[1] hath some stirring tale.
—Yet here thou sitt'st as meekly innocent,
As though thine eager lip had never quaffed
Hot streams of kindred blood.

Well pleased thou art
To hear no more the shout of border feuds,
Laying thy frontier annal at the feet
Of the two sister kingdoms, who with smile,
Arm locked in arm, survey their fair domain.
So may the God of love, bless them and thee.
Fresh flowers thou giv'st me from "Queen Mary's Walk,"
Rich red carnations, though to her thy gifts
Were but those bitter weeds and piercing thorns,
Which the poor prisoner plucks.

And so, farewell,
Carlisle! and peace be with thee. Thy sweet scenes
And the deep tones of thy cathedral-hymn,
Telling our sabbath of the choir of heaven,
Went with us as we journeyed.

Many a change
In that delightful landscape cheered the eye,

---

an extent not true of America. "Carlisle" undermines this view, showing European history to be violent and its celebration in literature by Romantic writers such as Sir Walter Scott to be glamorization. "Carlisle" contains a verse tale (from l. 41, "The long day ...") in the style of William Wordsworth, illustrating the consequences of war, reprinted by Sigourney as "To-Morrow." Sigourney's endnotes suggest that Carlisle and its environs, now peaceful and symbolizing the union of England and Scotland, long witnessed warfare between the two. "Carlisle" might also suggest to Americans that civil strife could similarly disrupt their Union and stain their landscape and history.

1 cuirass] torso armour of front and back piece

As onward o'er the pleasant banks of Clyde
We traced the barer hills and brighter streams
Of Caledonia, poor, perchance, in gold,
But rich in song; saw crowned with purple light
The Lady of Branksom's towers, the rolling Esk,
Where the impetuous young Lord Lochinvar[1]
Staid not for ford, the homes of Teviotdale
Fast by the Tweed, and last, the classic domes
Of beautiful Edina.[2] The long day
Sped hastily, and once, as the swift coach
Stopped at its destined goal, an ancient dame
Came from a neighboring cottage, with such speed
As hoary years could make, and earnestly
Scanning each passenger, with hurried tone
Demanded, "*Is he come?*"
"No; not to-day;
To-morrow," was the answer.
So, back she turned,
Lifting her shrivelled finger, with a look
Half-credulous, half-sorrowing, and still
Repeating, "*aye, to-morrow*," homeward went.

'Tis a sad tale. She and her husband led
A life of humble and of honest toil,
Content, though poor. One only son they had
Healthful and bright; and to their eyes he seemed
Exceeding fair. The father was a man
Austere and passionate, and loved his boy,
As fathers often do, with such a pride,
That could not bear the humbling of his faults,
Nor the slow toil to mend them. When he grew
To a tall lad, the mother's readier tact
Discerned that change of character, which meets
With chafing thought the yoke of discipline,
And humored it: but to the sire he seemed
Still as a child, and so he treated him.
When eighteen summers threw a ripening tinge
O'er his bold brow, the father, at some fault,
Born more of carelessness than turpitude,
In anger struck him, bidding him go forth

1 Lochinvar] title and subject of a literary ballad by Sir Walter Scott
2 The rest of this poem was republished by Sigourney as "To-Morrow."

From his own door. The youth, who shared too well
The fiery temper of his father's blood,
Vowed to return no more.
                                        The mother wept,
And wildly prayed her husband to forgive
And call him back; but he with aspect stern
Bade her be still, and harshly said, the boy
Was by her folly and indulgence spoiled
Beyond redemption. So she meekly took
The tear and prayer into her silent soul,
And waited till the passion-storm should slack
And die away. It was a night of woe;
But mid its agony she blest her God,
That, after hours of tossing, quiet sleep
Stole o'er the wrathful man. With the fresh morn
Relentings came, and that ill-smothered pang,
With which an unruled spirit bears its shame;
And then he bade the woman seek her son.
And forth she went. Alas! it was too late;
He was a listed[1] soldier, for a land
Beyond the seas, nor would their little all
Suffice to buy him back.[2]
                                        'Twere long to tell
How loneliness, remorse, and sorrow took
Their Shylock[3] payment for that passion-gust,
And how the father, when his hour was come,
Said, with his pale, pale lips and hollow voice,
"Would that our boy was here," and how the wife
In her kind ministrations round his bed,
And in her widowed mourning, murmured still
His dying words, "would that our boy was here."

Years sped, and oft her soldier's letters came,
Replete with filial love, and penitence
For his rash words. But then the mother's ear
Was tortured by the tidings, that he lay
Wounded and sick in foreign hospitals.

---

1 listed] enlisted

2 buy him back] Soldiers could buy out their remaining military service.

3 Shylock] In Shakespeare's *Merchant of Venice* Shylock lends money to a man on collateral of a pound of the man's flesh, and when the man cannot pay demands the collateral, but is outsmarted by a woman.

A line traced faintly by his own dear hand
Relieved her anguish. He was ordered home
Among the invalids. Joy long unknown
Sat on her brow. Again to hear his voice,
To gaze into his eyes, to part the hair
O'er his clear forehead, to prepare his food,
And nurse his feebleness,—she asked no more.
And so, his childhood's long-forsaken bed
Put forth its snowy pillow, and with care
She hung a curtain of flowered muslin o'er
The little casement, where he used to love
To sit and read. The cushioned chair, that cheered
The father's days of sickness, should be his,
And on the favorite table by its side
The hour-glass, with its ever changing sands,
Which pleased him when a boy.
The morning came.
Slow sped the hours; she heaped the cheerful fire
In the small grate, and ere the coach arrived
Stood, with a throbbing heart, expectant there.
"Is Willy come?" Each traveller intent
On his own business made her no reply:—
"Coachman! is Willy here?"
"No! No! he's dead!
Good woman! dead, and buried near the coast,
Three days ago."
But when a stranger marked
How the strong hues of speechless misery
Changed every feature, he in pity said,
"Perhaps he'll come to-morrow."
Home she turned,
Struck to the heart, and wept the livelong night,
Insensible to comfort: and to those,
Who came in kind compassion to her side,
Answering nothing.
But when day restored
The hour of expectation, with strange zeal
She rose, and dressed, and cast her mantle on,
And as the coachman checked his foaming steeds
Stood closely by his side. "Is Willy here?
Has Willy come?" while he, by pity schooled,
Answered "*to-morrow!*"
And thus years have fled;

And though her steps grow weaker, and the locks
Thinner and whiter on her furrowed brow,
Yet duly, when the shrill horn o'er the hills
Announceth the approaching passenger,
She hurries forth, with wild and wasted eye,
To speak her only question, and receive
That same reply "*to-morrow!*"
And on that
Poor, single fragment doth her yearning heart
Feed and survive. When tottering Reason sank
Beneath the shock of grief, maternal Love
Caught that one word of hope, and held it high,
And grappling to it, like a broken raft,
Still breasts the shoreless ocean of despair.

Monday, August 31, 1840.

[Sigourney's endnotes follow:]

"King Arthur's wassail cup." [l. 10]

Carlisle, principally distinguished as it was in border-warfare, had also, as it appears by ancient chronicles, its share in the festivities of olden time.

"The great King Arthur made a royal feast,
  And kept his merry Christmas at Carlisle,
And thither came the vassals most and least,
  From every corner of the British isle."

Also in an ancient ballad, in Bishop Percy's Reliques, the same allusion is made.

"In Carlisle dwelt King Arthur.
  A prince of passing might,
And there maintained his table round,
  Beset with many a knight,
And there he kept his Christmas,
  With mirth and great delight."[1]

"England's cloth-yard arrow." [l. 14]

Sir Walter Scott says, "In some of the counties in England, distinguished for archery, shafts of this extraordinary length were actually used;" and he thus alludes to them in Marmion.

---

1 Opening lines from "The Boy and the Mantle" in *Reliques of Ancient English Poetry*, ed. Thomas Percy (1765), a collection of ballads.

"Fast ran the Scottish warriors there
Upon the southern band to stare,
And envy with their wonder rose
To see such well appointed foes,
Such length of shaft, such mighty bows,
So large, that many simply thought,
But for a vaunt such weapons wrought,
And little deemed their force to feel
Through links of mail and plates of steel,
When rattling upon Flodden-vale
The cloth-yard arrows flew like hail."

"Queen Mary's Walk." [l. 24]

Some carnations, which were given us from a spot called "The Lady's Walk," we carried with us to Edinburgh, and they retained their freshness and beauty for several days after our arrival there. We visited the remains of the turret, in the castle of Carlisle, where Mary of Scotland[1] was held in confinement, when, after the battle of Langside, she decided to throw herself on the generosity of Elizabeth. We saw also the limits of the promenade, bounded on one side by the moat, where she was permitted to take her daily exercise, guarded by sentinels. Two large ash-trees formerly marked its extreme point, planted, according to tradition, by her own hands. They were numbered among the finest trees of Cumberland, until it was found necessary to cut them down, because they interfered with some architectural design;—I believe, with the construction of a bridge.

We spent some time in examining the Castle, and saw a glorious sunset from its heights. It was built in the reign of Edward the Third; and here his unfortunate grandson, Richard the Second, rested for a night, when making his humiliating journey, in the custody of the aspiring Bolingbroke, afterwards Henry the Fourth. Here, also, Fergus Mac Ivor[2] was imprisoned, and led forth to execution. They pretend to show the print of his hand in a rather soft stone, lining the walls of the cell where he was held in captivity. On the parapets, where the cannon are mounted, I observed a fine, ancient dial, with the following forcible inscrip-

1 Mary of Scotland] Mary, queen of Scots (1542–87) was a favourite literary figure for the woman destroyed by male-dominated political and sexual intrigue; she was forced to seek protection from Elizabeth I of England, who imprisoned her and eventually had her executed.

2 Character in Walter Scott's novel *Waverley* (1814).

tion in gold letters: "Hours and ages are nothing to the Eternal, but as for man, they fix his changeless doom for weal, or woe."

From WESTMINSTER ABBEY.[1]

"A throng is at thy gates."[2]

The contrast between the silence of this receptacle of the mouldering dead, and the ceaseless press and tumult of the living throng without, is strangely impressive. The restlessness and rush of the people, in the most populous parts of London, are among the best helps to a stranger in forming an idea of its magnitude. At first there is a dreaminess, an uncertainty whether one is, of a very truth, in the "world's great wilderness capital."[3] Parts of it are so much like what have been seen at home, that we try to fancy we are still there. Names, too, with which we have been familiar from the lispings of our earliest lessons in geography, or whose imprint was in the most precious picture books of our nursery, assist this illusion. Paternoster Row, Temple Bar, Charing Cross, The Strand, Fleet Street,[4] Bolt Court, from whose sombre windows it is easy to imagine Dr. Johnson[5] still looking out, are to us as household words. But when you see the press and struggle of the living mass, at high noon, through some of the most frequented streets, or when, on some thronged Sabbath in St. Paul's,[6] listen to the tread of the congregation, like the rush of many waters, upon the marble pavement of that vast ornate pile, you begin to realize that you are indeed in the midst of two millions of human beings. A kind of suffocating fear steals for a moment over you, lest you might never get clear of them, and breathe freely in your own native woods again; and then comes a deep feeling, that you are as nothing among them; that

1 Altered very slightly in the second edition (1844); Westminster Abbey: a large Gothic-style medieval church in London, and burial place of many notable Britons, including poets.

2 A throng ... gates] perhaps echoing Alexander Pope's "Messiah: A Sacred Eclogue" (l. 91), "See barbarous nations at thy gate attend"

3 "wilderness capital"] normally used to designate the main town of a newly opened frontier region of the United States

4 Paternoster Row . . . Fleet Street] area of London where many publishers and booksellers were located

5 Bolt Court ... Johnson] home of Samuel Johnson (1709–84), English writer and prototype of the modern man of letters, just off Fleet Street

6 St. Paul's] London's seventeenth-century neo-classical cathedral church

you might fall in the streets and die, unnoticed or trodden down; that with all your home-indulgence, self-esteem, and vanity about you, you are only a speck, a cypher, a sand upon the sea-shore of creation; a humiliating consciousness, heavy, but salutary.

Two millions of human beings! Here they have their habitations, in every diversity of shelter, from the palace to the hovel, in every variety of array, from the inmate of the royal equipage to the poor street-sweeper. Some glittering on the height of wealth and power, others sinking in the depths of poverty and misery. Yet to every heart is dealt its modicum of hope, every lip hath a taste of the bitter bread of disappointment. Death, ever taking aim among them, replenishes his receptacles night and day, while in thousands of curtained chambers, how many arms and bosoms earnestly foster the new-born life, that he may have fresh trophies. For earth and the things of earth, for fancies and forms of happiness, all are scheming, and striving, and struggling, from the little rill, working its way under ground in darkness, and silence, to the great crested wave, that with a thundering echo breaks on the shore of eternity.

21. From *Pleasant Memories of Pleasant Lands*, 2nd edition (1844).

THE ROSE GERANIUM.[1]

HOLD up thy head, thou trembling voyager!
  Vex'd by the storm-clouds, as they darkly roll,
Chid[2] by the fiercely tossing waves that stir
  Thy slender root, and try the timid soul;

Sad change from thy sweet garden, where the dew,
  Each morning glistened in thy grateful eye,
And where no rougher guest thy bosom knew,
  Than quiet bee, or gadding butterfly.

It grieves me sore, to see thy leaflets fade,
  Wearing the plague-spot of the sickening spray,
And know what trouble I for thee have made,
  Yet still bear on, meek partner of my way.

---

1 Not included in the first edition of 1842; first piece in the second edition, 1844; rose geranium: a woody plant with lobed rose-pink flowers and rose-like scent, used in perfumes and sometimes in cooking.

2 Chid] chided

For in thy life I keep the flowery chain
Of home, and its delights,—here on the lonely main.

Thursday, August 13th, 1840.

Flowers have a magic power in retracing the associations of other days.[1] Though our path may have led over the steep and thorny places of the world for many years, yet the unexpected sight of the pale grass-flowers[2] and yellow king-cups,[3] we gathered in childhood, brings back the cool fragrance of life's early morning. If the wearied traveller chance to find, in foreign climes, such plants as he culled by the singing brook of his native glen, the broad-leaved iris,[4] or the bright crimson lobelia,[5] straightway he is a boy again, and shreds them fondly into his mother's lap. The hoary woman, unto whom there remaineth little, save the arm-chair in the chimney-corner,—and the oft repeated counsel to her shouting grand-children,—if she see among its lustrous leaves the pure white Camella,[6] remembers the thrill, with which its damp petals drooped over her forehead at her bridal, and is lost amid the wanderings and dreamings of fairy-land.

The smile, the breath, of our familiar home-flowers restores to us the careless innocence of those days, when half in ignorance, half in faith, we planted the rootless stem of some rich blossom, that had been given us, and heaped the fresh soil tenderly around it, and watered it every moment, and visited it with hope, until it was as brown and dead as the mould, by which it was encompassed. They recall the reckless curiosity, with which we dug up the bulb of our tulip or tube-rose,[7] and found them busy at their work of germination, which our impatience interrupted, perhaps destroyed.

Distant places, and absent friends are brought near by the same talisman. The odor of a pressed flower, between the leaves of a long-closed book, brings back the voice, the form of the loved one who placed it there, whose home may now be in the tomb. I

---

1 The prose passage continues after the poem.

2 grass-flowers] a wide variety of plants are known by this name

3 king-cups] also known as buttercups, or marsh marigolds

4 broad-leaved iris] small iris with purple or mottled flowers

5 crimson lobelia] a perennial with thick upright stem and scarlet flowers

6 Camella] camellia, a popular evergreen shrub, originally from Asia, with white, red, or pink flowers

7 tube-rose] tuberose, plant of the lily family

had sought the sweet trailing arbutus,[1] among the wilds of my native place, when life was new, and a box of it recently performed a journey of many miles, to meet me. The moment it was opened, every breathing blossom spoke of the rocks, which we used to climb in pursuit of it, and of the rough falling waters that filled every pause in our merry voices;—and then suddenly my playmates stood beside me, their baskets overflowing with the gifts of early spring, themselves still young and spring-like, though on the heads of some I knew that the frosts had settled, and that over others rested the green sod.

Still more eloquent was a slender plant of the rose geranium, which accompanied me on my way to an Older World. It was taken from her quiet bed in her garden, by my little daughter, as the parting time drew near, with the remark, that "something green might look pleasant to me on the sea." And so it did. But I imagined not then the depth of communion it would call forth. For the home-spirit was in its heart, and it became to me as a friend. Sometimes, when night closed over the deep,—with those heavy sighs of the wind, which often betoken a coming storm, and the ship leaped and plunged amid the billows, as if seeking for a place to escape, or a depth to hide in, I have drawn closer to that meek plant, as if its love might comfort me. Or at waking in the morning, and raising my head from the coffin-like berth, where the dark hours had passed in such broken slumbers, as the hoarse lullaby of the surge induces, I have fixed my eyes first upon that solitary plant, and spoken softly to it, as to a child. Yet it was evidently in an uncongenial atmosphere, and the delicate branches grew sad, and faded. I numbered its leaves, but almost every day some of them grew sickly and fell, until at last, only a few were left clustering round a single graceful stalk.

We had been thirteen days and nights upon the great deep, and accomplished nearly two thousand miles of our watery journey, when I awoke at the grey hour of dawn. I remembered that it completed the first anniversary of the death of my beloved father, and beckoned its solemn imagery to meet me amid the waves. At once, every circumstance of that scene gleamed forth as in a picture. His venerable head resting upon its white pillow, the brightness of his beautiful hair, on which fourscore and seven winters had scattered no snows, his heavy breathing mingled with the gentle dropping of the summer-shower, upon the vine-leaves

1 arbutus] a flowering tree, in America also called ground laurel, or mayflower, regarded as a harbinger of spring

at his casement, and the measured tick of the clock, through that lonely night while bending over him, I hoped against hope, that the sudden illness might not be mortal, and that the form, which but the day before had moved with so vigorous a step, would yet rise up, and lean upon its staff, and come forth to bless me. The rain ceased, a circle of faint brightness foretold the rising of the sun, those precious lips, uttered again the sound of kind words,—the opening eyes told their message of saintly love, the lids fluttered and closed. There was no more breath.

A wail! Another—piercing and protracted, deeper even than that with which an only child mourns the last parent. It must be the wail of a mother. No other sorrow hath such a voice. Yet so abruptly it burst forth, amid deep and silent meditation, that for a moment memory was bewildered, and the things, which had been, mingled their confused tissue with things that are.

Among our passengers, was a dignified and accomplished lady, returning with her husband, an officer, from a residence of several years in Canada, to England, their native land. They had with them three little daughters, and in the course of those conversations, which beguile the tedium of sea-life, she had sometimes spoken of the anxiety with which her aged mother waited to welcome these descendants, born in a foreign clime, whom of course she had never seen; and so exquisite was their beauty, that it would not have been surprising, had a thrill of pride heightened the pleasure with which she painted the joy of such a meeting. The youngest was a babe of less than a year, and we, who often shared its playful wile, fancied that it had grown languid as if from some inherent disease. Yet its large black eyes still beamed with strange lustre, so that neither the parents nor nurse would allow that aught affected it, save what arose from the change of habits, incidental to the confinement of the ship. Yet, that night, the mother more uneasy than she was willing to allow, decided not to leave its cradle. In the saloon adjoining our state-room she took her place, and when we retired, the fair infant lay in troubled sleep. Yet even then, the spoiler[1] was nearer to it than the watchful mother, and ere the morning, he smote it in her arms. We found her clasping it closely to her bosom, as if fain to revivify it with her breath. Masses of glossy black hair, escaped from their confinement, fell over her shoulders, and drooped as a curtain over the marble features of the dead. Mingled with gasps of grief, that shook her like a reed, were exclamations of hope,

1 the spoiler] one of Sigourney's favourite terms for death

that hope, which clings and cleaves to the wounded heart, striking its fibres, wherever the blood-drop oozes, and striving, like a pitying angel, to staunch where it may not heal. "Constance, Constance! look at me! Oh my dear husband, she *will* live again. She has been sicker than this once, when you were away. Yes, yes, she will breathe again." Long she continued, thus assuaging her bitter sorrow, with this vanity of trust, and then we tenderly strove to loosen her convulsive grasp, from the lifeless idol. After we had prevailed, and it was borne from her sight, we still heard, in the pauses of the soothing voice, with which her husband sought to console her, the wild cry, "She will breathe again! I saw her sweet lips move, as they took her from me! My baby *will* live again!"

It was laid out on our sofa in the ladies' cabin, in a pure white robe, its brow surpassingly beautiful, and the deeply fringed lids, but imperfectly closed over its large lustrous eyes. The black lace veil of the mother, shaded its form and features, and through it was clearly visible the last green slip of my rose-geranium. It was my gift to the dead, and pressed into that little pale hand, not without a tear. This was the last office of that cherished plant, which had left its own home, in the quiet gardens of New-England, to do this service to faded innocence, and itself to die. Happy shall we be, if in the closing of our frail life, we, like this trembling voyager, leave behind a gleam of light and consolation, as the olive-leaf above the flood, or the dove whose last act was peace, ere it entered rejoicing into the ark, to be a wanderer no more.[1]

22. From *Poetry for Seamen* (1845).

THE WHALER'S SONG.[2]

THERE she lies!—There she lies!
Like a mountain-isle on Ocean's breast.
"*Where away?*" Just three points west,

---

1 In the Bible, book of Genesis, God floods earth to punish sinning humanity, but tells Noah to build an ark, or ship, to save himself, family, and certain animals and birds. In time, Noah sends a dove to seek land; it returns with an olive-branch, henceforth symbol of reconciliation.

2 The 1840s were the heyday of world whaling, with New England whalers hunting into the Pacific and supplying oil for lubricants and lighting, fat for candles, bone for corsets and other articles, and ambergris for perfumes.

Where the white surge meets the skies.
Head the vessel! Trim the sail!
Let us see this mighty whale.

There she blows!—There she blows!
Man the boats! for nothing stay!
Such a prize we cannot lose,
Stretch to your oars! away! away!
Grapple closer, careful steer,
Launch the harpoon, laugh at fear,
Plunge it deep, the barbed spear,
Strike the lance, in swift career,
Give her line! Give her line!
Down she goes, through the foaming brine,
Sponge the side, where the flying coil
Marks the monster's speed and toil;
But though she dives to the deepest ground,
Which the plummet fails to sound,
'Tis all in vain! All in vain!
She hath that within her side,
Will surely bring her up again.

Spout! Spout! Spout!
The waves are maddening all about,
Every billow on its head
Strangely wears a crest of red;
How she lashes the seething main,
In her flurry and her pain;
Take good heed, my hearts of oak,
Of her terrible flukes, as she tortured lies,
Lest they hurl us to the skies:
But lo! the pride of her strength is broke,
Heavy she lies, as a mass of lead,
The mighty-monarch whale is dead!

Row! Row! Row!
In our ship she must go,
Changed by fire to a liquid stream,
Over the broad Pacific's swell,
Round Cape Horn, where the tempests dwell,

Many a night and many a day,
Home with us, she must sail away,
Till we joyful hail once more,
Old Nantucket's treeless shore;
There when the fair whom we love to please,
Sit by the fireside at their ease,
Let them remember, if they will,
The hardy tar, who on seas afar
Risked his life their lamp to fill.

23. From *Scenes in My Native Land* (1845).[1]

From NIAGARA.[2]

UP to the Table-Rock, where the great flood
Reveals its fullest glory. To the verge
Of its appalling battlement draw near,
And gaze below. Or if thy spirit fail,
Creep stealthily, and snatch a trembling glance
Into the dread abyss.[3]
                    What there thou see'st
Shall dwell forever in thy secret soul,
Finding no form of language.
                    The vexed deep,
Which from the hour that Chaos heard the voice
"Let there be light,"[4] hath known nor pause, nor rest,
Communeth through its misty cloud with Him
Who breaks it on the wheel[5] of pitiless rock,
Yet heals it every moment. Bending near,
Mid all the terror, as an angel-friend,

---

1 A series of verse and prose accounts of various places in the northern United States.

2 The opening section of the book; see also "Niagara" (p. 152).

3 dread abyss] one of many references in the poem to the sublime, thought to be characterized by power, vastness, obscurity, and grandeur, beyond the power of language to represent, inspiring almost overwhelming awe, and causing morally beneficial suspension of self-awareness; often associated with the masculine; here given a religious turn, making Niagara an earthly manifestation of God.

4 "Let ... light"] god's command initiating creation of the earth and cosmos, in the Bible, Genesis 1.3

5 breaks it on the wheel] torture in which a victim bound to a wheel has his joints and limbs broken

The rainbow[1] walketh in its company
With perfect orb full-rounded. Dost thou cling
Thus to its breast, a Comforter, to give
Strength in its agony, thou radiant form,
Born of the trembling tear-drop, and the smile
Of sun, or glimmering moon?
                                        Yet from a scene
So awfully sublime, our senses shrink,
And fain would shield them at the solemn base
Of the tremendous precipice, and glean
Such hallowed thoughts as blossom in its shade.

This is thy building, Architect Divine![2]
Who heav'dst the pillars of the Universe.
Up, without noise, the mighty fabric rose,
And to the clamor of the unresting gulf
Forever smiting on its ear of rock
With an eternal question, answereth nought.
Man calls his vassals forth, with toil and pain;
Stone piled on stone, the pyramid ascends,[3]
Yet ere it reach its apex-point, he dies,
Nor leaves a chiseled name upon his tomb.
The vast cathedral grows, with deep-groined arch,
And massy dome, slow reared,[4] while race on race
Fall like the ivy sere, that climbs its walls,
The imperial palace towers, the triumph arch,
And the tall fane[5] that tells a hero's praise
Uplift their crowns of fret-work haughtily.[6]
But lo! the Goth dost waste them, and his herds

---

1 rainbow] caused by constant mist from the falls, and in the Bible (Genesis ch. 8) a sign of God's covenant not to use a cataclysm such as the great flood again to punish sinning humanity

2 Architect Divine] reference to a well-known argument for God's existence from the apparently intelligent design of the universe

3 pyramid ascends] Ancient Egyptian Pharaohs built huge pyramids as tombs, but in Sigourney's day their occupants' names remained unknown.

4 slow reared] Medieval cathedrals took centuries to build.

5 fane] temple, a common poeticism

6 The imperial palace ... haughtily] Roman imperial monuments, in ruins by Sigourney's day

The Vandal pastures mid their fallen pride.[1]
But thou, from age to age, unchanged hast stood,
Even like an altar to Jehovah's name,[2]
Silent, and steadfast, and immutable.
Niagara and the storm-cloud!
                    To the peal
Of their united thunder, rugged rocks
Amazed reverberate, through depths profound
Streams the red lightning, while the loftiest trees
Bow, and are troubled. Shuddering earth doth hide
In midnight's veil; and even the ethereal mind,
Which hath the seed of immortality
Within itself,—not undismayed, beholds
This fearful tumult of the elements.

Old Ocean meets the tempest and is wroth,
And in his wrath destroys. The wrecking ship,
The sea-boy stricken from the quaking mast,
The burning tear wrung from many a home,
To which the voyager returns no more,
Attest the fury of his vengeful mood.
But thou, Niagara, know'st no passion-gust;
Thy mighty bosom, from the sheeted rain,
Spreads not itself to sudden boastfulness,
Like the wild torrent in its shallow bed.
Thou art not angry, and thou changest not.

Man finds in thee no emblem of himself:
The cloud depresseth him, the adverse blast
Rouseth the billows of his discontent,
The wealth of summer-showers inflates his pride,
And with the simple faith and love of Him
Who made him from the dust,[3] he mingleth much
Of his own vain device. Perchance, even here,
Neath all the sternness of thy strong rebuke,
Light fancies fill him, and he gathereth straws

---

1 the Goth ... pride] Goths and Vandals: Germanic tribes who ravaged the Roman empire from the third to sixth centuries CE

2 Jehovah] Biblical name for God

3 made him from the dust] In the Bible, book of Genesis, God makes Adam, the first man, from clay, or dust, to which the body returns after death; dust also symbolizes fleshly weakness and desire.

Or plaiteth rushes, or illusive twines
Garlands of hope, more fragile still than they.

But in one awful voice, that ne'er has known
Change or inflection since the morn of time,
Thou utterest forth that One Eternal Name,
Which he who graves not on his inmost soul
Will find his proudest gatherings, as the dross
That cannot profit.
                                        Thou hast ne'er forgot
Thy lesson, or been weary, day or night,
Nor with its simple, elemental thought
Mixed aught of discord.
                                        Teacher, sent from God,
We bow us to thy message, and are still.

Oh! full of glory, and of majesty,
With all thy terrible[1] apparel on,
High-priest of Nature, who within the veil,
Mysterious, unapproachable dost dwell,[2]
With smoke of incense[3] ever streaming up,
And round thy breast, the folded bow[4] of heaven,
Few are our words before thee.
                                                  For 'tis meet
That even the mightiest of our race should stand
Mute in thy presence, and with childlike awe,
Disrobed of self, adore his God through thee.

"Deep calleth unto deep, at the noise of thy water-spouts."[5] Most appositely did the poet Brainerd, in his beautiful apostrophe to Niagara,[6] quote from the inspired Minstrel, "deep calleth unto deep."[7] Simple and significant also, was its Indian appellation, the "water-thunderer."[8] To the wandering son of the forest,

1 terrible] awe-inspiring
2 veil ... dwell] In ancient temples, such as Jerusalem's, a veil or curtain covered the holiest place, to which the high priest alone had access.
3 incense] used in acts of ritual and worship
4 bow] rainbow
5 The Bible, Psalms 42.7.
6 American poet John G.C. Brainerd (1796–1828), "The Fall of Niagara."
7 The Bible, Psalms (42.7), composed by David, the "inspired Minstrel."
8 One version of the meaning of the aboriginal word "Niagara."

"whose untutored mind
Saw God in clouds, or heard him in the wind,"[1]

it forcibly suggested the image of that Great Spirit, who in darkness and storm sends forth from the skies a mighty voice.

The immense volume of water, which distinguishes Niagara from all other cataracts, is seldom fully realized by the casual visitant. Transfixed by his emotions, he forgets that he sees the surplus waters of these vast inland seas, Superior, Huron, Michigan, and Erie, arrested in their rushing passage to the Ocean, by a fearful barrier of rock, 160 feet in height. He scarcely recollects that the tributaries to this river, or strait, cover a surface of 150,000 miles. Indeed, how can he bow his mind to aught of arithmetical computation, when in the presence of this monarch of floods.

Niagara river flows from south to north, and is two miles in width when it issues from Lake Erie. It is majestic and beautiful[2] in its aspect, and spreads out at Grand Island to a breadth of three miles, like a mirrored lake. At the Falls, it is less than a mile broad, and after emerging from its terrible abyss, flows on of a dark green or violet color, until it reaches the whirlpool. There, compressed to between 5 and 600 feet, it rushes upon a bed of sharp rocks, boiling and breaking with great velocity and suction. After many curves, it regains its original course, and having cleared itself of every conflict and trouble, glides with a placid loveliness to the bosom of Ontario. Altogether, it is a most noble river. Sprinkled with many islands, of a depth of 2 or 300 feet, and in some places unfathomable, it flows between banks sometimes 500 feet in height, having a descent of nearly 350 feet from its efflux at Erie, to its junction with Ontario. Not like those streams, which at some seasons run low in their channels, and at others swollen with a "little brief authority,"[3] inundate the surrounding country, it preserves the uniform characteristics of power and majesty.

---

1 Alexander Pope, *An Essay on Man*, Epistle I (1733), 95–96; echoed by American poet R.T. Paine (1773-1811) in "Bright is the sun beam": "E'en savage Indians, with untutored souls,/See God in clouds, and hear him in the winds" (*Works*, 1812, ll. 139–40).

2 Both sublime and beautiful, the latter characterized as pleasing, soothing, elevating, morally educative, and associated with the feminine, in contrast to the awe-inspiring, overwhelming, masculine sublime.

3 Shakespeare, *Measure for Measure*, 2.2.119, Isabella, of "man, proud man."

The Rapids commence about three quarters of a mile above the Falls. The river, after passing Grand and Navy Islands, becomes suddenly compressed, and opposed by ledges of rugged rocks. Over a succession of these it leaps with impetuosity. The total descent is not more than sixty feet, but the effect is grand and imposing. It is more picturesque[1] on the American shore, where the water is less deep, and the conflict more palpable.

These Rapids are exceedingly beautiful, and it is desirable to secure an apartment overlooking them, where the traveller, in the intervals of exploration, may contemplate them from his window. They are an appropriate preparation for the grandeur of the principal cataract, a preface to a volume of unutterable wonders.

The intersection of the river at the termination of the Rapids, by Goat Island, gives to Great Britain and America a distinct, though unequal partnership in this glorious cataract. The former, or Great Horseshoe Fall, has far greater breadth, and quantity of water. The latter has somewhat more height, and is surpassingly graceful, though less terrific than its compeer. The intervention of Luna, or, as it is sometimes called, Prospect Island, causes another subdivision on the American side, and forms the Central or Crescent Fall, a cascade of surpassing beauty. The Great Fall on the Canadian shore, is 2100 feet in extent, and 158 in height; the American 164 in height, and, including the Crescent Fall, has a breadth of more than 1000 feet. In comparing the British and American Falls, we cannot do better than to use the words of an English traveller, the Rev. Dr. Reed. "The character of one is beautiful, inclining to the sublime, that of the other sublime, inclining to the beautiful."[2]

A bridge of 150 feet, constructed with immense labor and peril, connects the main land of the American shore with Bath Island, from whence a shorter one of about thirty yards gives access to Goat Island. This extends half a mile in length, and a quarter in breadth, and is one of the most delightful spots that can be imagined. It is covered with lofty and magnificent trees, and in its rich mould[3] a great variety of wild plants and flowers find nutriment. It is an unspeakable luxury here to sit in solitary meditation, at once lulled and solemnized by the near voice of the everlasting torrent. It seems the most fascinating of all the haunts

1 picturesque] distinguished from both the sublime and the beautiful, as striking, interesting, and pleasing, but a lesser quality

2 Andrew Reed, *A Narrative of the Visit to the American Churches by the Deputation from the Congregational Union of England and Wales* (1835).

3 mould] soil

in this vicinity; the one where we earliest linger, and latest depart. We take leave of it, as from a being of intelligence, to whom we have given our heart. It has shielded us, when our senses were awe-stricken and overpowered, like the cliff where the prophet was hidden when that majesty passed by which none can "see and live."[1]

Embellishments have been spoken of for this island, rustic temples, and winding gravel-walks.[2] It would be a pity to see them here: a desecration to remove for them one of those trees which for ages have struck their roots deep in the soil, every green leaf baptized by the spray of the cataract. Modern decoration would but detract from its solemn beauty. A few seats placed here and there, where the sight of the falling waters best blend with their thunder-hymn, might be a convenience, as would also some improvements for the sake of those of weak nerves, in the carriage-drive around its shores.

At the entrance of this sweet and sacred solitude, a neat cottage, with a fine garden attracts the eye, where flowers, fruits, and other refreshments may be obtained from the worthy couple, natives of Caledonia's romantic clime.[3] It was pleasant to perceive the restrictions on a board placed over the gate, that the hallowed day of rest would be exempted from this traffic. Here, and at other places in the neighborhood, are a great variety of Indian fancy-work, in beads, bark, and porcupine quills, from whence keepsakes for friends at home may be readily selected. The vicinity of the Tuscaroras, Senecas, and Oneidas, with the industry of their females, keeps the market well supplied for its various purchasers.

The village of Niagara possesses sufficient accommodations in its large hotels, for the throngs of visitants who resort thither during the summer. It has two churches, several mills, and about 600 inhabitants. A descent of 200 feet by a stair-case brings you to the Ferry, which conducts to the Canadian shore. At the base of the first flight of steps is a delightful view of the American Fall. The beauty and grace of the watery column, so fleecy, so sparkling, so flecked with the brightest emerald hue, surpass all description.

---

1 The Bible, Exodus 33.20, where God tells Moses, "Thou canst not see my face: for there shall no man see me, and live."

2 rustic temples ... gravel-walks] ornamental features in the grounds of European and American country mansions

3 Caledonia] Scotland, then considered "romantic" or characteristic of romances of adventure appealing to the passions and imagination

The view from the boat while crossing the Ferry is unique and impressive. It gives the first strong idea of the greater magnificence that awaits you. You are encompassed by an amphitheatre of towering rocks and hills. Fragments of rainbows and torrents of mist hover around you. A stupendous column rises, whose base is in the fathomless depth, whose head wrapt in cloud, seems to join earth and heaven. It strikes you as a living personification of His power who poured it "from the hollow of his hand."[1] You tremble at its feet. With a great voice of thunder it warns you not to approach. The winds spread out their wings and whelm you in a deluge of spray. You are sensible of the giant force of the tide, bearing up the boat, which like an egg-shell is tossed upon its terrible bosom. You feel like an atom in the great creation of God. You glance at the athletic sinews of the rowers, and wonder if they are equal to their perilous task. But the majesty of the surrounding scene annihilates selfish apprehension, and ere you are aware, the little boat runs smoothly to her haven, and you stand on the Canadian shore.

Hitherto, all you have seen, will convey but an imperfect impression of the grandeur and sublimity that are unfolded on the summit of Table-Rock. This is a precipice nearly 160 feet in height, with flat, smooth, altar-shaped surface. As you approach this unparapeted projection, the unveiled glory of Niagara burst upon the astonished senses. [...]

[The narrative quotes Daniel Wadsworth's description of the view and continues the tour, including a visit to the Canadian side, and concludes:]

No one, unless impelled by necessity, should make a short stay at Niagara. A week scarcely suffices for its more prominent features. It should be seen not only at morn, at noon-day, and the sun-setting, but in darkness, and beneath the exquisite tinting of the lunar-bow. It is desirable so to arrange the excursion, as to meet there, the summer-moon at full. Those who have journeyed there in winter, pronounce the scenery to be gorgeous beyond all powers of the imagination.

The lover of Nature's magnificence will scarcely be satisfied without repeated visits to Niagara. The mind is slow in receiving the idea of great magnitude. It requires time and repetition to expand and deepen the perceptions that overwhelm it. This edu-

---

1 The Bible, Isaiah 40.12.

cating process is peculiarly necessary among scenery, where the mind is continually thrown back upon its Author,[1] and the finite, trying to take hold of the Infinite, falters and hides itself in its own nothingness.

It is impossible for Niagara to disappoint, unless through the infirmity of the conception that fails to grasp it. Its resources are inexhaustible. It can never expend itself, because it points always to God. More unapproachable than the fathomless ocean, man cannot launch a bark upon its bosom, or bespeak its service in any form. He may not even lay his hand upon it, and live.[2] Upon its borders he can dream, if he will, of gold-gathering, and of mill-privileges;[3] but its perpetual warning is, "Hence, ye profane!"[4]

Let none, who have it in their power to change their places at will, omit a pilgrimage to Niagara. The facilities of travelling render it now a very different exploit from what it was in the days of our fathers, who were forced to cut away with their axes the branches intercepting the passage of the rocky roads. Those whose hearts respond to whatever is beautiful and sublime in creation, should pay their homage to this mighty cataract. No other scenery so powerfully combines these elements.

Let the gay go thither to be made thoughtful, and the religious to become more spiritually-minded. Yet let not the determined trifler linger here to pursue his revels. Frivolity seems an insult to the majesty that presides here. Folly and dissipation are surely out of place. The thunder-hymn of the mighty flood reproves them. Day and night it seems to repeat and enforce the words of inspiration: "The Lord is in his holy temple: let all the earth keep silence before Him."[5]

---

1 Author] God

2 He may not ... live] In the Bible (Exodus ch. 19), God instructs Moses to call the people to mount Sinai to hear His commandments but forbids a hand to touch the mount until a trumpet sounds.

3 mill-privileges] the right to use water to drive a mill; an American usage

4 profane] secular, but also morally polluted, irreverent, or blasphemous

5 The Bible, Habakkuk 2.20.

24. From *Myrtis: with Other Etchings and Sketchings* (1846).[1]

THE YANKEE.[2]

"Strange phrase and quaint, but spirit shrewd,
And heart with pious thoughts embued."[3]

THERE is sometimes a period in the life of nations, as well as of individuals, when the energies work in diseased channels, and a morbid imagination pictures "destruction before them, and sorrow behind."[4] Such seemed the condition of the oldest colony, the mother of New England,[5] when about to pass the seventieth year of her existence.[6]

Within her borders she beheld a savage foe,[7] wronged and inexorable, the print of whose stealthy footstep was red with the blood of the defenceless. The fathers who had been her guides; the ancient priests, whose wisdom was as the Urim and Thummim[8] to the multitude, were with the dead. We, in whose minds respect for age is less deeply rooted than of old, can but imperfectly realize the "horror of great darkness"[9] that settled upon her soul as the last vestiges of that patriarchal race disappeared. One by one the stars were muffled, the beacon-lights withdrawn, and she left to steer her lonely barque amid the troubled waters.

---

1 A collection of thirteen pieces of prose fiction set in various times and places from antiquity to Sigourney's present, most centred on female protagonists exercising forms of domestic heroism.

2 First published as "Jehiel Wigglesworth" in the *Amaranth: A Literary and Religious Offering* for 1831, ed. J.H. Buckingham (Newburyport: Charles Whipple), 67–89, with a different opening section in place of the first five paragraphs here, and many other differences; Yankee: term of uncertain origin for an inhabitant of New England, and the northern states generally.

3 Not identified; possibly by Sigourney herself.

4 Adapted from James Beattie, "The Hermit," *Poems on Several Occasions* (1776), l. 36.

5 Massachusetts.

6 The story is set in the 1690s, at the time of the Salem witchcraft panic.

7 Savage foe] aboriginal peoples

8 Urim and Thummim] in the Bible, an oracle

9 The Bible, Exodus 15.12, of the patriarch Abraham asleep at sunset: "and, lo, an horror of great darkness fell upon him."

Other causes conspired to harass and depress the people: heavy taxation; the almost utter extinction of commerce; and a sea-coast infested by piratical cruisers. France, irritated by a recent invasion of Canada, menaced the colonies with her vengeance. "They were becoming," says Upham, in his Lectures, "the victims of political jealousies, discontent, and animosities; their minds were startled and confounded by forebodings of dark and dismal events; and, as it were, to crown the whole, and fill up the measure of their affliction and terror, it was their universal and sober belief, that the Evil Being[1] himself was in a special manner let loose, and permitted to descend upon them with unexampled fury."[2]

It was from the midst of this discomfort and gloom, this "fearful looking-for of judgment,"[3] that the delusion at Salem sprang forth.[4] Though not without precedent in an older continent, it derived peculiar elements of sternness and inveteracy from the locality and circumstances of its birth. Few of those influences that soften and unbend the minds of men were then in operation. Literature and science[5] gave but a feeble infusion of their spirit, and social intercourse seldom sparkled with hilarity. Seeds of religious dissension were vegetating, and whatever form of bitterness or superstition seized upon the mind, was pursued with the exclusiveness of monomania.

An isolated and ascetic state of feeling was doubtless nourished by the tardy and infrequent communication between the settlements. No post-roads or periodicals diffused intelligence, and, penetrating to the most remote solitudes, bound the extremities to the heart in strong and warm vitality. The adventurous traveler encountered not only fatigue, but peril, for he knew that he must pass dense and overshadowing forests, where the watchful Indian prowled. So slow was the transmission of news, that the awful tragedy at Salem, which commenced early in 1692, did not reach for several months a colony of Huguenots, planted

---

1 Evil Being] first of many euphemisms for Satan found here

2 Charles Wentworth Upham, *Lectures on Witchcraft* (1831), later recast as *History of Witchcraft and Salem Village* (1867); also a source for Nathaniel Hawthorne's *The House of Seven Gables* (1851).

3 From the Bible, Paul's letter to the Hebrews 10.27.

4 delusion ... sprang forth] reference to Charles MacKay, *Extraordinary Popular Delusions and the Madness of Crowds* (1841), an early work of social psychology, with a chapter on various witchcraft panics

5 science] knowledge

about forty miles from Boston.[1] Few in number, and occupied with those labors on which existence depended, vague rumors, as of some distorted and horrible dream, at length floated to their hermit residence.

It was at that period when autumn fosters the fading beauties of summer, and yet announces the approach of winter by infusing a slight chill into the evening atmosphere. The harvest of maize had been principally gathered and deposited in a rude tenement, which served as a public granary. Lights were seen there to glimmer, after they had one by one vanished from the surrounding habitations. A few men, employed in separating the golden sheaves from their investing sheath, still prolonged their pleasant toil, listening to the narrations of a hardy New England yeoman, who for the past year had assisted these more delicate natives of France in the ruder labors of husbandry. While in the midst of an animated description of the festivities of what he called a "real huskin' frolic,"[2] which he had sometimes shared among his own people, he was interrupted by a heavy knock at the door, and the sudden entrance of a wearied stranger. A word or two in an under-tone caused an exclamation of amazement.

"Why, Cousin Jehiel[3] Wigglesworth! it can't be you! in such torn and awful riggin'! Have the Indians come down upon Malden? and was you necessitated to fly for your life?"

"Indians, do ye say? What is a host of cowardly heathen to the terrible visitations of the spirits of darkness? We read in the Bible of only *one* witch of Endor,[4] and she busied herself with calling up the dead; but Salem town is full of witches, from one eend to t'other, and they do nothing but torment the living."

To the inquiry of his cousin respecting the reasons of his removal from Malden, their native place, he answered, "You know I come of age last winter, and so I told father he might as well get some work out of brother Titus,[5] who is a stout young-

---

1 Huguenots ... Boston] The Edict of Nantes granted religious toleration to Protestants, or Huguenots, in France, but after revocation of the Edict in 1685 a group, including forebears of Sigourney's husband, settled Oxford, MA, as depicted in "Legend of Oxford" in *Sketches* (1834).

2 frolic] party or merrymaking, here for communal husking of corn; an early nineteenth-century Americanism

3 Jehiel] name of several persons in the Bible, meaning "God's living one"; early Puritans often named children after Biblical characters

4 witch of Endor] name of a sorceress in the Bible, 1 Samuel 28.7

5 Titus] in the Bible, name of a helper of the apostle Paul

ster, and I would go and hire myself out a spell and 'arn a little money. I had heard of a minister in Salem, one Mr. Parris,[1] who wanted help, and I reckoned 'twould be a good notion to live with a minister, because, their portion not being in this world, they would not be likely to insist on so much hard slaving. But I was rather discomfited at our first meeting. He observed that he was particular in inquiring the character of *sarvants*, because he chose to have only those of good report. '*Sarvants!*' said I; 'I never was any body's *sarvant*, and I never mean to be.' So I turned to go off, thinking he was too mighty topping[2] for me. But he said over a text or two of Scripture, which made me as quiet as a lamb, how that we all had a Master in heaven, and that he only wanted me to be his *help*.[3] Then I felt ashamed that I had been so mad and hasty, and made an agreement with him, and lived quiet and peaceable, till I was carried to Salem jail."

"To the jail! to the jail! You don't say so! None of our relations ever come to such disgrace before! No wonder you look so exceedin' dumpish.[4] Tell me all that you did, without any prevarication."

"Cousin Jehoshaphat[5] Jones, have a little patience. Every thing in its right place. I guess you had better hear first consarning my dealings at the minister's. My business was to dig in the gardin, and to chop wood, and to take care of the dumb critturs, which consisted of an old horse, quite lean in flesh, and a cow with balls at her horns, 'cause she routed down fences when she could get a chance, and a flock of hens, which it was a power of trouble to watch and scare out of the neighbor's corn; moreover, to mind the minister's wife in all she directed."

"And was it really a great sight easier to live with a minister than to be on the good old farm at home? Did you get enough to eat?"

"I liked all well enough except the Sabba-day dinners; for then they never got any victuals. They are no upholders of fasting in Boston; they understood good eating and drinking there right well.

1 Rev. Samuel Parris, born in London, England, 1653; failed as sugar planter in Barbados and as merchant in Boston; became minister at Salem in 1689; involved in 1692 Salem witch trials because his daughter and niece claimed to have been tormented by Satan.

2 topping] domineering; an early nineteenth-century Americanism

3 help] specifically a hired labourer; a seventeenth-century Americanism

4 dumpish] sad, "in the dumps"

5 Jehoshaphat] name meaning "the Lord has judged"; in the Bible, fourth king of Judah

But Salem folks seemed to me more for skinching[1] and saving. However, there was really nothing worth complaining on, till them great and grievous trials come down like a clap of thunder. The minister's darter and his niece, who lived with them, both smart, sprightly gals of eleven or twelve years old, were brought all of a sudden under the power of the Evil One, and tormented just like the children of Mr. John Goodwin at North Boston, a few years before.[2] Cousin Jehoshaphat, did not you read that marvelous account published by a godly and larned minister?"[3]

"Yes, I did; but it seemed to me a deal more like their own ugliness than any other sort of witchcraft."

"Jehoshaphat Jones, just in that same way other bold ones blasphemed and made their mocks, but some of them got hung upon the gallows like proud Haman,[4] a spectacle to heaven and airth. It is true that them two gals was the most tormentedest critters that eyes ever beheld. Sometimes we'd find them a standing in brooks of water, saying that the Wicked One wanted to drown 'em; then they'd be a clinging to the tops of high trees, where they'd no way in natur' of getting, crying out that he commanded 'em to throw themselves down from thence."

"Jehiel, wasn't there apples or some sort of fruit on them trees? I guess I've seen children climb pretty decent high arter[5] green apples, without no supernatural help."

"Well, what should they run upon the ridge-pole of the barn, and bemoan themselves there for? You don't s'pose any green apples grew there, do ye? And when the poor souls set down to comfort themselves with a meal of victuals, who do you calculate[6] drew their tongues out of their mouths, and laid them all along upon their chins, so that they were not able to eat a single mou'ful?"

"I don't know. I guess they did not see any thing they liked on the table, and thought they'd make a push to get something more to their taste."

"Who do you reckon[7] run pins into 'em, and left the marks of

1 skinching] encroaching

2 few years before] in 1688

3 minister] Cotton Mather (1663–1728), *Memorable Providences, Relating to Witchcrafts and Possessions* (Boston, 1689)

4 Haman] villain in the Bible, book of Esther, who plots with his wife to kill Mordechai and the Jews in Persia but is foiled by queen Esther and hung with his ten sons on the gallows he had intended for Mordechai

5 arter] after; a colloquialism

6 calculate] think, suppose; an early nineteenth-century Americanism

7 reckon] think, suppose; an Americanism by the early nineteenth century, mainly in the Southern states

great pinches and bites on their innocent flesh? And what made 'em, when they was told only to do the least little chore, fall into fits like one about to die?"

"Why, Jehiel, I have made believe to be sick myself, when I was a small boy, and told to hoe corn or weed the gardin; but I was always mighty well if any play was going on. And I have seen bigger folks sarve their master in that way time and again. Who pinched and bit those gals, I don't undertake to say; but I rather guess, if the minister had given them a smart box on the ear, as father used to me, they'd gone to work and felt better."

"It is very likely, to be sure, that with your poor edecation you should know more of their case than all the wise and rich gentlemen who come to see and pity 'em, and the host of ministers too, who used to pray and exhort over 'em. And when them that was the most gifted, and could hold out the longest, were a putting up petitions, it was awful to see the sufferings of them children. Every inch of their flesh would tremble, as if the Evil Spirit was about to come out of 'em, but it was only because he was mad and tired to hear the precious saints communing so long with the Lord. Then the poor babes might not enjoy the comfort of saying the Lord's Prayer themselves; for they'd always be forced to leave out some part of it. And when Mr. Parris would say, 'Begin again, and say it right,' they'd be speechless. Neither was they permitted to read a single godly book, whereby their souls might 'a been comforted under their body's tribulation. The wicked sarpent would allow them to read silly stories and jeest books, to be sure, and if they was particular unchristian and bad, they'd giggle and shout till even the neighbors heard the racket. But when the Assembly of Divines' Catechize[1] was put into their hands, oh! such whooping and hollowing; and if it was not taken directly out of their sight, they'd have the terriblest fits, and scare the minister's wife nigh upon to death."

"Law,[2] Cousin Jehiel, as for that monstrous long catechize, I'd have screamed as bad as they, and had as many fits, if I could only frightened mother out of the notion of making me larn it."

"Jehoshaphat Jones, I feel bound to say unto you what holy Mr. Baxter saith in his preface to the book about John Goodwin's afflicted offspring: 'He that disbelieveth, must needs be a most

---

1 Catechize] catechism or book of religious instruction by question and answer, learned by rote, specifically the "Westminster catechism" approved by Presbyterian Calvinists ("Assembly of Divines") in 1648

2 Law] an exclamation from "lo" or "la," and later a version of "Lord"

obstinate Sadducee.'[1] I s'pose it will be of no use to certify you that there *was* a witch in our house; yea, a black wench, from a far-distant country, where, I'm told, they have daily dealings with Satan, as man with man, in buying, and selling, and trucking of goods. The afflicted girls, when in their sorest torments, would cry out upon Tituba;[2] and there would be the cruel jade, looking as much amazed as if she had never done any evil in her life. But she had manifested her ugly temper toward 'em before this calamity, by divers times discovering 'em in a closet where jellies and such like sweet trade[3] was kept, of which it was very natural that they should be just tasting a little, you know. They could not so much as hook a lump of sugar, or a spunful of molasses, but they'd hear her muttering, 'I'll tell mistress, for by-and-by sugar-pot and 'lasses-jug be empty, and she'll say, Tituba steal—Tituba tief.' So, don't all these doings plainly prove that she was moved of old, by the Father of malice against these poor children? Well, after things had gone on so for a long, lengthy time, they come to a detarmination to hold a court upon these dealings of Satan, and try if the authority of the town could not cast him out, since the godly ministers was not able. Oh! I never shall forget that dreadful day. Heads was as thick in the Salem court-house as green pease in a pod, but no more noise nor shuffling of feet than if all had been dead bodies. There, on a high seat, sot[4] Governor Danforth, looking exceeding solemn, and Governor Stoughton,[5] with eyes as sharp as a needle; and there was the Reverend Mr. Samuel Parris, with a pen to write down every word that should be said. I could not help thinking of the day of judgment. And when the crowd was so great that we could hardly breathe, the distressed children was brought in. Close behind them came Tituba, rolling up the whites of her eyes. Then they fell into the worst torments that I ever did see. It seemed as if the Wicked One put forth the whole of his power and spite in the presence of the honorable court. 'Who hurts you?' said his worship, the judge. 'Tituba!

1 Richard Baxter (1615–91), *The Certainty of the World of Spirits* (1691); in the Bible the Sadducees are a sect of Jews who oppose Jesus and test his orthodoxy with questions.

2 Tituba] South American aboriginal slave purchased in Barbados by Parris, accused by his daughter and niece of witchcraft and beaten by him until she "confessed," though she later recanted

3 trade] stuff, rubbish

4 sot] past tense of set, meaning sit; American dialect

5 Deputy Governor Thomas Danforth; Lieutenant Governor William Stoughton.

Tituba!' they both screamed at once; 'she afflicts us! She is going to ride on a broomstick now, and will stick pins in us.' Then they fell into such awful fits that the honorable court injoined the black witch to make confession of her wickedness. And she did confess, so far as this; that, when she was a slave among the Spanish, she larnt *how to find out a witch*. And was not that just the same as to be one herself? Their honors agreed it was next akin to it, and ordered her straightway to prison. After she got there, such a hardened sinner was she, that she denied having ever made a league with Satan, and said she would not have told the court what she did, only her master had[1] most grievously beaten her to make her confess, and, catching his eye in the court, she was afeard of the same punishment again, which was surely no worse than she desarved. And what a maracle it was, that, as soon as she was taken away, the poor, afflicted gals sot up, and looked pleasant and satisfied. But just as the crowd was beginning to clear out, the minister's darter betook herself to swooning again, and foamed at the mouth like a barrel of hop beer a working. And, Cousin Jehoshaphat, can you imagine my situation when I heard her exclaim, '*Jehiel Wigglesworth! Jehiel Wigglesworth! he afflicts me!*' Oh! I screamed as loud as she, and took to my heels to run right out of the court-house, thinking I'd get home like a streak of lightning to father's. But they seized hold of me, and dragged me before the judges. Things swum round me, and I was afeard the floor would cleave asunder, and let me into the suller. So I held fast on to the sheriffs, and they grabbed just as tight hold of me; so I was like a crutter shut up in a vice. But when the chief judge axed[2] me, in a terrible voice, 'How do you afflict this young maid?' I found marvelous strength to reply, 'Please your honor, I never did offend her, in thought, word, or deed, saving once, when, about six weeks ago, I s'pose I did occasion her some sort of worriment by telling her mother, who axed me the question, that I did see her take apples from a cart that brought some to the door to sell. But then she would not a took 'em if we had only a bought 'em for her to eat; and, as she declared she never touch'd one on 'em, I do s'pose she forgot it. So, 'cause my memory happened to be rather better than hers, she was huffy to me for two or three weeks, which was no more than natural, your honor; and then she seemed to get over her hard thoughts. Most

1 Sigourney's footnote: See page 56 of "Lectures on Witchcraft," by the Reverend C.W. Upham, published at Boston in 1831, and evincing much historical research.

2 axed] asked; dialect

sartingly,[1] this is the only time in which I ever crossed her since I have abode under her father's ruff.'[2]

"Then the court ordered me to walk straight up to her, and look her in the face; whereat she shrieked so, and vowed that I tore her vitals, that my heart misgive me, and I begun to wonder whether I had not, somehow or other, made a league and covenant with the Old One,[3] and known nothing about it. Howsoever, I would not confess, though they took vast pains to make me. Whereupon they said I was obstinate, and commanded me to jail. Then she come immediately out of her fits, and was as chirk[4] and cheery as a bird out of the snare of the fowler. Oh! the wearisome days and nights that passed over me in that house of bondage! But plenty of good company came there afore midsummer. We was like a bee-hive at swarming time. From the dens around I'd hear the poor prisoners bemoaning themselves, and saying, 'Oh! that we'd never told such a falsehood as to confess that we was witches, and so wronged our own souls.' And then the crying of children would ring in my ears, for there was some shut up there not over eight or ten years old. Father and mother got a seat in neighbor Lynch's wagon, and come down to Salem jail to see me. We was all cast down bad enough, to meet in such a dolesome hole. 'Oh, Jehiel,' said the old lady, 'confess! do, pray, confess! for they tell me all that confess they are witches get set at liberty, and all the rest are hanged without marcy, for a stiff-necked and hard-hearted generation.' 'Mother,' says I, 'would ye have me confess dealings with the Wicked Sarpent when 'taint true?' 'Oh! I don't know,' says she; 'but do be sure and save your life; there ain't nothing so bad as death.' 'Why now, mother,' says I, 'I remember you broke me of telling lies when I was a small youngster; I don't think I shall begin again at this time of day. And I guess there *is* something as bad as death, and worse too, namely, the lake that burns with fire and brimstone.' 'There,' said father, 'did not I tell you 'twould be so? Jehiel was always a good boy to larn the New Testament by heart; and now ye see he's got it in his heart. So give over tempting him, mammy.'"

"I should have thought," said Jones, "that Aunt Jemima[5] might

---

1 sartingly] certainly

2 ruff] roof

3 Old One] Satan; first recorded 1787; an Americanism in Sigourney's day

4 chirk] lively, cheerful; by Sigourney's day solely a New-Englandism

5 Jemima] another name from the Bible, Job's eldest daughter

have given you better advice. A professor o' religion as she is, too! She must have been worse blinded and bewitched than even you was."

"I felt desp'ate heavy," continued the narrator, "when our folks left me, and went and curled down in the corner upon my heap of straw. But I found some comfort in a bit of cold gammon, and bread and cheese they brought me, which was enough better than the jail victuals. The latter part of August, five of the prisoners was taken out and hanged. One of them was a grand minister, Mr. George Burroughs,[1] whom they condemned because he had e'enamost[2] the strength of a giant, which he must have got from the powers of darkness, for he was real[3] slim and slender made. But never shall I forget the awful 22d of September. Then we was all summoned to look out and see eight of our miserable comrades marched to the gallows. First walked Martha Corcy,[4] paler than ashes, whose husband had been pressed to death with heavy weights,[5] because he refused to plead when he was indicted before the honorable court. The next was Mary Esty, who writ the most beautiful letter to the judges and ministers, declaring her innocence. When she took the last leave of her husband, and children, and friends, she was said to look just as calm and holy as an angel. Close behind come Goody Parker, with her hood partly drawn over her face, and her lips moving in prayer, and Ann Pudeator, with the large tears like hail-stones rolling down her face, and Margaret Scott, with the ruddy bloom still upon her cheeks, whom all the young men had so admired for her beauty. There was Wilmot Read, too, with whom I had played at school, and Goodman Ward-well, who was accused by his own wife and daughter, and a broken-hearted man was he, with his head hanging down upon his breast. Last of all, with a fresh, goodly countenance, walked Molly Parker, stepping as light, as if she knew she was about to rise above her enemies to a heavenly home. She it was that spake so bold to the Reverend Mr.

---

1 Burroughs] formerly a minister at Salem

2 e'enamost] almost; late eighteenth- and early nineteenth-century Americanism

3 real] really, very; an Americanism by Sigourney's day

4 Martha Corcy] Mary Corey; the others are Mary Easty, Alice Parker, Ann Pedeator, Margaret Scott, Wilmott Redd, Samuel Wardwell, and Mary Parker

5 pressed ... weights] the only recorded instance in the American colonies of pressing, or *peine forte et dure*, originally designed to extract a confession and, if not, to kill; abolished in Britain in 1772

Noyes[1] when he bid her confess the sin of witchcraft. 'I am no more a witch than you are a wizard; and if you take away my life, God will give you blood to drink.'[2] Oh! how my heart sunk within me, and cold chills run through all my veins, to see them walking along with the bright sun, and the clear, blue sky over their heads, which they was never more to behold. And I said to myself, Make haste, Jehiel Wigglesworth, and get out of this strong hold, or you will be dealt with in like manner. In the arter part of that memorable day, there came a pious good minister to preach to the poor prisoners, and exhort them to sarch into the plague of their own hearts, while yet it was a time of hope. We, in the upper story, flocked together into the largest cell to hear him. He spoke exceeding well, and had a wonderful smooth delivery, but he'd only got as far as sixteenthly, when down fell Molly Lacey[3] in a fit, a curious talking creature, who had charged both her mother and grand-mother with witchcraft, and got them both into Salem jail with her. Down she fell, calling out the name of Mr. Willard,[4] a grand Boston minister, and the names of some of the highest powers of the state, saying they had a commission from the Prince of Darkness[5] to afflict her, and to burn her flesh from her bones with fire. Great was the stir indeed, and when I see the jailer was as busy as the rest on 'em, I watched my chance, and glided down stairs like a sperrit.[6] But when I reached the second story, the door was locked so tight that the Old Dragon[7] himself could not start it. I made for the window through which we had looked at the poor, condemned people in the morning, and lo! it was left a leetle open, to admit a morsel of air. 'Jehiel Wigglesworth!' said I, 'cast yourself down from thence. Ain't it as well to grind your bones to powder, as to have your neck stretched by these Philistines?'[8] So I snatched up the minister's broad-brimmed hat, which had been left on the stairway, and thrust it on my head, thinking I would not go into etarnity with a broken skull, if I could help it. But what do you think appeared just at that critical minute? A huge load of hay passing directly under,

---

1 Noyes] Nicholas Noyes (1647–1717)

2 Spoken by Sarah Good; Noyes reportedly died twenty-five years later of a hemorrhage.

3 Lacey] Mary Lacey, an accused witch

4 Willard] Samuel Willard, hung in early August 1692 for witchcraft

5 Prince of Darkness] Satan

6 sperrit] spirit

7 Old Dragon] Satan

8 Philistines] in the Bible, enemies of the Jews worshipping a different god

and nobody in sight. As quick as thought, I plumped down upon it, and kivered myself up in the cutest[1] manner. The boy who driv was wandering along in front, and gazing around, but hearing a strange sound as I plunged down, gave his cattle a stroke or two, and said, 'Gee up, Dimond. Haw! old crooked-horn! what d'ye start for? D'ye see any o' the Salem witches?' So whistling, he went on with his load, while the sweet smell of the new-mown hay, and the fresh air that I had not breathed so long, and the thought that I had got out of that dismal den of lamentation, though but for one half hour, even if they clawed me back the next, made both my heart and head so lightish, that I could scarcely keep from outright singing and shouting. But I took good care to hold the minister's hat well under the hay, lest some of his parishioners might know it and hunt me out. I obsarved the boy arter a while to be looking round, and calling 'Jehu, Jehu.' Thinks I to myself, Jehu and Jehiel are pretty much alike. So when we'd got past the house where I used to live, I takes courage, and says, 'What d'ye want? Don't ye see that I'm up here on the hay?' 'On the hay,' said he. 'How on airth did ye get there, and I not know it?' 'Why forty people might 'a got up and down, and stole half the hay too, while you have been lazing and gazing at every thing and every body.' 'You hain't done all your arrants,[2] have ye?' 'Yes, indeed, long ago.' 'Well, then, get down and drive the team. Don't you know master said, "Tim, you must drive till you get through the thickest of Salem town, and when Jehu has done my business there, he shall see to the cattle." So make haste and come down, for I'm as tired as a dog.' 'And don't you think I'm tired too, trotting through all the lanes like a camel, while you've been a loungin' along, more asleep than awake?' 'I declare you shall get down *now*, Jehu,' said the lad, beginning to climb up the load. 'I'll tell you what it is, Tim,' said I, 'the great pitchfork is here, and if you come up before I give you leave, I'll catch you on it. But if you'll only drive fast and good till we get out of sight of them housen[3] yonder, I've got a clever[4] clingstone peach[5] here that I'll give you, and you shall ride all the rest of the way.' 'Oh yes, to be sure, out of sight of them housen! Why, that ain't a quarter of a mile from the place where the man lives that's bought

1 cutest] acutest, cleverest; an early nineteenth-century Americanism

2 arrants] errands

3 housen] houses; used in English regions furnishing New England settlers

4 clever] agreeable, pleasing; by Sigourney's day an Americanism

5 Variety of peach, preferred in America, with flesh clinging to the stone.

the rowin.[1] You're a real cross-grained dog, to make me do more than master says.' So he walked along, muttering. When we'd got about through the thick-settled part, I called out suddenly, 'Oh! what a beast I am to forget. Run, Tim, run, as fast as ever you can, to Squire Larkin's store, at the second corner, and bring a small bottle of sperrit I left standing on the horse-block. I'm awful afeard somebody has drinked it up afore now. Come, gallop, that's a good fellow, and if you happen to take a small swig out on't, I won't tell master.' Off he set like a catamount;[2] and no sooner was he out of sight than I was down, and a running faster than he, for I was dumb afeard that he'd meet the real Jehu, and both together take arter me, like Jehu of old pursuing the false prophets.[3] I struck into the woods and hid till dark, and then took the road and traveled right manfully all night. It made me down-hearted to think I could not go to father's, for I know'd well that was the fust place they'd naturally sarch in for me, and I seemed to be in a worse fix than the returning prodigal.[4] While I was doubting where to shape my course, I remembered that Cousin Jehoshaphat Jones, who had always been a true frind, had hired himself out to some Huguenot bodies, who lived in an out-of-the-way sort of a hole, and thought if I could once get there, I might stand a good chance to be hid, in such an outlandish region. So I turned my steps hitherward. But oh! the torment of hunger that I've endured. Sometimes I have thought I could e'e-namost gnaw a sheep's head off, and eat it with all the wool on. But I have not been altogether easy in my mind, for fear the bears should eat me, when I dropped asleep in the woods, or some ugly rattlesnake give me a mortal bite, or the beastly Indians start out from behind some bush and scalp me. Yet have I been led through the wilderness in safety, through help from above. I hope the precious minister that I left preaching in the Salem jail will forgive me for hooking his hat. Its broad brim has been of vast use to me to dip up water from brooks, and fend off the rain and musquetoes. How real thankful I was, at last, to see a light glimmering here, and, looking through the cracks of the corn-house, to be

---

1 rowen] hay of the season's second growth

2 catamount] early nineteenth-century American name for cougar

3 Jehu ... false prophets] In the Bible, book of Kings, Jehu seized the throne of Israel and expelled worshippers of the god Baal.

4 prodigal] the Bible, gospel of Luke 15.11-32, where Jesus illustrates divine forgiveness for sin by the parable of the son who left home and dissipated his inheritance, but on returning was forgiven by his father

sure that it was indeed Cousin Jehoshaphat, by the side of a great pile of ripe ears. I doubt whether the poor critturs who was a drowning in the flood-time could have been much joyfuller to have set their feet in Noah's ark,[1] than I to behold my own blood-relation, and stretch my weary limbs on this floor."

When the narrator closed his recital, all his auditors expressed sympathy for his troubles, and gladness at his deliverance, and hastened to provide him with fitting refreshment, and a place of repose. It was afterward decided to offer him refuge among them, with such compensation for his services as should be deemed satisfactory, until "the indignation might be overpast."[2] For some time after this miserable delusion had subsided, he remained among the Huguenot colonists, grateful for their kindness, and pleased with their gentle manners and reasonable requisitions.

Afterward, returning to his native village, he settled for life in those peaceful agricultural employments to which his ancestors had been inured. He dwelt in rural comfort and happiness, and enjoyed the respect of his neighbors and friends. Some lingering of superstition continued through life to mingle with that shrewdness and simplicity which so often mark the Yankee character; and when, in long winter evenings, beside a blazing fire, he recounted to his astonished children the evils to which he had been exposed, and from which he was so remarkably rescued, he never failed to bespeak their gratitude that they had never been tempted to the sore sin of witchcraft, or brought under the visible and fearful dominion of the great Wicked One.[3]

25. From *Water-Drops* (1848).[4]

WOMAN'S PATRIOTISM.[5]

How shall we aid the land we love?
  O'er dusty tomes to pore,
And catch the warrior's wrathful mood
  From Amazonian lore?—

1 Noah's ark] In the Bible, book of Genesis, God punishes sinning humanity with a great flood but instructs Noah to build an ark, or large boat, to escape with his family and pairs of animals and repopulate the earth.

2 The Bible, Isaiah 26.20–21; Isaiah advises, "hide thyself as it were for a little moment, until the indignation [of God against sinners] be overpast."

3 Wicked One] Satan

4 Sigourney's collection of pro-temperance (i.e., abstinence) writings.

5 A reply to the growing women's rights movement initiated by Lucretia

To turbulence, or pride incite,
And quench of peace the angel light?
Relinquish for a meteor's glare
The boon of Love's protecting care?
Ambition's wind-swept heights assail,
And shun the sweet, secluded vale?—
No, sister, no.

How aid our land?—The boastful voice
  In public haunts to raise?
Or barter for a fickle fame
  Affection's priceless praise?
For "*Woman's Rights*" to clamor loud,
And dare the throng, and face the crowd?
Or wrapped in wild desire to roam
Forfeit those charities of home,
That pain can soothe, and grief control,
And lull to harmony the soul?—
No, sister, no.

In her own place, the hearth beside,
  The patriot's heart to cheer,
The young, unfolding mind to guide,
  The future sage to rear,—
Where sleeps the cradled infant fair,
To watch with love and kneel in prayer,
Cheer each sad soul with pity's smile,
And frown on every latent wile
That threats the pure, domestic shade,
Sister,—so best our life shall aid
The land we love.

Mott and Elizabeth Cady Stanton after they were denied admission as delegates to an 1840 English anti-slavery convention because they were women; first published, with slight differences, in the *Ladies' Wreath, A Magazine Devoted to Literature, Industry and Religion*, 1 (May 1846): 24.

26. From *Illustrated Poems* (1849).[1]

ORISKA.[2]

FAR in the west, where still the red man held
His rights unrifled, dwelt an aged chief,
With his young daughter. Joyous as a bird,
She found her pastime mid the forest shades,
Or with a graceful vigour urged her skiff
O'er the bright waters. The bold warriors mark'd
Her opening charms, but deem'd her still a child,
Or fear'd from their grave kingly chief to ask
The darling of his age.
A stranger came
To traffic with the people, and amass
Those costly furs which in his native clime
Transmute so well to gold. The blood of France
Was in his veins, and on his lips the wile
That wins the guileless heart. Ofttimes at eve
He sought the chieftain's dwelling, and allured
The gentle girl to listen to his tale,
Well framed and eloquent. With practised glance
He saw the love-flush on her olive cheek
Make answer to him, though the half-hid brow
Droop'd mid its wealth of tresses.
"Ah! I know
That thou dost love to please me. Thou hast put
Thy splendid coronet of feathers on.
How its rich crimson dazzles mid thy locks,
Black as the raven's wing! Thy bracelets, too!
Who told thee thou wert beautiful? Hast seen
Thy queenly features in yon mirror'd lake?
Bird of the Sioux![3] let my nest be thine,

---

1 A lavish and illustrated volume in a series including the popular male poets of the day, indicating Sigourney's status as a major American poet.

2 The first poem in the volume; Oriska is also the name of an Oneida aboriginal village in what is now New York state, near the site of the battle of Oriskany (1777) in the Revolutionary war. Oriska in North Dakota was named after the heroine of this poem (George R. Stewart, *American Place-Names*, New York: Oxford UP, 1970).

3 Sioux] the Lakota, inhabiting what became Minnesota and North and South Dakota

And I will sing thee melodies that make
Midnight like morn."
With many a spell he charm'd
Her trusting innocence; the dance, the song,
The legend, and the lay of other lands;
And patient taught his pupil's lip to wind[1]
The maze of words with which his native tongue
Refines[2] the thought. The hoary chieftain frown'd;
But when the smooth[3] Canadian press'd his suit
To be adopted by the tribe, and dwell
Among them, as a brother and a son,—
And when the indulgent sire observant read
The timid pleading of Oriska's eye,—
He gave her tenderly, with sacred rites,
In marriage to the stranger.
Their sweet bower
Rose like a gem amid the rural scene,
O'er-canopied with trees, where countless birds
Carol'd unwearied, the gay squirrel leap'd,
And the wild-bee went singing to his work,
Satiate with luxury. Through matted grass,
With silver foot, a frolic fountain stole,
Still track'd by deepening greenness, while afar
The mighty prairie met the bending skies,—
A sea at rest, whose sleeping waves were flowers.

Nor lack'd their lowly dwelling such device
Of comfort, or adornment, as the hand
Of gentle woman, sedulous to please,
Creates for him she loves. For she had hung
Attentive on his lips, while he described
The household policy of prouder climes;
And with such varied and inventive skill
Caught the suggestions of his taste refined,
That the red people, wondering as they gazed
On curtain'd window and on flower-crown'd vase,
Carpet and cushion'd chair, and board arranged

---

1 wind] follow a devious or sinuous course

2 Refines] polishes, makes more cultured and elegant, but also makes more subtle, or too subtle

3 smooth] pleasant and affable, or polished and elegant, but also insinuating, flattering

With care unwonted, call'd her home the court
Of their French princess.
A rich clustering vine
Crept o'er their porch, and 'neath its fragrant shade
Oriska sang her evening melodies,
Tuneful and clear and deep, the echoed truth
Of her soul's happiness. Her highest care
And dearest pleasure was to make his lot
Delightful to her lord; and he, well pleased
With the simplicity of fervent love,
And the high honour paid a chieftain's son,
Roam'd with the hunters at his will, or brought
Birdlings of brilliant plume, as trophies home
To his young bride.
Months fled, and with them change
Stole o'er his love. And when Oriska mark'd
The shadow darkening on his brow, she fear'd
The rudeness[1] of her nation, or perchance
Her ignorance had err'd, and strove to do
His will more perfectly. And though his moods
Of harshness or disdain chill'd every joy,
She blamed him not, for unto her he seem'd
A higher being of a nobler race;
And she was proud and happy, might she bathe
His temples in some fit of transient pain,
Or by a menial's toil advance the feast
Which still she shared not. When his step was heard,
She bade her beating heart be still, and smooth'd
The shining tresses he was wont to praise,
And fondly hasting, raised her babe to meet
His father's eye, contented if the smile
That once was hers might beam upon his child:—
But that last solace fail'd, and the cold glance
Contemptuously repress'd her toil of love.
And then he came no more.
But as she watch'd
Night after night, and question'd every hour,
How bitterly those weeks and years were notch'd
Upon the broken tablet of the soul,
By that forsaken wife.
Calm moonlight touch'd

---

1 rudeness] lack of culture and refinement

A fair Canadian landscape. Roof and spire,
And broad umbrageous tree, were saturate
With liquid lustre. O'er a lordly dome,
Whose halls had late with bridal pomp been gay,
The silvery curtains of the summer night
Were folded quietly.
A music-sound
Broke forth abruptly from its threshold stone,
Shrill and unearthly—not the serenade,
That thrills on beauty's ear, but a bold strain,
Loud even to dissonance, and oft prolonged
In low, deep cadence, wonderfully sad,—
The wild song of the Sioux. He who first
Awaking, caught that mournful melody,
Shudder'd with icy terror, as he threw
His mantle o'er him, and rush'd madly forth
Into the midnight air.
"Hence! Leave my door!
I know thee not, dark woman! Hence away!"

"Ah! let me hear that voice! How sweet its tones
Fall on my ear, although the words are stern.
Say! know'st thou not this boy? Whose eyes are these?
Those chestnut clusters round the lifted brow,—
Said'st thou not in his cradle they were thine?"

"How cam'st thou here, Oriska?"
"We have trod
A weary way. My father and his men
Came on the business of their tribe, and I,
Unto whose soul the midnight and the morn
Have been alike for years, roam'd restlessly
A wanderer in their train, leading our boy.
My highest hope was but to hear, perchance,
That thou didst live; and lo! a blessed guide
Hath shown me to thy home."
"Oriska, go!
I have a bride. Thou canst not enter here—
I'll come to thee to-morrow."
"*Wilt* thou come?
The white-hair'd chief, I fear me, fades away
Unto the Spirit-land!"
"I bid thee hence,

To thine abode. Have I not said to thee
I'll come to-morrow?"
With a heavy heart,
Through silent streets, the sad-brow'd woman went,
Leading her child.
Morn came, and day declined,
Yet still he came not. By her sire she watch'd,
O'er whose dull eye a filmy shadow stole,
While to her troubled question no reply
Rose from his palsied lip. Nature and age
Slept wearily and long. The second eve
Darken'd the skies, when lo! a well-known step—
He stood before her.
"Was it kind of thee,
Oriska, thus to break my bridal hour
With thy strange, savage music?"
"Was thy wife
Angry at the poor Indian? Not to speak
Harsh words I came: I would not think of thee
A thought of blame. But oh! mine aged sire,
Thou see'st him dying in this stranger-land,
Far from his fathers' graves. Be thou a friend
When he is gone and I am desolate.
Make me a household servant to thy wife.
I'll bring her water from the purest spring,
And plant the corn, and ply the flying oar,
And never be impatient or require
Payment from her, nor kind regard from thee.
I will not call thee husband,—though thou taught'st
My stammering lip that word when love was young,—
Nor ask one pitying look or favouring tone,
Or aught, except to serve and pray for thee
To the Great Spirit. And this boy shall do
Her will, and thine."
The pale face turn'd away
With well-dissembled anger, though remorse
Gnaw'd at his callous bosom!
"Urge me not!
It cannot be!"
Even more he might have said,
Basely and bitterly, but lo! the chief
Cast off the ice of death, and on his bed,
With clenched hand and quivering lip, uprose:—

"*His* curse be on thee! He, who knoweth where
The lightnings hide!"
Around the old man's neck
Fond arms were wildly thrown. "Oh, curse him not!
The father of my boy." And blinding tears
Fell down so fast, she mark'd not with what haste
The white-brow'd recreant fled.
"I tell thee, child,
The cold black gall-drop in a traitor's soul
Doth make a curse. And though I curse him not,
The sun shall hate him, and the waters turn
To poison in his veins.
But light grows dim.
Go back to thine own people. Look no more
On him whom I have cursed, and lay my bones
Where my dead fathers sleep."
A hollow groan,
Wrung by extremest agony, broke forth
From the old chieftain's breast.
"Daughter, I go
To the Great Spirit."
O'er that breathless clay
Bow'd down the desolate woman. No complaint,
No sigh of grief burst forth. The tear went back
To its deep fountain. Lip and fringed lid
Trembled no more than in the statued bronze,
Nor shrank one truant nerve, as o'er her pass'd
The asphyxia of the heart.[1]
Day after day,
O'er wild and tangled forest, moved a train,
Bearing with smitten hearts their fallen chief;
And next the bier a silent woman trod,
A child's young hand forever clasp'd in hers,
And on her lip no sound. Long was the way,
Ere the low roof-trees of their tribe they saw
Sprinkling the green; and loud the funeral wail
Rose for the honour'd dead, who, in his youth,
Their battles led, and in his wintry years
Had won that deeper reverence, which so well
The forest-sons might teach our wiser race
To pay to hoary age. Beneath the mounds,

---

1 asphyxia of the heart] stoppage of the pulse, or suspended animation

Where slept his ancient sires, they laid him down;
And there the gather'd nation mourn'd their sire,
In the wild passion of untutor'd grief;
Then smoothed the pillow'd turf, and went their way.

Who is yon woman, in her dark canoe,
Who strangely towards Niagara's fearful gulf[1]
Floats on unmoved?
Firm and erect she stands,
Clad in such bridal costume as befits
The daughter of a king. Tall, radiant plumes
Wave o'er her forehead, and the scarlet tinge
Of her embroider'd mantle, fleck'd with gold,
Dazzles amid the flood. Scarce heaves her breast,
As though the spirit of that dread abyss,
In terrible sublimity, had quell'd
All thought of earthly things.
Fast by her side
Stands a young, wondering boy, and from his lip,
Blanching with terror, steals the frequent cry
Of "Mother! Mother!"
But she answereth not.
She speaks no more to aught of earth, but pours
To the Great Spirit, fitfully and wild,
The death-song of her people. High it rose
Above the tumult of the tide that bore
The victims to their doom. The boy beheld
The strange, stern beauty in his mother's eye,
And held his breath for awe.
Her song grew faint,—
And as the rapids raised their whitening heads,
Casting her light oar to the infuriate tide,
She raised him in her arms, and clasp'd him close.
Then as the boat with arrowy swiftness drove
Down toward the unfathom'd gulf, while chilling spray
Rose up in blinding showers, he hid his head
Deep in the bosom that had nurtured him,
With a low, stifled sob.

---

1 Niagara] famous waterfalls between present day New York state and Ontario in Canada; favourite theme of Sigourney's, representing sublime nature as God's presence on earth; see pp. 152 and 203 here

And thus they took
Their awful pathway to eternity.—
One ripple on the mighty river's brink,
Just where it, shuddering, makes its own dread plunge,
And at the foot of that most dire abyss
One gleam of flitting robe and raven tress
And feathery coronet—and all was o'er,
Save the deep thunder of the eternal surge
Sounding their epitaph!

THE THRIVING FAMILY.[1]
A SONG.

OUR father lives in Washington,[2]
And has a world of cares,
But gives his children each a farm,
Enough for them and theirs.
Full thirty[3] well grown sons has he,
A numerous race indeed,
Married and settled all, d'ye see,
With boys and girls to feed.
So if we wisely till our lands,
We're sure to earn a living,
And have a penny, too, to spare
For spending or for giving.
A thriving family are we,
No lordling need deride us,
For we know how to use our hands,
And in our wits we pride us.

---

1 Published in the *Union Magazine* (1848). The poem resembles a political campaign song and alludes to increasing sectional divisions between North and South, non-slave and pro-slave regions; slavery was a prominent issue in the presidential elections of 1844 and 1848, exacerbated by debate over whether territories acquired in the war with Mexico (1846–48) should be slave or free. In 1864 Sigourney sent the poem, with some alterations, to the *Sandusky Register*, retitled "Our Union"; it seems to have been published with the editor's remark, "It will be perceived by the following patriotic Lyric that the much loved poet is awake with the times and sounding the clarion for the Union." (Lydia Huntley Sigourney Papers, US/CTH/SIGOL/1865—I.33, at the Connecticut Historical Society)

2 Washington] United States capital; father: President of the United States

3 thirty] number of states after admission of Wisconsin in 1848

Hail, brothers, hail,[1]
Let nought on earth divide us.
Some of us dare the sharp north-east;
Some, clover fields are mowing;
And others tend the cotton plants
That keep the looms a-going;
Some build and steer the white-wing'd ships,
And few in speed can mate[2] them,
While others rear the corn and wheat,
Or grind the corn to freight them.
And if our neighbours o'er the sea
Have e'er an empty larder,
To send a loaf their babes to cheer
We'll work a little harder.
No old nobility have we,
No tyrant king to ride us;
Our sages in the Capitol[3]
Enact the laws that guide us.
Hail, brothers, hail,
Let nought on earth divide us.

Some faults we have, we can't deny,
A foible here and there;
But other households have the same,
And so we won't despair.
'Twill do no good to fume and frown,
And call hard names, you see,
And what a shame 'twould be to part
So fine a family!
'Tis but a waste of time to fret,
Since Nature made us one,
For every quarrel cuts a thread
That healthful Love has spun.
Then draw the cords of union fast,
Whatever may betide us,
And closer cling through every blast,
For many a storm has tried us.
Hail, brothers, hail,
Let nought on earth divide us.

---

1 Hail, brothers, hail] 1864: Hail, Brothers of the banded States!
2 mate] equal, rival; a poeticism
3 Capitol] building completed in 1800, reconstructed by 1830; seat of the US Congress in Washington, DC

27. From *The Ladies' Wreath* (1851).[1]

THE CRUSHED MOUSE.[2]

I BEAR the trouble in my heart, of one
Who hath extinguished life;—yet not the sin
Of malice preconceived. And I confess
Without the form of witnesses,—or weight
Of circumstantial evidence, to spread
Close covered guilt before the jury-box
Where sit the twelve grave burghers, puzzled sore
Between the lawyers, and the bench, to give
A righteous verdict.
                    Now, the facts are these:—
The time of rest drew near,—and as becomes
A careful housekeeper,—I took my round
To see the bolts well drawn, and windows safe
That all might sleep secure. A closet door
Was left ajar,—and somewhat hastily
I closed the latch. But when the morrow came,
Lo! in its crevice caught, a tiny mouse
Lay pressed and lifeless.
                              And I did the deed!—
'Twas all in vain, to stroke its silken coat,
And praise its thin, transparent ears, and lay
Its fairy paw in my warm hand, and wish
The heart might beat once more,—for I had forced
The life that God had given, out of that cell
Which all man's wisdom ne'er could reconstruct
Or vivify.
          Yes, I,—whose care it was,
To keep a conscience pure from stain of blood,
Save of some gorged musquito,—or perchance
In childhood's thoughtless hours,—some gadding fly,
I, who had bade the spiteful wasp go free,
Whose sting still quivered from my swollen arm,
Swept down the web, and let the spider go,
Spared the piratical black ant, that wrecked

1 *The Ladies' Wreath: An Illustrated Annual*, ed. Sarah T. Martyn, 5 (1851): 32–33.

2 One of several poems humanizing small animals; compare to "The Mouse's Petition" by English poet Anna Laetitia Barbauld (1743–1825).

My cupboard's wealth,—I, who had turned aside
That even the hateful snake might pass unharmed,
And won from shouting boys, the hunted toad,
Marked out for torture,—gave all monstrous things,
Cockroach, and dragon-fly, and poplar worm,
Wide passport,—had at once destroyed the boast
Of a whole life.
                              Yes, I had rent the mesh
Of subtlest net-work nerves, and in those veins
Staunched the warm tide, that on from brain to heart,
Bore innocent joy.—
                                        And what was thine offence
Poor martyred mouse?—
                                                Merely to taste of what
We well could spare, and rear in secret nook,
Thy light-heeled offspring.—But 'tis vain to mourn
Thy fate, or my misdeed.
                                              And so farewell,—
Slight atom of a much enduring race,
Entrapp'd by cats and men. The feline claw
Bared of its velvet, hath been ever swift
To clutch thine ancestors.
                                                Scarce might they snatch
The silent rapture of the nibbled cheese,
In some dark pantry, ere the whiskered foe
With glaring eyeballs from his ambush sprang,
Awful as Jeffreys,[1]—to condemn unheard,
To spurn the plea for mercy, sport with pain,
And like a demon, glut himself with blood.
Say, ye who read the future,—Statesmen wise!
Who 'mid the wonders of our age have seen
The imprisoned water moving like a god,[2]
And on the trembling wire,[3] the human thought
Darting from zone to zone, and ancient crowns
Fall from anointed brows,[4]—is there no time

---

1 Jeffreys] George Jeffreys (1648–89), Englishman known as "hanging judge Jeffreys" for sentencing 320 accused rebels to execution or exile during the "bloody assizes" of 1685, following Monmouth's Rebellion

2 water moving like a god] steam power

3 trembling wire] the electrical telegraph, patented in the United States in 1837 by Samuel Morse

4 anointed brows] In 1848–49 revolutions shook or swept aside rulers in many places; anointing with holy oil was part of coronation ceremonies.

In this world's history, when the scale shall turn—
And the oppress'd and uncomplaining mouse,
Find some oasis, where the savory cheese
Shall swell like mountains and no cat be near?

28. From *The Ladies' Repository* (1854).

ARE THE AGED A PRIVILEGED ORDER?[1]

BY MRS. LYDIA H. SIGOURNEY.

METHINKS I hear some readers of this pleasant periodical exclaim, "What a singular subject this essayist has chosen! There must have been a paucity of themes that so bare a theory should have been resorted to."

But in reality, has age, that most unlovely season of life, any privileges, emoluments, or immunities, inherent in itself, to justify the assumption in our title? Let us examine.

It had, in ancient times, a distinction sanctioned by Divine authority. This, however, has, by some modern nations, been counted obsolete. Our own, which has been pronounced, by observant foreigners, deficient in the sentiment of respect, is perhaps not heedful of the command to "reverence the hoary head, and rise up before the face of the old man."[2] Waiving, therefore, any undue tenacity on this point, which, possibly, in a republic might be construed into an order of nobility, it might be as well for the aged to strike these colors[3] from the main-mast and be content to sail with the tide.[4]

After resigning this charter what remains? First, the wealth of experience. Take good note of possession.[5] Are not the whole beautiful and ever-moving world of the young in poverty for the want of it? See them searching, trying, tasting, snatching at garlands and grasping nettles and thorns, chasing meteors, fighting

---

1 *Ladies' Repository: A Monthly Periodical, Devoted to Literature, Arts, and Religion* 14 (November 1854): 481–82.

2 Misquoted from the Bible, Leviticus 19.32.

3 strike colors] lower flag (though the meaning here seems to be "sails")

4 sail with the tide] allow the ship to be carried out of port by the ebb-tide, without use of sails or other power

5 possession] self-possession, self-control

wind-mills,[1] in danger of being swallowed up by quick-sands. The evidence of others they will not take. The knowledge they need they have not attained. But the aged, through toil and hazard, through the misery of mistake, or the pains of penitence, have won it. It is theirs—gold dust, well washed, sometimes in fountains of tears. "Bought wit is best," says the proverb.[2] If they have bought theirs too dear, that is their own concern. They paid for it out of their own pockets. Young people need not grudge or despise it.

Have the aged any peculiar sources of revenue? These may, of course, be negative, as well as positive, in the things cast off, as well as in those amassed. They are supposed to have dissolved partnership with personal vanity, and that was always a losing concern. Time and toil spent at the toilet,[3] with the hope of admiration, are rescued for higher purposes. With them is no exciting consciousness of personal attraction, no bewilderment from flattery, no unamiable competition in the arena of fashion or extravagance. The full amount of gain, both in leisure and tranquillity, thus occurring, those who were once the most beautiful and the most vain are the best qualified to tell. Yet all might probably find some relief from thus loosening the clutches of self-conceit.

Does not Envy decline to follow the aged? One would think it were time. "Sixty years old," says a spirited author, "is a good era to write a book. We have then learned what mankind are, and Envy leaves us at peace." "Who is able to stand before Envy!" exclaimed the wise monarch of Israel.[4] Her leer unnerves action as much as her frown darkens merit. Age, however grave its companionship, should be welcomed if it puts to flight such an enemy.

Are not the aged respited from the bondage of money-getting? This is surely a gain, for the science of accumulation, as pursued in this land, is slavery. The hoary headed ought to taste the luxury of enfranchisement. Man, in the vigor of his prime, having made wealth his chief object of pursuit, rises early, and late takes rest, and eats the bread of carefulness;[5] but when he is solemnly assured that the time is near when he must leave behind what he

---

1 fighting wind-mills] reference to the hero of Miguel de Cervantes' *Don Quixote* (1605; 1615), who mistakes a windmill for a giant with flailing arms and attacks it

2 proverb] also found in Aesop's *Fables*, the Lion and the Ass, translated by Sir Roger L'Estrange

3 toilet] dressing-room

4 The Bible, Proverbs 27.4, by Solomon.

5 Man ... carefulness] echoing the Bible, Psalms 127.2

has gathered, he looks upward for rest. Happy if he may there contemplate treasures laid up in heaven.[1]

Is not the overmastering force of the passions broken for the old? Are they as irascible at opposition as when the rushing current of life, like a cataract, battled with all obstacles? The anger that shook the strong man like a reed, does it tarry with them? Are they, as of yore, led in blind captivity by

> "Love, Hope, and Joy, fair Pleasure's smiling train—
> Hate, Fear, and Grief, the family of Pain?"[2]

If a more serene, self-sustained philosophy is the concomitant of age, should it not be numbered among gifts for which to be grateful? If through their inevitable position they are recipients of that condensed, unrusting gold, styled experience, and are gainers in time and tranquil temperament, and are reprieved from many vexing labors, and lose some dangerous enemies, may they not justly lay claim to the immunities of a privileged order?

But not in exemptions alone do the advantages of age consist. One precious material ought to be more abundant with them than in life's earlier seasons. Absence of selfishness is one of the chief elements of happiness; and have they not more helps to become disinterested than at some other points of their pilgrimage? The young acquire accomplishments to be admired; the old strive to be agreeable that they may please or edify others. The young seek knowledge to become distinguished in future life; the old are impelled to devote to the good of others that which they have attained. The man of mature years is bent on the increase of wealth as a means of influence; the study of the old should rather be how to dispense it wisely. Their business is to shower back upon the earth the blessings they have received, having henceforth no further expectation, save of a couch upon her bosom. Their investments being less in hazard from her mutations, their happiness ought to be more independent and complete.

If to compensate for visible losses through the declension of time, there are correspondent gains less obvious yet vastly important—it concerns them to understand their comparative amount, that they may be able to balance the books, ere the Master calleth for an account of their stewardship.[3] An ancient writer has

---

1 Happy if ... heaven] echo of the Bible, Matthew 6.20

2 Alexander Pope, *An Essay on Man*, Epistle II (1733), ll. 107–108.

3 Master calleth ... stewardship] echoing the Bible, Luke 16.2

forcibly inquired, if it can be supposed that Nature, after having wisely distributed to all the preceding portions of life their peculiar and proper enjoyments, should have neglected, like an indolent poet, the last act of the human drama, and left it destitute of suitable advantages?[1]

No! unerring Goodness has not so ordained. Every season of human life has its inherent fitness for the end it was intended to serve. The charms of youth, like the blossoms of spring, glow among the grass blades and the boughs that are to be fruit-laden. Maturity toils with its reaping hook, and Age, like a favored guest, has a right and a rest in the garner. There it awaiteth *His* coming—the Lord of the harvest; not unmindful of its privileges, and ready to restore this mysterious gift of life when he shall call, that it may enter on a higher stage of existence, where there is neither decline nor death.

29. From *The Western Home, and Other Poems* (1854).

WILD FLOWERS.[2]

FLOWERS of God's planting!—Man doth call ye *wild*,
Though in your breasts a gentle nature lies,
And timidly ye meet the breezes mild,
Paying their love-kiss with your perfumed sighs.
Still, with unuttered speech,
More true philosophy ye teach,
Than they, your rich-robed relatives, who share
The florist's tender care,
And shrink with fretted nerves from the too buxom[3] air.

Methinks their polished petals hide
Some thrill of vanity or pride,
As the admiring throng
Through the rich green-house press along,
Where still they claim, in proud magnificence,
A warmer smile than Heaven's own healthful skies dispense,
Or lulled on beauty's breast
To a brief dream of rapturous rest,
Too soon—with pale, regretful eye
Fulfil their envied destiny, and die.

---

1 Nature ... advantages] Marcus Tullius Cicero, *Cato; or, An Essay on Old Age*, trans. William Melmoth (London, 1773), p. 10

2 Title in the book's Table of Contents is "Uncultured Flowers."

3 buxom] vigorous

But ye, in humble cell,
Cloven nook or grassy dell,
Or by the brooklet's shaded brim,
Turn in your trustful innocence to Him,
Who wisely metes the sun-beam and the rain;
Or else the plough-share's fatal pain,
Or even the crushing foot repay
With a forgiving fragrance—and beneath
The same loved skies that gave you birth,
On prairie broad, or purple heath,
Pass willingly away
From your slight hold on earth.

Perchance, with longer date
Gladdening the field-bee, at her work elate,
Ye nurse your buds, and give your winged seeds
Unto the winnowing winds, to sow them as they fly
In fertile soil, or mid the choking weeds
Or desert sands, where the rank serpent feeds;
Then, not of death afraid,
All unreluctantly ye fade,
Meek as ye bloomed at first, in glen, or forest-glade,
Bequeathing a sweet memory
Unto the scented turf, where erst ye grew,
And garnered in your souls the heaven-distilling dew.

Oh, fair, uncultured flowers!
The charm of childhood's roving hours,
Who seek no praise of man—have ye not caught
The spirit of *His*[1] lowly thought,
Who loved the frail field-lily—and the bird
By whom its breast was stirred?
And on his mountain-shrine
With eloquence divine
From its unfolded leaves, as from a text book, taught?
Yes—still ye show, in lessons undefiled,
The Christian life and death, though man doth call ye *wild*.

1 His] Jesus'

FALLEN FORESTS.[1]

Man's warfare on the trees is terrible.
He lifts his rude hut in the wilderness,
And, lo! the loftiest trunks, that age on age
Were nurtured to nobility, and bore
Their summer coronets so gloriously,
Fall with a thunder sound to rise no more.
He toucheth flame unto them, and they lie
A blackened wreck, their tracery and wealth
Of sky-fed emerald, madly spent, to feed
An arch of brilliance for a single night,
And scaring thence the wild deer, and the fox,
And the lithe squirrel from the nut-strewn home,
So long enjoyed.
He lifts his puny arm,
And every echo of the axe doth hew
The iron heart of centuries away.
He entereth boldly to the solemn groves
On whose green altar tops, since time was young
The wingéd birds have poured their incense stream
Of praise and love, within whose mighty nave
The wearied cattle from a thousand hills
Have found their shelter mid the heat of day;
Perchance in their mute worship pleasing Him
Who careth for the meanest He hath made.
I said, he entereth to the sacred groves
Where nature in her beauty bows to God,
And, lo! their temple arch is desecrate.
Sinks the sweet hymn, the ancient ritual fades,
And uptorn roots and prostrate columns mark
The invader's footsteps.
Silent years roll on,
His babes are men. His ant-heap dwelling grows
Too narrow—for his hand hath gotten wealth.
He builds a stately mansion, but it stands
Unblessed by trees. He smote them recklessly
When their green arms were found him, as a guard
Of tutelary deities, and feels
Their maledictions, now the burning noon

1 One of several poems protesting ecological destruction caused by westward settlement; see "Death Among the Trees" (p. 153).

Maketh his spirit faint. With anxious care,
He casteth acorns in the earth, and woos
Sunbeam and rain; he planteth the young shoot,
And props it from the storm; but neither he,
Nor yet his children's children, shall behold
What he hath swept away.
Methinks, 'twere well
Not as a spoiler or a thief to prey
On Nature's bosom, that sweet, gentle nurse
Who loveth us, and spreads a sheltering couch
When our brief task is o'er. O'er that green mound
Affection's hand may set the willow tree,
Or train the cypress, and let none profane
Her pious care.
Oh, Father! grant us grace
In all life's toils, so, with a steadfast hand
Evil and good to poise, as not to pave
Our way with wrecks, nor leave our blackened name
A beacon to the way-worn mariner.

POWERS'S STATUE OF THE GREEK SLAVE.[1]

BE silent! breathe not! lest ye break the trance;
She thinketh of her Attic[2] home; the leaves
Of its green olives stir within her soul,
And Love is sweeping o'er its deepest chords

1 A sculpture (1844) by the American Hiram Powers (1805–73) depicting a naked woman enslaved by the Turks at the time of the Greek War of Independence, with which Sigourney sympathized; Powers toured the statue in the USA in 1847–48, generating great public interest and many articles and poems. Anticipating controversy over the statue's nudity, Powers had the work "approved" by a group of clergymen. A New York exhibition took in $25,000; Powers sold several copies. The statue received much attention when displayed at the Great Exhibition in London in 1851. Thousands of smaller versions in bronze, plaster, and "Parian" were sold. Few American commentators connected Powers' Greek slave and American Negro slaves, but in his last version (1869), Powers put the slave in contemporary American manacles. Controversy continues: in 2005 Governor James Douglas of Vermont (Powers' home state) wanted to remove an antique lamp-replica of the statue from his desk as unsuited to be seen by schoolchildren visiting his office.

2 Attic] of Attica, region of Greece that includes Athens

So mournfully. Ah! who can weigh the wo[1]
Or wealth of memory in that breast sublime!

Yet errs he not who calleth thee *a slave*,
Thou Christian maiden?
Gyves[2] are on thy wrists;
But in thy soul a might of sanctity
That foils the oppressor, making to itself
A hiding-place from the sore ills of time.
What is the chain to thee, who hast the power
To bind in admiration all who gaze
Upon thine eloquent brow and matchless form?
We are ourselves thy slaves, most Beautiful!

THE MUSE.

THEY say that the cell of the poet should be
Like the breast of the shell that remembers the sea,
Quiet and still, save a murmuring sigh
Of the far-rolling wave to the summer-lit sky;
Tasteful and polished, as coralline bowers,
Remote from intrusion, and fragrant with flowers.

'Twould be beautiful, surely, but as for me,
Nothing like this I expect to see,
For I've written my poetry, sooth to say,
In the oddest of places, by night or by day,
Line by line, with a broken chain,
Interrupted, and joined again.
I, if paper were wanting, or pencils had fled,
Some niche in the brain, spread a storehouse instead,
And Memory preserved, in her casket of thought,
The embryo rhymes, till the tablets were brought:
At home or abroad, on the land or the sea,—
Wherever it came, it was welcome to me.

When first it would steal o'er my infantine hour,
With a buz or a song, like a bee in a flower,
With its ringing rhythm, and its measured line,
What it was I could scarce divine,

1 wo] woe; a deliberate archaism

2 Gyves] shackles

Calling so oft, from my sports and play,
To some nook in the garden, away, away,
To a mound of turf which the daisies crown,
Or a vine-wreathed summer-house, old and brown,
On a lilac's green leaf, with a pin, to grave
The tinkling chime of the words it gave.

At dewy morn, when to school I hied,
Methought like a sister it went by my side,
Well pleased o'er the fresh lanes to gambol and stray,
Or gather the violets that grew by the way,
Or turn my lessons to rhyme, and bask
In a rose, 'till I finished my needle's task.

When Winter in frost did the landscape enfold,
And my own little study was cheerless and cold,
A humble resource from the exigence rose,
And a barn was my favourite place to compose;
For there I could stow myself snugly away,
With my pencil and slate, on a nice mow of hay;
While with motherly face peeping out from her rack,
The cow munched her food, with a calf at her back;
And the fancies that there in that solitude wrought,
Were as chainless and bright as the palace-born thought.

When school years were o'er, and the tremulous ray
Of the young dawn of life took the tinting of day,
With ardour and pride I delighted to share,
By the side of my mother, her sweet household care.
My callisthenics[1] followed each morning, with zeal,
Were the duster and broom, and the great spinning-wheel;
No curve of the spine in that region was feared,
And of nervous diseases we seldom had heard.
So, singing along, with a buoyant tread
I drew out a line, as I drew out a thread.
Bees and bluebirds the casement flew by,
Yet none were so busy or happy as I;
The voice of my wheel, like a harp in my ear,
And the Muse keeping time with her melody clear,
And the joy of my heart overflowing the lay,
And my parent's approval each toil to repay.

1 callisthenics] physical exercises promoting beauty with strength

A season there was then the viol grew sweet,
And the maze of the dance was a charm to my feet,
For Youth and Joy, with their measures gay,
Beckoned me onward both night and day;
Yet oft in the soul was a secret tone
Winning away to my chamber lone,
And, lingering there, was a form serene
With a mild reproof on her pensive mien;
And though I feigned from her sway to start,
Having music enough in my own merry heart,
Yet her quiet tear on my brow that fell,
Was more dear than the dance or the viol's swell.

When life's mantling pleasures their climax attained,
And the sphere of a wife and a mother was gained,
When that transport awoke, which no language may speak,
As the breath of my first-born stole soft o'er my cheek,
While she slept on my breast, in the nursery fair,
A smothered lyre would arrest me there,
Half complaining of deep neglect,
Half demanding its old respect;
And if I mingled its cadence mild
With the tuneful tones of the rosy child,
Methought 'twas no folly such garlands to twine,
As could brighten life's cares, and its pleasures refine.

And now, though my life from its zenith doth wane,
And the wreaths of its morning grow scentless and vain,
And many a friend who its pilgrimage blest,
Have fallen from my heart and gone down to their rest,
Yet still by my side, unforgetful and true,
Is the being that walked with me all the way through.
She doth cling to the High Rock wherein is my trust,
Let her chant to my soul when I go to the dust;
Hand in hand with the faith that my Saviour hath given
Let her kneel at His feet mid the anthems of Heaven.

30. From *Past Meridian* (1854).[1]

CHAPTER XVII.[2]

The Pleasures of Winter.

> "And when the tinting of the Autumn leaves
> Had faded from its glory,—we have sat
> By the good fires of winter, and rejoiced
> Over the fulness of the gathered sheaf."
>
> WILLIS.[3]

WHAT a singular subject! The *pleasures* of winter. And what may they be? Some, with whom the imagery of frost and snow predominates, will be ready to say that it has none.

Surely it has been the most ill-treated season, decried by almost every one that could wield a pen or weave a couplet. The poets have been in league against it from time immemorial. Still it has some very respectable, shall I say desirable characteristics? It has not the fickleness of spring, whose blossoms so soon fall, nor the enervation of summer, when the strong men bow themselves, nor the imperious exactions of autumn, when the in-gathering[4] is a weariness, and may be a disappointment.

Do not speak with too much scorn of a wintry landscape. The wreaths of smoke rising high into the clear, blue skies, the pure, white covering under which nature reposes, the sparkling of the sinuous streams, where the graceful skaters glide, the groups of children, gathering rosier cheeks and merrier spirits from the heightened oxygen of the atmosphere, give to a winter morning in our sunny latitude cheering excitement.

Did you ever chance to look upon the glorious Niagara in the garniture of winter? And did not its solemn, solitary majesty, impress you more deeply, than when the green, waving woods, and the busy, gazing throngs, divided the absorbing sentiment?

Is not the wintry eve sweet, with its warm fires and bright lights, when families gather in a closer circle, and better love each other? Heart springs to heart, with fewer obstacles than in the

1 A series of essays reflecting on old age.

2 Slightly altered in the second edition (1856).

3 N.P. Willis, American poet, "January 1, 1828," ll. 14–17.

4 in gathering] harvest

more discursive seasons, when the foot is tempted to roam and the eye to wander. The baby crows louder after its father because it can sit longer on his knee. The youth has a lengthened tale for his lady-love, and the storm passes by unheard. Pleasant talk, and sweet song, and loud reading, vary the scene of household delights. Added cheerfulness and love are among the treasures of the wintry evening.

Shall we not avail ourselves of these hints, when the winter of life comes? Shall we not light up the cheerful lamp, and put more fuel on the flame in our cold hearts? They need not go out, though some are gone who were wont to feed them with fresh oil. We will keep love to our race, alive, till the last. Let its embers throw their warmth even into the dark valley. Yes, we will carry those embers with us, and relight them where they can never wane or expire.

The young are said to love winter. Let us strive to make them love us, when we become the personification of winter. We will redouble our offices of kindness, and our powers of entertainment, and see if we cannot melt the ice that has collected between us.

"Young men," says Lord Bacon,[1] "are to be happy by hope, and the old by memory." Yes, with us, are the pictures of the past, the winter gallery, whose landscapes fade not, and whose fountains still freshly murmur. Memory! she who hath sifted and winnowed the harvest of life, that she may know the true wheat. Memory, who hath stood by us when Hope and Love have so often rung the death-knell, and forsaken us,—may we be happy through her? The Lord be thanked if it is so. If, in looking back on all the way wherein He hath led us, she presents a predominance of correct motive, of earnest obedience, of forgiven sin, let us strike that key-tone of praise which shall re-echo through eternity.

Among the prominent joys of life's winter, are those of faith; a nearness, and shadowing forth of things unseen. It was at a festal gathering of the old and young, that the question was once proposed,—which season of human life was the happiest. It was freely discussed, with varying opinions. Then the guests decided that their host, a man of fourscore, should be the umpire. Pointing to a neighboring grove, he replied, "When vernal airs call forth the first buds, and yonder trees are covered with blossoms, I think how beautiful is spring. When summer clothes them with rich foliage, and birds sing among the branches, I say how beautiful is

---

1 Bacon] Francis Bacon, viscount St Albans (1561-1626), English lawyer, statesman, and philosopher

summer. When they are loaded with fruit, or bright with the hues of early frost, I feel how beautiful is autumn. But in sere winter, when there are neither verdure or fruit, I look through the leafless boughs as I could never do before, and see the *stars shine*."[1]

Stars of our God! beam more brightly into our souls, through this wintry atmosphere. For our home is near. And notwithstanding the Great Philosopher hath said that the old can be happy only through memory, we will be happy through hope also, yea, through that hope which hath no mixture of earth, the "hope that maketh not ashamed, and which is as an anchor to the soul."[2]

31. From *Sayings of the Little Ones, and Poems for Their Mothers* (1855).

From PART FIRST.

HUMOROUS, OR PECULIAR USES OF LANGUAGE.

"Harry, was that a love-pat, to your maid?" said a young mother.

"No. It was a strike."

"A *strike!* How is that?"

"I heard a battle-story told. I read some in a war-book too."

"What has that to do with your slap to Jane?"

"Why, it made me want to fight, Ma'am. And I thought likely the maid deserved to be striked. So, I striked her."

Poetical thoughts and forms of expression are sometimes noticed among the little ones, where there could have been neither prompting nor example. A child who had resided on a farm, among working people, from her birth, was once asked, in crossing a field, what was the cause of a gulley that traversed a portion of the grounds, and answered:

"It is the path where the stream used to walk."

Another, who had been accustomed to hear refined conversation, said, on removing from the sea-shore to a rural situation, that "she was sorry to lose the murmur of the waves."

---

1 William Adams (1706–89)? a similar quotation is attributed to him: <http://www.geocities.com/Heartland/Meadows/4939/Zbest001.html>

2 hope ... soul] conflation of Bible passages: Paul's letter to the Romans 5.5 and his letter to the Hebrews 6.19

Looking at the stars as they came twinkling one by one through the boughs of the trees, she exclaimed:

"See, there are angels' fingers pointing to us."

From PART SECOND.

HIGH PRINCIPLES, OR SWEET SENTIMENTS AND AFFECTIONS.

"Please, cousin Philip, do n't" But the wild, rude boy, was not ready to give over his cruel sport of chasing and throwing sticks at a homeless kitten, who filled the air with melancholy mewing. Then the little advocate ran after him into the yard, and laying her soft hands on his cheek, patted it with a sister's fondness, and said:

"Don't, cousin Philip, dear. *It's God's Kitty*."

The persecutor desisted. Then, after a few minutes thought, he took the poor, bewildered animal, and laid it in his little cousin Clara's arms. When he saw it cling confidingly to her, and knew she would be kind to the frightened creature, he went on to school with a new satisfaction in his heart.

Not long after, he saw a fine bird's nest in a tree, and climbed up to it. Just as he was taking the eggs, the mother robin flew round his head with mournful cries. "I suppose," thought he, "cousin Clara would say, 'that is God's robin.' What a strange little creature she is." So, down he got, and left the nest untouched. And he fancied that he felt her soft hand patting his cheek, and sang aloud with happiness.

Neither was this all the advantage that he derived from the gentle touch, and holy precept of the child-teacher. For when he became a man, and was sometimes tempted to sternness, or hard dealing, methought there was a soft hand on his cheek, and a sweet whisper in his heart, "Do n't, cousin Philip. It's God's creature."

From PART THIRD.

PIETY: OR WORDS PRECEDING DEATH.

A little one, just beginning to lisp, had been taught to say, "God will take care of baby." It was the only phrase of any length that she[1] knew. Sweetly the hallowed words dwelt upon those innocent lips.

1 she] in the original: he

Both parents were seized with a malignant epidemic, and ere their convalescence, the little one was attacked. Intelligence was continually brought to their bed-sides, of the state of the sufferer. Suddenly the fearful tidings came that she was death-struck. Feeble and agonizing, the father and mother were brought in their beds, and laid down by their darling. Faintly she unclosed her beautiful eyes, and whispered with an ethereal smile,

"*God will take care of baby.*"

From PART FOURTH.

POEMS FOR MOTHERS.

HOUSEHOLD FESTIVALS.

THE birthday of the precious child!
  With merry laughter fraught,
It graspeth in its little hand
  The toy it long had sought.

The birthday of the blooming boy,
  The maiden fair and sweet,
Where treasured gifts and woven flowers,
  And hallow'd blessings meet.

The birthday of the silver-haired!—
  The nurslings climb their chair,
While kiss, and offered token speak
  Of filial love and care.

The birthday of the absent!—Thought
  On winged scroll shall fly
Where distant zones enwrap the earth,
  Or mountains meet the sky,—

Shall bear above the ocean-waves
  That black with anger frown,
A love its waters may not quench,
  Nor all their billows drown.

The birthday of the dead! Be sure
  That sacred day to keep;
Send portions to the sick and poor,
  And comfort those who weep:

Wrap garments round the shrinking form,
  Home for the orphan find,
And bid the light of knowledge beam
  O'er the untutored mind:—

Spread wide the page that speaks of God,
  Speed on the mission band,
O'er western vales, or Asia's wilds,
  Or far Liberia's strand:—

Give teachers to the prairie-child,
  Give hope to soul forlorn;
Speak kindly words to erring hearts,
  That feel the sting of scorn:—

Remember those who climb the shroud,
  And plow the boisterous main,
Breathe pity through the prison-gate,
  O'er sin's despairing train:—

To all mankind, be deeds or prayers
  Of pure good-will be given;
So shall the birthdays of the dead
  Help thine own soul to Heaven.

THOUGHTS IN A CHURCH-YARD.

I have enriched this soil. Flesh of my flesh
Is here deposited.
                    Crushed at my feet
A casket lies, that love's true essence held.
  Oh, mother! mother! what a thrilling tide
Flows o'er me at thy name.
                    Thy tender cares,
Thy footstep wearied in this thorny vale,
The sculptured beauty of thy pale, pale brow,
Where gentle death restored what pain had marred,
The smooth, benignant forehead, and the smile
That curved the perfect lip. Let me sit down
On thy green sepulcher, and talk with thee.
Still sounds thy thrilling death-moan in my ear,
Oh, mother! mother!

Yet it is not well
To mourn supinely. Rather let us pay
To our own little ones that debt of love
Which nothing earthly, save a mother's heart,
Can comprehend or cancel. Let us strive
The good we have received to render back
Into the bosom of the rising race;
So shall we keep Heaven's law.
Sad harp![1] be still.

32. From *The Ladies' Repository* (1855).[2]

MEMORIES AND LEGENDS OF CONNECTICUT.

NUMBER III.

BY MRS. L.H. SIGOURNEY.

MISS TABITHA'S FARMING.

IN most ages of the civilized world it has been fashionable to satirize females who have continued exempt from matrimony. Sometimes this wit, if analyzed, leaves an element of praise. A young lady is more neat or systematic than her companions, and forthwith it is prophesied she will be an "*old maid*;" whereas, neatness and adherence to system are among the most commendable virtues of her sex. After all, is the lot of unmarried females justly deprecated? If they miss the more tumultuous joys of life, they also escape its correlative trials. If prone to sympathy and to take part in the burdens of others, as they often are, they rank among the most excellent of the earth. Their good impulses have a better chance, from more leisure and unchecked force, of being brought into perfect action.

A clergyman from New England, who exercised for several years his sacred profession in one of our new western states, said, "I love my situation, and the frankness of our warm-hearted people; but painfully feel in my congregation the want of two

---

1 harp] symbol of the poet's or bard's genius for song, or poetry

2 *Ladies' Repository: A Monthly Periodical, Devoted to Literature, Arts, and Religion* 15 (December 1855): 725–27; the same periodical had published Susan W. Jewett's "An Old Maid's Reflections on Woman's Rights," vol. 14 (April 1854): 161–64.

important classes—hoary-headed men, with whom is experience, and unmarried females who are ever doing good to all."

The history of our own times, as well as the private record of friendship, is rich in examples of their benevolence, intellectual effort, and piety. Still licensed sarcasm pronounces them selfish, odd, and eccentric. Selfish! what human being can be more disinterested than the sister who devotes herself to aid the domestic cares and training the offspring of her nearest kindred? except the daughter, who yet more nobly gives her life as the stay and comfort of aged parents. Odd and eccentric! Do these charges mean any thing more than that, standing alone, as they do, unsheltered by husband or children, their peculiarities are made more manifest?

But let this matter be as it may, my present business is to give a few traits of one formerly belonging to this fraternity, who gloried in her condition, and its inherent independence, and, being, perhaps, suspicious of the scorn of mankind, set herself, somewhat on the Ishmaelitish principle,[1] against them. Miss Tabitha,[2] or, as she was occasionally rather irreverently called, Aunt Tabitha, was a lady of a certain age, by which is meant an age not to be inquired into. She guarded this sacred point with as much vigilance as the Romans their vestal fire.[3] A very capable person was she; straight as a dart, and smart as a steel-trap, and prompt in repairing any ravage of time as the Russians at Sevastopol.[4] If a tooth got dilapidated, suddenly appeared a new one in its place. She studied the reigning modes of apparel, and, with needle and shears, was skillful in all kinds of repair, or transmigration.[5]

She professed a contempt of the ruling sex, and great pity for the oppression of her own, and had truly a strong fancy for managing things in her own way. Having received the gift in fee simple[6] of a small freehold, she felt it her duty, when she first came into possession, to assume the entire charge of it. So she

1 Ishmaelitish principle] the Bible, Genesis 16.12, saying of Ishmael, "his hand will be against every man, and every man's hand against him"

2 Tabitha] in the Bible, Acts of the Apostles 9.36, a female disciple "full of good works and almsdeeds," raised from the dead by Peter

3 vestal fire] In ancient Rome priestesses of the goddess Vesta were to be virgins and maintain the temple's sacred fire.

4 Sevastopol] During the Crimean war (1854–56), the Russians were famous for quickly repairing damage to the bastion of Sevastopol.

5 transmigration] recycling or altering

6 fee simple] legal phrase: indefinite and unlimited possession, without limitation to any particular kind of heirs

dismissed the tenants, for she did not like the doings of men, and hoped to exhibit grounds taken care of as they should be. Forthwith she made war on sundry trees, and exulted over their fallen trunks like Semiramis or Boadicea.[1]

Certain plats of long-established turf she directed to have dug up and planted. Stakes were driven, and cords stretched, and beds laid out at her bidding. Trenches and holes were excavated according to her admeasurement.[2] She was determined to drop her peas and beans herself, for she hoped she had some practical knowledge, as well as these men who monopolized all the power of earth, and all the glory of it. As for gardens, she had observed they always sowed too thick or too thin. So at it she went, with a pair of huge masculine gloves drawn over her attenuated hands. At it she went, working fast and valiantly. Out came the hot sun, and into her face mounted the color, till it seemed enveloped in a case of red flannel. In a day or two there was bitter grunting and complaining. She had gotten the crick in the back, and her doctor's bills came to more than her garden stuff would sell for.

"Aunt Tabitha," said one of the neighbor's children, "what makes your cabbages all so full of holes?" "Holes! what do you mean?" Whereat, peering sharply through an eye-glass, for she never indulged herself in spectacles, she exclaimed, "It is them villainous hens. They shall be shut up."

At sunset there was a fierce chasing by Miss Tabitha's second self—a colored woman, who, like her mistress, had been growing young for a matter of thirty years. Nearly breathless was Ebony, when she paused and announced that they were at last all locked up in the barn. After sitting in council, and taking fully into view that there was a small yard surrounded by a high fence, where the aforesaid poultry might take fresh air, and disport themselves as health should demand, it was decided to keep them close prisoners of state during the remainder of the summer. This penal statute was pronounced sufficiently merciful, considering their many willful depredations.

The next morning, bright and early, some two dozen hens were seen actively scratching among the garden beds. By dint of flying and boosting the whole clumsy family had gotten over the palisades. Aunt Tabitha said something scarcely audible about joiners[3] and a higher inclosure; but disliked to call in the aid of

1 Semiramis] semi-legendary warrior queen of ancient Babylon; Boadicea, or Boudicca: first-century CE British queen resisting Roman invasion

2 admeasurement] apportioning, measuring out

3 joiners] carpenters

men, and fell back upon woman's rights, proposing to clip their wings with a large pair of shears. So the dark-browed woman—who, some of the shrewd ones said, ruled her mistress—commenced a running fight, and by sundry screeches heard within the barn, appeared to be carrying into effect the sentence of mutilation. Nevertheless, a few light heeled, half-grown chickens eluded her pursuit, and, roosting nightly on the highest trees, contrived through the day, by hiding, dodging, and purloining, to take care of themselves and form a colony of malcontents.

Miss Tabitha had a commercial taste. She thought it one of the wrongs of her sex that men should take it upon themselves to do the buying and selling of this whole round world.[1] Perambulating her premises to discover their affinities with the market, she fixed her choice upon certain rows of currant bushes.

"How much better they look than when men had the care of them! Not a withered spray or a yellow leaf. *I* know what pruning means."

The long fruit-stalks put forth abundantly; and ere the berries were as large as pin's heads she had mathematically apportioned their products, paying no attention to the antique adage of counting unhatched chickens.[2] So many pecks she would sell for jellies, and so many for wine. And in imagination her purse was already dropsically[3] distended with bits of silver, "current money of the merchant."[4] But the fair leaves began strangely to shrink and blister. Worms were busy there. At first the system of excision was resorted to till the branches threatened to be left bare. Then the reddening fruit grew pale, and some of it fell to the ground, and the poultry, getting a taste, leaped up and ate the remainder.

Aunt Tabitha was a lover of turnips. She bought a quantity of seed, inquiring earnestly for the best bearers. Remembering the crick in the back and the doctorial stuff, an Emeraldine[5] was smuggled within the walls to sow. She designated, with an imperative air,

---

1 round world] echo of Shakespeare, *Antony and Cleopatra*, 5.1.15, spoken by Octavius referring to the death of Mark Antony

2 unhatched chickens] proverbial: "don't count your chickens before they're hatched"

3 dropsically] from dropsy, a disease involving swelling due to the body's retention of fluid, but also slang for money paid as a tip or bribe

4 current money of the merchant] the Bible, Genesis 23.16, describing money Abraham paid Ephron for a piece of land; picked up and widely circulated by Adam Smith, *The Wealth of Nations* (1776), book 1, ch. 4

5 Emeraldine] humorous circumlocution for Irish labourer (Ireland was called the Emerald Isle; two paragraphs down: "he of the Verdant isle")

the spaces where the seeds were to be deposited, marking each with a small stake. Soon there came a request for new supplies.

"More seed!" she exclaimed; "he has had enough to stock a farm. I shall buy no more!"

So several spots were left bare. Young Ireland[1] could not make them hold out, and murmured as the ancient people did when told to make brick without straw.[2] The sun shone and the showers fell, and up came the green turnips. As soon as they opened their sheaths they saw they were in evil case. The land was too strait[3] for them, and they fell to crowding and quarreling. Some stood on each others' backs, and jostled for a place like politicians. Narrow and tall as grass blades they pushed upward into the air, having no possibility of expansion. He of the Verdant Isle was sent for and rebuked, and bade to thin the turnip patches. Whereupon he filled sundry large baskets with masses torn up at discretion, or, rather, indiscretion. And the hens, issuing surreptitiously from their retreat, seized upon the bare places with delight, and, wallowing there in temporary nests, uprooted the remainder. So there was an end of Aunt Tabitha's turnip tops.

It so happened that the first season of her farming was marked by a superabundance of rain. Her corn became broken-backed, and her potatoes spread out long, sickly arms, and lay sprawlingly upon the ground. She perceived that the harvest would be small; yet in this she was no worse off than her neighbors. But not to be better than they—her men-neighbors, too—there was the rub.

Though disappointed, she was too proud to repine, and trusted to another year for more brilliant prosperity. As the vernal season again approached, she resolved to devote her attention more exclusively to the culture of grass and fruits, which she thought might yield a more immediate revenue. But the soil happened not to be in a good condition to favor her first-named hope. It proved unusually propitious to the growth of burdocks and mullens.[4] Indignantly she uprooted a quantity of these interlopers, and scattered clover-seed. Yet Nature, with obstinate partiality, fostered her wild children, and refused to nourish the exotics.[5]

---

1 Young Ireland] another joking reference to the Irish labourer; in fact the name of a group of Irish political agitators in the 1840s

2 brick without straw] referring to the Bible, Exodus 5.18, where the Egyptians punish the enslaved Jews by compelling them to make bricks without straw, thus increasing the difficulty of the task

3 strait] narrow, restricted

4 mullens] or mulleins

5 exotics] foreign plants, not naturalized

Nolens volens,[1] outspread the tough-stalked white daisy, and the hard-wooded yellow-dock, and the hard-headed mullen, while the prickly thistle took stand in every corner, turning the edge of the mowers' scythes, and causing those who had purchased the hay in advance to demand a large discount.

But Miss Tabitha looked on her loaded fruit-trees, and found comfort. A few fine peaches had she, from which she had scrupulously removed every yellow leaf, and caused the roots to be refreshed with the soap-suds of the weekly washings. It so happened that a regimental training was to coincide felicitously with their perfect ripeness, and they were to be disposed of on very advantageous terms to a fruit vender. But other eyes it seems had taken note of them as sufficiently ripe a few nights earlier, and in the morning nothing was found but a few hard peaches on the topmost limbs, and the ground strewed with those partly eaten, mixed with quantities of the stones and trampled leaves. All search was fruitless. The only comfort was in blaming the masculine sex, who were by nature pirates and marauders.

Still Aunt Tabitha's spirit did not fail. Like a true hero, it seemed to gather strength from defeat. A plenty of apples had she. To them she turned as a last resource. To them also turned a multitude of boys for their anticipated reflection. Deep pockets, and large baskets, and dark nights favored their spoliations. They were not removed all at once, like the peaches, but by detachment. The lady of the manor would have sat up and watched, but the orchard was too distant from the house. She meditated setting man-traps, but was afraid of falling into them herself. What should she do? There was no resort but to apply to a neighboring justice of the peace. It was a shame that there were no female justices.

But he undertook her cause so zealously that some of the nimble-footed urchins failed to escape, and were brought to condign punishment. Passing then from one extreme to the other, as the mind is sometimes prone to do, she sought his advice in all her movements. She would neither plant nor harvest without his counsel. As the distance rendered it inconvenient to consult as frequently as it was deemed expedient, it was at length the mutual conclusion that the justice should transfer his residence to that of his client.

This he was the more ready to do, inasmuch as his last daughter had recently married and he was averse to a stranger-house-

---

1 Nolens volens] willing or not; from Latin

keeper, and thought he discovered in the lady in question some resemblance to his deceased wife. She also considered him an exception to her expressed opinion of the sex at large, and had been convinced by his arguments that the yoke matrimonial might be borne without wholly compromising the rights of women. So there was an end of Miss Tabitha's farming.

33. From *Lucy Howard's Journal* (1858).[1]

PREFACE.

THE rush of progress in our native clime is without parallel in its transforming and effacing power. The sound of the woodman's axe yields to the hum of the village springing amid fallen trunks. The city forgets the primeval forest over whose roots it rises. Every generation takes with it to the grave some trait or treasure which it might be curious to restore or useful to cherish.

The inner habitudes of the last half century are already becoming matters of tradition. Yet, as far as they are mingled with the domestic nurture of females, it is well to preserve their semblance; for if obsolete as precedents, they will become points of historic interest. Those elementary details which, from their simplicity or minuteness, seem to need excuse, involve principles or affections which have given to New England homes stability and comfort, as well as that affluence of virtue which has enabled them to cast freely to the young West germs that cause its wilderness to blossom as the rose.

Hartford, Conn., Sept. 1st, 1857.

LUCY HOWARD'S JOURNAL.

Wednesday, August 1st, 1810.

THEY have given me a nice blank-book for a journal. I've written my name and the date as well as I possibly could. What more to put in it I'm sure I don't know.

---

1 A partly autobiographical novel of a young New England woman who settles in the West with her husband.

The schoolmistress says we must all keep journals. She gives several good reasons for it. But what a child of ten years, unless she's wiser than I, can find that's worth writing down, I can't for my life see. I think nobody would care to read it after it was written.

There has been a great storm to-day, with thunder and lightning. I've got nothing else to say. I wish I could get along without this journal, as I used to do; but mamma says I must obey my teacher always.

Somebody has called a journal a map of life. A rude outline I am afraid mine will be. An irregular coast; an island uninhabited; Mountains of the Moon;[1] rivers rising nowhere and emptying nowhere; "Great cry and little wool."[2] Never mind. Let me try to do as well as I can.

I had a grand time in the arithmetic hour this morning at school. I did so many sums, and so fast, that my hand trembled, and my heart beat quick; but it made me happy. I do like those studies that one is sure of. You have only to go straight ahead, and work, and take pains, and all will come right.

My teacher says
  "No day without a line."
I wish to keep her rule
While I am in her school;
  So here is mine.

If I kept school, I think I'd try to make every body have a good time; for if children get mad, they won't learn. If they are very cold, or very warm, or very tired, and you say to them "*study, study!*" and look cross all the time, they are apt to think hard. Then there is no doing them any good till they get into a better

---

1 Mountains of the Moon] in central Africa

2 Great ... wool] proverbial; an action incurring great trouble for little result: "He who shears his hogs will have great cry and little wool"

mood. If teachers would only just look pleasant, and speak pleasant, and not get mad themselves, what a nice place school would be!

I hope I did not write unkindly yesterday. When I read it over this morning it seemed just like a slap of slander. I am afraid I did not feel pleasant myself, and that made me think others were not so. An old lady used to say, When you complain of things around, most likely something goes wrong within. I'll try to carry a sunbeam in my heart to school to-day, and see what that will do.

Tuesday, January 1st, 1811.

Here is a New Year's day, and my birth-day, too.[1] I should suppose I might have some decent thoughts on these two events. So I have, but 'tis such an awful trouble to write them down. As soon as I take a pen away they fly. My strongest impression at present is, that it's terribly cold. I was half frozen in going to school this morning, and not much better off after I got there. We took turns, indeed, in standing at the fire, but the wood was green, and the sap ran out in streams upon the hearth, and the chimney smoked so fiercely that we all shed tears.

They have sent me to a man's school. My mother was induced to believe that it was more thorough, and would be better for me in the end. I'm sure I hope it will. But I love to be taught by ladies, because I always have been. I am awfully afraid here to look up. The gentleman is said to be very learned, and has not been long out of college. It seems so strange to hear him calling me Miss Howard, seeing my name in school has always been Lucy. At first I did not know who he meant, and did not answer, and looked all round the seats to see who Miss Howard was. [pp. 5–9]

I wonder if it is wrong to write poetry. Some wise people say it is a waste of time, and that poets are always poor. I do not wish to waste time, which is so precious; and I am not willing to be poor and beg. But when any thought keeps singing in my ear, just like a bee, I do write it down, and it comes in rhyme. If I try to

1 my birth-day, too] Lucy was born 1 January 1800.

drive it away, it flies round my head, as if it meant to sting me. I have quite a pile of such things hid away. I hope mother will not find them. I never tried to conceal any thing from her before. [...]

I love to go to school in a snow-storm. It makes me jump about, and feel so light and gay. I am not philosopher enough to tell the reason. [pp. 14–15]

I have great comfort with my friend Mary Ann. We are side by side in most of our studies, and always one in heart. I have seen her more than usual during this vacation, and love her better than ever. She is like a sister, as far as I know what a sister would be; at any rate, she is one to me. When we enter school, as our seats are not together, we always smile upon each other; and if any thing goes hard in our lessons, we look into each other's loving eyes, and seem to get light and strength. After school, if we are not obliged to hasten home, I walk with her to her door one day, and she with me the next. She is so beautiful, and her thick, raven hair so glossy. Sometimes I think she is an angel. I wish we might go to school together all the days of our lives.

Some of the girls laugh at us. Others say, they wonder what we find in each other so very remarkable. They wish to give us names significant of our preference. One of the boys said that neither sacred or classic story gave an instance of female friendship, so that the only way would be to form a feminine to David and Jonathan, or Castor and Pollux, or Beaumont and Fletcher.[1] So, thinking himself very witty, he exclaimed, "For the present, we can do no better than to call them Miss David and Miss Jonathan. But which of them, do you suppose, will brandish the sling and stone? for I don't believe either, for all they're such famous scholars, would have the pluck to kill Goliath."[2]

Alas! alas! what shall I do? It is decided that I must not go to school any more. How can I write such words? How can I believe them?

1 David ... Fletcher] famous pairs: David and Jonathan: close friends in the Bible, first book of Samuel; Castor and Pollux: in ancient legend twin warriors, sons of Zeus; Francis Beaumont (1584–1616) and John Fletcher (1579–1625): collaborators on numerous plays

2 kill Goliath] In the Bible, 1 Samuel 17.50, the young Israelite David slew the giant Goliath, hero of the Philistines, in single combat.

People have been talking to mother. They say I am a good scholar in French and in Latin, in Algebra, History, and all the common branches,[1] and that there's no more for me to learn. 'Tis not true. I am just a beginner. To be sure, I've taken pains to get my lessons well. I wish I had not. I wish I had made mistakes at the public examination. I wish I had mumbled when I read or spoke, so that they could not have heard me.

I wonder if this does not come from getting the medal. I'd rather never have had it, nor any of my other prizes.

Grandfather says, when he was young, the women did not go to school so much, and were better housekeepers, and had better health. I don't see why their housekeeping, or their health either, should be helped by being dunces. "You polish and polish," he says to mother, when talking about my education, "but will the foundation be stronger?" Oh dear! I don't wish to hear any of their arguments to this end. I expected to have been a pupil much longer. I feel as if I knew nothing yet as I ought to know. [pp. 60–62]

I wonder if I could not write a novel. I think I might, though I have never read one. Mamma has not been willing that I should occupy my time with them. I suppose I must take Earls and Countesses, and several singular people, and beauty and love, and dangers and escapes, and perils and quarrels, and shake all up together, and the end would be matrimony. A great deal of uncommon action to arrive at a common condition. And then, I understand, all the romance vanishes. [pp. 75–76]

I am convinced that a journal is an assistant to intellectual improvement. I think also it aids in the formation of character. I should not be surprised if it made life seem longer; for the time that I review, even by my very imperfect one, reminds me of a road where there are waymarks and milestones. Every line that is written recalls events and feelings that cluster about it, and might else have been forgotten. It strings the pearls that otherwise, lying loose, might be trodden upon and swept away. I was unwilling to begin it from ignorance, but now, if it were taken away, I should feel as if something had been lost that was important and appreciated.

---

1 common branches] reading, writing, spelling, grammar, arithmetic, geography

A journal, to have its full value, should be kept sacred. The thought that it is to be scanned by other eyes destroys its use. It ceases then to be a means of self-improvement, of solitary communion. The moment you cogitate how to make what you record there agreeable or witty, you are tempted to represent yourself better or wiser than you really are, and its end is frustrated. If vanity or display have any thing to do with a journal, they will uproot all its usefulness. I speak of its moral influence, which should always have the highest place. Setting this aside, it might still have a sort of statistical value as a register of passing events.

My dear Mary Ann joins in our historical readings when she can get time from her school, where she still continues. It is delightful when she comes, for then we question each other about the substance of what we have been reading together, and sometimes I recapitulate what I have read in the interval, so that she may have the advantage of all. It seems a little, too, like an exercise in classics, which vastly pleases me, for my heart still turns back to school-days with a hankering love, notwithstanding I am so very happy in my housekeeping.

She was asking me about my progress in it, and praising some jellies of my making, of which she begged me to give her the recipe. Being in her debt for a poetical morceau[1] or two, I thought I would write it in rhyme:

Cut in pieces four calves' feet,
  Put four quarts of water to them,
Make them subject to a heat,
  That to two quarts shall subdue them.

Strain the fluid; let it rest
  All night long from toil and trouble;
Then from foot and forehead take
  Sediment and oily bubble;

Lay it in the pan once more,
  With a pint of wine to boot,
Acid juice of lemons four,
  Sugar that your taste shall suit;

---

1 morceau] piece

Beat the whites of twice four eggs
  To a snowy froth; and then,
Watchful at your kitchen range,
  Boil for minutes three times ten;

Take it off, and add a cup
  Of cold water to restore it,
Pass it through a flannel bag,
  And in crystal glasses pour it.

CODICIL.

When you compound this jelly, friend,
  I'd simply hint to you,
From motives of economy,
  To make a custard too,
For there are yolks of eggs, you know,
Which 'twere not well away to throw.

So beat them all with sugar fine,
  A quart of boil'd milk use,
And when 'tis tepid, stir them in,
  With flavoring as you choose;
Then in small cups of china bake it,
Or in deep dish a pudding make it. [pp. 86–88]

I have partaken of the holy communion.[1] Side by side with her who nurtured my infancy and him who guided her own, I have received the symbols of dying and redeeming love. I saw in their loved eyes tears of joy, and blessed them, and blessed God.

I feel that I have given myself up entirely to Him. But have I not been His from the beginning? What more can I be now? Only His by my own consent and deed. His by the consecration of my poor services—by the open promise of allegiance until death. Oh, may these not be words of course,[2] but living, lasting principles. [p. 105]

---

1 holy communion] a rite that recalls Jesus' sacrifice for humanity's sins, signifies the communicant's participation in Christian society, and for first communion symbolizes transition from childhood to adulthood

2 of course] customary

To-day, February 8th, is the two hundred and twenty-third anniversary of the execution of poor Mary, Queen of Scots.[1] What a strange and sad romance was her life! A strong contrast there was between her luxurious training and regal life in France, and the rudeness[2] of her native realm, to which, in her young widowhood, she returned. It must have been like coming from the sunny tropics to the Arctic Zone, and the bears too. She seems to have had no wise advisers, and to have been thrown upon treacherous friends. No wonder that she committed errors. I do not wish to excuse, or speak lightly of them, but her long captivity and violent death make us forget the spirit of blame in sympathy.

In faded beauty, who so meekly bends,
And with weak step the scaffold's height ascends?
Why do those stern-soul'd guards exulting bring
The daughter, wife, and mother of a king?
Oh, broken lily of the Stuart line,
Unfriendly blasts and adverse fate were thine.
By flattery nurtur'd, and to folly lured,
How deeply hast thou err'd! how much endured!
Slow, wasting years the captive's bars between,
And the sad memories of a fallen queen.
Lo! one brief struggle, and one savage blow,
Blot out thy charms, thy charges, and thy woe. [pp. 108–09]

It is so much easier to write poetry than prose. I don't mean that high poetical thoughts would be easy to find; but for such thoughts as you happen to have, rhyme is a great help. It hovers like music around you, and beguiles the toil. It is like the song the bees sing when they are abroad at their work. I suppose that amuses them while they are getting their honey. So is the rhythm of the measure to the mental bee, as it stores a little sweetness in its hive. [p. 111]

---

1 Mary, Queen of Scots] Mary (1542–87) married the dauphin of France, was widowed young, and returned to Scotland. A Catholic, she resisted the Protestant Reformation there, had love affairs, became a pawn of Scottish baronial factions, and fled to England, where her cousin, the Protestant Queen Elizabeth, had her imprisoned and eventually executed as a potential threat. She came to represent the price women paid for indulging passion and engaging in the male domain of politics.

2 rudeness] lack of culture and refinement

Some say that female domestic occupations are unfavorable to mental improvement. I think they may be so mingled as to help each other. A consciousness of doing one's duty gives vigor to every thing. That versatility which can turn from one employment to another, and apply itself to all with zeal, and not waste time in the transition, is valuable, and may be cultivated. [p. 115]

Alas! my blessed mother is very sick. She was seized several days since with chills, followed by a high fever. I am not willing to leave her for a moment.

The physician says she has a modification of typhus, which was prevalent here. Some of her pensioners had it. I think she might thus have been exposed. [p. 119]

Our dear physician has pronounced the crisis over.

> "Oh, God of grace!
>   Henceforth to Thee
> A hymn of praise
>   My life shall be." [p. 121]

Henry Howard graduated some time since with honor. He has fine talents, and was always an excellent scholar. His uncle, who has directed his education since his father's death, does not wish him to study a profession, and has placed him in a bank here, with which he is himself connected. I regret not seeing him as formerly, for we have been friends from childhood. He seems to spend what leisure he has in Emily's company. When I see them they are cold in their manners, and distant as strangers. The rumor of his engagement abroad is, I presume, unfounded.

The intimacy one forms with a Journal is remarkable. It seems as a living friend. It is always ready for us, and has no occupation but our concerns. As soon as we have formed the habit of resorting to its to its society, it gets a strange sort of power over us. It remembers for us, and gives new life to scenes and emotions which might else have been forgotten. It never speaks a word, yet it has a reproving power, so that we respect it. If we should persevere in evil doing, I think we should be afraid to meet it. I don't see how a very wicked person, if they told it the truth, could keep in its company. I believe that, by little and little, it would grow very confidential, and that we might lay words upon its silent brow that would scarcely be uttered to those who have ears and voices. [pp. 133–34]

There is something very soothing in the search and linking of poetical sounds. Sometimes they so beguile the mind that the thought which should give them solidity escapes. The "tinkling cymbal"[1] amuses, and the sense become secondary, or takes flight. Nevertheless, this writing of rhymes is a fascinating, and may be a useful thing. [p. 139]

[Lucy visits Washington with her family.]

Politics seem to me but another name for strife; and, as Falstaff says of honor, "Therefore I'll none on't."[2] One of the privileges of our sex is that they may keep clear of such matters. Our wisdom, even if we were not Christians, is to be peace-makers. Now it is our duty. What a mistake to feel that we are injured by being excluded from an active part in the arena! Thrice blessed is our own quiet sphere of duty, where, in making others happy, we find our own truest joy. [pp. 144–45]

We are all so interested in attending the debates of Congress. I fancy that I can tell from what section of our country the representatives are when they first come forward to speak. The New England and the Southern members have a marked idiosyncrasy, and I think the Western men have a freedom and bravery of manner, as if caught from their broad, unsettled regions. It is beautiful to see them, as brethren of one common family—more beautiful than if they were all alike. Legislating as they do for the good of the whole, each has some little sacrifice to make, which adds moral elevation to their bond of brotherhood. [p. 147]

[They travel on to Baltimore, Philadelphia, and New York.]

What a busy, bustling city is this same New York! How full of vitality and progress. The people hurry through Broadway as if

---

1 The Bible, 1 Corinthians 13.1: "Though I speak with the tongues of men and of angels, and have not charity, I am become as sounding brass, or a tinkling cymbal."

2 In Shakespeare's *Henry IV Part 1*, 5.1.139.

there was a bailiff at their heels. I wonder how they got into this fast way of walking. Not from their Dutch ancestors, I fancy. The grave old burgomasters and thrifty vrows,[1] could they trundle about here again, would scarcely believe this to have ever been New Amsterdam.[2]

Immense capacities for commerce has this powerful metropolis. Already it numbers one hundred and twenty thousand inhabitants. Grandfather says that, before the Revolution, Boston and even Newport had precedence; but since that period its growth has been astonishing. Perhaps nothing will limit it but the island on which it stands. I am bewildered by its unresting activities; the more so for having just come from Philadelphia, where people take time to sleep, and sometimes to think too. Men from all regions of the earth congregate here, and all, with one consent, agree in chasing each other.

Some noble institutions I have visited in this city, and am glad of the opportunity of seeing them. I was thankful for safe arrival in it, and more especially thankful to get safely out. [pp. 156–57]

[Lucy is engaged to Henry Howard.]

I know not how I could ever have been worthy of the love of so pure and ardent a heart, such a vigorous and accomplished mind. Indeed, I am not worthy. It is God's unbounded mercy. A new strength seems to have inspired me, as if all life's troubles would be light, all its clouds silver-lined, through the aid of this kindred spirit. [p. 159]

Our wedding was quiet and simple.[3] It would not have been proper, on account of recent bereavement,[4] that it should be gay or festive. Invitations were given to those only who had peculiar claims. The circle was therefore select, but pleasant and sympathetic.

The rooms were beautiful with flowers. Our little conservatory gave forth all its wealth and fragrance. The hyacinths[5] were in full glory, in bulb-glasses and in pots; and the English ivy, climbing out of its baskets, almost covered the principal windows.[6]

---

1 vrows] housewives

2 New Amsterdam] Dutch settlement on Manhattan Island (1625), becoming a British possession in 1674

3 The wedding took place on Lucy's birthday, 1 January 1818.

4 bereavement] Henry's uncle died

5 hyacinths] bulbous plants with a drooping spike of bell-shaped flowers

6 English ivy grows aggressively and is now regarded as a pest by many.

Heliotrope and mignonnette,[1] Henry's favorites, were so disposed among the rich crimson roses as to have a good effect. Mary Ann's taste and assistance were freely lent. She and Egbert stood up with[2] us at the solemn ceremony.

"Can a maid forget her ornaments, or a bride her attire?" asks the prophet.[3] I was gratified that the entire simplicity of mine was approved by those whom I best love. A pure white dress, a fair white rose in the bosom, white rose-buds and orange-flowers wreathed in the hair—that was all. I was so glad not to be absorbed in preparing an elaborate costume, or for the excitement of a large and strange company, at an era so sacred. My grandfather's blessing and my mother's embrace, after the thrilling, hallowed ceremony, and their sweet welcome of my beloved to their heart of hearts, I can never forget while memory holds her seat.[4] [pp. 176–77]

[The couple take a delayed honeymoon at Niagara Falls.]

Niagara! God's voice! God's voice! Let man keep silence.

That fathomless flood! That torrent falling night and day! Have they never rested! Will they never run out? Hath it been so from the beginning? Will it be so until the end? No other symbol can there be of God's eternity. [p. 191]

[While at Niagara, they visit the Canadian shore.]

Here we are, in the dominions of his majesty, the British king. No perceptible change in ourselves by being under a monarchical government. There is doubtless in us Americans an innate love to the good old mother-land. It was inculcated on our ancestors as a part of their religion, and, though the war-cloud dashed it with bitterness and stained it with blood, it is not dead. I trust she will be proud of her high-spirited offspring by-and-by. These

1 Heliotrope] plants with flowers that follow the sun, in Sigourney's day including sunflowers, marigolds, etc.; mignonette: plant of African origin with spike-like clusters of fragrant yellow-white flowers, popular from the mid-eighteenth century

2 stood up with] acted as bridesmaid and best-man; an Americanism

3 The Bible, Jeremiah 2.32; also referred to in Sigourney's account of her own wedding in *Letters of Life* (1866).

4 seat] an account resembling Sigourney's in *Letters of Life*, here p. 297

Canadian subjects of George of Brunswick are less intelligent, and wiry, and wide awake than the Yankees. They seem an industrious, well-disposed people, not made uneasy by a surplus of ambition. [pp. 196–97]

[Lucy devises a plan of benevolence.]

It seems as if I might be useful by instructing poor little girls, were it only in the use of the needle. Many home-virtues are connected with that simple implement, and much wretchedness has it power to prevent; but, unless acquaintance with it is formed in early life, it is seldom resorted to with pleasure or profit. After a family consultation, there has been full consent that I should undertake such a plan, and once a week have as many of these neglected children as our back parlor will conveniently contain. [p. 205]

Methinks the African race have warmer affections and more lasting attachments than our hirelings of other nations. Probably I have formed my judgment from our faithful Amy. So long has she served us and been interested in our welfare, both as a family and as individuals, that I feel as if she were our own flesh and blood. To be served from the heart is a luxury, a privilege for whose continuance we should give thanks to God. [pp. 220–21]

[Lucy discovers she is pregnant.]

Can it be possible that for four weeks I have cherished this gem in my heart? Not like the mother of Moses, hiding from the footstep of foes,[1] but amazed at the weight of my own great happiness. [p. 229]

[Lucy bears a son.]

How wonderful the exquisite workmanship of God in this miniature of humanity! Breathing, moving, opening its eyes, unfolding its tiny fingers, every change is a study of which I never tire. The first night after his birth I could not sleep for watching him. I had never seen so young an infant before. I was not kept waking by pain, but

1 Moses ... foes] In the Bible, book of Exodus ch. 2, Moses' mother sets him adrift in a waterproof basket to avoid an Egyptian decree to kill all newborn Jewish males.

by the curiosity of wondering love. I said to myself, "Am I in a dream? Is this *my* baby?" I feared that the breath, heaving the little breast, might stop, and, when any slight sound stirred the lips, exclaimed, "God's mystery! God's mystery!" [p. 231]

The only bequest of value to Henry from his uncle was a large tract of land at the far West.[1] He is bound by the conditions of the will to dispose of it to some person who will settle upon it and improve it, unless he will do this himself. The time has arrived for the decision, and he feels that he can not understandingly make it without a view of the premises; so he leaves with little warning, that he may avail himself of the company of an intelligent gentleman who visits that vicinity for a somewhat similar purpose. How can I part with him? How can I be divided from him so long? The journey and change of scene may be favorable to his health, which is not very firm. Selfish heart, be silent. [p. 241]

[The Howards leave to settle in the West.]

It was the early gray of the morning when the stage-horn summoned us. There must be no waiting. All things were ready. The baby, roused from his usual slumbers, looked wonderingly around. Let me not think again of the parting embrace. *No, never.* [p. 261]

[They reach the end of public transportation.]

We have purchased an immense covered wagon and a powerful pair of horses. It is astonishing how much may be stowed away in these houses upon wheels, and yet have space for our persons. Henry has engaged another vehicle of equally formidable size, with a practical driver, to accompany us to our place of destination, carrying additional varieties of what the Scotch call "plenishing," and also a small tent, as we are to pass one night on the way out of the reach of habitations. That will give quite an Oriental feature to our cavalcade.

What a unique and wonderful object is a prairie! We have now a far better view of it than we could have had in the rapidity of stage-coach traveling. It is impossible to describe to one who has

1 far West] at this time (around 1820) reaching the Mississippi river

never seen it the effect on the mind of its interminable extent, its unbroken level, varied only by waving grass, and coarse, gorgeous flowers. [pp. 265–66]

We occasionally see one of the cone-roofed wigwams of the Indians, but scarcely any marks of their being inhabited. I have always felt a great interest in our poor aborigines. A few of the men have sauntered listlessly by us in the course of the day. They had a sulky look, and did not return our salutations. The guide said that the remnants of the neighboring tribes were at variance, and had recently had an affray which put them both in bad humor. As evening approached we passed from the prairie into a region with more of the characteristics of a forest. It was delightful to be again in the company of the protecting trees. The road was sometimes obstructed by fallen trunks or branches, so that traveling was slower and more laborious, and, ere the setting sun cast his last golden rays, we selected a fitting place for our nightly encampment. The tired horses were unharnessed and turned out to forage, the poles planted, and the tent pitched with great celerity. A fire was kindled, tea made, a comfortable supper partaken of, and a bed spread in our greenwood dormitory, with proper precautions against the dampness of the earth. Sandy[1] and the guide were to act as sentinels, occasionally taking rest in the wagon, and Henry, sometimes in the tent and sometimes without, took superintendence of the whole. I perceived that each one put his gun in order. As darkness deepened, they replenished the fire as a protection against wild beasts, for we had seen now and then the red eyes of the panther glaring down upon us through the woven branches.

Oh, the solemn grandeur of that night in the forest! Methought it was God's temple, and He visibly near. We, poor emmets at His footstool, cast out from the fellowship of our kind, from the pride of a strong shelter with bolts and bars, were still in the hollow of His hand, girt about with His immutable strength. Through the dark, lofty arches of interlacing trees, reddened by the fitful flame, it might almost seem that there were glancing wings, and a voice, "He giveth his angels charge over

1 Sandy] a Scottish gardener who emigrates west with the Howards; Americans regarded Scots gardeners as the best

thee. They bear thee up in their hands, lest thou dash thy foot against a stone."[1] [pp. 268–69]

We supposed that we had bought every article essential to our simple mode of life, as far as the limits of two carriages would suffice for freight. Yet, what should we happen to forget? Hear it with horror, all ye in the shape of housekeepers. *A broom!* Yes, that indispensable appendage of all notable women.[2] What was to be done? Behold the Indian ingenuity! Orra,[3] of her own accord, was seen dividing thin slips of whitewood into narrow, pliant splinters, which, after forming into an even mass, she bound firmly around a smooth handle prepared for her by Sandy, having seen this work done by the women of her tribe for market among the whites. Even the Scotchman pronounced it "cannie,"[4] and seems to be laying aside some of his prejudices against the "evil race of Injuns." [pp. 274–75]

To have but few books is an advantage. They are better prized, more thoroughly read, more frequently meditated upon and talked about, so that their contents are more likely to be appropriated or their wise suggestions adopted. What we considered a privation, because we could bring with us but a small selection, may therefore prove a gain. From the luxury of periodical literature we are indeed excluded; but important intelligence reaches us after a while, and the habit of much miscellaneous reading, though it may entertain, does not strengthen or discipline the mind. Whoever reads without the intention of remembering—indeed, what it is impossible to remember and logically arrange, will find his retentive power growing inert, as masses of ill-assorted food impair digestion.

How the magic of correspondence softens the pain of separation. Every package of letters from the East brings the loved circle around us. Rivers and mountains no longer divide us. We sit among them and hear their voices. We speak and are answered. Our habit of writing a little every day of whatever occurs, and

---

1 The Bible, Psalms 91.11–12.

2 notable women] common phrase denoting women skilled in every branch of housework, but often implying no knowledge beyond that

3 Orra] an abandoned aboriginal youth whom the Howards took in

4 cannie] Scots for "clever"

sending the sheets when they are filled, gives much of the freshness of living intercourse, and an indwelling with each other, as though we led our existence in two places. Is not this sort of double life a gain? a multiplication of sympathies? Continually I bless my dear Father in Heaven for His protecting care of our earliest home, and that His mantle over all its inmates is love. [pp. 284–85]

It is amusing to see with what miserable accommodations some of the surrounding inhabitants are satisfied. Almost like a mushroom the log-house rises. The growing tree of to-day may find itself to-morrow part and parcel of the roof that shelters a family, a fixture in the wall where the board is spread and the cradle rocks, or hammered into the shrine of the Lares and Penates.[1] With the Eastern people, however poor, there is a laborious effort to add to their internal comforts. Compelled to bring but few with them, they never rest until they have obtained more, or conformed in some measure to the habitudes of early life; but the native dwellers are content. They are satisfied to take their food from maple blocks, or to sit at the table on stumps of basswood. Free and easy are they; and if any improvement is suggested, they say, "This way will do a while. I reckon we'll try it *a section*."[2] Great are they at borrowing. Orra sometimes brings their requests with amazement.

"Will mistress lend her rolling-pin, her chopping-tray,[3] her tea-kettle?"

A large woman came this morning for a washtub, which she took upon her head as if it were an egg-shell; but, suddenly returning, said,

"I forgot to borrie some knives and forks, and a platter big enough to hold the meat and saase too, cause we expect a stranger-man to dinner."

With as much readiness as they request will they oblige. The simplicity of their colonial life induces a fellow-feeling not known where the ceremonious and artificial prevail. Still, civilization and refinement make advances, and progress, in many respects, comes onward with such a whelming tide that these regions can not long be called young or new. What is entirely essential to the women who emigrate hither is a spirit of bravery and cheerful-

---

1 Lares and Penates] the household gods in ancient Roman culture

2 section] while, space of time; by italicizing the expression Sigourney indicates she considered it a regionalism or colloquialism

3 chopping-tray] a shallow wooden dish

ness. The burden of the childrens' quaint old song would be a fitting motto for them, "Come with a good-will or not at all."[1] Come with a determination to bear up boldly, to despise trifles, to take part in every duty with a smiling face, and, when things do not go to your mind, see if you can not find a bright side, or "some soul of goodness in them,"[2] and all will go well enough. [pp. 287–89]

Poor little Willie! Poor little Willie! I could better have borne to yield him back whence he came than to see him suffer. Might it but have pleased his Heavenly Father to have taken his own, like some transplanted flower, that I need not have looked upon the struggle with the Destroyer, and the ghastly white settling over those cheeks of rose.

Short and sharp was the way, dear lamb, to thy Shepherd and the fold of rest. [p. 294]

That little billow upon the green sward! White blossoms begin to crest it. I see it when I rise in the morning. The moon silvers it with long penciled rays. My child! My child!

"He is not there—he has arisen."[3]

[...]

The settlement is enlarging itself beyond our most sanguine hopes. Here and there, sometimes in spots where they might have been least expected, rises the roof of the emigrant. Volumes of blue, curling smoke mingle gracefully with the solemn groves. I am amazed at the mushroom vitality with which they spring up and finish themselves. In less time than is allotted to the digging of a Yankee cellar,[4] walls are upreared, floors laid, children's heads peep out at the windows, and the bee-hive work of busy life goes on. It is true, they do not, as the Scotch say, "fash them-

---

1 Song dating to the seventeenth century and attributed to "Mother Goose," known as "Boys and Girls [or Girls and Boys] Come Out to Play."

2 Shakespeare, *Henry V* 4.1.4–5, King Henry: "There is some soul of goodness in things evil,/Would men observingly distill it out."

3 From the Introit to the Easter mass.

4 Yankee cellar] shallow excavated area beneath a house, less than a full cellar; commonly used to store preserved or dried foods

selves"[1] with much decoration or any great array of what we call creature comforts, but all the purposes of hardy, healthful existence seem accomplished. In due time there will doubtless be progress in what is more refined. "First the blade, then the ear, then the ripe corn in the ear."[2] [pp. 301–02]

Now my blessed mother will come to us. She will dwell under our own roof. We shall be sundered no more. Have I ever before written words so full of joy? Shall not the whole of my life below be one unmixed strain of gratitude to God? [p. 308]

I am thankful that we have been enabled to do something to improve the premises, originally so rude,[3] ere my mother saw them. The inclosed grounds in the immediate vicinity of the house might seem to have really been under longer cultivation. Fruit-trees have been set out, a garden of esculents[4] is in full prosperity, vines encircle the rustic piazza[5] and trellises, and a rich morning-glory,[6] from home-seeds, looks in at my window. Immense flocks of poultry flourish in their own proper domain; beautiful cows add healthful luxuries to our table; fine horses are ready to bear us wherever the still improving roads invite. On every one of these objects I now look with an interest unknown before, saying perpetually in my heart, my mother will see, my mother will share them.

Sandy, who has remarkable constructiveness, has made, out of common boards, sofas, toilet-tables, and a variety of seats, which, with the aid of Orra's needle, I have covered with rich, highly glazed chintz.[7] Recently, also, we have been able to procure pretty paper for our walls; and Henry, who determined, soon after our arrival, to have carpets, procured them at a great

1 From Elizabeth Hamilton's bestseller *The Cottagers of Glenburnie* (1808), in which Mrs Mason exhorts the villagers to good housekeeping but they declare they can't be "fashed," or bothered.
2 The Bible, Matthew 4.28.
3 rude] unfinished
4 esculents] edible plants
5 piazza] normally, public plaza or square; here, veranda of a house; an Americanism in this sense
6 morning-glory] originally tropical, a climbing plant with trumpet-shaped flowers that open in the morning and close at evening
7 chintz] cotton fabric dyed with floral patterns, usually of five colours

expense of transportation, so that I hope my dear mother may find her Western home not comfortless, nor wholly devoid of taste. [pp. 309–10]

The poetical element, like the religious one, is a source of happiness. It may be so cultivated as to soothe suffering, to refine enjoyment, and to sublimate our whole nature. I speak of only the very limited measure in which I have been enabled to taste it. Those who have taken deeper draughts can better set forth its Bethesda properties;[1] but often throughout my not yet very long life have I thus apostrophized the spirit of poetry:

> I bring a broken spirit. Make it whole
> With the sweet balm of song.
> To her I spake
> Who rules the spirit's inborn harmonies.
> And not in vain; for as she struck her harp
> Of varied symphony, and claimed response,
> Forthwith the brooding sadness fled away,
> And, sitting at her feet, I was made whole. [p. 317]

Henry is busying himself with a good and great plan.[2] It occupies his thoughts and conversation. It is to lease, at low prices, small portions of his lands to industrious settlers, for whom he will put up simple but convenient tenements, keeping in view a pleasant degree of external uniformity. Afflicted as he has been, he says he renounces the desire of becoming rich, but will enrich his country as far as he is able by a thrifty, meritorious population. He is determined to admit only such as have a correct moral character, and are willing to work. His wish is that they should derive subsistence for their families, or the principal part of it, from their leased lands, and to furnish employment on his own, at fair wages, for such time as they can spare. To that end he is to devote large expanses to the culture of grain, lest their own element of bread should fall short, and to cover his pastures with sheep, whose fleeces will be salable in distant markets. He con-

1 Bethesda] pool near Jerusalem's Temple where Jesus healed the sick

2 great plan] Plans of managed settlement, often utopian or radically egalitarian in character, were common in American westward expansion. Though philanthropic and patriotic, Henry's plan is also paternalistic, transforming him from farmer living on his own produce to rentier living on rents from others, and thus into a gentleman, of higher social status ("lord of the manor" later in this passage).

templates, also, that each household, according to its ability, should sustain domestic manufactures for the supply of its own coarser and necessary fabrics. Sandy is entranced with delight at being told a Scottish weaver has decided to come, and I have been almost equally uplifted at hearing that a physician and merchant from our own native region may be expected, each of whom are also to take a glebe[1] for cultivation. Henry, with his ardent fancy, already sees this Laconian[2] community in full operation, and intends to offer agricultural and horticultural premiums at the earliest possible opportunity. But his colony is not Utopian,[3] for applications have been already made, though he wisely examines credentials so scrupulously ere he accepts, that it will scarcely increase too rapidly to be healthful. I tell my lord of the manor that I have also some private ambitious views to gratify, and foresee among the children who will thus come together materials for such a kind of school as cheered our dear old home. He assures me that I shall be advanced to the honor of domineering over them for one afternoon in the week, but that his plan, when completed, comprises a school-house and regular teacher, as well as a clergyman and church. May God grant him life and strength to mature his designs, for I am sure they spring from unselfish motives and a pure patriotism. If his purposes and prayers could be perfectly illustrated, he would, in the words of the eloquent prophet, "make the wilderness an Eden, and the desert a garden of the Lord."[4]

I believe home-happiness to be the secret of national prosperity. Men who have not this fountain of peace, this wing of love

1 glebe] parcel of land supporting a clergyman (usually) or other professional, directly through produce or indirectly through rent

2 Laconia] ancient Greek city-state of Sparta with a simple, martial society based on small self-reliant farms rather than on cash crops and trade, in contrast to Athens, city of urban culture and luxury; both Sparta and Athens exploited slave labour.

3 not Utopian] By this time there were many utopian experiments in communal and communistic agrarian living in the United States, often with a religious basis, such as those of the "Shakers" in New England, New Harmony in Indiana (founded 1814), the Oneida Community in New York state (founded 1844), and the Amana colonies of eastern Iowa; viewed with suspicion by mainstream society, such communities were often harassed and persecuted by local and state governments.

4 The Bible, Isaiah 51.3.

folded around them, are more ready for "treasons, stratagems, and spoils."[1] Herein is the patriotism of woman and her privilege. Not to wrestle at the ballot-box; not to shout in popular assemblies; not to steer the ship through the blackening tempest, nor sound the trumpet for the battle-field,[2] but to cheer and charm at board and hearth-stone; to teach the sanctities of deathless affection; to breathe heaven's melodies over the cradle-sleeper; to fashion by holy example every soul under her roof for a realm of harmony and peace. Homes thus ordered, sprinkled over a land, are as dew-drops, giving freshness and beauty; as the hidden salt, preserving the great heaving ocean in health and purity. Who can desire more honor than thus to be priestess at the shrine of the household affections till she finds her place among "an innumerable company of angels, and spirits of the just made perfect, whose names are written in heaven?"[3]

In my stated[4] perusal of the Scriptures this morning, I was impressed with the great beauty of a promise in the Divine name which occurs in the thirty-fourth chapter of Ezekiel: "I will seek that which was lost, and bring again that which was driven away, and bind up that which was broken, and strengthen that which was sick."[5] Methinks it would be an excellent text for a consolatory sermon, as comprehending the prominent varieties of human suffering with their merciful antidotes. A passage in the thirty-seventh chapter of the same book, at the sixteenth and seventeenth verses, furnishes a natural foundation for the structure of a discourse on national union, should any dissension ever arise among these banded states, this spreading, happy, and prosperous family; which may our Almighty Protector avert.[6] The

1 Shakespeare, *The Merchant of Venice* 5.1.85, Lorenzo, describing the preoccupations of the man who has "no music in himself"

2 battle-field] reference to women suffragists and anti-slavery campaigners, opposed by Sigourney; see p. 225

3 Adapted from the Bible, Hebrews 12.22–23.

4 stated] of regular, not casual occurrence

5 The Bible, Ezekiel 34.16.

6 The passage reads: "Moreover, thou son of man, take thee one stick, and write upon it, For Judah, and for the children of Israel his companions: then take another stick, and write upon it, For Joseph, the stick of Ephraim and for all the house of Israel his companions: And join them one to another into one stick; and they shall become one in thine hand." Sigourney applies the passage to the breakdown in the political compro-

prophet from whom I have quoted, though overshadowed in eloquence by Isaiah, and surpassed in pathos by Jeremiah, has occasionally great vigor and picturesque power. He seems, also, to have been an observer of dates, or of that minuteness in chronology which I so much regard, as he thus records the period of one of his visions: "In the five-and-twentieth year of our captivity, in the tenth day of the month, in the fourteenth year after the city was smitten, in the self-same day, the hand of the Lord was upon me."[1] Sometimes I find striking texts which ministers seldom use. Would not this from Kings, "Then he said, What title is that I see? And the men of the city told him, It is the sepulchre of the man of God,"[2] be a good one at the funeral obsequies of a distinguished saintly person? And might not the solitude and meditation which are salutary after any great affliction be enforced by the description of Moses: "While the cloud tarried upon the tabernacle, remaining thereon, the children of Israel abode in their tents?"[3] The question of the lawless Danites to the recreant priest of Micah, "What *makest* thou in this place? and what *hast* thou here?"[4] might be made to rebuke that venal spirit which counts the gain of money above the gain of godliness; and the accepted prayer of Jabez, "Oh that Thou wouldest keep me from evil, that it may not grieve me,"[5] shadows forth that elevation of spirit above the ills of time which should be sought for by those whose home and heritage are in heaven.

People who enter on the roughnesses of Western life will do well to divest themselves as soon as possible of enervating associations. This is not merely an accomplishment, but a species of self-defense—a heart-shield. "Forgetting the things that are behind" is essential to a brave "pressing onward to those that are before."[6] "Behold, all things are become new,"[7] says the wondering house-

mises from 1820 to 1854 that preserved the Union by admitting one new state that allowed slavery for each new one that banned it; the breakdown led to the secession of the Southern slave states and outbreak of Civil War in 1861.

1 The Bible, Ezekiel 40:1.

2 The Bible, 2 Kings 23:17.

3 The Bible, Numbers 9.22.

4 The Bible, Judges 18.3.

5 The Bible, 1 Chronicles 4.10.

6 The Bible, Paul's letter to the Philippians 3.13.

7 Paul's second letter to the Corinthians 5.17: "Therefore if any man be in Christ, he is a new creature: old things are passed away; behold, all things are become new."

keeper, who, entering her rude mansion, misses the carpeted floor and the marble mantel-piece. Yes; but it is of no use to complain or to compare. The direction to the nephew of Abraham and his emigrating family, "Look not back," is appropriate to you;[1] for, though you might not, like his wife, in case of disobedience be turned into a pillar of salt, you might, perchance, become a stumbling-block to those around, or be reminded of the regrets of the good lady who said, "*I'm a stumbling-block to myself.*"[2] Go ahead and work. See where there is any good to be done, and do it. Look aloft, and gather strength, and wear the smile of the "angel who came and sat under the oak at Ophrah while they were threshing wheat,"[3] or of him who found Hagar a wanderer in the wilderness, and comforted her.[4] [pp. 320–25]

All the way in which God has led me from my birth has been full of love. All the discipline I have had has been but for my soul's good. Already I can see it has fitted me more rationally to enjoy earth's happiness. Ever in view, as a consummation, is God's reserved happiness. In the glimpses of that noontide glory, how beautiful to walk through this silvery moonlight below, admiring the foundation and the columns of the "temple not made with hands,"[5] catching even in its vestibule some echo of its

---

1 In the Bible (Genesis ch. 19), before God destroys Sodom for its wickedness he sends angels to lead away Abraham's virtuous nephew Lot with his wife and daughters, enjoining them not to look back; Lot's wife disobeys and is turned into a pillar of salt.

2 Perhaps Jeanne Françoise Fremyot, Baronne de Chantal (1572–1641), known as St Jeanne de Chantal; mentioned in Mary Shelley's *Eminent Scientific and Literary Men of France* (1838) and a biography of her was published in New York in 1852.

3 The Bible, Judges 6.11: God sent an angel instructing Gideon, who was threshing his wheat at Ophrah, to liberate the Jews from Midianites' oppression, inflicted as punishment for sinfulness; presumably the angel smiles in anticipation of the good news that Gideon has not yet heard.

4 In the Bible, book of Genesis, Abraham's infertile wife Sarah has her maid Hagar bear Abraham a son, Ishmael, but then has Abraham expel Hagar into the wilderness, the first time for arrogance (16.1–16) and a second time with Ishmael (21.8–21), whom Sarah sees as a threat to the rights of the son, Isaac, she has finally borne herself; on each occasion an angel visits Hagar in the desert assuring her that she will survive and her son will found a distinct tribe.

5 In the Bible, gospel of Mark, 14.58, Jesus is falsely accused of threatening to destroy the Temple made with human hands and erect another "made without hands."

high celestial symphony, "Holy, holy, holy, Lord God Almighty, heaven and earth are full of the majesty of Thy glory."[1]

The homeless child, the unshelter'd guest,
  Whom thou on earth didst cheer,
Perchance, when cares no more infest,
Shall rise in Heaven among the bless'd,
And greet thee to that realm of rest
  Which sorrow comes not near.

[These verses mark the end of Lucy's narrative; after her death, her story is concluded.]

She whose intimacy we have so long shared through these pages thought not to write in her journal, "*These are my last lines.*" Prescience was not hers. [...]

She lingered not to press the mother-kiss on those innocent brows. For her the parting scene had no terror. She saw in death only the moment when the soul draws near to its Father, the stream returns to its Source.

THE END.

34. From *The Daily Counsellor* (1859).[2]

JANUARY II.[3]

"In the beginning, God created the heavens and the earth."

GENESIS, i: 1.

GOD spake,—and startled chaos fled
  With ancient night away,
The slumbering elements arose,
  Obedient to His sway.

---

1 From the Protestant Episcopalian Book of Common prayer.

2 A series of Bible passages with poems and commentaries, for each day in the year, some poems previously published in the annuals the *Christian Keepsake* (1837), the *Ladies' Wreath* (1847), and the *Waverley Garland* (1859); with a sermon (1845); in the *Illustrated Family Christian Almanac* (1854); and in the anthology, *Hymns for the Circle* (1855).

3 A rewriting of the Biblical creation story; for an earlier similar work see "The Creation" in *Moral Pieces, in Prose and Verse* (1815), p. 66 here.

The kingly Sun came forth in state.
  The stars their courses wove,
And, like a timid bride, the Moon
  Look'd from her bower of love,

Fair Eden spread its cultured bound,
  While through its stainless green
Man, and his dear companion[1] walk'd,
  Sole rulers of the scene.

So, thus in the beginning rose
  This universal frame,
Glad Nature singing hymns of praise
  To her Creator's name.

Oh! Maker of the earth and skies,
  Remember me I pray,
This dying form,—this living soul,—
  And cast them not away.

FEBRUARY IX.[2]

"A deep sleep from the Lord was fallen upon them."
1ST SAMUEL, xxvi: 12.

THEY fell asleep. The weary heat
  And burden of the day
Oppress'd them, and their failing feet
  Have halted by the way.

Some, in the hallowed place of graves,
  Some, where the prairies spread,
And some, in ocean's coral caves,
  Have found a dreamless bed.

While others, 'mid the Arctic pines,
  And over drifting snows,
Or where the sunny tropic shines,
  Share undisturbed repose.

---

1 Man ... companion] the first couple, Adam and Eve

2 Reminiscent of Felicia Hemans's "England's Dead," but representing the scattered dead of American global missionary work rather than of British global empire.

Let grief forego her hopeless cares,
  Nor in despondence weep,
A holy hush should sure be theirs
  Whom God hath laid to sleep.

JUNE XIV.

"They have laid their swords under their heads."

EZEKIEL, xxxii: 27.

UNDER their heads they have laid their swords,
  Who turn'd the nations pale,
With the threat and boast of their banner'd host,
  And their masses of moving mail,
At their stern command mov'd the warrior band,
  The soldier struck his tent,
And with stifled sigh from his home to die
  The youthful conscript went,
They stirr'd the sleep of the desert deep
  With trumpet and battle-cry,
Scattering men's bones mid the sands and stones
  To bleach 'neath a wintry sky,
The wave of their hand was the law of the land
  Where their conquering legions swept,
Like the voice of a god was their tyrant nod.
  Yet they slumber in dust, unwept.

Under their swords they have laid their heads,
  They shall trouble the earth no more,
They molder away, like the coarsest clay
  Of the serf that their livery wore,
No vine they bade, with its clustering shade,
  O'er the quiet hillocks spread,
But they ravaged the plain with its ripening grain
  That the poor man's children fed,
They led the fire over tower and spire
  And village in rural pride,
They drench'd the soil with the blood of toil
  Till it shrank from the loathed tide,
They have gone, they are fled, like a dream they have sped,

They have acted their gorgeous[1] part,
They have left a name on the tomb of fame,
And a curse in the living heart.

35. From *Gleanings* (1860).

UP AND DOING.

"We can't afford to wait."
BISHOP CLARK.[2]

Lo! from the wild, the city starts,
And on the prairie's breast
Spring dome, and tower, and spire, like dream
Of Araby the blest,[3]
And they who fall behind the age,
Or move with snail-like feet,
Are in these days of progress deem'd
Defunct, or obsolete.

The world grows busy, and expects
Her sons to do the same,
She makes the boiling water work,[4]
And yokes the winged flame,
She bids the mightiest elements
Her varied will obey,
And calls the lightning from the skies
Her whisper'd words to say.[5]

The idle man is like the dead[6]
Who can no burial find;

---

1 gorgeous] magnificent, splendid, but also gaudy, showy

2 Thomas March Clark (1812–1903), rector of Christ Church, Hartford, Sigourney's church, before being made bishop of Rhode Island in 1853.

3 Araby the blest] Milton, *Paradise Lost*, 4.162, but widely circulated

4 boiling water work] reference to steam power

5 And calls ... to say] reference to the electrical telegraph, patented in the United States in 1837 by Samuel Morse

6 Sigourney's footnote: "The idle are a peculiar kind of dead, who cannot be buried." ARABIAN PROVERB [also used elsewhere by Sigourney; from Maxims of Imam Hazrat Ali (599–661), "Learning"].

Ill fares it in the race, with those
 Who halt and look behind;
Even she, who backward gaz'd of old,
 Was petrified,[1] we read,
And how can we afford to wait
 'Mid all this railroad speed?

The tares are growing in the field,
 Though we supinely sleep,[2]
And he who sows no seed betimes
 May hope in vain to reap,
The Prince of Evil[3] never lags,
 Nor loiters o'er his prey,
And they must needs be wide awake
 Who think to bar his way.

The pagan people fade and fall
 In ignorance and night,
Without a cheering ray from heaven
 The dreary grave to light,
The ready mission-ship but asks
 Our bounty for its freight,
Hark! to the cry of dying souls—
 They can't afford to wait.

If there's a duty unfulfill'd,
 A blessed word unspoken,
Haste! ere the hour-glass of our days
 Is wasted, spent, or broken,
Nor let procrastination lend
 Its burden to our fate,
We can't afford to wait, my friends,—
 We can't afford to wait.

---

1 petrified] reference to the Bible, book of Exodus, where Lot's wife's is turned to a pillar of salt for ignoring God's command not to look back as she flees the city of Sodom, destroyed by God for its sinfulness

2 The Tares ... sleep] referring to Jesus' parable on constant vigilance against sin, in the Bible, Matthew 13.25: But while men slept, his enemy came and sowed tares [weeds] among the wheat, and went his way.

3 Prince of Evil] Satan

THE SEWING MACHINE.[1]

Click!—click!—click!—
  There in a pile they lie,
Shirts and bosoms and collars,
  Heap them still more high.
Table cloths, towels and sheets,
  Off in a trice they glide,
With all the countless articles
  Of household use and pride.

Click!—click!—click!—
  Cloak and surplice and stole,
Counterpane, curtain and quilt,
  In ceaseless current they roll,
From the wonderful magician
  That there in the corner stands,
Transcending old Briæreus,[2]
  With all his hundred hands.

No more the thoughtful husband
  Need hasten to his trade,
With handkerchiefs unhemm'd,
  And wristbands broken and fray'd,
Even the matron findeth leisure,
  Though with many a labor tried,
To read the daily paper,
  And something else beside,

While the astonished mother
  Can keep in neat array
Her rude and rosy urchins
  That in the gutter play,
Coats and jackets and pants
  Are quicker made anew
Than the laundress can restore the old
  To their primeval hue.

---

1 There were earlier forms of sewing machine but the American Elias Howe patented the first reliable one of the modern type in 1846, and Isaac Singer began manufacturing the first commercially successful machine in the 1850s. The machine enabled greater industrialization of clothing manufacture and the establishment of sweatshops employing women.

2 Briæreus] in Greek legend, a creature with a hundred hands and fifty heads, who fought against the Titans

The lover, when he presseth
  The hand of his lady fair,
No longer finds her finger rough
  With the needle's furrowing share.[1]
And the thin and pallid sempstress,
  With endless stitching worn,
May sleep before the midnight,
  And rise refresh'd at morn.

What a blessed age we live in,
  Sisters, and daughters, and wives;
With all the lights of science
  To lengthen out our lives.
And be the time thus rescued,
  Not spent in folly's strife,
But fit ourselves and others
  For a higher, better life.

BREAKFAST.[2]

Breakfast!—Come to breakfast!
  Honest friend is he,
More than gourmand Dinner,
  More than tinsel Tea,
More than stolid Supper
  Dragging in its train,
Dizzy-head, and night-mare,
  Or paralytic pain.

Breakfast!—Come to breakfast!
  Little ones, and all,
How their merry footsteps
  Patter at the call,
Break the bread,—pour freely
  Milk that cream-like flows
A blessing on their appetites,
  And on their lips of rose.

---

1 share] ploughshare

2 Previously published in *Breakfast, Dinner, and Tea: Viewed Classically, Poetically, and Practically*, ed. Julia C. Andrews (New York: D. Appleton and Company, 1859).

Breakfast!—It reclaims us
  From realms of death-like sleep,
From wild and dream-land wanderings
  Wherein we laugh or weep,—
It giveth strength for labor,
  It giveth zeal for play,
New vigor to the student,
  Fresh spirits to the gay.

Breakfast!—summer breakfast!—
  Throw the casement high,
And catch the warbler's carol
  On glad wing glancing by,
Set flowers upon your table
  Impearl'd with dew-drops rare,
For still their fragrance speaks of Him
  Who made this earth so fair.

Breakfast!—winter breakfast!—
  Recruit the blazing fire,
Heap coal upon the glowing grate
  Or fill the furnace higher,
Though drifting snows descending
  May whiten field and bower,
Where loving hearts are true and warm,
  King Frost hath little power.

Dinner may be pleasant,
  So may social tea,
Yet, methinks the breakfast
  Is best of all the three,
With its greeting smile of welcome,
  And its holy voice of prayer,
It forgeth heavenly armor
  To foil the hosts of care.

Breakfast!—early breakfast
  The Sun's new rising ray,
Doth lend a secret magic
  To speed you on your way,
But let one hour of morning
  Go by you on the track,
And Franklin says "you'll toil all day,
  But never get it back."

Breakfast!—Come to breakfast!—
  Some there are, who hear
No such household-music
  Ringing in their ear;
Wilt thou from thy store-house
  Cheer them when they pine?
Shedding blessed sunbeams
  On their day, and thine?

36. From *Selections from Various Sources* (1862).[1]

USE OF BIOGRAPHY, TO HISTORY.

"HISTORY without the companionship of her sister, Biography, is an inexorable riddle: for in the individual character of rulers and princes, in their passions, interests, and good or bad principles, can alone be traced the springs of outward and visible actions that history records."—*Miss Strickland; from "Life of Queen Mary."*[2]

PRECEPTS OF QUEEN CHRISTINA.[3]

"THE past is gone: the future may never come: the present is but a point; yet on that terrible point hangs Eternity."

"THE ocean is the type of truly great souls; however agitated the surface may be, the most profound tranquility reigns beneath it."

"MEN should seek in themselves the commencement of ancestral distinction."

---

1 A commonplace book, or collection of favourite quotations, of the kind kept by many at the time, and recommended by Sigourney as a way of disciplining reading and memory.

2 Agnes Strickland (1796–1874), English author of several histories, including a multi-volume *Lives of the Queens of England* (1840–48).

3 Queen Christina] Christina Vasa (1626–89), queen regent of Sweden, raised like a boy, later dressed in men's clothes, led an unconventional life, abdicated her throne in 1654 to become a Catholic; sources include a biography in Anna Jameson's *Memoirs of Celebrated Female Sovereigns* (1834) and Margaret T. Taunton's *Christina, Queen of Sweden: A Brief Notice of Her Life, Conversion, and Death, with Her Maxims* (1862).

SONG.

"THIS faculty of imagination, has lifted me up when I was sinking, and kept my head above water. Its results cheer me, for I feel that they have enabled me to give pleasure to others. I am thankful to God, who gave me this faculty, and it is a part of my religion, to defend the gift, and profit by its possession."

Charlotte Bronte.[1]

THE PROVISONS FOR LIFE.

"THE bread of life, is love;
The salt of life, is work;
The sugar of life, is poetry;
The water of life, is faith."

Mrs. Jameson.[2]

FROM MRS. HEMANS.[3]

"OH Searcher of the Soul! in whose dread sight,
  Not the bold guilt alone that mocks the skies,
But the scarce own'd unwhisper'd thought of night,
  As a thing written with the sunbeam lies."

"IT was a fearful, yet a glorious thing
  To hear the hymn of martyrdom, and know
That its glad stream of melody could spring,
  Up from the unsounded depths of human woe:"

"FOR she had made no deeper love her guest,
  'Mid her young spirits dreams than which grows
Between the nurtur'd of the same fond breast,
  The shelter'd of one roof, and so it rose
    Twin'd in with life."

---

1 Charlotte Brontë (1816–55), English novelist and poet; passage adapted from Elizabeth Gaskell, *The Life of Charlotte Brontë* (1857), ch. 18; letter to W.S. Williams, 21 September 1849.

2 Jameson] Anna Brownell Jameson (1794–1860), English art historian

3 All six selections from English poet Felicia Hemans, *The Forest Sanctuary* (1825): part 1, stanzas 26, 71, 39, 63; and part 2, stanzas 50 and 51.

"JOY for the trembler! Thou redeem'd one joy!
Young dove set free."

"YES! I am he that look'd and saw decay
Steal o'er the fair of earth, the ador'd too much,
It is a fearful thing to love what death may touch."

"HOW dear the image and the thought of those
Before us gone; our lov'd of early years
Gone where affection's cup hath lost the taste of tears!"

RELIGION IN THE FAMILY.

"WE might picture many blessed scenes in the Christian household,—children grouped around a pious mother listening to her soul teachings, perchance, aged grand-parents benignantly looking upon the efforts of those whom they have trained to fill their places. Here are sons and daughters, brothers and sisters, all intent upon fulfilling their duties at home and abroad, faithful in the discharge of worldly business, yet in subordination to the higher interests of the immortal soul.

"In this period of innovation and revolution, injudicious efforts are making to break up the foundations of society, and to bring woman forward in unwonted places and situations. Her true friends should advocate her advancement in all knowledge and wisdom, suitable to her character and duties, to guard her rights of property and personal liberty, as far as may consist with the organization of society; man being divinely constituted the head of the family, and the protector of woman."

Mrs. A.H.L. Phelps.
From "Christian Households."[1]

FAME.

"IT were no recompense for wasted life
That men should breathe my name in empty sound,
And when the heart is broken with the strife
And toil of earth, the solemn sleeping mound
That pillows me, be haunted by a throng

1 Mrs Almira Hart Lincoln Phelps (1793–1884), science writer and author of the pamphlet *Christian Households* (1858).

Who knew me not, save in my fleeting song;
The enfranchised soul should seek a higher aim,
Nor droop its pinions down so low as earthly fame."

Mrs. Ann S. Stephens.[1]

37. From *Letters of Life* (1866).[2]

From LETTER X.

LOVE AND MARRIAGE.

[...] as years glided onward, with their changes, I was no stranger to the language of love, nor unsusceptible to its sentiment. Manly beauty and grace I appreciated, but the chief attraction was in intellect and knowledge. My most valued associates were of the latter order. I had also a *penchant* for the company of men considerably older than myself. This arose from several motives. I had always been taught to respect seniority. I gained from their experience more information, and felt secretly more at ease in their company, because I thought there could be no suspicion of their partiality, or of my seeking to create it. Ever had I been exceedingly sensitive to aught that bore the appearance of forwardness in my own sex. It seemed to me treason against their native refinement and their allotted sphere. So I still think; and, however the modes of association may vary with differing generations, can never respect any woman who boldly seeks the attentions, or invades their province whose part it is to make advances, to legislate, and to bear rule. Perhaps I might have been deemed fastidious, but have never been able to lay aside my creed.

I had still a deeper reason for avoiding serious advances. My mind was made up never to leave my parents. I felt that their absorbing love could never be repaid by the longest life-service, and that the responsibility of an only child, their sole prop and solace, would be strictly regarded by Him who readeth the heart.[3] [...]

---

1 First published in the *Ladies' Wreath* (1847), 240; Ann Stephens was Sigourney's personal friend, and author of numerous works of poetry and prose fiction, including *Malaeska* (1860), the story that launched the firm of Beadle and Adams' dime novels, the most widely distributed form of cheap book in the nineteenth-century United States.

2 Sigourney's posthumously published autobiography.

3 Him ... heart] God

Still, I was sometimes sorely tempted, and my faith ready to fail. At a time when my religious convictions were peculiarly strong, I painfully studied the case, whether I ought not to take part in mission labor in a foreign clime. The literal application of the passage was warmly pressed: "He that loveth father or mother more than me, is not worthy of me."[1] "Not worthy of me! Not worthy of me!" rang like a dirge in my soul. But the surge of feeling subsided, and in deepened humility I decided that, without any worthiness whatsoever, I must cling to my Saviour's cross.

Sundry times, also, I came near being caught in the clerical net, but broke through. Fascinations of a more ambitious character had likewise their scope and sway. Still my slight bark was guided, though sometimes veering, to keep its pole-star in view. [...]

But the blind archer,[2] though oft repulsed, and long held in subjection, bided his time. One might have supposed that, for me, this time had passed. A quiet school-dame, most happy with her scholars and friends, having surmounted the period of youth's romantic enthusiasm, and addicted to "maiden meditation, fancy-free,"[3] might have been thought no fit mark for his arrow.

Nevertheless, as I plodded my way to and from my school-house, a pair of deep-set and most expressive black eyes sometimes encountered mine, and spoke unutterable things. They were the property of a gentleman of striking physiognomy and the elegant manners of the olden school. Their dialect might not have made a lasting impression on one whose every thought and faculty were bespoken by her daily occupation; but ere long a letter came—a letter of touching eloquence and the fairest chirography.[4] From this there was no escape. It was like a grappling-iron, not to be evaded. Wherever I turned, its words followed me as living creatures—an image of the wheel seen by the entranced prophet, full of eyes, that gazed wherever he went.[5] To love-letters I had been no stranger, yet nothing like this appeal had caused such perturbation, and captivity of thought. Its writer I had occa-

1 The Bible, Matthew 10.37.

2 blind archer] In ancient myth, Cupid's arrows inspired love in those they hit.

3 Shakespeare, *A Midsummer Night's Dream* 2.1.164, Oberon's speech.

4 chirography] style or character of writing, in Sigourney's day considered an indication of character and culture

5 eyes ... went] the Bible, Ezekiel 1.15–18

sionally met in select parties, with his wife, a being of angelic loveliness and beauty, who had gone to a higher and congenial sphere.

[She consulted her patrons, Mr and Mrs Wadsworth, who urged her to accept the offer of marriage; she then asked permission of her parents, who approved.]

I gave scope to the new affection, so long repressed or chastised, and its sway was pervading and delightful. Every task was achieved with new vigor, every obstacle surmounted as with double strength. Indeed, it seemed as if nothing remained worthy the name of task or obstacle, so perfectly did *couleur de rose* overspread all things. The refrain of an ancient sacred melody echoed in my secret thought a perpetual melody:

> "O God of grace!
>   Henceforth to Thee
> A hymn of praise
>   My life must be."

I was as one wrapped in the tissued drapery of a pleasant dream. What came the nearest to awakening me as a stern reality, was the necessary dissolution of my cherished school. [...]

"Can a maid forget her ornaments, or a bride her attire?"[1] asked one of the prophets of Israel. I should have been thankful to have been allowed to forget mine. Such purchasing, devising, driving of needle and shears, dealing with mantuamakers, milliners, and sempstresses, had never before entered into my history. I was humbled by it. I analyzed it as an inherent selfishness, a weak compliance with the tyranny of Fashion. It struck me that an event so sacred, so entwined with eternal destinies, should be less marked by trifles and trappings. Nor could I witness without regret the consequent and almost entire absorption of a moderate sum laid aside from my school-earnings, and mentally devoted to my dear, deserted parents.

One of the brightest of June mornings shone upon our nuptials. Every leaf and flower was redolent of dew and sunshine, as the bridal procession set forth. [...]

---

1 The Bible, Jeremiah 2.32; God asks, "Can a maid forget her ornaments, or a bride her attire? Yet my people have forgotten me days without number."

It had been my resolution to utter audibly the responses required of me. Yet I was not aware, until hearing the clear, impressive enunciation of him who stood by my side, that my lips gave no sound. The power of articulation had fled. The presence of the throng had no influence. It did not enter my mind. I seemed wrapped in a dream, and to have no personal identity with surrounding things. The congratulations that succeeded the ceremony, the world of flowers that were pressed upon me and showered around, seemed cheering and beautiful; but I could not think them mine. It seemed an illusion, though without the loss of self-command. What first restored full consciousness, was the blessing of an old lady of ninety—Madam Lathrop, a connection of my earliest benefactress—and the fervent glance of her still lustrous eye. Her voice touched the sealed fountains of other years, and I was again myself. [...]

From LETTER XIII.

LITERATURE.

My literary course has been a happy one. It commenced in impulse, and was continued from habit. Two principles it has ever kept in view—not to interfere with the discharge of womanly duty, and to aim at being an instrument of good.

My journals, which I have already mentioned were begun at an early age, were usually made the repositories of my poems, in the order in which they were composed. Those systematic records became a sort of necessity of my existence. They seemed an adjunct in religious progress, and to justify the adjuration with which one of them is consecrated:

"Give me Thine aid calmly to look upon the changes that are appointed me, and to love the little streams fed hourly from the fountain of Divine Mercy; and to hope that, when I fade, as I soon shall, like the grass, I may be renewed in the image of a glorious immortality."

After my establishment in a school at Hartford, through the influence of Daniel Wadsworth, Esq., he and his lady, my lovely friend, requested a sight of my journals, which had been usually kept in sequestration. He made selections from their contents which he persuaded me were adapted to the public eye; and I adventured, under his guardianship, on what was in those times, and in our part of the country, a novel enterprise for a female.

[Sigourney gives an account of each of her books as they appeared in succession, and turns to her publication in magazines.]

There was a long period, after I became a writer for the public, when periodical literature flourished abundantly. The monthly magazines in particular became almost a legion. Every position, occupation, and age of human life seemed to have its own exponent. This, after a series of years, regulated itself, and such as were essentially ephemeral disappeared. Some, whose embellishments were original and tasteful, continued to stimulate the fine arts, and a few established Reviews to hold a high guardianship over the interests of literature.

On this sea of miscellany I was allured to embark, and, having set sail, there was no return. I think now with amazement, and almost incredulity, of the number of articles I was induced by the urgency of editors to furnish. Before I ceased to keep a regular catalogue, they had amounted to more than two thousand. Some of these were afterwards comprehended in selections, though enough for several volumes must still be floating about, like seaweed among the noiseless billows. They were divided among nearly three hundred different publications, from the aristocratic "Keepsake" of the Countess of Blessington, and the classic "Athenæum" and "Forget-Me-Not" of London, to the "Coachmakers' Magazine," the "Herald of the Upper Mississippi," the "Buckeye Blossom" of the West, and the "Rose-Bud" of the factory girls at Lowell.[1] Promptitude was the life-blood of these contributions. Hungering presses must be fed, and not wait. How to obtain time to appease editorial appetites, and not neglect my housekeeping tactics, was a study. I found the employment of knitting congenial to the contemplation and treatment of the slight themes that were desired, and, while completing fifteen or sometimes twenty pairs of stockings yearly for our large family, or for the poor, stopped the needles to arrest the wings of a flying

1 *Keepsake*, literary annual (1828–57), ed. F.M. Reynolds, Caroline Sheridan, and Marguerite, Countess of Blessington; *Athenæum* (1828–1921), respected literary magazine; *Forget Me Not* (1823–47), elegant literary annual, ed. Frederic Shoberl; *Coachmakers' Magazine* (1856–57; under similar title to 1871), published at Columbus, Ohio; *Western Adventurer, and Herald of the Upper Mississippi* (1837–38), published at Des Moines, Wisconsin Territory (later Iowa); *Buckeye Blossom* (6 July to 14 September 1839); *Rose Bud* (1832–1900s), Lowell, Massachusetts.

thought or a flowing stanza. Still, I always corrected, and rewrote more than once, these extemporaneous effusions, not considering it decorous to throw crude matter at the head of the public.

This habit of writing *currente calamo*[1] is fatal to literary ambition. It prevents that labor of thought by which intellectual eminence is acquired. [...]

With the establishment of a poetic name came a host of novel requisitions. Fame gathered from abroad cut out work at home. The number and nature of consequent applications were alike remarkable. Churches requested hymns, to be sung at consecrations, ordinations, and installations; charitable societies, for anniversaries; academies and schools, for exhibitions. Odes were desired for the festivities of New Year and the Fourth of July, for silver and golden weddings, for the voyager wherewith to express his leave-taking, and the lover to propitiate his mistress. Epistles from strangers often solicited elegies and epitaphs; and though the voice of bereavement was to me a sacred thing, yet I felt the inefficacy of balm thus offered to a heart that bled. Sometimes I consoled myself that the multitude of these solicitations bespoke an increasing taste for poetry among the people. But to gratify all was an impossibility. They would not only have covered the surface of one life, but of as many as ancient fable attributed to the feline race. I undertook at one time to keep a statement of the solicitations that showered upon me. A good-sized manuscript book was thus soon filled. It was commenced during what dear Mrs. Hemans[2] used to call the "album persecution." It was then the fashion for school-girls, other youthful personages, and indeed people of every age, to possess themselves of a neatly-bound blank book, which was sent indiscriminately to any one whom they chose, with the request, or exaction, of a page or more in their own handwriting.

Of those who were so unfortunate as to be known as rhymers, it was expressly stipulated that it must be original. Sometimes there would be a mass of these cormorant tax-gatherers in the house at the same time. To refuse compliance was accounted an offence, or an insult. I commuted the matter with my imperative engagements as well as I could, by setting aside a peculiar portion of time for these enforced subsidies. Happily this custom is now obsolete, having been merged in the slighter impost of autographs.

---

1 *currente calamo*] with a running pen: extempore, without deliberation

2 Mrs. Hemans] Felicia Hemans (English, 1793–1835), the most widely read woman poet of the nineteenth-century English-speaking world; Sigourney was often referred to as the "American Hemans."

I feel an inclination to give you a few extracts from the manuscript catalogue before alluded to, which was not long continued. Perhaps they may amuse you, my sweetly patient friend.

Some of them, you will observe, are not strictly poetical requisitions, but sprang from a position among poets.

Requested to write dedication poems for three nicely-bound volumes, brought by strangers. [...]

To obtain an accomplished female teacher for the children of a member of Congress, at the far South. [...]

Desired to assist a servant-man not very well able to read, in getting his Sunday-school lessons, and to "write out all the answers for him, clear through the book, to save his time." [...]

A list of the female poets who have written in all languages, a statement of their births and deaths, with information of the best editions of their works, and where they may be obtained, for a gentleman resident in a distant State, who thinks of undertaking a compilation of feminine literature. [...]

To punctuate a manuscript volume of three hundred pages, the author having always had a dislike to the business of punctuation, finding that it brings on a "pain in the back of the neck." [...]

A new periodical desires a "touching tale, a bit of poetry, and an address to its readers," to be sent in the course of the week, and the printing to be stayed for the contributions. [...]

Solicitation from the far West, that I would "write out lengthy" a sketch of the loves of two personages, of whom no suggestive circumstances were related, one of whom was a journeyman tailor, and the name of the other, "Sister Babcock," as far as the chirography[1] could be translated. [...]

To draft a constitution for a society in a distant State, whose object is to diminish the reluctance of young people to the writing of compositions. [...]

To be umpire of a baby-show in the city of New York. [...]

A monody for the loss of a second wife, fortified by the argument that I had composed one at the death of the first. [...]

If there is any kitchen in Parnassus,[2] my Muse has surely officiated there as a woman of all work, and an aproned waiter. Lacking firmness to say no, I consented so frequently, that the right of refusal began to be counted invidious. Those who

---

1 chirography] style of writing

2 Parnassus] mountain in Greece, in ancient legend home of Apollo and the Muses, who inspire poets

requested but a few verses considered them, what they appeared to be, a trifle. Yet "trifles make up the sum of human things,"[1] and this trifle involved thought, labor, and time. This habit of yielding to persuasion occasionally led to the curtailment of sleep, and of meals, as the poems which were to be sung in public audiences must be ready at a specified period, and frequently a very brief notice was accorded me. Sometimes I have been urged to send copies of long printed poems to strangers, that they might possess them in my own handwriting. Though there is always a degree of pleasure connected with obliging others, yet the extent of my own facility or folly in this respect might be rebuked by the common sense displayed in other occupations.

Do we go to a milliner, and say, "You have earned a good name in your line. Make me a bonnet and a dress. I should prize them as proofs of your skill?" Do we tell the carpet manufacturer, "You assort your colors better than others. Weave me a carpet for my study?" Do we address the professed cook with "You have a high reputation. I am to have a party. Come and make my jellies and confections?" Would these functionaries, think ye, devote time, toil, and material to such proposals, without compensation? I trow not. But a truce to this diffuse matter of custom-work.

My epistolary correspondence is extensive, and exceeds a yearly exchange of two thousand letters. It includes many from strangers, who are often disposed to be tenacious of replies, and to construe omission as rude neglect. I have no aid from amanuensis or copyist since the marriage of my loved daughter, or any listening friend to whom I may take the liberty of reading an unpublished production. Yet, if ever inclined to account so large a correspondence burdensome, I solace myself with the priceless value of the epistles of long-tried friendship, with the warm vitality often breathing from young hearts, and the hope of disseminating through this quiet vehicle, some cheering thought or hallowed principle.

My literary course has been a happy one. Its encouragements have exceeded both my expectations and deserts. Originating in impulse, and those habits of writing that were deepened by the solitary lot of an only child, it gradually assumed a financial feature which gave it both perseverance and permanence.

This, which at first supplied only my indulgences, my journeyings, or my charities, became eventually a form of subsis-

1 trifles ... things] Hannah More, "Sensibility: An Epistle to the Honourable Mrs. Boscawen" (1782), l. 293

tence; and now, through the income of its accumulated savings, gives ease to the expenditure of my widowhood, and the means of mingling with the benevolent enterprises of the day. Pecuniary gain has flowed in upon me rather from abroad than at home. With the exception of the initiatory volume, sheltered under the patronage of my venerated friend, Mr. Wadsworth, scarcely any profit has accrued to my literary labors in this vicinity, or indeed in the whole of my own New England. On the contrary, some severe losses have occurred. To the States of New York and Pennsylvania I am mainly indebted for the remuneration of intellectual toil, and gratefully acknowledge them as benefactors.

Fame, as a ruling motive, has not stimulated me to literary effort. It has ever seemed to have too flimsy a wing for sustained and satisfactory flight. Candid criticism, and the voice of friendship, have been coveted correctives and tonics. Still the only adequate payment are the hope and belief that, by enforcing some salutary precept, or prompting some hallowed practice, good may have been done to our race.

I ought to speak with more emphasis of the encouragement kindly addressed to me since first, as a timid waif, I ventured into regions then seldom traversed by the female foot. It has breathed upon me from highways and hedges, from boughs where nesting birds reared their young, from the crested billows, and the islands of the sea. Thanks be to Him who hath thus touched the hearts of my fellow-creatures with kindness toward me! [...]

Yes, my literary course has indeed been a most happy one. At an age surpassing threescore and ten, I still pursue it with unimpaired delight and unspectacled eyes. Through its agency, and the Divine blessing, I feel no loneliness, though my household contains only servants, with the exception of occasional guests. Praise be unto Him who hath led me all my life long unto this day; and if any good fruit shall ever spring from the seed He hath enabled me to sow, to His name be all the glory.

Appendix A: Letters and Manuscripts

[Editor's omissions and emendations are enclosed in square brackets.]

Abbreviations

CHS Connecticut Historical Society, Hartford, Connecticut
HBSC Harriet Beecher Stowe Center, Hartford, Connecticut
LHS Lydia Huntley Sigourney

1811–19: Discipline: Rules of Lydia Huntley's School.[1]

<u>Rules of the School</u>

1st Every day will begin and end with a perusal of the Scriptures and prayer. Each scholar will attend to these with seriousness and solemnity, and endeavour to recollect and repeat a part of the Sacred History, that may be read.
2[d] Each scholar must attend the appointed hours as punctually as possible:—enter and leave the room with politeness, and in going and returning from school, observe the rules of propriety and decorum.
3[d] All Conversation in school, except with the Instructress, is forbidden.
4th Every scholar must remain at her respective seat without disturbance, and preserve her books, paper, and desk neat, and free from ink.
5th After reading, each one is required to tell what she recollects, and those sufficiently advanced in writing, will keep a blank book to contain pieces learnt, composed or extracted, and likewise an account of her progress in her several studies.
6th Every scholar must come provided with necessary articles that the disturbance of borrowing may be avoided.
7th Spelling is attended every night. She who gains the head of the class, and has behaved throughout the day with propriety, is entitled to the office of Monitress the ensuing day.
8th The duty of the Monitress, is to exhibit an example of propriety of behaviour, to observe if the rules are violated by any, and

1 Undated manuscript; LHS Papers (US/CTH/SIGOL/1865—I.24), CHS.

to recommend those who pay attention to them, and are diligent in their studies.

9th The Monitress is entitled to respect from her companions, while she discharges the duties of her office, and acts as an Assistant to her Instructress.

10th She who has excelled in exemplary deportment throughout the week, shall be chosen to the honour of Saturday Monitress, and the young lady who has sustained most frequently the office of Monitress during the quarter shall be presented with a premium when it closes.

11th For impropriety of behaviour, or transgression of the rules, the offender loses her place in the class, and thus removes herself further from the honourary office of Monitress, and from the esteem of her Companions.

12th These rules are intended to promote order in school, and to advance the improvement and happiness of its members. She who preserves them with the greatest care will gain the rewards allotted to merit, and the affection of her Instructress.

1821: Self-Discipline: Questions for "Self-Examination."[1]

Self-Examination.

1. — Did I address myself in morning Devotion, to Him[2] who alone giveth strength to persevere in the path of duty? — | | | | |
2. — Have I endeavoured to advance the real good of the children during the past day, uninfluenced by false indulgence? — | | | | |
3. — Have I consulted just economy, in any plan, or expenditure? — | | | | |
4. — Have I performed any thing in the way of domestic industry? — | | | | X
5. — Have I remembered that I had a mind, and read anything with a view of obtaining information? — X X | | |
6. — Have I obtained any knowledge which I did not possess this morning? — X | | | |
7. — Have I written anything worthy of a rational being? — | | | | |

---

1 Questions in ink; scores after each question in pencil; LHS Papers (US/CTH/SIGOL/1865—I.35), CHS.

2 God.

8. — Have I disturbed my husband with complaints of ill health, or like the Roman borne pain in silence,— because she was the wife of Brutus?[1] — | | | | |

9. — Have I censured, where I might have excused, or commended? — X X X X X

10. — Have I imparted to others, a single pious sentiment, or moral precept for the direction of conduct? — X | | | X

11. — Have I followed the example of the Psalmist.— "morning, —evening,— and at noon, will I pray, unto thee, and lift up my hands with thanksgiving."[2] — | X | | |

12. — Have I shewn to any one an expression of tenderness,—a deed of kindness, or an act of relief? — | | | | X

13. — Have I attempted or desired to do any good? — X X | | X

14. — Have I endeavoured to cherish a sense of God's goodness, recounted his blessings,—or felt the love of my Redeemer? — X | X X |

15. — Have I laboured to transfer my affections to that state, where there is neither error,—wound,—or disappointment? — X X X | |

16. — Have I remembered "from whence I have fallen,"[3] and been repentant & humble, & prayed for submission to the Divine will? — X X | | X

17. — Have I recommended my parents, my husband, my family, to God's care? — | | | | |

18. — Can I now look upon circumscribed usefulness, upon the opportunities of doing good that were once so dear to me,—upon my neglected manuscripts,— and perceiving the hand of a Father in all things,—say "his will be done?"[4] — | | | | |

19. — Do I this night realize the shortness of life, & the approach of Death? — | | | | |

20. — Have I read this paper with solemnity before retiring, prayed of the Almighty, to forgive my errors,—and to bless this habit of Self-examination, and to lead me in the way everlasting? — | | | | |

---

1 As portrayed in Shakespeare's *Julius Caesar* (2.1.293–95), Portia tells her husband Brutus that she is superior to other women because she is the daughter and the wife of heroic republicans.

2 Echo of the Bible, Psalms 55.17.

3 Echo of the Bible, Revelation 2.5: "Remember whence thou art fallen, and repent ..."

4 From the Lord's Prayer, the Bible, Luke 11.2.

Deeply have I felt the inutility of all mental determinations;—be thou my strength,—my guide,—my portion,—Oh Thou, Almighty.—

L.H. Sigourney.

Hartford, Sunday, April 8th
1821. —

1827: Opinions: Housework and Hemans.[1]

Your letter, my dear Jane, and that of sister Ann, by Mr Furber, were exceedingly welcome, & the details they contained of all our friends in Boston, seemed once more to place me in the midst of that beloved circle. This morning you have been on my mind more than usual, and I almost fear to shock your romantick feelings, by acknowledging that it was during the ablution of my silver, or what is emphatically termed <u>Saturday work</u>, that your image was so remarkably vivid.—I flattered myself that you were engaged in the same employment, and this created a powerful sympathy,—and as piece after piece was presented to me, I gazed in spirit upon your bright eyes, and remembering the cheerfulness and resolution which you always brought to such domestick avocations, derived benefit from your example.—So having thus been profited by you, I determined as soon as everything was in order, to take my pen and tell you the oddity of this my obligation, which I do with a hand trembling with fatigue, and a frame fully sensible of the luxury which a chair can impart. When I last wrote you, dear sister, I was not able to answer your question with regard to Mrs Hemans,[2] which I am now happy to have it in my power to do.—I have just finished the perusal of her two volumes, with more delight than I have in my whole life experienced, from reading the same quantity of poetry.—She seems to me to have opened a new era in this department of the imagination, as fully and decidedly as Walter Scott[3] has in another.—I have been almost as much struck with the felicity of her choice of

---

1 LHS, Hartford, 10 March 1827, to Jane C. Sigourney, Boston; James Marshall and Marie-Louise Osborn Collection, Beinecke Rare Book and Manuscript Library, Yale University, folder 13804.

2 Felicia Hemans (1793–1835), English poet with whom Sigourney was often compared, as the "American Hemans."

3 Walter Scott (1791–1832), Scottish poet and author of the Waverley Novels.

subjects,—as with the charm of numbers, and purity of sentiment which she blends with all.—How much did I wish for you, my dear Jane, while reading the "Forest Sanctuary."[1]—Did you see an uncommonly fine review of Mrs Hemans in the Christian Examiner,[2]—perhaps for November?—If you have not, I wish you would do me the favour to read it on my recommendation, as in my opinion it stands next to Dr Channing[']s review of Milton's last treatise,[3]—for its forcible elucidation of the true elements of poetry.—Will you mention in your next, some of the smaller pieces of Mrs Hemans, to which you give the preference?—I cannot willingly resign the pleasure of sometimes mingling and measuring tastes with you, notwithstanding the envious obstacles which interpose between us.—I have long been accustomed to admire,—"The voice of Spring,"—"The treasures of the Deep,"—"Bring Flowers,"—"The Revellers," "The Sunbeam,"—"The graves of an household,"—"Tasso & his sister,"—"Bernardo del Carpio,"—"The Invocation,"—"England's Dead,"—& a number of others which have at different times appeared in our periodical publications.—I could with pleasure fill several pages in praise of this the greatest of poetesses,—and certainly among the greatest of modern poets.—

————Since my last letter to you, I have read Dr Channing's sermon which you was so kind as to send, with great care, and with equal astonishment at the powers of mind which it displays.—I have been in the habit of reading but little controversial theology, from the impression that it sometimes leads us either to foster or repel peculiar opinions, to the detriment of christian charity, but such a production I should always value, were it only as a specimen of intellect, eloquence, and beauty of style.—I have often thought, dear sister, that in our age of high illumination, it was no great effort of discovery, that men might arrive at one home of bliss, th[ough] they should choose different paths thither; and [that? page torn] it need be no such mighty sacrifice to extend the [? page torn] & open the heart in love, to those whose system of fai[th] should vary from our own.

———I was very sorry to hear that your Aunt Parsons had been such a sufferer.—I hope that she has ere this entirely recov-

---

1 Long narrative poem (1825) by Hemans.

2 Published in Boston.

3 Unitarian clergyman William Ellery Channing (1780–1842), review of John Milton, "Treatise on Christian Doctrine"; Channing was an admirer and correspondent of Hemans.

ered.—My best love to our Mother and Mary. I shall answer dear Ann's letter, as soon as I can find anything interesting to communicate. I think you were mistaken, dear, in mentioning that Frederick wrote last.—I have received none from him, since sending one the past winter, with an oration of Mr Hillhouse,[1]—which I hope reached him safely.—Remember me affectionately to him, & likewise to sisters Elizabeth & Ann, with their husbands,—to Ann Carter, & James, with all in their household, of whose health we are all grateful to hear such good accounts.—

The weather is growing very fine, dear sister,—would that you were here?—My husband, Betsy, and the children are well, and desire to be remembered to all.

Ever your affectionate sister, L.H. Sigourney

1827: Home Life: A Husband's "Appeal"—Be Less a Poet and More a Wife.[2]

My beloved wife,

I come to you in the spirit of deep self-abasement. I come to you in the spirit of kindness, & conjugal affection. I come to you, my wife, in the spirit of prayer; for on my knees have I implored, and repeatedly, the direction & blessing of the Almighty on the application I am about to make to you. [...]

The first years of our marriage, may it yet be blessed, you may remember that, in addition to the sentiments of love, & esteem I entertained for you, I took a pride in admiring the talents with which your mind was adorned, & the efforts, then only occasional, of your poetical imagination. You may remember too, not only my admiration of the powers of your mind, but the satisfaction, & patience, with which I cooperated with you in preparing your "Traits," & your "Sketch,"[3] & the pleasure, with which, in

---

1 Probably James Hillhouse (1754–1832), Connecticut lawyer and politician.

2 The document may have been designed to state Charles Sigourney's case should his wife have recourse to the law; also, though addressed to her, the document may not have been actually delivered to her; extracts are from the longer of two drafts of "Appeal" by Charles to Lydia Sigourney, dated "October —, 1827"; LHS Papers (US/CTH/SIGOL/1865—II.7), CHS.

3 Her poem *Traits of the Aborigines of America* (1822), with extensive notes by Charles Sigourney, and her prose fiction *Sketch of Connecticut, Forty Years Since* (1824).

the former work, I anticipated, what did not follow, an honourable, & successful sale. This, my wife, pardon me if I say it, was the more meritorious, as, in both cases, I surrendered my own opinions, as regarded the publication of the works, to your wishes. Nevertheless, our minds, to a certain degree, to the period of the publication of the "Traits," were one; & I endeavoured, by every means in my power, not merely to uphold your character, but to extend your reputation. To this time, however, you restrained, within the limits of what I deemed propriety, your desire of publick attention. But, when, afterwards, I began to perceive your great susceptibility of praise, and, as I thought, your passion for literary distinction increasing, I perceived also that it led you occasionally, without any motive I agree beyond self-gratification for the moment, & thinking no evil, into conduct I could not reconcile with my ideas of the delicate propriety which should ever mark the female character;—that, at first it occupied, as appeared to me, too large a share of your thoughts,—then excluded other duties, & feelings, as of inferior importance,—and, finally, like avarice, growing by what it fed on, usurped, & engrossed your whole mind. Then it was that I, by degrees, drew ba[ck] and feeling, as well as perceiving, the injurious operation of this passion on the feminin[e] part of your character, on your conjugal affections, & domestick habits, I gradually abstained from administering fuel to a fire I believed would consume your happiness; and finally did, indirectly, what I could to check it's progress, & thereby prevent the growth of habits which, however they might augment your individual reputation & interest, I was convinced would not contribute to domestick quiet.

These, then, being my opinions on this subject generally, in your own case, my dear wife, what is it I think I have to regret, & complain of? [...] It is, that the ambition for literary distinction seems now to be occupying nearly all your thoughts, & threatens to destroy your conjugal character:—that the apparently unconquerable passion of displaying yourself is the secret principle which of late influences your conduct, & may be traced in very much which you do:—that it begets a lust of praise which, like the appetite of the cormorant, is not to be satisfied:—that it leads you to prefer the flatteries of the parasites who hang upon you, to the good opinion, and plain but steady esteem of your husband:—that it leads you to despise, as you have repeatedly avowed, the conversation & society of your own sex, and will lead you, probably, for the next step (if not already the case) to despise that of your husband:—and, on the other hand, that it leads you to prefer, and, in defiance of that modesty, & reserve, which should ever be the ornament of your sex, to court, to make advances to, to solicit the notice, & correspondence, or in another word the praise of, literary men, whose civilities, & flatteries (to a lady especially) may most surely be obtained by the bribe of flattery to begin with.——

[...] This forwardness after men, not for their persons it is true but their minds, would have led a Sappho, or a Mary Wolstonecraft[1] into serious errour, had there been any at hand who possessed the ability, & the inclination to have taken advantage of it, and might have led even you into temptation, had you not been guarded by the cold, & petrifying shield of Minerva.[2]—— [...]

And have you a right, my wife, in fine, to be surprised that I am displeased if, when returning at night, weary from my customary place of labour, I find you with * * *, whose visits are too pointedly exclusive for me to appropriate any part of the compliment of them to myself [...]

And Have you a right to be surprised at my being displeased at your carrying on a private, I might almost say a clandestine correspondence with him (I say clandestine, for both your notes, & his answers are carefully kept from all other eyes)—applying to him for trifling services, seemingly as an excuse for writing, which your husband could perform with equal facility,—writing him notes which he pronounces "delightful," & then either concealing, or destroying, his replies?—The woman who is innocent, & yet adopts concealment, the usual resort of the guilty, has no right to be surprised should she be doubted. Nor can she have a right to be surprised should her conduct provoke comment. You sometimes censure Elizabeth to me for her inclination for the company of young men, & running after the College students.[3] Furnish not the daughter with an example, & an apology for the conduct you impute to her, by putting it into her power to alledge the mother was "running after" the professors.

[...] As to my imagining any thing criminal, or likely to be so, I should feel myself entitled to the fullest measure of your con-

---

1 Sappho, sixth-century BCE Greek poet who became a figure for self-destructive female passion; Mary Wollstonecraft (1759–97), English feminist and author of *A Vindication of the Rights of Woman* (1792), who became a figure for coincidence of unorthodox social views and scandalous private life.

2 Roman virgin goddess of wisdom, depicted wearing armour.

3 Presumably at Washington (later Trinity) College of theology.

tempt, & should despise myself, could I presume to insinuate it. I own, however, I have doubts of your general discretion I did not formerly entertain, & think your imagination, & feelings, often times, overpower your judgment, & lead you astray. [...] But it is impossible, I think, you can be so absurd as to impute to me the vulgar, & mean jealousy, which regards the person[1] of the object. Because you know full well what it is which would forbid almost the possibility of my suspecting you of what could not very well happen.——But, if you impute to me jealousy of your affections, I own I have it, &, what is more, I glory in the avowal. A man is not fit to have a wife, if he does not love her. And if he does love her, can it be a matter of indifference to him whether her affections are wholly his, whether they are divided with another, or whether they rest on objects & pursuits foreign to his domestick happiness, & which, like the insatiate kine, swallow up every thing else?[2] Oh! my wife, my beloved wife, if I were indifferent to you, then indeed would your conduct, so long as it were not greatly imprudent,[3] be a matter of indifference to me. [...] Was it not for the fourth time that, on friday night, you proposed, or declared your willingness to agree to, a Separation? Such propositions I have always resisted, from a regard to your reputation, as well as to our united happiness, & feeling it was in anger you made them. [...] My dearest wife, I will not part with you, as you propose. Your affection, purified from the alloy with which it is commingled, I value beyond any other earthly blessing, & feel that it is a pearl of great price, which must not be thrown away. I will not give it up without a struggle. [...]

I have thought, my dear wife, if you could hear it without pain, & without taking offence, it might be the part of a friend to inform you the publick are already taking the liberty to pass those criticisms on your character, which your placing yourself on the conspicuous point of observation you have chosen has in fact invited them to do. I have heard, within a year past, & without either soliciting, or going out of my way for them, of remarks made concerning you, by respected persons, but some of whose names I do not know altho' represented as friends of us both, which, perhaps, it were proper should be repeated to you. A lady & gentleman, visiting us, some years since, "saw enough to satisfy

1 Body, physical self.

2 Pharaoh's dream in the Bible, Genesis 41.2–4, in which seven lean kine (cows) eat up seven fat kine.

3 Inserted in other draft: "& actually licentious."

them all was not right," in reference to the appearance of the children: A lady declining to visit you alledged as a reason, "you were always in the clouds": Another thought you had "been very much injured by flattery":—A gentleman, making some comments on the publication of your book, & circumstances connected with it, observed "he shall not like it, if you were his wife[")]:—Another expressed the opinion I had "run a great risque in marrying a woman so wise in her own conceit as to think she could never do wrong": while another uttered the exclamation "the Lord deliver me from marrying a Poetess." [...]

It is not, my dear wife, that I have a decided objection to your writing, & improving the elegant accomplishments you possess. It is not that I object to your publishing what you write, provided it be in moderation, and, as your simile expresses it, "like the Sun behind a cloud, yourself unseen." But I object to the excess, & the abuse of this talent, the consequent immoderate desire of constantly appearing before the publick, & the immoderate desire of notoriety which follows, which amounts, in fact, to a mental disease. [...]

I do object, and it has given me very great pain, to seeing your name bandied about in the newspapers, & magazines;—the burthen of paragraphs, & the praise of the witling;—in the mouths of printers, & publishers, artists, & shop boys;—subjected to the levities, & freedoms it's conspicuous situation invites;—exposing you to be pointed out in the streets, like a stage player or artist, like a Percival or a Madame de Stael,[1] with a kind of meretricious distinction, as "Mrs. Sigourney the poetess," a distinction by which, it has appeared to me, you would be more flattered to be known, than by the modest & humble one of the respectable wife of Mr. S. [...]

I do object that you sink the woman, & the wife, in the writer; that you appear to be more anxious, and better pleased to be known for talents as an author, than for virtues as a wife, & a mother;—that those who will flatter the first have more influence with you, & seem to occupy higher ground in your regard, than your husband. [...]

I do object to the great appropriation of your time, & thoughts, to your poetical pursuits, from the effect, I think, it has

1 Susanna Percival Mountfort Verbruggen (c. 1666–1703), one of the first professional woman actors, famous for playing low-life parts; Germaine de Staël (1766–1817), French novelist, cultural commentator, and centre of an intellectual circle, leading a life apart from her husband.

already had, & must continue to have, on your health, & temper,—as nourishing a restless & morbid spirit, loathing the common food of life, in it's quiet enjoyments, as too tasteless & insipid for it's sublimated appetite, & craving perpetually something new to excite, & stimulate it's pampered desires;——a malady, which the health equally of the mind, & the body requires to be cured. It needs not the formality of argument to shew that the rack of the imagination produces a corresponding tension of the nerves, & that, from the days of Horace[1] to the present time the poetical fraternity have been, proverbially, marked by an increased irritability of temperament.

[...] As if the example of the Miss Wrights,[2] or the Mary Wollstonecraft's were worthier of imitation by you than that of Cornelia, mother of the Gracchi, or Milton's beautiful pattern of feminine, & conjugal excellence[3] [...]——

[...] Is it, I say, to be wondered at if, by degrees, my own mind became weaned from it's first inclination to indulge, & aid, you in your peculiar pursuits, which occupying so undue a proportion of your thoughts, I began to consider as the bar to my domestick comfort, & happiness, & poetry itself as my enemy?——and to say to myself were you less of a poet, how much more valuable would you be as a wife?——

[...] There may be a spiritual seduction, as well as a corporeal one,—a seduction of the mind, & affections, as well as of the person. And the publick may be the seducer, as well as an individual.—Who wants, or would value, a wife, who is to be the publick property of the whole community?—She who wishes to belong to the publick never should consent to be the private possession of any individual man. She, who is infatuated with the ambition of literary eminence, & to whose happiness popular applause becomes in consequence indispensable, bows down to the God of her idolatry elevated in her own breast, & can neither

1 Quintus Horatius Flaccus (65–27 BCE), Roman satirical and amorous poet.

2 Frances Wright (1795–1852) and her sister Camilla; Frances Wright, a Scottish-born reformer and follower of the British socialist Robert Owen, established a utopian community at Nashoba, Tennessee, but created scandal by supposed practice of free love and Wright's attacks on organized religion.

3 Cornelia, first-century BCE daughter and mother of heroes of republican Rome; Milton's Eve, in *Paradise Lost* book 9 a pattern of conjugal virtue and obedience until tempted by Satan.

"love, honour, or obey"[1] a common mortal.—It is a most dangerous situation for a married woman, where she yields but her person, & the exterior concessions of married life to her husband, & goes elsewhere to seek her chief pleasures, & gratifications, from the society, & flatteries of others, and from sources foreign to the domestick fireside. It requires not the spirit of prophecy to foresee the result of such a course. The small remains of affection will soon be weaned from him from whom you seek not your happiness. Indifference will succeed. Distaste, & dislike ensues,—then aversion,—domestick discord,—hatred,——!——!——

Turn then, my dear wife, ere it be too late, & escape from the gulph which is threatening to draw you into it's vortex. Return to the affections of your husband, and he will receive you, will cherish, and "comfort, honour, & keep you, forsaking all others,"[2]—for none other does he love, as he loves you. [...]

your husband, who ever loves you,

C. Sigourney.—

1837: Doing Business: Letter to the Editor of a Religious Annual.[3]

My dear Sir,

The articles which were contributed to your Sunday School Annual, about which you inquire in yours of the 1st of this month, are at your service for that work, however long its publication may be deferred.—I have no objection to their being used in the "Sabbath School Visitor," if you prefer this designation, but shall not be able, from a great press of writing, & but little time,—to furnish any others for your Annual.—You will be the best judge, where they will have the most hope of being useful.—If you wish to divide them,—and take one for each publication, I have no objection.—The price, about which you inquire,—is $2. a page for all articles accepted in Annuals,—at least as far as I have ever been connected with them, either as contributor, or

1 Echo of the marriage service.

2 Another echo of the marriage service.

3 LHS, Hartford, 28 September 1837, to the Rev. Asa Bullard, Secretary of the Massachusetts Sunday School Society, Boston; LHS Papers (US/CTH/SIGOL/1865—I.5), CHS.

editor.—Wishing success in all your labours of piety, to benefit the rising generation, and diffuse the knowledge and love of the Gospel,

I remain yours with respect,

L.H. Sigourney.—

1847: Doing Business: Record of Receipts for 1847.[1]

1847.

"Columbian Lady's & Gentleman's Mag."

1. Louisa Wilson, a prose tale, 9 sheets
   offered at $50. . . . Jan 8th
2. The Royal Clock. . . . . March 27th

paid. —

New Volume

1. "Reef Sails." — } May 31st
   Epitaph on a Young Lady }
2. The Ivy . . . . Sept 11th
3. Aurora . . . . Nov 10th

Wrote Jan 5th 1848, to say
I should draw in 10 days for payment.
Bill protested.
Afterwards I received it.

1847

"Forget Me Not."—London.—

1. Welcome to Wisconsin. . . March 27.
2. Nature's true Friends . . . 27.
3. Emigrant's Tale. 123 lines . . April 28

Union Magazine. Israel Port. NY

---

1. Needle, Pen & Sword. May 13th
2. On planting a Row of
   Shade Trees . . June 18th

Recd payment for these two poems. Aug 23d

1. Young Prison Visitants pd Sept 9th
2. The Early Crocus pd Oct 8th
3. The Thriving Family pd Nov 16th

---

1 Folded half sheet of blue paper with white paper paste-in, in Sigourney's hand; LHS Papers (US/CTH/SIGOL/1865—I.31), CHS.

4. Responsibility. — Dec 9th

Written Jan 5th 1848, to say
I will draw in 10 days for $20—
Recd 20. Jan 8th

Family Circle & Parlour Annual

1. Death of a pious Child Oct 20
Paid $ 5.
2. Death of a Young Teacher Nov 22
Recd 3 volumes —

"Tuthill's Annual."—Phila.

1. La petite Sourd Muet . . . March 30.
$10: received payment. July 3d

Ladies Wreath

1. Storm-Sails Nov 19th

Southern Literary Messenger
1847

1. View from Griswold Hill Nov 27th
Recd $ 5: & 5—

1847
"Gospel Messenger" N. York.

1. ["]The Lord passeth by." July 12th
2. Unknown Heirs. — Aug 14th
3. The Autumnal Storm. Sept 28th
Recd $ 6. Dec 28th

Graham's Magazine.

1. The Rainbow . . Nov 25th
2. Lat Pet [? or Pct?] . . Dec 5. —
unpaid — Dec 31. 1847.
pd Nov. 1848 [altered to 1847?]

1855: The Price of Fame:
Description of the Poet's Writing Table.[1]

[...] I wish you could look in upon me, and see how the writing table in my den is covered with things collected and heaped up, during my absence. Here is one large book from the post office,

---

1 LHS, Hartford, 13 December 1855, to Mrs Sarah P. Baldwin, Fremont St., Boston; LHS Collection, HBSC.

and 42 weekly & monthly periodicals,—besides 3 notes of invitation,—several scores of cards, and 29 letters. As Mr Baldwin is such a man of business & so systematic, I will mention some of the localities & subjects of the latter, thinking they might possibly amuse him.—

4 from the Autograph-hunting gentry, of various States;
1 from Charleston, SC;—
1 from Alexandria, V^{a};—
1 from my publisher in Buffalo;—
1 from a Western Publisher, desiring an introduction for a work he is about to issue;—
1 from Iowa, respecting the building of a Church;—
1 from the Western Education Society, wanting aid;—
1 from a clergyman, soliciting for a sick seaman, and his destitute family;—
1 from Philadelphia, wanting a Tale for a periodical, without delay;—
1 soliciting patronage for a peculiar kind of morocco-work,[1] and for its maker;—
1 requesting a hymn to be sung at an approaching Sunday School anniversary, for the reason, that one had been furnished for 4 previous years;—
1 wishing a poem for the sixtieth anniversary of a marriage;—
1 from the Department of State at Washington;
2 from the Legation at St Petersburgh;
4 from Oroomiah,[2] in Persia;—
7 from New York, and different parts of Connecticut, on business, friendship, or nothing at all. [...]

1 Items made from a fine grained leather.

2 Site of an American Congregationalist missionary station.

1861: Self-discipline:
From "Memoranda of Employments."[1]

1861

Holy Father, increase my industry, and its beneficial results.

LHS

Spring Memoranda.

March.

	Pages.	Lines.	Vols.	Garments	Calls made	Rec[d]	Letters Rec[d]	Written.	Total.
Sat. 2	120	120	2	1 pair hose	10	50	36	34	70
9	90	40	2	0	8	22	28	22	50
16	115	50	2	0	0	35	30	30	60
23	80	20	0	0	6	34	25	25	50
30	95	20	0	0	6	34	36	34	70
	500	250	6	1	30	170	155	145	300

200

April.

	Pages.	Lines.	Vols.	Garments	Calls made	Rec[d]	Letters Rec[d]	Written.	Total.
Sat 6	80	30	6	0	7	33	27	13	40
13	90	150	0	0	10	35	26	24	50
20	75	50	1	0	8	32	26	19	45
27	55	20	1	1 pair hose	20	35	11	14	25
	300	250	8	1	45	135	90	70	160

				200 May.					
Sat 4	100	100	1	1 hose	3	52	10	20	30
11	55	50	1	48 Towels	9	51	14	16	30
18	75	0	1	0	16	34	17	18	35
25	70	200	1	0	10	25	20	25	45
	300	350	4	49	38	162	61	79	140
				200					

Aggregate, during Spring of 1861.

Pages Written . . .	1100	in 1860	1050
Lines of Poetry . . .	850		600
Volumes read . . .	18		15
Garments made . . .	51		10
Calls & Visits Exchanged . .	600		600
Letters do— do— . .	600		600

Hartford, Friday May 31st 1861 LH Sigourney

1 Folded sheet covering years 1860 and 1861; LHS Papers (US/CTH/SIGOL/1865—I.35), CHS.

Appendix B: Views and Reviews of Sigourney and Her Work

1815: Review of Her First Book: Exhortation to Become a National Poet.[1]

THE mass of poetry is constantly accumulating in the world. The English have of late years furnished a larger quantity than any other nation, but we have not been idle. We however consume less paper, and absorb less capital. Our contributions are generally in modest duodecimos, with small type, and narrow margin; in England, large types, wide margins, and black-letter ornaments, decorate the pompous volume of quarto dimension. The only difference is, that dulness here is attired with plainness and frugality, and there, accompanied with ostentation and expense. We are strongly inclined to believe, that when four or five of their candidates for fame are withdrawn from the lists, that those who remain, would not be found superiour to ours, except numerically. [...]

The volume before us contains a mixture of prose and poetry, of which, the latter we think the best. [The review quotes several poems.]

One great negative merit of these poems is, that they are almost wholly free from any false taste, from any thing either in thought or style, that is turgid or vulgar. There is much freedom and facility in the manner, a correctness and harmony in the features, though generally tinged with melancholy; that make us strongly wish, that the writer would devote herself to some work of greater scope and higher character than any of these occasional verses.[2] [...]

After considering the indications of genius, afforded by these disconnected poems, the variety and facility of versification they discover, joined to what we have heard of the fair author's solid acquirements, and her power and habit of severe application, we should, if our advice were a little more imposing, earnestly counsel her to devote her mind to some more considerable undertaking. We have in the way of subjects, a rich and various mine that has hardly been opened. Let it be remembered, how

1 From a review of Lydia Huntley, *Moral Pieces, in Prose and Verse* (1815), in *North American Review* 1 (April 1815): 111–22.

2 Sigourney's next work would be a long historical, descriptive, and didactic poem, *Traits of the Aborigines of America* (1822).

much the genius of Scott[1] has struck out from his Scottish highland chiefs, and the border warfare with England; where both men and events are almost beneath the dignity of history; from what rude materials has he constructed and polished his most successful productions! How much more important, how much more varied, how vastly superiour in picturesque effect, the events that took place on our frontiers, in the course of the seventeenth, and beginning of the eighteenth century! [...] and then the magnificence of the scenery,—the cataract,[2] in its gigantick magnificence, that might receive all the waterfalls of Europe united, without perceiving the addition; the lakes whose shores for a century and a half, have been rendered illustrious by so many memorable combats of different nations, all give dignity to the theme.[3] [...]

1829: Sigourney's Poetry in an Emerging American Literature.[4]

[The essay surveys American poets to the late 1820s.]

From a review of the character of these early and imperfect endeavors in the rhyming art, and of our literature generally, down to a very recent date, we perceive the perfectly spontaneous growth of every branch of polite[5] letters among us. The common incitements to literary exertion, rivalry and the prospect of fame and emolument, cannot be said to have exerted any material influence in prompting the efforts of American writers. Authors have been too few to create competition, and the public, to whom they addressed themselves, too much occupied with matters of direct practical interest to bestow any high consideration upon the talents which are exerted only in the embellishment of life.

---

1 Sir Walter Scott (1771–1832), best-selling poet and novelist.

2 Niagara Falls, subject of several later works by Sigourney.

3 Sigourney did write several historical poems about armed conflicts in the making of the United States, but consistently denounced warfare.

4 From Samuel Kettel, *Specimens of American Poetry* (1829), Introduction and the biographical sketch of Sigourney; three typographical errors silently corrected.

5 Polished, refined.

Hence we have never known till the present day such a thing as a professed[1] author. All the talent and industry of the people have been called into the field of active employment, and the most of what has been written among us consists of such productions as were executed in the early days of our authors, before the serious business of life was entered upon; or in such leisure moments as were snatched from constant and laborious occupations. We have obtained therefore only the unripe fruits of their youth, or the imperfect performances of casual moments. The cultivation of literary talent has moreover been retarded by the state of dependence as to literature, in which we have continued, to the writers of Great Britain. Without searching for causes which lie deep in the character of our nation, we may assert that the "bales and hogsheads"[2] of learning which our friends beyond the ocean speak of having supplied us with, have been dealt to us in such abundance that the great stimulus to exertion has been wanting, and no pressing necessity has thrown us upon our own resources.[3] Still the feeling of patriotism must prompt the desire that native genius should be conspicuous in every high career of human intellect, and that a national spirit in the liberal arts should be encouraged, as instruments to nourish the civic virtues and give scope to the energies of mind among our countrymen. That this has not hitherto been effected, can hardly excite surprise in any one acquainted with our history. While we have been filling this wide land with people, it is not remarkable that as a nation, we should have found little leisure to cultivate the refinements of intellectual taste. [...][4]

[From the biographical sketch of Sigourney:[5]]

---

1 Professional, in the sense of earning a living from writing.

2 Widely quoted phrase from the British writer Sydney Smith: "But why should the Americans write books, when a six weeks' passage brings them, in their own tongue, our sense, science and genius, in bales and hogsheads?" "Travellers in America," *Edinburgh Review* 31 (1818): 132–50; Smith went on to predict that the United States would produce epics and other major literature once it had completed expansion to the Pacific.

3 In the absence of an international copyright agreement, American publishers usually did not pay foreign authors, making their works cheaper to reprint than those of American authors.

4 Vol. 1, pp. xlvii–viii.

5 Vol. 2, pp. 204–07.

It is an omen of favorable import to our national literature, that the claims of female talent have been ably advanced, and readily acknowledged. The value of such an accession to its interests, cannot fail of being duly estimated in an age, which is enjoying the pure and delightful breathings of Mrs Hemans' poetry and the strong practical sense of Miss Edgeworth.[1] To these cherished names we do no discredit, when we associate with them that of the accomplished lady, of whom we now speak. [Briefly discusses her early volumes.]

Upon none of the volumes, however, which have been the subject of our remarks, does the literary reputation of our author depend. Our specimens, the first excepted, have all been written since 1824. Within that period, she has exhibited a rapid improvement, and we rejoice to say, that this improvement is yet in full career. It is in the department of fugitive poetry—an appellation, certainly, most inappropriate, when applied to much which has been written under that name in this, its golden age, that Mrs Sigourney has reaped her most enduring laurels. It is no disparagement to her talents, to say, that this is the field for which they are best adapted. The highest living talent has been exerted in it, and found its recompense. To be classed with Watts, and Hervey, and Bryant, and Halleck,[2] and Mrs Hemans, is an association, of which the most successful votary of the muse, in any age, might justly boast. Only less popular than the last of these gifted minds, the productions of our author have been widely wafted with hers, on the wings of the periodical press. There is indeed, no other shape, in which the widest popularity may so well be combined with the most permanent endurance. [...]

The prevailing attributes of Mrs Sigourney's poetry are tenderness and religious feeling. She is an ardent lover, an accurate observer, and an eloquent revealer of the charms of nature. A most captivating tone of plaintiveness mingles with every breath-

---

1 Englishwoman Felicia Hemans (1793–1835), most popular and respected woman poet in the English-speaking world at that time; Maria Edgeworth (1768–1849), respected Anglo-Irish fiction writer, author of "national tales" and books for children.

2 Isaac Watts (1674–1748), English clergyman, education writer, and writer of numerous popular hymns; James Hervey (1714–58), English clergyman and author of widely read devotional *Meditations and Contemplations* (1746–47); William Cullen Bryant (1794–1878), American moral and patriotic poet and newspaper editor; Fitz-Greene Halleck (1790–1867), American poet in the style of Byron.

ing of her harp—but it is a plaintiveness which we may safely admire and cherish, for it never sinks into sadness. She loves to sing of "decay and death"—but it is that she may mingle with the mournful strains which they awaken, the cheering promise of renovated life and beauty.

We confidently refer the reader, for ample confirmation of all that we have said, to her last volume of poems.[1] Had Mrs Sigourney written no more than our "Specimens" exhibit, she would still possess undoubted claims to the proud title of the American HEMANS.[2]

1835: Sigourney and the Growing Moral Influence of Women Writers.[3]

[...] The literary empire, like almost every other, has been divided; the sexes are beginning to share it pretty impartially; nor would it be safe to say that woman's portion of it is less fertile or less wisely governed than the other. We should hold him to be rather indiscreet, to say the least, who should at this day make the experiment of casting reproach or ridicule on female writers, unless the circumstances of the case were pretty aggravated; if things shall continue to go on as they have done for the last twenty years, it is by no means certain that these writers will not constitute a majority of the whole number, and, acting in the spirit of the republican principle, manage matters at their own discretion. [The review considers British women writers, including Felicia Hemans.]

While the literature of Great Britain has been thus adorned by female intellect, our own has not been slow to partake of the regeneration; there is no doubt that the amount of woman's literary effort, in proportion to the whole, is greater here, and has done more to elevate the national character and her own, than in any other country; and it should be remembered that those who have labored longest have not yet reached the meridian of their powers, and that what they have already done is not to be taken as the full measure of what they have it in their power to do.

---

1 *Poems* (1827).

2 Sigourney received more space in the anthology than any American poet except Timothy Dwight and Joel Barlow, and the same space as John Neal and William Cullen Bryant.

3 From a review of Lydia Sigourney, *Poems* (1834), and Hannah Gould, *Poems* (1835), in *North American Review* 41:2 (October 1835): 430–54.

[The review praises Catharine Maria Sedgwick, Lydia Maria Child, Eliza Leslie, and Sarah Josepha Hale, and continues:]

[...] So great a change could not come over the form and fashion of literature, without producing some important changes in its spirit; and in one respect, the alteration is already visible. By a beautiful illustration of justice, it appears to be reserved for woman to do for Christianity in some degree what Christianity did for her, when it raised her to her just position in the social scale, and enabled her to become a bright example of its own beatitude. Such have, accordingly, been the aim and tendency of female literature in general; we may confidently believe that it will continue to be found on religion's side; and if such should be the fact, it would be treachery to the great purpose of our being not to welcome it, as a momentous and restoring power. Whoever believes that the ultimate end of science is to instruct, and that of poetry to please, mistakes the matter greatly; the true and only worthy object of literary effort, and all scientific research is, to purify the heart while they enlarge the mind, and thus to render both, according to their humble measure, worthy of the Source[1] to which they owe their powers. [...] These are truths, which woman is in far less danger of forgetting than man, from whose memory the pride of intellect or the hope of applause, so frequently obliterates them.

If such is to be the religious character of female writers, their moral influence will of course be great and happy; this result is equally assured by their social position, and their prevailing qualities of mind and heart. The spirit of man is militant, and whatever be the cause he is engaged in, strikes for victory; passion sweeps over his purest purposes, and leaves the heart a desert; interest, the god of this world, takes possession of the abandoned dwelling-place; rivalry and envy blight, like a summer frost, his generous emotions; and vanity, the gilded serpent, whispers her temptations not vainly in his ear. [...] But the gentle voice of woman addresses that heart, when its earliest thoughts may be easily inclined to good, in the soothing accents of interest and tenderness, in the fireside lesson, in the music of the infant hymn; before it has gone forth to wrestle with temptation, but not before the education for eternity is begun. [...] By a peculiar happiness of position, she is in a great degree removed from the influence of those infirmities of the mind, which the world are now dis-

1 God.

posed to regard as the evidences of its power. [...] She cannot comprehend, how the intelligent and haughty can be brought to wear the iron fetters of political party with no less triumph, than if they were badges of sovereignty, instead of slavery; she is slow to understand, how the Christian can obey to the letter all the commandments, except the one expressly given by the Author of his faith;[1] she is reluctant to believe the humiliating truth, that the applause of mankind is to be won by employing the gifts of God in hostility to Him who gave them. We may surely venture to indulge the hope, that her influence will mitigate the wild excitement of the chase for wealth and fame, tranquillize the angry passions which constantly rebel against the necessary ills of our condition, and convince men that the way of wisdom is the way of pleasantness and peace.

[The review speculates on women's future contribution in moral "romantic fiction" depicting social relations and everyday life, and then turns to Sigourney's poetry:]

Without devoting her attention exclusively to poetry, or engaging in the composition of any extensive work, Mrs. Sigourney has continued from time to time to give to the public, principally through the medium of the magazines and annuals, a variety of productions, by which she has acquired a high rank as a popular and useful writer.

The volume before us is a collection of the poetical productions, which the author has thought proper to publish in a more permanent form. Some of its contents were written at a very early age; others, as she herself assures us, were composed at later periods, amidst domestic occupations or maternal cares; and the greater portion of them were suggested by passing circumstances, and may be regarded as extemporary in their nature. [...] Such writings do not ask nor admit of the display of some of the very highest attributes of poetry, and to these Mrs. Sigourney presents no claim. The excellence of all her poems is quiet and unassuming. They are full of the sweet images and bright associations of domestic life; its unobtrusive happiness, its unchanging affections, and its cares and sorrows; of the feelings naturally inspired by life's vicissitudes from the cradle to the death-bed; of the hopes that burn, like the unquenched altar fire, in that chosen

1 The Ten Commandments, in the Bible, Exodus 20.3–17.

dwelling place of virtue and religion. The light of a pure and unostentatious faith shines around them, blending with her thoughts and giving a tender coloring to her contemplations, like the melancholy beauty of our own autumnal scenery. [...] Mrs. Sigourney's habitual tone of thought is pensive, but not melancholy; serious, but not severe; and her views of life, without being joyous, are not shaded by repulsive gloom. Every subject she touches is made the fountain of calm reflection, which is often striking, and always pure. If she do not often excite the reader to enthusiastic admiration, she generally leaves a strong impression of her power, and never fails to inspire respect for the qualities of her mind and heart.

Mrs. Sigourney's versification is, in general, correct and sweet; although, in this respect there are occasional instances of want of care. The effect of short pieces, like the greater part of her's, very much depends upon the delicacy and perfection of their finish; in those of greater magnitude, the attention is withdrawn from minute defects, or they are lost in a comprehensive survey of the general proportions; as an imperfection, which would pass unheeded in a panorama, is at once detected in a cabinet picture. Her writings in blank verse are, however, remarkable for the music of their flow. In their style of thought and expression, they remind us of those passages of Cowper,[1] where the movement of the verse is in perfect keeping with the gravity and tenderness of the subject. Like him, she is attracted only by Nature's soothing and gentle aspects; her spirit holds no communion with the elements in their wrath; she takes no delight in witnessing the whirlwind and the storm; she looks on all the seasons, as they change, not to people them with images of gloom, but to draw from them whatever of happiness and instruction they can give. [...]

Great as Mrs. Sigourney's merit certainly is, she has not yet displayed it with so much effect as she may and will do, if she shall be inclined to render poetry a more exclusive object of pursuit. Thus far, it has evidently been little more than the amusement of her leisure hours; with less divided attention, she has the power of accomplishing higher and better things. [...]

---

1 William Cowper (1731–1800), English poet of religious devotion and domestic life, a major influence on Sigourney.

1836: Edgar Allan Poe Explains Sigourney's Popularity.[1]

[...] There are two kinds of popular reputation,—or rather there are two roads by which such reputation may be attained: and it appears to us an idiosyncrasy which distinguishes mere fame from most, or perhaps from *all* other human ends, that, in regarding the intrinsic value of the object, we must not fail to introduce, as a portion of our estimate, the means by which the object is acquired. To speak less abstractedly. Let us suppose two writers having a reputation apparently equal—that is to say, their names *being equally in the mouths of the people*—for we take this to be the most practicable test of what we choose to term *apparent popular reputation*. Their names then are equally in the mouths of the people. The one has written a great work—let it be either an Epic of high rank, or something which, although of seeming littleness in itself, is yet, like the Christabelle of Coleridge,[2] entitled to be called *great* from its power of creating intense emotion in the minds of great men. And let us imagine that, by this single effort, the author has attained a certain quantum of reputation. We know it to be possible that another writer of very moderate powers may build up for himself, little by little, a reputation equally great—and this, too, merely by keeping continually in the eye, or by appealing continually with little things, to the ear, of that great, overgrown, and majestical gander, the critical and bibliographical rabble.

It would be an easy, although perhaps a somewhat disagreeable task, to point out several of the most popular writers in America—popular in the above mentioned sense—who have manufactured for themselves a celebrity by the very questionable means, and in the very questionable manner, to which we have alluded. But it must not be thought that we wish to include Mrs. Sigourney in the number. By no means. She has trod, however, upon the confines of their circle. She does not *owe* her reputation to the chicanery we mention, but it cannot be denied that it has been thereby greatly assisted. In a word—no single piece which she has written, and not even her collected works as we behold

1 From "Critical Notices" of Sigourney, *Zinzendorff, and other Poems* (1836), Hannah Gould, *Poems* (1835), and E.F. Ellet, *Poems; Translated and Original* (1835); *Southern Literary Messenger* 2 (January 1836): 112–17.

2 Samuel Taylor Coleridge, "Christabel" (1816), a fragmentary poem of Gothic-style enchantment.

them in the present volume, and in the one published some years ago, would fairly entitle her to that exalted rank which she actually enjoys as the authoress, *time after time*, of her numerous, and, in most instances, very creditable compositions. The validity of our objections to this adventitious notoriety we must be allowed to consider unshaken, until it can be proved that any multiplication of zeros will eventuate in the production of a unit.

We have watched, too, with a species of anxiety and vexation brought about altogether by the sincere interest we take in Mrs. Sigourney, the progressive steps by which she has at length acquired the title of the "American Hemans." Mrs. S. cannot conceal from her own discernment that she has acquired this title *solely by imitation*. The very phrase "American Hemans" speaks loudly in accusation: and we are grieved that what by the over-zealous has been intended as complimentary should fall with so ill-omened a sound into the ears of the judicious. We will briefly point out those particulars in which Mrs. Sigourney stands palpably convicted of that sin which in poetry is not to be forgiven.[1]

And first, in the *character of her subjects*. Every unprejudiced observer must be aware of the almost identity between the subjects of Mrs. Hemans and the subjects of Mrs. Sigourney. The themes of the former lady are the unobtrusive happiness, the sweet images, the cares, the sorrows, the gentle affections, of the domestic hearth—these too are the themes of the latter. The Englishwoman has dwelt upon all the "tender and true" chivalries of passion—and the American has dwelt as unequivocally upon the same. Mrs. Hemans has delighted in the radiance of a pure and humble faith—she has looked upon nature with a speculative attention—she has "watched the golden array of sunset clouds, with an eye looking beyond them to the habitations of the disembodied spirit"—she has poured all over her verses the most glorious and lofty aspirations of a redeeming Christianity, and in all this she is herself glorious and lofty. And all this too has Mrs. Sigourney not only attempted, but accomplished—yet in all this she is but, alas!—an imitator.

And secondly—in points more directly tangible than the one just mentioned, and therefore more easily appreciated by the generality of readers, is Mrs. Sigourney again open to the charge we have adduced. We mean in the structure of her versification—in the peculiar turns of her phraseology—in certain habitual expres-

1 Poe goes on to describe Hemans' work inaccurately, and to overstate the similarity between Sigourney's subjects and style, and those of Hemans.

sions (principally interjectional,) such as *yea! alas!* and many others, so frequent upon the lips of Mrs. Hemans as to give an almost ludicrous air of similitude to all articles of her composition—in an invincible inclination to apostrophize every object, in both moral and physical existence—and more particularly in those mottos or quotations, sometimes of considerable extent, prefixed to nearly every poem, not as a text for discussion, nor even as an intimation of what is to follow, but as the actual subject matter itself, and of which the verses ensuing are, in most instances, merely a paraphrase. These were all, in Mrs. Hemans, mannerisms of a gross and inartificial nature; but, in Mrs. Sigourney, they are mannerisms of the most inadmissible kind—the mannerisms of imitation. [...]

Having expressed ourselves thus far in terms of nearly unmitigated censure, it may appear in us somewhat equivocal to say that, as Americans, we are proud—very proud of the talents of Mrs. Sigourney. Yet such is the fact. The faults which we have already pointed out, and some others which we will point out hereafter, are but dust in the balance, when weighed against her very many and distinguishing excellences. Among those high qualities which give her, beyond doubt, a title to the sacred name of poet are an acute sensibility to natural loveliness—a quick and perfectly just conception of the moral and physical sublime—a calm and unostentatious vigor of thought—a mingled delicacy and strength of expression—and above all, a mind nobly and exquisitely attuned to all the gentle charities and lofty pieties of life.

[The review considers strong and weak passages in "Zinzendorff," and more briefly discusses "Female Education," "The Pholas," "Friends of Man," "Filial Grief," and "Poetry," before discussing Gould and Ellet.]

1840: Differences between Male and Female Writers.[1]

Between authors and authoresses, taken generally, there are some differences. The following, it appears to me, are a few of them.

There is much more sameness in the style and tone of sentiment throughout the works of females: for instance, how very much alike, in their general character, are all the productions of Mrs. Hemans and Miss Landon.

1 From "Thoughts and Reflections, Number I" by "G.," in *Southern Literary Messenger* 6 (March 1840): 213–19.

They have less versatility of talent; not being so often distinguished for writing well on many different subjects. This proceeds from their being acquainted with fewer branches of knowledge than men generally are: and indeed the first mentioned quality may be owing to the same cause. For the greater the extent of our knowledge, the more extensive will be the field for inferences, deductions, and figures of speech: and hence our manner will be varied according to the relative amount and variety of that knowledge.

They are generally more diffuse—from their having been accustomed to pay attention to many small things, with which men have scarcely any thing to do: they are hence led to mention, and sometimes dilate upon, things that men would scarcely notice.

In works depicting society they are generally superior; for they necessarily devote much more time and thought to it than men do. Hence, perhaps, in some measure, the superior excellence of the works of Miss Edgworth, Miss Burney,[1] &c. In conversational scenes they are superior, for a similar reason.

Lastly, there is generally a certain polish—a certain purity and refinement of feeling, about their productions, which those of few authors possess. James in his last novels—the Robber, Charles Tyrrel, and the Gentleman of the Old School[2]—approaches perhaps as near to this peculiar polish as any other author.

It is a singular coincidence how many female writers there are of the present day whose names begin with an S, viz: Mrs. Sherwood, Sommerville, Shelley, Sigourney, Seba Smith, Miss Strickland, Sedgwick, Sinclair, Stickney,[3] &c.

---

1 Maria Edgeworth (1768–1849), Anglo-Irish fiction writer and writer for children, and Frances Burney (1752–1840), English novelist and dramatist, both known for fiction depicting social life.

2 Popular and prolific English novelist G.P.R. James (1801–60), author of *The Robber* (1838), *A Gentleman of the Old School* (1839), *Charles Tyrell; or, The Bitter Blood* (1839), and others.

3 Mary Sherwood (1775–1851), prolific English writer of Evangelical fiction for young people; Mary (Fairfax) Somerville (1780–1872), English mathematician and popularizer of science; Mary Shelley (1797–1851), English novelist and author of *Frankenstein* (1818); Elizabeth Oakes Smith (1806–1868), American writer and feminist; Agnes (1796–1874) and Elizabeth (1794–1875) Strickland, popular English historians; Catharine Maria Sedgwick (1789–1867), American fiction writer; Catherine Sinclair (1800–1864), English novelist and children's writer; Sarah (Stickney) Ellis (1799–1872), English writer on education and the condition of women.

The same quality appertains to Madame De Stael—the most talented of women: and to Sappho[1]—Sappho, sole star among the ancient poetesses, that yet sends a few rays of light through the dark abysm of the past.

1843: Call from the South for "a Mrs Sigourney" to Represent Slavery Positively.[2]

"LET me write a people's songs, and he who will may write their laws."[3] The sagacity of this saying cannot be too much applauded. Before the discovery of the printing press, the only access to the minds of any people was through their ears. In those days, the *orator* was omnipotent; or, if his power admitted a rival, that rival was the *minstrel.* The arts of rhetoric, the graces of poesy, and the charms of music, were alike resorted to, as means of chaining attention, engaging sympathy, and enlisting the passions of the multitude. [...]

The press has lent its aid to diffuse the influence, and perpetuate the fame of the orator and poet; but it has, at the same time, become the rival of both. No man can be an orator or a poet, who is not born so; and the rare and marvellous endowments necessary to the constitution of either character, gave, to those who possessed them, a divided empire over the minds of men. This monopoly of intercourse with the public mind they no longer enjoy; and now, thanks to the press, it may be successfully approached by the sober moralist, the stern jurist, and the homely utilitarian, through an avenue open alike to all.

Yet the essential wisdom of the adage quoted above is not even now to be questioned. The same idea may be expressed in other words, with equal truth, at this day. What is that idea? That he

---

1 Germaine de Staël (1766–1817), French novelist and political and cultural writer, author of *Corinne* (1807), whose heroine was an influential figure for the Romantic poetess as national bard; Sappho: sixth-century BCE woman poet, made by Romantic culture into a figure of the female author as victim of her passions.

2 From review of *A Brief Enquiry into the True Nature and Character of Our Federal Government ...*, by "a Virginian" (Petersburg, 1840), in *Southern Quarterly Review* 3 (April 1843): 407–31 (407–09).

3 Originally in Andrew Fletcher of Saltoun (1655–1716), "An Account of a Conversation Concerning a Right Regulation of Governments for the Common Good of Mankind," in *Political Works* (1737), where "songs" are "ballads," but the statement was proverbial by this time.

who commands the avenues, through which alone the minds of a people may be reached, exercises over them a power greater than that of the mere written law. In this reading age, that avenue is the press; and it is as true at this day, as that adage ever was, that "he who writes a people's books, need not care who makes their laws."

Of the truth of this, the history of the constitution and government of the United States affords a remarkable and interesting proof. Every one versed in political science perfectly understands why it is that the business of authorship in the United States has heretofore been left to northern writers. But whatever be the cause, such has been the fact, and the consequences have been such as might have been anticipated. Books, intended to form the minds, the habits, and the manners of the rising generation, are put into the hands of our children; and, in these, we look in vain for any lessons adapted to such of our institutions, and the relations growing out of them, as are peculiar to ourselves. There is nothing, for example, in any other society, analagous to the relation between the white child and his negro nurse, or that between the half-grown boy and the gray-headed family servant. Yet, from these it is that we imbibe some of our best, as well as earliest lessons of feeling and of manners; and these lessons it should be, in part, the office of the schoolbook to enforce and ratify. On this point, however, all we have are silent; or, if they speak, it is in profound ignorance of the subject. All connected with it, that the boy finds in books, is at variance with his experience; and this contrariety of influences produces confusion in his mind, caprice in his feelings, and inconsistency in his conduct. We are persuaded, that a book made up of authentic anecdotes of the incidents of the nursery, and the adventures of my young master, in the servants' hall, and the stable yard, would be one of the most amusing and instructive that could be compiled. What a theme for the candid mind of Mrs. Sigourney, if she could trace the history of one day, in the life of the little urchin, from the moment he opens his eyes, and springs, kicking and chuckling, to his nurse's arms, to that, when he cons over to her his evening prayer; and, patting her face with his little hands, sinks to sleep on her bosom. Her sleepless vigilance to guard him from fault or hurt, the ready address with which she soothes his petty griefs, and calms his petulance, and subdues his waywardness, all these are beautiful; and the heart must be obdurate, indeed, which is not made better by witnessing them. We may be asked, wherein does this case differ from that of any other nurse?

and the answer is found in the complicated relation of the nurse to the family of her little charge. His father bears a sort of paternal relation to herself; the elder brothers and sisters had formerly been her pets, as he now is; she feels a mother's interest in all of them; and they, together with her own children, form, for her, one family; while the master and mistress are the common parents of all. And this relation is not a thing of a day. It has come down from generation to generation, and gains strength in every transmission. We repeat that it is an *hiatus valde deflendus*[1] that in all our school-books there is nothing to cherish and perpetuate the holy affections engendered in this relation; and thus to check the growth of pride, arrogance and selfishness, by keeping alive this sympathy between the highest and lowest.

When the boy advances towards manhood, and begins to study the political institutions of his country, he experiences, without perceiving, a similar want. The books in which he must study them are all composed by writers from a section of the union[2] where all men, in every occupation and in every gradation of society, are aware of a common interest, to establish a reading of the constitution highly favorable to their purposes, and, for the same reason, and, in a more than equal degree, injurious to ours.

1843: Sigourney's Popularity a Sign of Low American Taste.[3]

The public judgment, (in our country at least,) is not likely to be passed upon metrical labors of any kind—particularly those which involve the higher standards of criticism. The taste for the fine arts, particularly poetry, is in very low condition in our country. The only poetry which takes the popular ear, is that which never tasks the popular thought. Simple common-places, gracefully expressed, like those of Longfellow, or clumsy versions of the Psalms, such as Mrs. Sigourney gives us in seldom-ceasing profusion—things which we read as we run—which never arrest us on the highway, are preferred far before Milton. A select circle, a sacred few, indeed, expect better things and occasionally find them; but these seldom utter themselves in print. The ordinary critic of the Reviews and Magazines is one who, if unprompted

1 A deficiency greatly to be deplored (from Latin).

2 The Northern non-slave states.

3 From review of "Mathew's Poems," *Southern Literary Messenger* 9 (December 1843): 715–20 (716).

by private interest or friendship, rarely runs counter with popular taste; and the poem to which the vulgar million give the go-by, he is also prepared to pass, either with similarly contemptuous indifference, or with an hostility which deems itself perfectly safe in its assault upon a performance, which the great majority will never read, for the revision of his judgment.

1849: Strengths and Limits of Sigourney's Poetic Mind.[1]

THIS edition of Mrs. Sigourney's Poems is uniform with the superb Philadelphia editions of Longfellow, Willis, and Bryant,[2] the fact of a poet's appearing in so beautiful a dress being of itself evidence of fame. The reputation of Mrs. Sigourney, indeed, is so well established, that she may be said to occupy a place from which she can neither be depressed by detraction nor elevated by panegyric. [...] This edition of her poems is composed partly of judicious selections from her former publications, and partly of new poems, and it conveys a much better impression of her powers than would be gained by a scrutiny of her complete works.

The volume contains about a hundred poems. They are on a variety of subjects, and in a variety of forms, but they all bear unmistakable marks of one mind, looking at nature and human life from one position. Their leading peculiarity is devotional sensibility, and their leading charm the extreme, the translucent purity of thought and feeling displayed in the expression of the religious and domestic affections. As is the case with most female poets, Mrs. Sigourney's powers act with intensity only on those subjects which have fallen within her own experience, or which spontaneously fasten on her womanly sympathies. She does not evince that masculine imagination, by which the mind passes out of its own individual relations of sex and person, and animates numerous and widely different modes of being. Her poems not only declare her at once to be a woman, but a woman who, as far as regards composition, has disciplined her mind into one or two moods, and persists in seeing every thing under their conditions. [...] Her mind, therefore, is not flexible and impassioned, but didactic; and fancy, feeling, understanding, and imagination all

1 Review of Sigourney, *Illustrated Poems* (1849), in *North American Review* 68:2 (April 1849): 496–503.

2 The popular American poets Henry Wadsworth Longfellow (1807–82), Nathaniel Parker Willis (1806–67), and William Cullen Bryant (1794–1878).

obey rules, —obey them, it is true, without strain or struggle, and almost with the quickness of instinct, but still in this obedience manifesting subjection, not sovereignty.

It is evident that a religious mind, thus subject to the higher powers, and at the same time confined within its own realm of thought and emotion, would perceive nature and human life always in their relations to God, but would have the range of its perceptions narrowed by the limitations of its own personality. We have, therefore, to make one or two more distinctions in considering Mrs. Sigourney as a poet of the religious and domestic affections, before we can reach the source of her merits or defects.

The truth of the all-pervading presence of a conscious Deity in nature, and of a Providence in the sorrows and joys of mankind, seems to have been fixed in her mind as a doctrine before it was felt as an overpowering conception or emotion; and, consequently, she rather goes to nature and life prepared to look and search for the signs of divine presence, than to be amazed by having the overwhelming truth suddenly flashed into her mind from without, through the vital processes of imagination. Accordingly, though she has a deep and thoughtful feeling of holy things, her hymns rarely rise to the raptures of holy passion, in which the soul, by a divine disinterestedness, seems to dissolve its whole individual being into one ecstatic song of adoration. This last mood of mind, the highest and grandest exercise of imagination, and the perfection at once of what is purely religious and purely poetical, it is no disparagement to Mrs. Sigourney to say she does not possess; for it is the loftiest and finest frenzy of the seer and the bard. But while a comparatively small number of religious poets reach this intense realization of Deity, it is approached just in proportion to the flexibility and objectiveness of the poet's imagination. Now, Mrs. Sigourney's mind being didactic rather than lyrical, her devotional feeling rarely gushes out in pure song, with the speed of an irrepressible instinct, but approaches more the character of a steady and quiet faith, in which the soul serenely believes rather than rapturously burns, and meditates more than it imagines. The poetic faculty, therefore, most at work in her thoughtful and devotional moods, is fancy, illustrating the truth *from* nature and life, rather than imagination[1] presenting it directly *in* nature and life.

1 A hierarchical distinction formulated by the English poet Samuel Taylor Coleridge in his *Biographia Literaria* (1817), ch. 14, becoming a critical commonplace: "... good sense is the body of poetic genius, fancy its drapery, motion its life, and imagination the soul ..."

In thus speaking of Mrs. Sigourney's poetry, as didactic, we by no means insinuate that it is prosaic, but simply that it is neither lyrical nor narrative in spirit, though much of her verse is cast in these forms. Religious thought relating to divine things, considered apart from its poetic expression, is vital or mechanical according as it directly conceives the objects of contemplation, or apprehends and applies a doctrine respecting them. In Mrs. Sigourney's book, we have illustrations of both, but more of the former than the latter. She has brooded long enough over her own experience and sympathies to give them vitality, and the poems which truly represent her own mind not only possess life, but communicate it. A healthy moral energy is diffused generally through her poems, which steals into the reader's mind through subtile avenues lying beyond his consciousness, and declares the presence of a poet gifted with the power of inspiring strength in the very heart of weakness and lassitude. This is a great poetic excellence, however limited may be the range of its exercise, and that Mrs. Sigourney possesses it cannot be denied or even contested. [...]

The pervading devotional tone to which we have referred, finds its finest and holiest expression in celebrating the domestic affections. The mode in which her mind acts in this province, however, illustrates what we have previously said of her mental processes. The poems entitled "To-morrow," "Unspoken Language," "The Emigrant Mother," not to mention others, are full of true pathos, and reach and penetrate the heart as inevitably as any in Wordsworth;[1] but though sufficiently tender and deep to bring moisture into the eyes even of a reviewer, we shall find, on a sharp scrutiny, that, though names are used and persons indicated, there is really nothing there but qualities. The purest types of the affections are grasped in all their firmness and delicacy, but there is no combination of them with those other human elements which, in their union, produce character. The consequence is, that we have no representations of the affections as modified by sex, age, nation, position, or character. With remarkable distinctness of conception and decision of expression, we have presented to us the type, but it is given in its simple unity, abstracted from all individuality. We assert confidently, that in this volume there is not displayed one trait of character but that of the author

1 William Wordsworth (1770–1850), widely respected English poet of nature and common life, whose plain style Sigourney adopted in such poems as "To-morrow" (here p. 191).

herself. [...] The long poem of "Pocahontas," the most beautiful of all the tributes to the heroic Indian princess, is still simply a fervid expression of the impression made by the story on the mind of the writer, without any clear vision of the scenes and characters of the story as they were in themselves. [...]

But this peculiarity of bringing out a quality at the expense of all character, which we have indicated as a limitation of Mrs. Sigourney's genius, is probably a chief source of her influence over the hearts of her readers. She is thus enabled to stamp a deep impression of one affection, at least, on the mind; and by detaching it from the other elements of character, by making a person stand simply for an emotion, she has completely mastered one prominent source of the pathetic. [...]

1853: Southern Attack on Sigourney as a Representative of Northern Literature and Art.[1]

[The article attacks lavishly produced picture-and-poetry books.]

Do tell, is all the *Miss Nancy-ism* of the northern cities to be applied to books professing to illustrate the Bible? Is all the proverbial humbug, the sorry namby-pamby, the mighty nothingness of their own grandiloquence, the effete tea-inspired poetry of their Sigourneys, the sorriest daubings of their numerous Raphaels and Titians,[2] to be hung around the Bible, as the gloomy long moss of Louisiana is hung around the stately cypress?

[The article then attacks Sigourney's contribution, the poem "Eve."]

The venerable Mrs. Sigourney has had the heart to perpetrate nearly a hundred lines, for this book, of wild, varied, Pindaric, Southeyish,[3] common-place rhymes about Eve and Cain and Abel. It is unaccountable to us how grown up people *can* have the heart

---

1 Review of *Some Sacred Female Portraits*, ed. Rev. H. Hastings Weld (1848), in the *Southern Literary Messenger* 19 (November 1853): 659–64.

2 Raphael (1483–1520) and Titian (c. 1490–1578), Italian painters much admired in the United States at this time, and invoked by American painters.

3 Pindar (522–433 BCE), Greek lyric poet known for his rich language; Robert Southey (1774–1843), poet and biographer, known for his long stanzaic narrative poems on historical subjects.

to write such things on such subjects; unless it may be that the book-maker tells them he must have *so much* poetry, and they spin on, until they have spun *so much* and stop. [...] We sincerely believe that it is not an utterly unattainable pitch of social excellence for northern ladies, to employ what ever gifts nature may bestow upon them, in good uses, without stirring up civil strife, or seeking and winning ovations from the rivals and foes of their country; to be geniuses without being traitresses; to be sensible and earnest without fanatic fury; to be informing and powerful without malice; and to be eloquent and readable, without hatred to the people of any of the States of the Union. If not, then our dear northern aunts and cousins would greatly better not meddle with the pen at all, but remain in woman's more legitimate and noble sphere—that is, be the comforters of the blue noses, and knit stockings.

[The article then discusses the book's many illustrations, and concludes by calling for a Southern literary and artistic secession from the North.]

We here bring to a close this little piece of criticism, (in the sourness of which we take pleasure only so far as it is deemed to be a part of justice,) with the expression of the deliberate opinion that Southern art will be higher, nobler, better every way, when it shall declare and maintain a total revolt from all vassalage and all pupilage to the Northern part of this confederacy. The analogies of history declare clearly that Southern mind, Southern scenery, Southern air, and Southern skies, are, to say the least and to speak moderately, not inferior to Northern, for all the high dreams of genius. We can not stand at all in such departments of human effort, if we cannot stand on a foundation of our own forming. If we wish for models at all, other than those which earth, cloud, sky and hallowed history hold out, in painting, poetry, sculpture or architecture, then they must be better models than those with which the Northern cities furnish us. [...]

1855: Sigourney One of the Established "Literary Women of America."[1]

[...] One trait in her literary productions can not fail to strike the attention and call forth the commendation of every reader, and that is the constant preservation of her womanly identity. She never loses the woman in the writer. Sometimes contact with the public, through the press, tends to obliterate the shrinking delicacy of woman's nature, or it becomes overtopped by the subtile spirit of ambitious aspiring. Contact with the public for nearly forty years has wrought nothing of this in Mrs. Sigourney; nor has the applause murmured by myriad tongues in both hemispheres. Her womanly delicacy gilds every page traced by her pen, and sheds a beautiful halo around her genius. For this we commend her; and in this she is a more happy example of what a female writer ought to be than almost any other that the age has produced.

One great cause of the preservation of this character, is to be found in the fact that she uniformly employs her pen with one great and paramount object; namely, that of doing good. [...] Mere freaks of imagination she never essays. She always has a lesson to teach, a moral to inculcate, or a religious sentiment to nurture—the object is apparent throughout, and she never once deviates from it. The solidity of her reputation, the affectionate regard in which she is held by the wise and good everywhere, result, in a great measure, from her almost instinctive adherence to this great principle. This is the reason why her name has become a household word in all lands where Christian virtues are cherished. [...]

It has sometimes been objected that Mrs. Sigourney rarely ever looks at nature or human life from any other than one position.[2] To us this objection has no force so long as it is conceded that that position is the true stand-point from which all just views of nature and human life are to be obtained.

[The essay discusses her large number of poems of mourning, and continues:]

---

1 "The Literary Women of America: The Genius and Writings of Mrs. Sigourney," By the Editor [Rev. D.W. Clark], *Ladies' Repository* 15 (March 1855): 176–78, referring mainly to Sigourney's *The Home in the West, and Other Poems* (1854).

2 See above, 1849.

There is a translucent purity of thought and feeling displayed in all her delineations of the domestic and religious affections. Her sympathies are here poured forth with all the intensity of her womanly nature. Her constructive power, her creative genius, though not of the highest order—not of that order that stands aloof from the ordinary modes of human thought, and refuses the practical lessons of experience, is by no means deficient. In her prose writings she displays a distinctness and breadth of perception, a force of argument, an aptness of illustration, and a ready command of choice and expressive words which indicate no ordinary powers of mind. She describes nature, too, and deciphers its great lessons with a delicate and truthful appreciation. These traits make her prose publications popular and useful. Poetry is her true element. Here she is at home, and her genius brightens in the smile of the muses. [...] Her prose writings will live long and do much good; her letters to mothers, to young ladies, to her pupils, and that genial, delightful production—Past Meridian—are works that will not soon die. But her fame will rest on her poetical and not on her prose writings. In the world of literature, in coming ages, she will be known as a *poet*; nor will it be by that name almost invidiously attached to her—though kindly intended—"the Mrs. Hemans of America;" for Mrs. Sigourney has as true an identity in the world of literature as Mrs. Hemans; and we doubt not that her recognition, by future ages, as a truly inspired poet will be as hearty and as enduring. [...]

1855: A Transatlantic View: Sigourney and other American Poets Will Revolutionize the World.[1]

[...] The impulse which the Poets of America may have already given to the great work of organization which has been so rapidly effected in their country, cannot with any accuracy be determined, and though it would be equally as difficult to hazard an opinion on the amount of their future influence on Transatlantic

1 "The Poets of America: First Paper," *Irish Quarterly Review* 5 (June 1855): 193–220, reviewing London editions of Henry Wadsworth Longfellow, William Cullen Bryant, and Oliver Wendell Holmes, and *The Poetical Works of Mrs. L.H. Sigourney*, ed. F.W.N. Bayley (London: George Routledge and Co., 1851); a second paper (*Irish Quarterly Review* 5, September 1855: 561–90) discusses John G. Whittier, Edgar Allan Poe, James Russell Lowell, Thomas Buchanan Reid, and N.P. Willis.

society, it is wonderfully evident that such influence will be immense. Greatness of capacity, apparently justifiable as such a basis would be, does not form the groundwork of this belief, which, on the contrary, has naturally grown from observing the adaptation of that capacity, to the wants and aspirations of the people, and from the unceasing vigilance with which it cherishes the bulwarks of the country's freedom. We search in vain through the records of European Literature, for instances such as the majority of these Poets afford us, where each inspiration of the Bard, seems consecrated at the shrine of public utility, and transferred into an oracle for the dispensation of the most invaluable truth. In like manner we are completely unsuccessful in discovering any other generation of Poets, who have been so generally distinguished for the vestal purity of their patriotism, or their manly advocacy in its behalf. The care with which those subjects are selected, most calculated to improve the intellect, and the heart, the paternal solicitude which is evinced in their treatment, and the practical ameliorations they suggest, have rendered the Poetry of America sacred, and have embued its people with a reverence for their Poets totally distinct from the admiration which their genius has elicited. [...]

But while we eulogise their merits, let us not shut our eyes to their imperfections. In common with the whole race, a peculiar species of emphatic egotism, which decidedly does not tend to impart elevation to the subject, is strongly apparent in a great number of the productions of American Poets. This injurious weakness it is to be hoped, and, indeed, expected, will gradually wear itself away: while it lasts it must act as a weighty drag chain on even the most splendid efforts, and cannot but deteriorate their merit. Another disadvantage under which these Poets labor, is the want of a native style, sufficiently robust and dignified: their deficiency in this respect obliges them to fall back on the idioms, and rythmical peculiarities of the mother country, which consequently lessens the compass of their originality, and the raciness of their expression. Time, however, the great teacher, will rectify this defect, for, as their ideas become more settled, and their character more developed, the increased improvement will necessarily be reflected in their literature.

[...] The mind prone to anticipation soon arrives at that period when the influence of this benignant teaching will have produced a plenteous harvest, already grown ripe beneath its fructifying rays; and unlike the cynic who asseverated that man never advances, but is constantly moving around a cycle of instincts, to whose grovelling propensities, Prometheus like, he is chained, it will behold in the open womb of the future, the transfiguration of humanity, comparatively redeemed, as it will then have been, from the degrading stigma of its present vices, such as war, lust, fraud, intemperance, assisted in its heavenward course by the spirit of wisdom, and the intensity of brotherly love, its symbols the horn of plenty, and the olive wreaths of the Minerva of peace.

[The review considers Longfellow and Bryant and turns to Sigourney:]

Mrs. Sigourney is a poetess possessing, in a remarkable degree, those qualities which entitle the possessor to the rank of a first class writer. Her vigorous comprehensiveness, lofty aspirings, brilliant fancy, philosophy, and philanthropic zeal, coupled with her sublime references to Almighty perfection, and the grand moral tendency of her poetry, unite in claiming for her an amount of admiration which enables her to hold one of the highest places among the poets of her country.

In like manner the patriotism which she has always evinced, her Spartan veneration for virtue, and scathing denunciations of crime; her deep-rooted love of nature, and the elegance, compass, and power of her language, have all had their share in accomplishing the universal success which her writings have obtained. [...] Truly her brilliant talents not only elevate the standard of intellectuality which dignifies her sex, but must naturally inspire its members with expectations, in which their widened influence, and far extended importance as a class, are conspicuously distinguished.

It is exceedingly questionable whether Sigourney would not gain from a comparison with her poetic sister, Felicia Hemans. Many would esteem her an equal in fancy, grace, and rhythmical beauty, while in vigor and range of comprehension she is most undoubtedly superior. [The review discusses "Oriska" and briefly mentions a number of other poems, and concludes with a consideration of Oliver Wendell Holmes.]

1871: Already Relegated to the Past.[1]

Fifty years ago, there were few female poets in the United States. Indeed, there were few women who had any place in literature;

1 "Current Literature" (review of Lucretia Maria Davidson, *Poems*, in *Overland Monthly and Out West Magazine* 6 (March 1871): 290–96 (294).

and literature itself occupied but a small space in the crowding activities of the time. Mrs. Sigourney, Miss Sedgwick, Mrs. Lydia Maria Child,[1] and a few other women whose names now are found only in the ancient catalogues of American authors, were delighting the generation with their works; and the eager "announcements of new books," made by the slow publishers of the day, read comically now, in the midst of the prodigal outpouring of books of poetry, romance, travel, biography, philosophy, and speculation—good, bad, and indifferent—with which the world is flooded.

1 Catharine Maria Sedgwick (1789–1867), American fiction writer; Lydia Maria Child (1802–80), novelist and education writer.

Select Bibliography

First Publication of Sigourney's Single Works, Collections, Major Revisions, and Significant Republications

Moral Pieces in Prose and Verse. By Lydia Huntley. Hartford: Sheldon & Goodwin, Printers, 1815.

The Writings of Nancy Maria Hyde, of Norwich, Conn. Connected with a Sketch of Her Life. Norwich: Printed by Russell Hubbard, 1816.

The Square Table. Hartford, 1819. No. I. Hartford: Samuel G. Goodrich, 1 Sept. 1819. No. II. *The Square Table, or Meditations of Four Secluded Maidens Seated Around It*. Hartford, November 1819.

Traits of the Aborigines of America: A Poem. Cambridge: University Press, 1822.

Sketch of Connecticut, Forty Years Since. Hartford: Oliver D. Cooke and Sons, 1824.

Poems. By the Author of "Moral Pieces in Prose and Verse." Boston and Hartford: S.G. Goodrich, 1827.

Biography of Pious Persons; Abridged for Youth. 2 vols. Springfield: Merriam & Little, 1832.

Evening Readings in History. Springfield: G. and C. Merriam, 1833.

The Farmer and Soldier: A Tale. L.H.S. Hartford: J. Hubbard Wells, Printer, 1833.

How To Be Happy: Written for the Children of Some Dear Friends. By a Lady. Hartford: D.F. Robinson, 1833.

The Intemperate and the Reformed. (First by Sigourney; second by Gerrit Smith.) Boston: Seth Bliss, 1833.

Letters to Young Ladies. By a Lady. Hartford: P. Canfield, 1833.

Memoir of Phebe P. Hammond, a Pupil in the American Asylum at Hartford. Prepared for the Press by Mrs L.H.S. New York: Sleight & Van Norden, Printers, 1833.

Report of the Hartford Female Beneficent Society. Hartford, 1833.

Poetry for Children. By the Author of "How To Be Happy." Hartford: Robinson & Pratt, 1834.

Poems. By Mrs L.H. Sigourney. Philadelphia: Key & Biddle, 1834.

Lays from the West: Poems. By Mrs L.H. Sigourney. Collected and arranged by the Rev. Joseph Belcher. London: Thomas Ward, 1834.

Sketches. By Mrs Sigourney. Philadelphia: Key & Biddle, 1834.

Tales and Essays for Children. By Mrs L.H. Sigourney. Hartford: F.J. Huntington, 1835.

Zinzendorff, and Other Poems. By Mrs L.H. Sigourney. New York: Leavitt & Lord; Boston: Crocker & Brewster, 1835.

History of Marcus Aurelius, Emperor of Rome. By Mrs L.H. Sigourney. Hartford: Belknap & Hamersley, 1836.

Olive Buds. By Mrs L.H. Sigourney. Hartford: William Watson, 1836.

Stories for Youth; Founded on Fact. Published for the American Peace Societies, and Sunday Schools. Hartford: William Watson, 1836. (Apparently two pieces by Sigourney, "The Farmer and Soldier," signed L.H.S., and "Ode on Peace," signed Mrs Sigourney.)

The Girl's Reading-book: in Prose and Poetry; for Schools. By Mrs L.H. Sigourney. New York: J. Orville Taylor, 1838.
Letters to Mothers. Hartford: Hudson & Skinner, 1838.
Select Poems. By Mrs L.H. Sigourney. Third Edition, with Illustrations. Philadelphia: Frederick W. Greenough, 1838. (A new edition of *Poems*, 1834.)
The Boy's Reading-book in Prose and Poetry, for Schools. By Mrs L.H. Sigourney. New York: J. Orville Taylor, 1839.
The Works of Mrs. Hemans, with a Memoir by Her Sister, and an Essay on Her Genius by Mrs. Sigourney.... Philadelphia: Lea and Blanchard, 1840.
Pocahontas, and Other Poems. By Mrs L.H. Sigourney. London: R. Tyas, 1841 (and a few weeks later in New York: Harper & Brothers).
Poems, Religious and Elegiac. London: R. Tyas, 1841.
Pleasant Memories of Pleasant Lands. By Mrs L.H. Sigourney. Boston: James Munroe, 1842.
Poems. Philadelphia: John Locken, 1842.
The Child's Book: Consisting of Original Articles, in Prose and Poetry. By Mrs L.H. Sigourney. New York: Turner & Hayden, 1844.
The Lovely Sisters. By Mrs L.H. Sigourney. Hartford: H.S. Parsons, 1845. (Apparently a rewriting by Sigourney of *Memoir of Margaret and Henrietta Flower*, by the Rev. Mr Stone, 1835.)
Poetry for Seamen. By Mrs L.H. Sigourney. Boston: James Munroe, 1845.
Scenes in My Native Land. By Mrs L.H. Sigourney. Boston: J. Munroe, 1845. London: H.G. Clarke, 1845.
Myrtis; with Other Etchings and Sketchings. By Mrs L.H. Sigourney. New York: Harper & Brothers, 1846.
The Voice of Flowers. By Mrs L.H. Sigourney. Hartford: H.S. Parsons, 1846.
The Weeping Willow. By Mrs L.H. Sigourney. Hartford: H.S. Parsons, 1847.
Water-drops. By Mrs L.H. Sigourney. New York: Robert Carter, 1848.
Illustrated Poems. Philadelphia: Carey and Hart, 1849.
Gertrude Russel; or, Parental Example. New York: Oliver & Brother, 1849. (Contains Sigourney's "The Apples of Sodom," "Twins," and "Patriarch and the Vine.")
Whisper to a Bride. By Mrs L.H. Sigourney. Hartford: H.S. Parsons, 1850.
The Poetical Works of Mrs. L.H. Sigourney. Ed. F.W.N. Bayley. London: George Routledge, 1850.
The Coronal; or, Pencillings in Poetry and Prose. By Mrs L.H. Sigourney. London and Edinburgh: Thomas Nelson, 1850.
The Poetical Works of Mrs. L.H. Sigourney. London and Edinburgh: T. Nelson and Sons, 1851.
Letters to My Pupils; with Narrative and Biographical Sketches. By Mrs L.H. Sigourney. New York: Robert Carter & Brothers, 1851.
Examples of Life and Death. By Mrs L.H. Sigourney. New York: Charles Scribner, 1852.
Olive Leaves. By L.H. Sigourney. New York: Robert Carter & Brothers, 1852.

The Faded Hope. By Mrs L.H. Sigourney. New York: Robert Carter & Brothers, 1853.
Memoir of Mrs. Harriet Newell Cook. By Mrs L.H. Sigourney. New York: R. Carter, 1853.
Past Meridian. By Mrs L.H. Sigourney. New York: Appleton; and Boston: J.P. Jewett, 1854.
The Western Home, and Other Poems. By Mrs L.H. Sigourney. Philadelphia: Parry & McMillan, 1854.
Sayings of the Little Ones, and Poems for Their Mothers. By Mrs L.H. Sigourney. Buffalo: Phinney; and New York: Ivison & Phinney, 1855.
Mary Rice and Other Tales. By Mrs L.H. Sigourney. London, Edinburgh, and New York: T. Nelson and Sons, 1855.
Biographies of the Great and Good. Glasgow: William Collins, 1855.
Examples from the Eighteenth and Nineteenth Centuries. First Series. By Mrs L.H. Sigourney. New York: Charles Scribner, 1857.
Lucy Howard's Journal. By Mrs L.H. Sigourney. New York: Harper & Brothers, 1858.
Wild Flowers Drawn and Colored from Nature. By Mrs C.M. Badger. With an Introduction by Mrs L.H. Sigourney. New York: Charles Scribner; London: Sampson Low & Son, 1859.
The Daily Counsellor. By Mrs L.H. Sigourney. Hartford: Brown & Gross, 1859.
Gleanings. By Mrs L.H. Sigourney. Hartford: Brown and Gross; and New York: D. Appleton, 1860.
The Man of Uz, and Other Poems. By Mrs L.H. Sigourney. Hartford: Williams, Wiley & Waterman, 1862.
Selections from Various Sources. By Mrs L.H. Sigourney. Worcester: John H. Turner, 1863.
The Transplanted Daisy: Memoir of Frances Racillia Hackley. By Mrs L.H. Sigourney. New York: Printed by Sanford & Haroun, 1865.
Letters of Life. By Mrs L.H. Sigourney. New York: D. Appleton, 1866.

Biography

Baym, Nina. "Sigourney, Lydia." *American National Biography Online*. <http://www.anb.org.login.ezproxy.library.ualberta.ca/articles/16/16-01504.html>.
Haight, Gordon S. *Mrs. Sigourney: The Sweet Singer of Hartford*. New Haven: Yale UP, 1930.
Teed, Melissa Ladd. "A Passion for Distinction: Lydia Huntley Sigourney and the Creation of a Literary Reputation." *New England Quarterly* 77:1 (March 2004): 51–69.

Criticism

Baker, Dorothy Z. "Ars Poetica/Ars Domestica: The Self-Reflexive Poetry of Lydia Sigourney and Emily Dickinson." *Poetics in the Poem: Critical Essays on American Self-Reflexive Poetry*. Ed. Dorothy Z. Baker. New York: Peter Lang, 1997. 69–89.
Baym, Nina. "Reinventing Lydia Sigourney." *American Literature* 62:3 (September 1990): 385–404.

Bogan, Louise. "The Heart and the Lyre." *Selected Criticism*. New York: Noonday Press, 1955. 335–42.

De Jong, Mary G. "Lydia Howard Huntley Sigourney." *Legacy: A Journal of American Women Writers* 5:1 (Spring 1988): 35–43.

Finch, Annie. "The Sentimental Poetess in the World: Metaphor and Subjectivity in Lydia Sigourney's Nature Poetry." *Legacy: A Journal of American Women Writers* 5:2 (Fall 1988): 3–18.

Giffen, Allison. "Dutiful Daughters and Needy Fathers: Lydia Sigourney and Nineteenth-Century Popular Literature." *Women's Studies: An Interdisciplinary Journal* 32:3 (April–May 2003): 255–80.

Loeffelholz, Mary. *From School to Salon: Reading Nineteenth-Century American Women's Poetry*. Princeton and Oxford: Princeton UP, 2004.

Okker, Patricia. "Sarah Josepha Hale, Lydia Sigourney, and the Poetic Tradition in Two Nineteenth-Century Magazines." *American Periodicals* 3 (1993): 32–43.

Petrino, Elizabeth A. "'Feet So Precious Charged': Dickinson, Sigourney, and the Child Elegy." *Tulsa Studies in Women's Literature* 13:2 (Fall 1994): 317–38.

Wood, Ann Douglas. "Mrs Sigourney and the Sensibility of the Inner Space." *New England Quarterly* 45:2 (June 1972): 163–81.

Zagarell, Sandra A. "Expanding 'America': Lydia Sigourney's *Sketch of Connecticut*, Catharine Sedgwick's *Hope Leslie*." *Tulsa Studies in Women's Literature* 6:2 (Autumn 1987): 225–45.

——. "'America' as Community in Three Antebellum Village Sketches." *The (Other) American Traditions: Nineteenth-Century Women Writers*. Ed. Joyce W. Warren. New Brunswick, NJ: Rutgers UP, 1992. 143–63.

Contexts

Bennett, Paula Bernat. *Poets in the Public Sphere: The Emancipatory Project of American Women's Poetry, 1800–1900*. Princeton: Princeton UP, 2003.

Brown, Susan. "The Victorian Poetess." *The Cambridge Companion to Victorian Poetry*. Ed. Joseph Bristow. Cambridge and New York: Cambridge UP, 2000. 180–202.

Burke, Martin J. *The Conundrum of Class: Public Discourse on the Social Order in America*. Chicago and London: U of Chicago P, 1995.

Douglas, Ann. *The Feminization of American Culture*. 1977; New York: Doubleday, 1988.

Finch, Annie. "The Poetess in America." *Able Muse*. <http://www.ablemuse.com/current/a-finch_poetess.htm>.

Kelly, Catherine E. *In the New England Fashion: Reshaping Women's Lives in the Nineteenth Century*. Ithaca and London: Cornell UP, 1999.

Kete, Mary Louise. *Sentimental Collaborations: Mourning and Middle-Class Identity in Nineteenth-Century America*. Durham and London: Duke UP, 2000.

Kramer, Michael P. *Imagining Language in America From the Revolution to the Civil War*. Princeton: Princeton UP, 1992.

Lueck, Beth L. *American Writers and the Picturesque Tour: The Search for National Identity, 1790–1860*. New York and London: Garland Publishers, 1997.

Mandell, Laura, ed. "The Transatlantic Poetess." *Romanticism on the Net* 29–30 (February–May 2003). <http://www.erudit.org/revue/ron/2003/v/n29/index.html>.

Marshall, Susan E. *Splintered Sisterhood: Gender and Class in the Campaign against Woman Suffrage*. Madison: U of Wisconsin P, 1997.

Matthews, Glenna. *"Just a Housewife": The Rise and Fall of Domesticity in America*. New York: Oxford UP, 1987.

McGill, Meredith L. *American Literature and the Culture of Reprinting, 1834–1853*. Philadelphia: U of Pennsylvania P, 2003.

McKinsey, Elizabeth. *Niagara Falls: Icon of the American Sublime*. Cambridge: Cambridge UP, 1985.

Mellor, Anne K. "The Female Poet and the Poetess: Two Traditions of British Women's Poetry, 1780–1830." *Studies in Romanticism* 36.2 (1997): 261–76.

Nelson, Dana D. "Women in Public." *The Cambridge Companion to Nineteenth-Century American Women's Writing*. Ed. Dale M. Bauer and Philip Gould. Cambridge and New York: Cambridge UP, 2001. 38–68.

Olwell, Victoria. "'It Spoke Itself': Women's Genius and Eccentric Politics." *American Literature* 77:1 (March 2005): 33–63.

Pattee, Fred Lewis. *The Feminine Fifties*. New York: D. Appleton-Century, 1940.

Petrino, Elizabeth. "Nineteenth-Century American Women's Poetry." *The Cambridge Companion to Nineteenth-Century American Women's Writing*. Ed. Dale M. Bauer and Philip Gould. Cambridge and New York: Cambridge UP, 2001. 122–42.

Rothman, David J. *The Discovery of the Asylum: Social Order and Disorder in the New Republic*. Rev. ed. New York: Aldine de Gruyter, 2002.

Ruttenburg, Nancy. *Democratic Personality: Popular Voice and the Trial of American Authorship*. Stanford: Stanford UP, 1998.

Ryan, Mary P. *The Empire of the Mother: American Writing about Domesticity 1830–1860*. New York: Haworth Press, 1982.

Shi, David E. *The Simple Life: Plain Living and High Thinking in American Culture*. New York and Oxford: Oxford UP, 1985.

Walker, Cheryl. *The Nightingale's Burden: Women and American Culture before 1900*. Bloomington: U of Indiana P, 1982.

Zboray, Ronald J. *A Fictive People: Antebellum Economic Development and the American Reading Public*. New York and Oxford: Oxford UP, 1993.